EMIGRATION IN POLISH SOCIAL-POLITICAL THOUGHT, 1870–1914

BENJAMIN P. MURDZEK

EAST EUROPEAN QUARTERLY, BOULDER
DISTRIBUTED BY COLUMBIA UNIVERSITY PRESS
NEW YORK

1977

EAST EUROPEAN MONOGRAPHS, NO. XXXIII

Benjamin P. Murdzek is Professor of History at
Oregon State University, Corvallis, Oregon

EAST EUROPEAN MONOGRAPHS

The *East European Monographs* comprise scholarly books on the history and civilization of Eastern Europe. They are published by the *East European Quarterly* in the belief that these studies contribute substantially to the knowledge of the area and serve to stimulate scholarship and research.

1. *Political Ideas and the Enlightenment in the Romanian Principalities, 1750–1831.* By Vlad Georgescu. 1971.
2. *America, Italy and the Birth of Yugoslavia, 1917–1919.* By Dragan R. Zivojinovic. 1972.
3. *Jewish Nobles and Geniuses in Modern Hungary.* By William O. McCagg, Jr. 1972.
4. *Mixail Soloxov in Yugoslavia: Reception and Literary Impact.* By Robert F. Price. 1973.
5. *The Historical and National Thought of Nicolae Iorga.* By William O. Oldson. 1973.
6. *Guide to Polish Libraries and Archives.* By Richard C. Lewanski. 1974.
7. *Vienna Broadcasts to Slovakia, 1938–1939: A Case Study in Subversion.* By Henry Delfiner. 1974.
8. *The 1917 Revolution in Latvia.* By Andrew Ezergailis. 1974.
9. *The Ukraine in the United Nations Organization: A Study in Soviet Foreign Policy. 1944–1950.* By Konstantin Sawczuk. 1975.
10. *The Bosnian Church: A New Interpretation.* By John V. A. Fine, Jr. 1975.
11. *Intellectual and Social Developments in the Habsburg Empire from Maria Theresa to World War I.* Edited by Stanley B. Winters and Joseph Held. 1975.
12. *Ljudevit Gaj and the Illyrian Movement.* By Elinor Murray Despalatovic. 1975.
13. *Tolerance and Movements of Religious Dissent in Eastern Europe.* Edited by Bela K. Kiraly. 1975.

Acknowledgements

I am indebted to many people who have helped me in a variety of ways. I would like to express my affectionate regard to my former preceptors, especially Ernst M. Posner and Samuel L. Sharp, who originally conceived the subject of this research and who presided over its initial development. I wish to extend my thanks to Professor Tadeusz Kotarbinski of the Polish Academy of Science for his sustaining encouragement and to Zbigniew Daszkowski, Henryka Jankowska, Miroslawa Kociecka and Zofia Zydanowicz for the many courtesies extended to me in the National Library in Warsaw.

I have benefitted from the wise counsel and generous assistance of many friends and colleagues, including Kenneth F. Lewalski, Hans Rogger, Richard Astro and John V. Byrne. My special thanks to George Barr Carson, Jr. and William Appleman Williams for their invaluable suggestions in the preparation of the manuscript. My wife, Marguerite Murdzek, has patiently labored through the many revisions of the manuscript as typist, grammarian and editorial counselor.

This publication would not have been possible without the financial assistance I have received from the Oregon State University General Research Fund, the Oregon State University Foundation and The Kosciuszko Foundation.

I have attempted to adhere scrupulously to the original orthography of the sources I have used in the footnotes and listed in the bibliography. The lack of Polish diacritical markings is a consequence of circumstances beyond my control.

Contents

Introduction

As originally conceived, this project was intended as a broadly statistical study of the multi-directioned population movements in those areas of east-central Europe populated predominantly by Polish-speaking peoples—an area which, because of its lack of political identity and for the lack of a better designation, is frequently referred to as "historical Poland." [1] On the political map of late nineteenth century Europe it included the five northern and eastern administrative districts of Prussia (Danzig, Marienwerder, Bromberg, Posen and Oppeln), the ten westernmost provinces of Russia (Warszawa, Kalisz, Kielce, Lomza, Lublin, Plock, Piotrkow, Radom, Suwalki and Siedlce) and the province of Galicia in Austria. Its scope was to include an examination into the causes and effects of the various population movements as well as their direction.

Chronologically, it was to be loosely delimited by the years 1870 and 1914. There appeared to be some justification for this delineation since it seemed to encompass a coherent historical period. In Prussia, its beginning was approximately marked by the establishment of the German empire and the administrative reorganization that followed. In Galicia it roughly coincided with the beginnings of that area's autonomous existence together with that of its parliamentary body, the *sejm*. In the Kingdom, where the year 1870 has been generally accepted as a chronological milestone in the economic history of that area, it also roughly corresponded to the administrative reorganization of the ten gouvernements involved.

The year 1914 not only marked the beginning of the first World War, but also introduced abnormal factors affecting the movements of population. Its conclusion marked a new era in the political history of Poland and a new era in the history of its population movements. Finally, it was within the limits of this period that the three politically separate sectors of "historical Poland" experienced the most extensive shifts of its population—movements which included the mass migrations to the United States and elsewhere.

While the chronological scope of the project offered no difficulties and, indeed, seemed to be logically and historically coherent, the national and statistical character of the undertaking proved to be fraught with difficulties. The area under consideration was occupied by a wide variety of ethnic, cultural and lingual groups. There appeared to be no single criterion for the determination of "Polish" population. Each had its inconsistencies and, frequently, contradictions. A lingual norm had only a qualified validity because it excluded bi-lingual children and descendants of Polish-speaking elements in the Prussian districts as well as much of the older Jewish population in the Kingdom and Galicia. In both the latter sectors the situation was further complicated by the presence of a considerable number of Ukrainian, Lithuanian and Byelorussian population.

Religious affiliation, as a test, had even more serious limitations. Christianity as a standard of "Polishness" left the question largely unanswered in the Prussian districts and excluded substantial portions of the population in both Austrian and Russian Poland. While Roman Catholicism had some validity as a measure of nationality in the provinces of West Prussia and Posen, it failed in the Polish-speaking areas of Prussian and Austrian Silesia. In Russian and Austrian Poland it suffered from the same disabilities as the lingual criterion.

This confusion was compounded by the growing temper of nationalism that developed in the last decades of the nineteenth century and the prewar years of the twentieth. Neither the agencies charged with the compilation of statistical data nor scholars occupied with its interpretation were immune to the nationalistic pressure. This was especially the case after 1904–5 which experienced the development of increasingly militant national irridentism in all sectors. As a result, the large volume of laboriously compiled nationality statistics, never too accurate, becomes even less creditable. The result, in most compilations and studies, seemed to be "a battle of numbers." A disparity in data led to a disparity in conclusions even among Polish scholars and was compounded when it involved Polish, German, Russian or Ukrainian studies in areas where their national interests or aspirations conflicted.

In the face of these apparently insoluble differences and in view of the questionable validity of nationality statistics in the first place, it seemed well advised to abandon the original, "Polish" orientation of the project and treat it broadly enough to encompass all of the population living in "historical Poland" without regard to nationality, ethnic composition, cultural distinction or religious affiliation.

Even with these delineations removed, however, the available data imposed some serious restrictions and difficulties for any essentially statistical study. While the requisite statistical data for the pertinent areas of Prussia[2] and Austria[3] were readily available and reasonably creditable, those for the pertinent provinces of Russia required so many reservations that they tended to lose their validity in general.[4]

Nor was the heavy hand of nationalism apparent in statistical compilations and studies alone. Non-statistical monographs on migration and, indeed, almost all literature touching upon it, became increasingly permeated with bias. Studies of emigration, lacking the requisite bases in objectively compiled and objectively appraised statistical data, seemed to become increasingly more or less expressions of opinions and attitudes on emigration. These attitudes seemed to be largely conditioned by patriotic aspirations, political ambitions, economic interests, ethnic hostilities and various combinations thereof.

This realization inevitably forced a further reappraisal of the scope and nature of the project of research. It seemed, in the given circumstances, that a descriptive, analytical and historiographic rather than a statistical project was indicated. Since attitudes and opinions alone did not exercise apparently decisive influences in the movements of populations, it was decided to broaden the scope within this already delimited area by including some of the outstanding policies of the ruling authorities which directly or indirectly, by accident or design, influenced the shifts of population in the political areas concerned. These measures, because of their official sanction, and for reasons of convenience, could appropriately be called "policies." Within the limitations imposed by this definition, it seemed germane to include the colonization program and the regulation of foreign immigration into the Eastern Marches by the Prussian government. The former, intended essentially to arrest the emigration of German-speaking elements and in turn to facilitate the emigration of Polish-speaking elements, could, in a sense, be called an emigration policy even though it was intended to foster the immigration of Germans. The latter, calculated to arrest the permanent increment of Polish-speaking elements from Russian and Austrian Poland, seemed clearly to be an immigration policy. An attempt was made to place the evolution and implementation of these policies in their historical context.

Within the same definition of "policies" a consideration of such varied measures as tariff schedules, reprisals against revolutionaries, the colonization of Siberia, the May Laws in the Western Governments and the operations of the Peasant Bank seemed to be warranted in the Kingdom. A consideration of these policies still left a considerable segment of opinion untapped. This was the influence exercised by the traditionally ruling classes of the Polish population and included their stand not only on the movements of population, as such, but also such measures as peasant credit facilities, the break-up of landed estates (parcelation) and other measures which in one way or another influenced and were related to those movements. These segments of Polish society, because of the political disabilities imposed upon them by the Russian authorities, were largely incapable of enforcing their will. Their position on migrations, in general, and measures related thereto therefore remained legally unenforceable. For this reason they were defined as "attitudes."

In Galicia, because of the comparative degree of autonomy enjoyed by the Polish population, this distinction between policies and attitudes was less apparent. Therefore, the action of the *sejm* on such issues as credit facilities, employment bureaus, entail legislation, parcelation, education and industrialization, could legitimately be called policies related to and affecting emigration. Nevertheless, lacking a politically independent status, some measures pertaining to emigration could not be officially enforced. These measures which failed to receive sanction by the central authorities in Vienna could be said to have remained largely in the category of attitudes.

Whether attitudes or policies, neither came into existence in a void. All of them gained currency and were implemented in a given historical context. Therefore, with due regard to the hazards implicit in any attempts to establish positive causal relationships, some attempt was made to fathom the motives underlying the various measures and attitudes which in their way were related to the movements of population. Since most of the measures and some of the attitudes developed in particular sectors independently of the others, the format of the first part of the text has been established along the lines of the political boundaries of that period. This is the justification for the organization of the first seven chapters. Nevertheless, most attitudes and many of the conditions conducive to migration were not particularly peculiar to any given sector but were, to a greater or lesser degree, common to all areas. Furthermore, Polish writers and commentators on the subject began to treat it as such shortly after the turn of the century. This is the justification for the eighth and ninth chapters. Such a procedure also lent itself well to a closer examination of the changing character of some of the attitudes, in general, and ideas of causes and effects of emigration, in particular.

The last chapter is intended as a general summation as well as a critical examination of some of the basic premises of those who had been instrumental in formulating policies or expressing attitudes on the subject of migration or measures pertaining to it. Although the postwar years in independent Poland were admittedly outside of the chronological limits already established, in view of the fact that its existence represented a triumph of the national ideal and because of the fact that many of the prewar ideas of causality were directly or indirectly conditioned by their lack of political autonomy, it was felt that at least a cursory examination of the attitudes and policies on population, in general, and emigration, in particular, was warranted. In a sense, independent Poland offered an ideal laboratory for testing the validity of many of the prewar attitudes and rationales. The closing of many traditional outlets in the postwar years also offered some check on ideas of effects of both seasonal and overseas emigration.

The overall picture that seems to emerge from this examination is one in which the spokesmen for the *status quo*—which in all sectors originally represented the interests of the landed gentry—initially ignored any public discussion of emigration in its inaugural stages, being generally guided by the precept of "let sleeping dogs lie." With minor modifications they and their spokesmen persisted in their opposition to peasant emigration—both continental and overseas—throughout the period under examination.

By the last decade of the nineteenth century, however, the phenomena of emigration could no longer be ignored. This was fostered by the nationalistic confrontation ("the fight for the land") that was developing in the Prussian provinces, the massive "Brazilian fever" that manifested itself in Russian Poland and, especially, the growing currents of liberalism, peasant populism, and socialism that were beginning to challenge the ideological monopoly that the landed interests heretofore enjoyed. This decade saw the emergence of the issue from obscurity to widespread public discussion in the legislative assemblies (Galicia), monographic literature and, especially, the periodical press. By way of reconciliation with the inevitable, the spokesmen for the dominant gentry were increasingly converted to the idea of the "regulation and control" of emigration. In this view they were frequently joined by the spokesmen of middle-class liberalism. One of the singular influences in this change of attitude appears to have been the very considerable economic impact of the increment of emigrant earnings and remittances. Indeed, in the Prussian provinces these savings, especially from the emigrants in the industrial areas of Rhineland and Westphalia, appear to have been the determining factor in reversing the German policies of expropriation and displacement of the Polish-speaking elements. There, as elsewhere, returning emigrants frequently located their savings in land. This gave stimulus to the pattern of parcelation which, temporarily at least, reversed the process of pro-letarization. Though originally viewed with serious qualms by those who saw the breakup of estates as a threat to the existence of that class of landowners, more perceptive observers saw this development as the reason for the enhancement of land values and a means of redemption from the pervasive indebtedness with which that class was burdened. Precisely how consequential were emigrant earnings to all sectors of prewar Poland is impossible to establish. Numerous students of the subject, however, were increasingly disposed to argue that these earn-ings and remittances were fundamental to the fiscal solvency of the respective sectors. Indeed, a few held that the emigrant was the para-mount object of regional export and his earnings, as such, the most significant and consequential economic factor of that era.

The revolutionary ferments in the Kingdom in 1904 and 1905 marked the emergence of militant currents of national irredentism in all sectors of prewar Poland and, accordingly, inaugurated changes in the rela-tively liberal attitudes toward emigration. To the degree that liberals and social democrats were converted to these sentiments, they too increasingly became the proponents of "regulation and control." This climate of opinion contributed to the organization of provincial em-ployment bureaus and the Polish Emigration Society (P.T.E.) in Galicia and similarly structured efforts in the Kingdom. A clearly de-finable "politics of emigration" gained currency especially focused on controlling the massive seasonal emigration to Germany and using it as an economic counter toward the advancement of their ends. Even on the imperial level, both in Vienna and St. Petersburg, the idea of regulation and control gained some adherents usually with the view of capitalizing on the profitable transport of the overseas emigration.

This conjunction of vested interest and national interest not infre-quently reduced the interests of the emigrants to secondary priority. Containment of emigration, though rationalized on the humanitarian grounds of protecting the emigrants from mistreatment and exploita-tion, was never successful. Legally, when possible, extra-legally, when necessary, the emigrant was guided by his intelligence and instincts to seek a better life for himself and his children—expectations which his country, in its socio-economic circumstances, could not satisfy.

I. Prussia and the Poles

I

Prussian Policies Affecting Emigration— From Assimilation to Displacement

The German policy toward both emigration and immigration in that area formerly called Greater Poland was an aspect of the larger policy of the government toward the Polish question in general and the Eastern Marches question in particular. Since the historical experience of the German Empire during the years following its formation up to the outbreak of the first world war was substantially defined by Otto von Bismarck, the population policy in the Eastern Marches is best comprehended as an aspect of the greater configuration of factors which motivated his leadership.

To Bismarck, as to many other German statesmen, past and future, the presence of numerous Polish-speaking elements in this area was of considerable concern. The question of Poland could never quite be disregarded. Since the Congress of Vienna, it was one of the chief forces which bound the partitioning powers in common interest. In time, as the international framework began to change and the problem of Poland began to decline from its primacy, there followed shifts in the policy of the German government toward its foreign-speaking subjects. It is within this changing framework of international relations, specifically the relations of the German empire with Russia, that Bismarck's "Polish Policy" in the eastern Prussian provinces can, to a degree, be understood.[1]

The territorial boundaries of Prussia established at the Congress of Vienna came to be regarded as a categorical imperative to the existence of Prussia. The consolidation and conservation of this gain was regarded by Prussian leaders as an indispensable condition of their power. Any prospect of a revived Polish state needs must threaten its very existence. A revived Poland would inevitably press for a corridor to the Baltic—a contingency which, if realized, would split the Prussian domains. To obviate this possibility became one of the underlying motives in the foreign and domestic relations of all the conservative statesmen charged with the destinies of Prussia.[2]

The thesis of incompatibility of coexistence of Prussia and an independent Poland, so eloquently enunciated by Bismarck, had been substantially formulated long before he ascended to the leadership of Prussia and the German Empire.[3] That these territorial acquisitions bound that country in a community of interest with Russia was also generally accepted by others charged with the security of Prussia before him.[4] It is significant that one of the characteristic manifestations of Russo-Prussian solidarity was the greater or lesser intensity with which these powers undertook to assimilate their newly acquired minority elements. Shifts in their relationships were immediately reflected in their policies toward the Polish elements within their borders. Conservative Prussian elements consistently identified the interests of their state with harmonious relations with Russia and frequently gave concrete expression of this solidarity as an assurance to her eastern Slavic neighbor.[5] In time it came to be regarded as a political barometer of their amity or discord.[6]

To be sure, Prussian foreign policy was not exclusively, not even primarily, predicated on the "Polish Question." During the nineteenth century numerous other bones of contention developed to ruffle the community of interest established at Vienna. Probably the foremost was Russian efforts to prevent unification of Germany. But even during this period of anti-Russian tendencies, the question of a revived Poland could not be ignored. Any prospect of a war with Russia inevitably caused the problem to recur.

A Polish buffer state under the tutelage of Prussia was sure to enlist the support of Polish national elements in all the three sectors of former Poland and might, quite conceivably, weigh heavily in the balance of military operations.[7] This contingency, however, was regarded only as a lesser of two evils—the greater evil being the prospect of Russian armies in Berlin.[8] Better than both these contingencies was a harmonious relationship with Russia.

It was within this framework that Bismarck embarked upon his aggressive policy against the Catholic hierarchy in the Prussian domains, commonly referred to as the *Kulturkampf.* The master diplomatist was, of course, not ignorant of domestic pressures favoring this move. Like his foreign policy in regard to Russia, his domestic policy toward Germanization and security had a historical background which traced back to Frederick II and his ministers. Like his predecessors, his domestic program of Germanization was directed almost exclusively against the Polish gentry and the Polish Catholic hierarchy. Like a score of German statesmen and writers before him, he saw in these Polish elements the exclusive keepers of the Polish national ambitions—the unreconstructed and implacable enemies of the Prussian state. There was no lack of German documentation to substantiate his position.[10]

Between the policy of the *Kulturkampf* and that inaugurated by the establishment of the Colonization Commission in 1886, there were some significant changes. The former, as it applied in Prussian Poland, was in conformity with the traditional internal policy toward the Polish minority. It was directed against the gentry, Catholic clergy and their respective retainers. Its attitude toward the mass of Polish-speaking peasantry was still largely one of benevolent paternalism. The higher German-Protestant culture was intended to accrue to their best interest—an attitude in accordance with the traditional view of the Teutonic mission. The nationalism and idea of the state of Frederick II, Eduard von Flottwell and other ideological progenitors of Bismarck were in accord with these concepts. Loyalty and conformity to the wishes of the majority were required—there were, however, no concerted efforts at forcing lingual and cultural assimilation. These latter were never regarded as a threat to the security of the Prussian state.[11]

Imperceptibly, however, the nationalistic ideology began to assume more uncompromising tones.[12] The security of the state was still the watchword but there was progressively less room for compromise with lingual or cultural sensitivities of the Polish minorities. The liberal policy of Germanization of the past was proving itself a failure. The Polish-speaking elements were not only successfully resisting assimilation but were even assimilating German-speaking elements around them. Emigration of Germans to western Germany and abroad was adding to this imbalance. The border regions of the German empire, instead of becoming German bastions against the Slavic incursions, were areas of infiltration by those elements. The policy of the removal of the alien elements inaugurated in 1885 and the colonization program inaugurated in the following year were defensive measures adopted within the framework of this newer type of nationalism.

The ministerial directive of March 26, 1885, aimed as it was against Austrian and Russian subjects residing within the borders of Prussia, was an expression of Germany's immigration policy. The Settlement Law *(Ansiedlungsgesetz)* of 1886 which established the Colonization Commission *(Ansiedlungskommission)* was directed against the allegedly growing preponderance of Polish-speaking elements in the eastern Prussian provinces and, as such, may be regarded as an expression of that government's emigration policy. Both were predicated on a new concept of nationalism and security.[13]

Several developments, each with a historical background, conspired to affect this ideological transformation. The powerful flowering of a united German empire, its unchallenged political and military hegemony in Europe, its economic expansion and prosperity, could not have been without influence on the formulation of the public opinion in regard to the "Polish problem." The triumph of Bismarck's policy awakened nationalistic drives which dictated not only the loyalty to the state of its minority groups but their complete assimilation—lingual and cultural. The foremost theoretical exponent of this new nationalism was Heinrich von Treitschke. Since 1863, in his lectures, he expounded the concept that it was the duty of the state to amalgamate all cultural and lingual minorities within its borders into that of the ruling group. "There is a natural tendency for the concept of nationality and the concept of the state to coincide." He observed this tendency in all culturally advanced states of the West.[14] The sense of cultural mission seemed to have a greater sanction than ever before. Everywhere was evidence of this great social and intellectual accomplishment.

There were, moreover, disquieting observers who saw threats to the security of these accomplishments—observers who were heard with increasing frequency in their pronouncements regarding the eastern border regions and the menace that the Polish-speaking elements constituted. The antagonisms called forth by the *Kulturkampf* gave opportunity to various bureaucrats to voice their complaints against Polish intractability. An indictment of this sort was expressed by the Minister of Education, Karl Gustav von Gossler, in 1882. He maintained that the Polish elements, to a greater extent than ever before, were directing their energy and organization toward the rebuilding of an independent Poland within the boundaries of 1772; that there was irrefutable evidence that the Poles were preparing for such a contingency—preparing economically, financially, mentally and morally; that the nationalistically aggressive Polish Catholic clergy were winning more and more formerly avowed Germans into the Polish Catholic fold. He deplored the growing Polish exclusiveness as exemplified by their separate establishment of credit and banking facilities, agricultural associations and organizations dedicated to the boycott of German physicians, lawyers and artisans.[15]

Outside the frontiers of the empire equally alarming developments provided the defensive impulse for the reception of the new concept of state and nationalism. The Russian nationalism of the reign of Alexander III made itself intensely felt not only by the old German settlements on the Baltic but also by the more recently established German settlements in Russian Poland. In Galicia, the short period of autonomy was sufficient to remove the effects of almost a century of Germanization by the government. In Bohemia the Slavic elements were waging a bitter war on Germanism. Taaffe's Austrian ministry signalized notable retreats of Germanism in Hungary and Carinthia. The future of the Germans, bounded on the north and east by Slavs, seemed to be in imminent danger. In this war of extermination it was only logical for the Germans to put their own house in order, especially with reference to the Eastern Marches.

All these fears and sentiments found eloquent expression in Eduard von Hartmann's article in 1885. This outspoken journalist-philosopher effectively synthesized the traditional Slavic policy with the new currents abroad in the land. It was his conviction that Germanism after a centuries-long history of advance was no match for aggressive Slavic nationalism. The way of Germanic salvation lay in the complete and unremitting Germanization of all minorities within its borders—this especially in the Eastern Marches. All vestiges of Polish culture and tradition should be immediately removed. An effective policy toward this end would be the importation of German settlers into that area and the transport of Polish agricultural workers to German colonies abroad.[16]

This threat to Germany in general and the Eastern Marches in particular was substantiated by statisticians. Friedrich J. Neumann, basing his article on demographic materials, found that up to the sixth decade of the nineteenth century the German-speaking element was on the increase in Posen province but that the contrary was the case at present. The cause of this development was neither a higher natural increase of the Polish elements nor a higher volume of German emigration, but rather a process of "Polonization" that was being carried on chiefly through the instrumentality of the Polish Catholic clergy. Though German land ownership was on the increase, its owners were frequently absentees, while those who leased or administered their holdings made no effort to displace the Polish workers with German.[17]

Albert von Randow viewed the problem of the Eastern Marches from a broader perspective. Taking the matter up in Schmoller's publication in the beginning of 1886, the crux of his thesis was that every state must take care to assimilate all those of its component elements who resist incorporation and whose ambitions are in opposition to

that of the state. Such was the problem in the eastern Prussian provinces. The growing ascendancy of the Polish elements was not, according to Randow, the result of their assimilatory capabilities but rather
the result of natural movements of population which throughout
central Europe were on the move from east to west, to the capital cities,
to the industrial and commercial centers. This process was especially
apparent in East and West Prussia, in Posen and in Silesia. The
German elements were emigrating westward and their places were
being taken by Jewish and Slavic elements from Russian and Austrian
Poland.[18]

From the above excerpts it is evident that the authors, whether
inciting anti-Slavic antagonisms or reiterating traditional anxieties regarding the security of the border regions, all were touching upon a
real demographic problem facing the empire. The great increases of
population and recurrent economic crises, together with the transformation from an agricultural to an industrial economy, resulted in the
creation of the most troublesome problem for the government—the
effective utilization of a surplus labor force. A clear warning of these
developments was the growing volume of overseas emigration which,
in view of the nascent state of the German colonies, was threatening
the loss of a considerable portion of this increase to foreign countries.

Bismarck was doubtless aware of these changing sentiments. Though
he did not entirely share them, he knew how to use them in his greater
scheme of reference within the framework of the international play of
forces. More than anything, his desire was to reestablish congenial
relations with Russia. This relationship had been under varying strains
and vicissitudes throughout its existence since the Congress of Vienna.
The Berlin Congress and the frustration of Russia's Balkan ambitions
was a recent and dramatic development which added a new note of
discord. Russia's more recent disposition toward a friendly reorientation toward France further disquieted the Iron Chancellor. As a means
of reopening the "wire with St. Petersburg" and at the same time satisfying the clamor of domestic nationalists, Bismarck concurred with
the issuance of the ministerial decree of March 26, 1885, which aimed
at removal of all alien nationals (specifically Russian and Austrian
subjects) living in the Eastern Marches. That this decree concurred
with that of the most vocal elements of German nationalists was only
incidental to its purpose of being an overt and traditional manifestation of Russo-German friendship and community of interest. As was
his habit, he judged public affairs from a governmental rather than
nationalistic viewpoint.[19]

The policy of removals, decreed by Robert von Puttkamer, Minister of Internal Affairs, on March 26, 1885, was aimed at foreign elements within the eastern Prussian provinces, and as such may be said to signalize the more stringent policy of the government toward immigration from the eastward.[20] This policy was to remain more or less the norm until the outbreak of the war—departures from this established norm, however, being made grudgingly in the interest of expediency and Junker self-interest.[21]

Ostensibly motivated "in the best interest of German culture and German security,"[22] its result was the forcible removal from the eastern provinces of Prussia all Polish seasonal immigrants employed in German agriculture and all other foreigners living there who could not show proof of German citizenship. The developing tide of seasonal immigrant workers from Austrian and Russian Poland was almost completely arrested. This decree and supplementary directives were further calculated to prohibit future settlement of alien elements within the boundaries of Prussia. It has been variously estimated that this decree, vigorously enforced until 1890, accounted for the removal of approximately 30,000 to 40,000 population. Some, faced with the alternative of returning to Austrian or Russian Poland, emigrated abroad.[23]

As the stratagem to "reopen the wire to St. Petersburg," if such it was, the decree of March 26, 1885, must be regarded as a failure. Bismarck's program of deporting "subversive" alien elements satisfied neither his critics at home nor had its expected effect upon the Russian government. The hardships that the removals caused elicited shocked surprise and disapprobation among many thinking Germans. A parliamentary opposition developed in the Reichstag, led by the Centrists—still smarting from Bismarck's *Kulturkampf*—liberals and Social Democrats supported by the Poles, Hanoverians, Danes and Alsatians. On January 16, 1886, the majority of that body condemned the measure as unwarranted in its extremes.[24]

To this setback (for Bismarck) at home was added the unanticipated news that the Panslavic and anti-German elements in Russia had regained the ascendancy and roundly condemned the measure as a typical manifestation of German barbarism. Hard upon the heels of the attack of the Russian periodical press came the news of Russian reprisals against German settlers in Russian Poland. A series of imperial directives prohibited or made it difficult for foreigners to acquire, lease or otherwise use land in the Russian empire.[25] The new configuration of factors on the international scene was replacing the traditional ones that had united the co-authors of the Holy Alliance.[26]

But before this singular manifestation of Russia's new orientation became widespread and its significance to the traditional political alignments obvious, Bismarck again embarked upon an offensive against the Polish minorities within Prussia's borders. Furthermore, Bismarck's censure by parliament could be interpreted in Russia that, though the Chancellor sought to maintain amicable relations with Russia, the representatives of the majority of the population, counting on the imminent outbreak of war, sought to placate the Polish nationalistic elements and win their support against Russia. Bismarck, therefore, hurried to advance another reassurance of friendship toward Russia by undertaking another anti-Polish offensive against the Prussian Poles. This was the famous *Ansiedlungsgesetz* of 1886.[27] Incidentally, it was also consistent with the new temper of nationalism developing at home. These elements found the removal policy useful but, in itself, insufficient to arrest the declining proportions of German-speaking elements in the Eastern Marches. These developments were especially distressing to the National Liberal party. That party's press had been for several years discussing the most effective means of offensive against the Polish elements along the border marches. By 1885, at its annual congress, it had adopted a platform favoring "the establishment of hereditary German landleases on national domains with the help of the government." [28]

Randow had also suggested several alternatives. In his view, the danger of Polonization was only temporarily arrested by Bismarck's removal policy. Such temporary expedients were not likely to have lasting results. It was imperative that conditions be created for the German elements living there which would permanently tie them to the soil and remove their impulse to the westward. His elaboration on this theme was an exact anticipaton of the program that was to be adopted by the *Ostmarkenverein* at a later date.[29] The German language should be more extensively utilized in all social and official relationships; all government administrative and judicial agencies should be staffed by German personnel unable to speak the Polish language. This would tend to force the Polish-speaking population to learn German. A greater emphasis should be put on teaching German in the schools. The heretofore inability of the German residents to satisfy their cultural needs should be immediately corrected by the establishment of universities, higher agricultural and business schools, museums, theaters, etc. The German element should be further aided by government bonuses for government workers and judges, scholarships for German students, organization of German trade and agricultural associations, adequate mortgage and credit facilities and a program of public works. Randow placed special emphasis on German colonization and settlement. He viewed the growing preponderance of large German landholds in Posen province with some qualms, since the large German landholders seemed to care little for the nationality of their employees—many of them even seemed to prefer Poles. For this reason, the government should buy large tracts of land and by parcelation to German farmers create from them farmsteads settled by Germans. The Prussian parliament would certainly not object to a special fund in the defense of German interests in the East.[30]

This was approximately the point of view which was adopted by the government. According to the statistics advanced by Minister of Agriculture Lucius (von Ballhausen) when the project was under deliberation in the parliament, in the western provinces of Germany large landholds of 100 hectares or more were gradually disappearing. They represented less than six percent of the whole. On the other hand, they reached 55.3 percent in Prussian Pomerania, 47.1 percent in West Prussia and 55.3 percent in Posen province. Any program of internal colonization, therefore, must be undertaken in the provinces with predominantly mixed population. The aim of the proposed law was to create a self-sufficient peasant class and a numerous group of laborers. He was not prepared to venture whether the hundreds of thousands who yearly emigrated abroad would constitute suitable material for the undertaking. A portion of them would doubtless prefer to settle there.[31]

Thus, gradually, the arena of anti-Polish operations was slowly shifting from the sphere of church, administration and school to the arena of economics and was concentrated around the problem of internal colonization.[32] This idea was given final formulation by the president of the Bromberg District, Christoph von Tiedemann. In a memorial addressed to Bismarck for his information, he emphasized that thanks to the depressed circumstances in which the Polish large landholders found themselves at that time, the government had an opportunity to acquire their lands at unusually low prices. By this means the government could acquire and create large domains or by progressive parcelation establish numerous German elements in these border regions.[33] Though this program to strengthen German elements in border regions interested the Chancellor sufficiently to have reference to it incorporated in the speech from the throne,[34] Bismarck was still not clear on the best method to put it into effect. In his conversations with Tiedemann, the Chancellor suggested several alternative measures, including revocation of right of assembly, restraint of the press, and even the advisability of breaking up the territorial unity of Posen province among the adjoining ones. None of these proved feasible or advisable; both agreed that the purchase of Polish large landholds by the government was probably the best procedure. Tiedemann suggested the sum of 10 million marks for this purpose. The Chancellor expressed the doubt that such a sum would be granted either by the Minister of the Treasury or the lower house.

It was at this auspicious moment that a new factor entered upon the scene—one that made it a gigantic operation. The leader of the National Liberal Party in the Prussian parliament, Johannes von Miquel, having heard of the intentions of the government, warmly embraced them and pledged the support of his faction for at least a 100 million mark fund. Furthermore, the National Liberal Party answered the suggestion made in the speech from the throne by a motion expressing its readiness to supply the government with every means to defend Germanism in the eastern provinces of Prussia.[35]

Around the implementation of this program developed a discussion which illustrated the various ideological currents abroad in the land. They ranged from those that prevailed in the past to the newer ideological concepts of nationalism. The discussions and debates ranged from reminiscences of former conflicts of the two nationalities to venturesome speculations on those to come. The most telling argument of the proponents of this law was the fear of the possibility of losing both Posen and West Prussia to a revived Poland at some future date. This danger could be circumvented by restraining the advancing process of Polonization in those lands. This could be the only answer to the offensive undertaken by aggressive Slavicism which was uprooting the German element in Bohemia, destroying it in the Russian Baltic provinces, and conducting a program calculated to counteract it in Russian Poland in order to more effectively menace the German eastern boundaries. The Polish concentrations in Prussia had the character of a strategically planned program aimed at the unity of Prussia. Why was the increase of Polish population especially apparent in the districts of Thorn and Strasburg? "There is evidence [in this development] of a certain system," expounded von Rauchhaupt, *Landrath* from Delitzsch. "Actually in this place where the districts of Thorn and Strasburg are situated, West Prussia is at its narrowest, most closely approaches the Baltic and the most strategic place where a Polish wedge can split East and West Prussia." It was folly to permit the Eastern Marches to be so saturated with the Polish elements as to imperil its ability to defend itself—Posen lay too close to Berlin.[36]

To these expositions from the floor were added those of the representative of the government, Puttkamer. He likewise raised the spectre of an independent Poland, which was to say, the destruction of united Prussian nationhood. His testimony likewise illustrated that the teachings of Treitschke had reached beyond the classrooms and had established themselves into the highest official spheres. In the course of its historical development, said Puttkamer, Prussia incorporated other national elements. "To these segments of foreign population we are and ever had been ready to acknowledge full and free rights of our citizenship, but . . . nothing more. . . . The Prussian state cannot agree to the return to these foreign national segments of an autonomous existence within our territories. We are a German nation and we would be betraying our historical mission were we to allow any concessions which would be contrary with the purely German character of our nation." [37]

A like ideological transformation was evident from the discussion on the most effective means to counteract the threat to Germanism posed by the growth of Polish population. The majority of the National Liberals, however, held that existing agencies had been found unequal to the task—the most effective program would be mass colonization of German peasants. Doctor Wehr, *Landes-Direktor* from Danzig, cited the example of Frederick the Great: the colonies that he established in West Prussia with Westphalian settlers had to that day resisted Polonization. "If the government undertakes this program systematically, in 10 or 15 years there will be no further necessity of any such discussion on the so-called Polish matter." [38] Tiedemann reached even further back into history. He saw the question at issue as "the thousand year old conflict, specifically, who is to rule in the area between the Elbe and the Vistula: Germans or Poles." That the result favored the Germans was not entirely resolved by the sword but also by colonization.[39] Doctor Enneccerus, Professor of Law at the University of Marburg, put special emphasis on the peasant character of this colonization. The owner of a large domain could never win the influence over his surroundings as could the peasant. The latter, having hired one or two Polish hands, would force them to learn German, not being himself in danger of Polonization. The immigrants from Germany should not only be given the soil but ready farmsteads for which they could pay rent.[40]

By and large, the upper house, that stronghold of conservative tradition, was disposed toward the more moderate traditional approach to the problem. Udo, Count Stolberg-Wernigerode, for example, held to the view that the most effective counter-agencies to spreading Polonism were still the schools and the army.[41] Dr. Heinrich Dernburg, Professor of Law at the University of Berlin, who moved for the support of the government's border policy in the upper house, assured his listeners that the issue was not Germanization but rather the defeat of Polish irredentism. Cultural pluralism was the aim. Complete assimilation was neither practical nor possible.[42] August von Bethmann-Hollweg, *Rittergutsbesitzer* from the district of Flatow, expressed corresponding sentiments, citing Flottwell's memorial to make his position clear.[43]

From the parliamentary discussion, it is evident that two contrary methods in treating the subject of the Eastern Marches were contending. The one represented the methods dictated by historical tradition; the other was the representative of future sentiments. Both agreed upon the necessity of strengthening the Eastern Marches, but, while the one denied the wisdom or necessity of total assimilation, the proponents of the latter view took a more uncompromising view in accord with the newer ideological temper of nationalism.

Bismarck's position within this conflict of ideologies seemed to be traditional and moderate. In his various pronouncements, both in and out of office, he still called upon Frederick II, Flottwell and Grolman as his authorities—those exponents of the dictum *divide et impera* as it related to the Polish elements.[44] In the conflict of alignments that developed on the question of the implementation of the law, his views seem to have oscillated in several directions. On one occasion he expressed the thought that the best means of obviating emigration of indigenous German population would be by a policy of small loans and by making purchases of land from them. Later he expressed the opinion that the creation of small landholds *(Kuhbauern)* should be limited. In both cases he was forced to give ground by the parliamentary majority and especially the National Liberals who made German colonization a foremost tenet of their political faith. Though he subsequently concurred with the program of the president of the commission for the creation of leaseholds from 25 hectares and bigger, he regarded this order as "truly false, and its motivations . . . as stupid. . . ."[45]

Later, when out of office, he could elaborate freely on his position toward this program. He stated quite frankly that it was not his intention of settling German dwarf-landholders *(kleine Leute)*. He favored the keeping of these newly acquired lands as national domains. The question of their settlement would be subsequently dictated by later developments. He reiterated his contention that he did not regard the Polish peasant as a menace to Prussian security. Whether the agricultural workers on these domains were Polish or German was beside the point. The *bête noire* on the Polish question almost to his very end remained the Polish landed gentry and Polish Catholic hierarchy. He appears to have been indisposed, publicly at least, to reduce any Polish-German antagonisms to the level of inherent racial antagonisms.[46] The benefits of this program, as Bismarck conceived it, would ultimately accrue to Germans and loyal Poles alike, the latter's loyalty shored up with strong ties of material self-interest. Ideologically he appeared to be closer to Frederick II, Flottwell and Grolman rather than the new Hartmanns, Miquels and Treitschkes. The tragedy of the Junker conservative was that he was drawn into the camp of the nationalistic dogma of the National Liberals. In time it became the criterion of loyalty and patriotism espoused by the court, the manor, the bureaucracy and the great masses of the German population, and, in turn, was instrumental in uniting the Polish minority front of gentry, clergy and peasant. The final capitulation to the new currents of nationalism was Bismarck's admission on the eve of his death that "On the basis of many years of observation and consideration, the prince [Bismarck] regards all Poles, especially the gentry, the clergy and, last but not least, the Polish peasant as elements to whom conspiracy and political intrigue not only have become a necessity of life but for which they show a high level of perfection and competence; [these aptitudes] dedicated to the service of the idea of nationalism, never permit them to rest but serve as impulses to ever newer machinations." [47]

The *Ansiedlungsgesetz* of 1886, as it was finally adopted, provided for the establishment of a Colonization Commission *(Ansiedlungskommission)* with a fund of 100 million marks which was to buy up lands from Polish landed gentry, divide them into economically feasible parcels, and sell them to German colonists on favorable terms. With the money received from these purchases the Colonization Commission was to buy up more lands, parcel them and sell them to other German settlers. As viewed by its proponents, the costs would be minimal since the Commission's operations would be thus self-sustaining. It was theoretically estimated that by 1907 the Commission would be able to return the original funds appropriated for it by the law to the national treasury and, if necessary, still carry on its operations on the profits realized from the sales of the land.[48]

These sanguine hopes were soon forced to adapt themselves to practical economic realities. Since the policy of the Commission was to buy from Poles and sell to Germans, its choices of lands were limited. Lands sold by the Poles were often of marginal quality and had to be improved at considerable cost before they could be sold. Thus their costs were increased to the colonists who showed a marked reluctance to avail themselves of the proffered lands. In time this resulted in a marked tendency to lease out lands when they could not be sold.[49] Furthermore, the Commission had predicated its program on acquisition of Polish lands at minimal cost. Their very program of operations, however, had a tendency to increase the prices. It was expected that land could be had for about 560 M. per hectare — actually the price already averaged 568 M. per hectare in the first year and continued to increase progressively. By 1900 the price was averaging more than 800 marks and an impossible situation was developing in which there was a growing demand by indigenous German farmers to be "expropriated" also.[50]

One of the foremost causes of this increase in land costs, besides that inherent in the Commission's operations, was the defensive activity which its discriminatory features had called forth among the Polish-speaking elements. If the German nationalists regarded the waging of their offensive on the economic level as a logical extension of the traditional program of Germanization, their Polish counterparts were not long in adapting themselves to these new views. The changed ideological orientation of German nationalism could not but call forth a Polish counterpart.[51]

Every attack against the Polish nationalists, specifically the landed gentry and Catholic hierarchy, was interpreted by the Polish press as an attack against all the Polish-speaking elements. Though the Polish peasant, for practical purposes, cared little who occupied the office of Archbishop of Gniezno-Poznan, the inflamed press and his equally impassioned parish pastor gave him to believe that their cause was his. The reports of the hardships, both real and fabricated, that the removals of 1885 caused their co-nationals served as a dramatic illustration of the uncompromising extremes the government was capable of adopting. These measures could call forth his personal anxieties and fears by association. The discriminatory features of the colonization law, however, struck at the very basis of his existence—his land. Thus, like its German-speaking counterpart, the great Polish mass of peasantry was drawn into a nationalistic crusade from which it had largely abstained in the past. To every measure taken by the government and its nationalistic spokesmen, there developed a Polish countermeasure.

The period saw the revival of agricultural "circles" among the Polish rural elements, aimed chiefly at spreading information on improved farming methods. By 1888 a Land Bank *(Bank Ziemski)* was created in Poznan for the purpose of buying up landholds and settling Polish peasants upon them. After 1890, numerous "Land Associations" were established on a provincial scale, some on the cooperative principle, others as private investments to buy up and parcel the lands to their Polish clients. Many of these were adjuncts of the *Bank Ziemski* or closely associated with it. The press and the pulpit enjoined the peasant to resist German annihilation in every way. There followed a revival of the most impassioned patriotic symbolism — the land on which they lived was given a sacred character — "the land of our Fathers." The vocal elements created a state of public opinion which regarded the sale of Polish land to Germans as the grossest breach of faith — a sell-out to the enemy. Those who sold their "birth right" were regarded as traitors to the common cause and publicly denounced and ostracized. Emigration came to be regarded as akin to desertion.[52]

This polarization of nationalistic forces and their concentration upon the acquisition of land could not do otherwise than put a premium upon its value. At a time when many Polish and Prussian landed gentry were "land poor," when the competition of American and other overseas grain producers was forcing them from their European markets, such a development at home was their salvation. It could not, however, be called fortuitous.

Though they may have disclaimed the motives of their more outspoken nationalists in the parliamentary deliberations on this law, they were nonetheless its consistent supporters. The Junker landowners, as the ruling clique in the Prussian parliament, stood to gain much by this new "Germanization" policy. The Commission was paying them disproportionately high prices for their holdings — the contemplated program of buying up lands by the government to establish "national domains" would have been even more profitable for them. Furthermore, since they were more or less localized in the areas to the east of the Elbe and therefore in the area predominantly occupied by Poles, the national policy of the government coincided with their class interests. A government which repeatedly calls its citizens to battle with "that most dangerous menace to Germanism" must perforce favor German elements in those areas, the front line of which was composed of these Junker elements. Thus the Junker prestige would be enhanced as "the guardian of the Eastern Marches" and his own class interests would be identified with the national interests of the

German empire.[53] In addition to enhancing the value of their lands, the program would also build up the local labor supply which was being diminished by emigration.[54]

The Polish landed gentry found itself in a correspondingly felicitous situation. Though they protested against the discriminatory features of the legislation, their opposition was more nominal than real. As the traditional keepers of the "national flame," they were beyond the reaches of the censures that might have been leveled at them for selling their "birth right." That many of them did avail themselves of this means of extricating themselves from a declining economic situation is attested by the periodical reports of the Colonization Commission.[55]

The organization of Polish counter-efforts likewise gravitated to their material interests since the market situation that these efforts created enhanced the value of their land. The success of the Polish "Land Bank" and many of the subsequent "Parceling Associations" was largely assured, having now the support of the *szlachta*. They, on the one hand, found their economic salvation in selling some of their land holdings at inflated prices to meet pressing debts—thereby salvaging at least a part of their holdings—and, on the other hand, assured themselves of a cheap and readily accessible labor force. This latter advantage resulted from the fact that most of the parcels of land sold to the Polish peasants were small and insufficient to assure them an independent economic existence. Since their capital accumulations were small, usually the result of several years of migrant farm or industrial employment in western Germany, their dwarf landholds served to anchor them to the soil and impeded their mobility. Their wage bargaining power was thereby considerably reduced and, in a sense, they became "clients" of the Polish manor.[56]

The rise of Caprivi to power was followed by a reorientation in the government's Eastern Marches policy which may be regarded as a return to the older, pre-Bismarckian concepts of colonization and Germanization. The progress of colonization was not achieving the sanguine hopes of its formulators and the flow of emigration to the westward was continuing unabated. In spite of the protective tariffs on grains from abroad, the large landowner found himself in a progressively insolvent situation.[57] The immigration restrictions against the Russian and Austrian subjects instituted in 1885 were only adding to his difficulties.[58] Furthermore, the Russian government appeared to be entering upon a conciliatory policy in its relations with the Polish peasantry, as evidenced by the establishment of the Peasant Bank in Russian Poland.[59] Viewed from the classical standpoint of Russo-

German relations on the Polish question, this development could only have increased Prussian anxieties.

At the international level this period (1890–1894) was characterized by a reduction of trade barriers; on the domestic level by the termination of anti-Socialist laws. Its policy regarding the Polish minorities was a return to the traditional moderation: there was a relaxation in regulations restricting the use of the Polish language which had originated in the 1870's; Stablewski was appointed the archbishop of Poznan-Gniezno. The policy of total exclusion of Polish immigrants inaugurated in 1885 by Bismarck was modified and its policy of emigration, as reflected in its land policy in the Eastern Marches, was characterized by the passage of the *Rentenguter* legislation.[60]

This legislation, passed by the Reichstag in 1890 and supplemented in 1891, provided for a liberal program of government loans for the establishment of middle landholds in the eastern Prussian areas. Its administration was turned over to already existing "General Commissions" who were authorized to grant government loans to all Prussian subjects, whether Polish or German, seeking to acquire middle and small landholds by means of so-called "land-leases." The continued existence of these leaseholds was guaranteed by a stipulation which provided that they were to be left entailed to one heir who was provided with favorable credit facilities to reimburse any co-heirs.[61] This law applied to all of Prussia, and was doubtless calculated to win the Polish-speaking peasant to the cause of the government by tying his economic fortunes with Prussia. In this sense, it was meant to "steal the thunder" raised by the Polish nationalistic elements against the discriminatory operations of the Colonization Commission.[62]

The progress of the nationalization of the Polish peasant, however, had reached a point where this motive of the government failed in its realization. The Polish nationalists were ready to point out that the odious Colonization Commission was continuing its discriminatory program unimpaired. Furthermore, the growth of the Polish Land Bank and parceling associations had provided the Polish peasant with sufficiently favorable credit facilities to obviate recourse to General Commissions.[63] Finally, the stipulation of the *Rentenguter* laws regarding entail ran contrary to the Polish peasant's traditional inheritance practices.[64]

In any case, the more nationalistic Prussian elements, after a brief set-back, were again in full voice and threatening Caprivi's shaky tenure. The incompatability of the purposes of the Colonization Commission and the General Commission were quite obvious to even the casual observer. As a result, the Polish peasant, even when he sought to avail himself of the provisions of this law, found himself increasingly frustrated by bureaucratic and administrative regulations. After the fall of Caprivi, the General Commissions were forced to fall in line with the policy of the Colonization Commission, as its adjunct. They were not permitted to grant loans to Poles without express permission from the Colonization Commission.[65]

The Caprivi period represented a brief reversal for the forces of extreme nationalism from which they returned with renewed vigor. It likewise represented the last vigorous assertion of the traditional nationalism as it pertained to the Polish minority elements in Prussia. Thereafter this policy, as to Germanization, colonization, and emigration, became progressively uncompromising. The factions that had made common cause with the National Liberal party in the passage of the *Ansiedlungsgesetz* and had previously acquiesced to the removal decree found themselves in a position from which they could not retreat. As traditional guardians of the security of the Prussian state, the Junkers could not take second position, even ideologically, to that of the National Liberals. As a class, their *raison d'être* was predicated on this historical tradition.

An organized expression of the revival of rampant nationalism was the establishment of the "Association for the Advancement of the German Nationality in the Eastern Marches" *(Verein für Forderung des Deutschtums in den Ostmarken)* on September 28, 1894. Popularly known as the *Ostmarken-Verein* by the Germans and *Hakata* by the Poles (after its founders Hansemann, Kennemann and Tiedemann), it centralized and coordinated within its orbit the new offensive against "the aggressiveness on the part of the Poles."[66] This organized movement of German nationalism in the Eastern Marches, representing a reaction to Chancellor Caprivi's conciliatory policy,[67] made the German colonization program, begun in 1886, the central tenet of its faith throughout its twenty-five years' existence.[68] Numbering among its members such distinguished Germans as von Treitschke, Gustav Schmoller, Bernhard Erdmannsdorffer, Karl Lamprecht, Ernst Haeckel and Max Weber,[69] it collaborated with other nationalistic movements and patriotic organizations, such as the Pan-German League, the Navy League, the Colonial League, the German Society for Northern Schleswig, the German Language Association, and the General German School Association. Numerous groups of patriotic German women were organized as auxiliaries to the all-male Hakatist societies.[70] Through their press and the frequent memorials that they addressed to the Reichstag, they established themselves as the most vigilant guardians of the new nationalistic orthodoxy. Whenever the program of the Colonization Commission showed signs of bogging down, they rallied to the cause by whipping up enthusiasm for its greater financial support.[71] As a means of accelerating and extending the program of the Colonization Commission, Hakatists participated in private enterprises formed for the purpose of colonizing Germans on eastern farm lands. One of the earliest of these was the German *Landbank*, a corporation founded in Berlin in 1895 with a capital of 20 million marks largely supplied through the *Disconto-Gesellschaft* of which Hansemann's father was the head, and devoted to the creation of farms for Germans. Like its Polish counterpart, the *Bank Ziemski*, it found the patriotic business of multiplying farmsteads in rural Poznan and West Prussia exceedingly profitable.[72]

Though it devoted its energies chiefly to the cause of increasing German settlers in the rural regions, the *Ostmarken-Verein* did not overlook the challenge to Germanism posed by the ever increasing proportions of Polish-speaking population in the towns and cities of eastern Prussia. According to Tims, "Business patronage, financial services and the recruitment of fresh blood for the German middle classes were . . . the three primary fields in which the H-K-T leaders proposed to render defensive aid to the Germans in the towns of Posen and West Prussia."[73] "Eastern Marches novels" were encouraged and subsidized and literary contests were sponsored to "awaken interest in the Polish threat in the East." German versifiers were likewise recruited to the national cause.[74]

By this program of government and private subsidization and colonization, the nationalists hoped to reverse the demographic trend which was decreasing the German-speaking proportions in the rural and urban areas in eastern Prussia. They hoped not only to arrest the tide of German emigration but, by removing some of the causes, to reverse it. On the issue of emigration of Prussian Poles, their policy seems to have followed the logic dictated by their cause. Every Pole whose land was purchased by the Colonization Commission was a potential emigrant, whether it was to the industrial areas of Germany or abroad. In a like position were the grown sons and daughters of the prolific Poles who could not acquire sufficient land on which to establish their families. According to one investigator, Tiedemann even entered into negotiations with government representatives and an agent of the North-German Lloyd concerning the possibility of promoting Polish emigration from the Eastern Marches to Canada, in

1904. The difficulty of such a project lay in preventing the Germans from being attracted overseas at the same time.[75]

Meanwhile, the program of acquisition of land and colonization by the Colonization Commission continued with varying fortunes but undiminished vigor. If anything, even more determined efforts were indicated. In an article published in 1894, Richard Boeckh had shown that, according to the most recent statistical data, the Polish-speaking population had, since 1860, continued to increase more rapidly than the Germans. This, according to him, was due to: (1) a higher birth rate among the Poles; (2) the greater rate of German emigration, and (3) the continued "Polonization" of many Germans living in those eastern districts.[76]

Quite obviously, therefore, the danger was far from removed. Indeed, it seemed to be on the increase in spite of the efforts heretofore expended by the government and interested parties. Furthermore, the operational funds of the Colonization Commission were rapidly being exhausted. The "struggle for the soil" called forth by the contending nationalists, had tended to increase progressively the prices asked for land and resulted in correspondingly higher prices that the Commission was obliged to charge its German settlers. At these inflated prices there was a marked reluctance among many prospective clients to avail themselves of the Commission's services. Others, willing to take up the land, were lacking in the requisite funds. Hence, there was a growing disposition of the Commission to unload some of its holdings in the form of lease-holds.[77] In either case, there was an insufficient return on its investment — the operational capital was frozen in the land. By 1898 its original fund of 100 million marks was exhausted and recourse to the government was necessary if it was to continue its program. The task begun by the nationalists had by this time acquired its own momentum and, despite some scattered and isolated doubts, another 100 million marks was voted to continue its program.[78] Again in 1902 more funds had to be appropriated for this purpose.

The Land Law of 1902 was aimed at extending and facilitating the policy of German colonization undertaken by the law of 1886. In the campaign for German control of rural Poznan and West Prussia, it was calculated to get more land from the Poles and to out-colonize them. Passed in the spring of 1902, it provided for an appropriation of an additional 150 million marks for the Colonization Commission and, in a new departure, set apart an additional 100 million marks for the purchase of Polish estates, which were to be kept intact as state property and leased in comparatively large units to German farmers.[79]

The "struggle for the soil," however, had by now been joined in earnest by the great base of the Polish peasantry. The unprecedented expansion of German industry in the western provinces afforded them heretofore incomparable sources of capital accumulations. These savings, which the Prussian Pole accumulated in the Rhine province or Westphalia, were frequently lodged in Polish banks or parceling associations to provide security for himself in his old age. The Commission found itself in the middle of this economic spiral which it had been instrumental in creating. By 1904 it was in need of further funds.[80]

The Land Law of 1904 was passed in response to the apparently losing race that the Hakatists and the Colonization Commission were waging with the Polish cooperatives and banks in colonizing the Eastern Marches with their respective nationals. As Tims summarized it, this bill "was so drafted as to give the government the power to make it virtually impossible for a Polish peasant or laborer to live on any plot of land that he might in the future acquire. Anywhere within the field of operations of the Colonization Commission the authorities were empowered to forbid a Pole to erect or remodel a dwelling house on any part of a newly subdivided farm."[81] The task of pushing this legislation through the upper house of the Landtag fell not to a Junker *Rittergutsbesitzer* but to the economist Schmoller, a member of the *Ostmarken-Verein* since its beginning. According to Schmoller, "patriotic Germans must stand united when the existence and future of the state were in question," and that, "the *salus publica* took precedence over considerations of equal justice to all citizens, classes or national groups."[82]

This measure, a logical extension of the law of 1886, likewise failed to achieve the expectations of the German nationalists. In fact, it was more than a failure since its results were diametrically opposed to what they had hoped to achieve. The Polish peasant, since he could not get a building permit on a newly acquired plot of land, was perforce obliged to direct his land hunger to purchasing existing *German* farms, thereby displacing a resident German. Hence, in effect, the law proved to be a "boomerang against the other side of the German program, repopulation [with German peasants]."[83]

The Hakatists and like-minded Germans were quick to realize this shortcoming. By 1905, they had already begun to raise the standard of outright expropriation. As formerly, their arguments raised the alarm of the continued losses sustained by Germans in the "struggle for the soil."[84] A logical extreme of its antecedents, this law ran into unexpected opposition in the upper chamber of the Landtag. Its precedential potential seems to have sobered the heretofore acquiescent Junker landowners. They refused to give it their sanction to the very end and, as formerly, the task of chief spokesman for its passage fell to Schmoller.[85]

The new Land Law of 1908, popularly called the Expropriation Act, authorized the Colonization Commission to expropriate from private owners a maximum of 70,000 hectares of land within carefully delimited areas in Poznan province and West Prussia. With it went an appropriation of 225 million marks—a total of 675 million marks since 1886.[86] It represented the highwater mark of Germany's policy toward its Polish-speaking subjects begun by Bismarck. As an instrument of its population policy toward its Polish-speaking subjects in that area, it formally proclaimed the *Ausrottungskrieg*—a policy it formerly stoutly disavowed.[87]

II

Prussian Policies Affecting Immigration— From Total Exclusion to Rigid Control

The policy of deportation and total exclusion inaugurated by Bismarck in 1885 was soon found to be at odds with the interests of large landowners in Prussia. That they were early cognizant of its ramifications was evident from the alarms that it called forth in wide circles of Prussian society and the vote of censure which it called forth in the parliament.[1] The die, however, had been cast and Bismarck was unaccustomed to retreating from a position he had once taken. During the remaining years of his tenure in office, the policy of total exclusion of Polish immigration remained in effect and the flow of immigration was practically halted.

Meanwhile, the flow of emigrants from the eastern districts continued toward the urban and industrial centers (especially western Germany) in such proportions that it was regarded as a "flight from the land."[2] This depletion of the labor reserve, in the absence of sufficient replacements from either at home or abroad, was felt intensely by the large landowners—especially since the introduction of the profitable sugar beet culture. This root crop, carried on an extensive scale, required large numbers of field hands for its planting, weeding and harvesting. In the absence of sufficiently numerous and cheap labor, this promising segment of Prussian agriculture was threatened with collapse.[3]

Thus it was that one of the earliest measures taken by the Caprivi ministry in 1890 was the suspension of the directive of March 26, 1885.[4] With this move the government changed its immigration policy, as it related to the Poles in the Russian and Austrian sectors, from one of total exclusion to one of rigid control—a policy which, with progressive intensity was to be followed until the outbreak of World War I.

Since the opening of the borders to Polish immigration from the Kingdom and Galicia was likely to result in a large influx of that population and since such a development was patently contrary to the

German population and settlement policy on her eastern borders, the measure that suspended the law of 1885 also provided that the Polish-speaking immigrant must leave Prussia each year by the 15th of November.[5] Such a policy of a purely seasonal stay was found to be acceptable to the large landowners and still satisfied the clamor of the extreme nationalists. In this way Polish immigrants could be effectively utilized as a labor force but would not add to the problem of Germanization of the Eastern Marches, a problem that was sufficiently impeded by the indigenous Polish-speaking Prussians. Furthermore, such a policy comported with the best interests of the German employers. Since the character of their agricultural operations was seasonal, the employers would not be obliged to care for their employees during the winter slack season.[6]

Having gained recognition of their needs, the agricultural interests pressed their advantage yet further. A Polish worker who availed himself of the opportunities opened by the relaxed immigration policy by seeking employment in German industry was obviously defeating its purpose, in the eyes of the Junker landowner. As a consequence of this possibility, the areas of his employment were rigidly circumscribed by provincial regulations supplementing the general law in the border areas—usually to agriculture or industries directly related to agriculture.[7] Several thousand workers profited from this policy as early as 1891. In Poznan province alone 7,814 workers from Russian Poland and 85 from Austrian Poland were imported in that year.[8] Thereafter, with only infrequent setbacks, the number of these seasonal immigrants increased progressively.[9]

The landed interests did not cease from pressing their advantage. As a result of their continued pressure on the government, in 1898 the Prussian parliament was induced to extend the legal sojourn of the seasonal immigrants by two weeks where their need could be established. In such areas, the length of their seasonal stay was extended from April 1 to December 1. In areas where this concession was deemed still insufficient, the landowners were advised by the Minister of Agriculture, Baron von Hammerstein, to seek workers from other countries.[10] Nevertheless, further concessions were made in 1899 and 1900. The period of legal sojourn was extended from February 1 to December 20.[11] Further concessions on this point, despite continued representations by German agricultural interests, were denied. On the contrary, the government thereafter sought by various means to displace Polish seasonal immigrants with either Germans living abroad or with other nationalities. During the following years German landholders actually did make an effort to attract non-Polish workers, especially Germans from the Banat.[12] The excessive dependence of German agriculture upon Polish immigrant labor was disquieting to the nationalists.

This revision of immigration restrictions was also attended by a relaxation of the policy of forcible removals of alien residents of the Eastern Marches. Caprivi's government still refused to give authorization for settlement of immigrants from Russian and Austrian Poland, but neither did it forcibly remove them. As a result, a certain number of Russian and Austrian subjects settled in Prussian Poland, especially in the border counties.

The fall of Caprivi resulted in the return to Bismarckian policy toward permanent Polish immigration and the renewal of a program of removals in 1895. This second period of removals, corresponding chronologically with the Hohenlohe chancellorship, reached sizable proportions in 1898. Concentrated in the provinces of Poznan and Silesia, the total removals were estimated at 2,000 population. A number of Galician laborers was forced to leave Upper Silesia in spite of the voices raised in the Reichstag against it by Silesian delegates and notwithstanding the official representations made by the Austrian government.[13]

A return to the Bismarckian policy of total exclusion of all immigration, however, was out of the question. While the excessive dependence upon Polish immigrant labor may have been disquieting to the nationalists, the economic solvency of the landed gentry was predicated upon precisely such a cheap labor supply. Partly as a result of the growing anxieties, but primarily to encourage the immigration of German peasants living in Galicia, Russian Poland and elsewhere in Europe, to the Eastern Marches, there came into existence in 1903 an organization called the *Zentralstelle zur Beschaffung deutscher Ansiedler und Feldarbeiter*. The initiative for its organization was supplied by the *Ostmarken-Verein* in cooperation with other nationalistic organizations. In time it was to become the semi-official instrument of the Prussian immigration policy. Besides encouraging the remigration of Germans dispersed outside the empire, it set its goal to displace as many Polish seasonal workers as possible with those of other nationalities.[14] With this end in view, it entered into negotiations with representatives of Ukrainian nationalists to encourage immigration of Ukrainians from eastern Galicia.[15] Such a program was pregnant with political possibilities since the position of these Ukrainian elements in Galicia corresponded to a remarkable degree with that of the Polish-speaking ones in Prussia.[16]

As an organization to encourage remigration of Germans, this organization did not enjoy much success. By 1905 it abandoned German colonization as its primary function and concentrated its efforts almost exclusively on supplying Prussian agriculture with a sufficient foreign labor force. Reorganized thus, it changed its name to *Deutsche Feldarbeiterzentralstelle* and removed its base of operations from Poznan to Berlin. Within this delimited area of operation its function was twofold: to serve the economic interests of Prussian agriculture by providing it with a sufficient immigrant labor force and, simultaneously, to control this immigration in such a way as to best serve the German national interest in the Eastern Marches. Subsequently it changed its name to *Arbeiterzentrale* and extended its operations to include seasonal immigrants for some German industrial establishments.[17] Under the protection of the Ministry of Internal Affairs, this organization hoped to centralize control over the supply of foreign labor and thereby remove the competition for labor between the various provincial *Landwirtschaftkammern* and numerous private agencies engaged in recruitment of immigrant labor—a competition which tended to raise the cost of labor.[18] The nationalists had now come around to the point where in their immigration policy they were working for the Prussian *Gutsbesitzer*.

The transition, however, was slow and painful. The instincts of the hard core of Hakatists dictated a policy of total exclusion. As late as the turn of the century, *Die Ostmark,* the official organ of the Hakata, proclaimed its stand on the question of immigrant agricultural labor with the following demands: (1) the prohibition of the use of immigrant Poles as domestic servants; (2) abolition of the reduced railway rates which encouraged immigration; (3) more careful supervision of immigrant labor; (4) a more vigorous German colonization program, and (5) total restriction of Slavic immigration at some future date "when economically feasible."[19] In a conflict between nationalistic guardianship against the "Polish peril" and the interests of the landed gentry, the militant nationalists had to make repeated concessions. Only on the subject of careful surveillance, *i.e.,* control, over the immigrant Poles, to prevent their permanent settlement in Prussia, was the government prepared to follow their advice. On the numerous other aspects concerning Polish immigration, the Hakatists, in their relation to the policy of the government, found themselves in the position of endorsing measures already adopted. Thus, their manifesto was no more than what the Prussian government had already been doing since 1892. On the issue of the length of the season which

the immigrant workers were permitted to stay in Germany, the Hakatists actually endorsed an extension of the period allowed by the
government.[20]

By sponsoring the *Deutsche Feldarbeiterzentralstelle,* the government had abandoned all hope of restriction and entered upon a
program which, on the one hand, encouraged seasonal immigration
and, on the other, exercised an increasingly rigid control over it. It
frankly espoused the cause of the landed interests. Beginning with
1905, the previously passed regulation forbidding employment of
Polish seasonal workers in factories and other industrial enterprises in
designated districts was adopted throughout Prussia.[21]

The *Deutsche Feldarbeiterzentralstelle* as an avowedly economic
agency exerted every effort to gain monopoly control over the entire
field of immigrant labor. In this way it apparently hoped to be able to
establish fixed wage norms. This tendency was evident from resolutions passed by a conference of its officials with representatives from
various Prussian *Landwirtschaftkammern* on October 22, 1908, which
stressed the need for elimination of harmful competition among the
various employment agencies functioning in this field. As a result of
official pressure, the local agricultural councils were obliged to submit.[22] The submission, however, was never entirely complete. Many
German employers preferred to do business with private agencies
either at home or abroad. In time, as the practice of seasonal migration became well established, an increasing proportion of migrants
undertook the journey of their own accord, usually to places where
they had worked previously. Not infrequently a peasant with some
experience in seasonal migration recruited a group from his or a
nearby village and directed them to an employer with whom he had
contracted to supply a specific number of field hands.[23]

Failing to acquire monopoly control over seasonal immigrants, the
Feldarbeiterzentrale entered upon a program of recruitment which, by
increasing the labor supply as much as possible, would correspondingly decrease the wages and conditions of employment, thereby
serving the best interests of its German clients.[24]

In the meantime, however, the rapidly growing volume of Polish
immigration had to be controlled with even greater vigilance. By disposition of the Prussian Ministry of Internal Affairs of December 21,
1907, all seasonal workers from Russia, Austria-Hungary and countries to the eastward were obliged to register at border stations provided for that purpose and receive proper identification papers. This
ministerial directive was supplemented by another on December 30,

1908, which extended this ruling to include all foreign seasonal immigrants. The entire administration of this policy was given over to the *Deutsche Feldarbeiterzentrale.* Authorization papers *(Legitimationskarte)* were made compulsory throughout Prussia and the greater part of the Reich. An immigrant found without these papers was immediately liable to deportation by the police authorities.[25] By 1911 this organization had established 51 border stations in localities through which the migrant tide passed. Twenty-three of these, under five inspectorates, were located along the Russian and Austrian borders and each of them had its territory of competence explicitly prescribed to preclude overlapping.[26]

By this act the government had established the *Arbeiterzentrale* as the final arbiter in the regulation of seasonal immigration. Though still ostensibly an employment agency intended to act as immigrant labor broker, it was in effect an immigration commission with power to restrict entry into the Prussian borders for whatever reason it might choose. During the two seasons of 1907/1908 and 1908/1909, identification papers were denied to 9,869 applicants for various reasons.[27] Nor did the *Arbeiterzentrale* ever forget its greater mission in the service of Prussian nationalism and the security of the Eastern Marches. Its representatives sought in every way to encourage and facilitate the immigration of Ukrainian Galicians. Among other preferences that were granted this group of Austrian subjects was their exemption from the so-called *Karenzzeit* regulations which required the immigrant Poles to remove themselves beyond the borders of the German empire each season for a short period.[28] Neither did they come under the regulations which excluded the immigrant Poles from employment in German factories and industries.[29] To preclude any confusion on these points, the identification papers of each of the various national groups were issued in different colors — those of the Poles, whether from Austria or Russia, were red — those of the Ukrainians were yellow and all remaining nationalities were white.[30]

Whether Pole, Ukrainian or otherwise, every seasonal immigrant had to show proof of definite employment, usually in the form of a written contract, before he was issued the *Legitimationskarte.* In the absence of a contract, the *Arbeiterzentrale,* in its capacity of employment agency, was prepared to draw one up for him. These contracts nominally intended to protect the employer as well as the employee were, in fact, heavily weighted in favor of the former. Whether drawn up by the *Arbeiterzentrale,* other agencies or by the employer himself, it was the almost universal practice to include in the contract a clause whereby the immigrant worker waived the right to seek redress of any grievances arising from his employment in the civil courts. Any questions arising from conditions of employment or wages were adjudicated by arbitration courts provided either by the local agricultural councils or the *Arbeiterzentrale*. As the area of competence of the latter agency was progressively extended, in time their arbitrational bodies almost completely displaced those of the agricultural councils. In either case, since both bodies were controlled by the agricultural interests, only in cases of flagrant abuse could the immigrant hope for equitable redress of his grievances. Even this recourse could be easily circumvented by the employer by the simple expedient of declaring the termination of the labor contract and reporting this action to the police authorities, in which case the immigrant's identification card was revoked and he was summarily and expeditiously removed beyond the border.[31]

To protect the employer from contract breaking on the part of the immigrant, the former was authorized to withhold a certain amount of the latter's wages, usually about three marks per week or ten marks per month, until the sum amounted to about thirty marks. This bond was returned to the immigrant upon fulfillment of the contractual agreement. Failure to do so resulted in its forfeiture. Since the importation of an immigrant laborer represented a certain investment to the employer — the commission he paid to the public or private agency which supplied him and the transportation costs from the border to the place of employment — it was argued that such a practice was justified. It served, however, to great advantage for an unscrupulous employer who could report his employee to the police authorities and have him removed, thereby forfeiting to the employer the accumulated bond. Theoretically, this practice, in the case of such an employer, could be repeated indefinitely to his great financial advantage. The nationalistic press voiced numerous complaints, in the early stages of this immigration, against the Polish immigrant as a contract breaker. Their validity is impossible to establish. Very likely there was a measure of truth in their alarms. Some immigrant Poles were doubtless irresponsible, others were as yet unimpressed with the idea of the sanctity of contractual commitments, and others still were likely incited to break their contracts by unprincipled employment agents in order to give the agents opportunity to mediate another job placement and thereby earn another commission. That contract breaking was not a practice peculiar to the Polish seasonal agricultural worker, however, is evidenced by the similar complaints voiced by German agriculture in the early 1890's, levelled against Brandenburgian harvesters.[32] Many of them openly advocated importation of "more tractable" Poles precisely to correct these unhappy occurrences.[33]

The strictures incorporated into the labor contracts were supplemented by government regulations calculated to control this immigration. For practical purposes, the seasonal agricultural worker was excluded from legal guarantees and protective legislation which had been progressively accruing to the German industrial worker since the 1870's. Thus, the right of coalition, long since recognized in industry, was denied to agricultural workers.[34] Circumstances which gravitated especially against the interests of the Polish seasonal agricultural workers were those which largely excluded him from the benefits provided by the existing compensation laws. The immigrant Pole, like all others, was required by law to contribute periodically from his wages into the established insurance and compensation funds. However, in the event of an accident resulting in his loss of life or capacity to work, neither his heirs nor he himself could fully benefit from either fund, since the law provided that the recipient of these benefits, or his heirs, must have a place of permanent residence in Germany. Inasmuch as the immigration regulations enforced the seasonal departure of all Polish immigrants and since another law prohibited him from immigrating with his family and thereby establishing their residence in Germany, for practical purposes he was excluded from the protection provided by the compensation laws. In practice, this obviously flagrant circumvention of the compensation laws was resolved by the payment to his heirs of an equivalent of his three years' wages. Not until the outbreak of the war were adjustments made to repair this impossible legal situation.[35]

Notwithstanding the comprehensive policy of regulation enforced by the German authorities and despite the combined efforts of public and private Polish agencies in the other two sectors to boycott Prussia,[36] seasonal migrations to that country progressively developed in volume in the decades preceding the war. The relaxation of immigration restrictions during the Caprivi period resulted in an influx of a couple of tens of thousand *Sachsengängerei* in 1891. Thereafter, with minor exceptions, their volume increased until by the turn of the century the Kingdom alone was supplying approximately 120,000 migrant workers annually. In the years immediately preceding the war their number was conservatively estimated at about four hundred thousand per annum from both the eastern sectors of pre-war Poland.[37]

II. Russia and the Poles

III

Russian Policies Affecting
Polish Emigration

In that sector of pre-World War I Poland known to the Poles as
"The Kingdom" and commonly referred to as Russian Poland, the
policies of the ruling authorities which affected the movements of its
population were, if anything, more varied than those of the Prussian
authorities in Greater Poland. Directly, or indirectly, all those policies
which touched upon the social, economic, political, cultural and religious life of its subjects contributed to the cumulative configuration of
circumstances which underlie the shifts of population in any given
area. Thus, such policies as the industrialization of the country, the
tariff schedules, the construction of railroads, military conscription,
land reforms, the confiscations and reprisals against the revolutionary
elements, the nationalities policy in the eastern governments of Russian
Poland and the "Western Governments" of European Russia, the
colonization policy in Siberia and the credit policy for the peasants
were more influential in determining the volume and direction of
migrations than such directly pertinent measures as the passport
policy or border restrictions.

The industrialization of European countries has historically been
conjoined with immigration as well as internal migrations. Far from
imposing impediments to immigration, such countries not infrequently
have offered a variety of special privileges and emoluments to encourage the inflow of skilled factory personnel. Such was the case in
Russian Poland throughout the greater part of the first half of the
nineteenth century.

The official policy of the ruling authorities toward immigration of
industrial personnel coincided with and was a concomitant of a
program aimed at industrializing Russian Poland. As far back as the
Commonwealth period, efforts were made to facilitate inflow of foreign
capital and otherwise to encourage industry and manufacture. By way
of attracting industrial elements, foreign artisans and craftsmen were
offered all manner of emoluments by the authorities, who frequently

built their homes, assigned them land for garden crops and improved the land for establishment of their colonies. This policy, inaugurated during the reign of Stanislaw Augustus, was continued during the period of the Duchy of Warsaw (established by Napoleon) and the autonomous existence of the Congress Kingdom (1815–1831).[1]

By act of March 2, 1816, the Polish government of the Congress Kingdom reaffirmed the former privileges granted the immigrants and extended them. Every immigrant artisan was exempt from all public taxes for six years, his sons were exempt from military service and, in crossing the border, he was freed from any tariffs on his goods or equipment. Should he become dissatisfied with his new life, the authorities were instructed, upon his request, to facilitate his return home.[2] Government agents were authorized to send their emissaries abroad, on a commission basis, to encourage this immigration. Private immigrant agents vied with those of the government in this practice.[3] As a result of these exceptional laws and privileges, these precursors of industrialism settled in the cities and towns of Russian Poland, created their small manufacturing establishments and laid the groundwork for such later industrial centers as Lodz, Zgierz, Tomaszow, Pabjanice, Ozorkow, Sosnowiec, Zyrardow and others.[4] During the ministry of Drucki-Lubecki (1821–1830) especially, this policy of the Polish authorities became a part of a comprehensive economic program for the fiscal, agricultural, commercial and industrial development of the country.[5] Woycicki, citing Schmoller as his authority, stated that about 250,000 German immigrants alone came to the Kingdom during the decade 1818–1828. They were mostly small scale manufacturers, artisans and craftsmen from Prussia and Silesia as well as weavers from Bohemia.[6]

In practical operation, this policy was continued during the Vice-regency of Paskiewicz (1831–1844). Not until the sixth decade of the nineteenth century was there any evidence of departure from this policy. Throughout these formative years of industrial capitalism in Russian Poland, the ruling authorities, whether Polish or Russian, sought to promote manufacture.[7] When an emigration of miners from Dabrowa Basin to Silesia developed in the 1850's, to escape military service, the Director of Finance prevailed upon the Czar to issue the Decree of October 28, 1856, exempting all miners employed in government establishments from military service. This privilege was extended to those in privately operated mines in August, 1862.[8]

Though not as comparatively numerous as in previous decades, by 1870 there was still a notable influx of German "masters" and workers, together with financiers, engineers and directors. The authorities, however, had ceased to encourage this immigration. Nevertheless, inasmuch as most of the large industrial enterprises were owned and operated by foreign, especially German, interests, skilled German industrial workers still received preferential treatment by their co-nationals. As one author put it, "faced with the alternative of earning their bread in a distant hemisphere, the German skilled worker preferred to establish himself in close proximity to his fatherland."[9] As a result of this influx of industrial personnel, at first encouraged and later unrestricted, the character of the industrial centers assumed a decidedly foreign cast. Especially considerable was the proportion of German elements in some industrial areas. Thus, in 1887 it was estimated that about three-fourths of the industrial workers in the Sosnowiec district were Germans. In the mining industry near the Silesian border, the German elements were so numerous that, according to one writer, "even the language of the Polish elements underwent considerable Germanization." By 1880, even the Russian authorities expressed deep concern over the hazards posed by the large concentrations of German elements along its borders. Shortly thereafter an administrative order was issued restricting the settlement of foreign elements along the border areas and aimed primarily at eliminating this hazard. In 1891, the Russian authorities instructed the employers of Lodz to remove from their employ such supervisory personnel and masters who lacked a "suitable competence" in the Polish or Russian language, or face deportation. Though this directive remained largely unenforced, it illustrated the changing policy of the government as it related to German industrial immigrants.[10] The influx of German elements into Russian Poland decreased considerably by the turn of the century and practically ceased in the years preceding the war — not as a result of bureaucratic impediments which, for practical purposes, were ineffectual, but rather as a result of an accelerated influx of indigenous elements into the industrial establishments.[11]

This changing policy of the Russian government toward industrial immigration into Russian Poland was but an expression of the changing policy of that government toward the industrialization of Russian Poland in the last decades of the nineteenth century. The shift in Russian policy from one of encouraging industrialization in Russian Poland to one favoring the central Russian provinces was attended by a concomitant change in the movement of population. This changing policy was illustrated by the changing tariff schedules as they related to Russian Poland.

As already mentioned, during the period of comparative autonomy after the Vienna settlement in 1815, the policy of the Polish authorities in Congress Poland was to encourage the inflow of capital investment and immigration. This trend was briefly arrested after the November Uprising (1830–1831) when a tariff barrier was established between the Congress Kingdom and the rest of the Russian empire. This policy had the total effect of seriously restricting the most important market outlets for the products of the factories of the Kingdom. The heretofore flourishing woolen, cotton and linen manufacture declined. The increment of foreign capital also declined. In this declining situation many craftsmen and workers, together with their manufacturing establishments, moved to Russian areas beyond the trade barriers.[12]

This recession, however, was arrested in 1850 with the removal of the trade barriers in that year. This had the effect of incorporating Russian Poland into the general economy of the empire and creating felicitous conditions for the revival of trade and commerce. The Russian markets opened by the removal of the trade barriers were fully utilized, especially so when the sea blockade of the Russian empire during the Crimean War both increased the need for the textile products of Russian Poland and practically gave them the monopoly of the overland trade with the Russian empire.[13]

Concomitant with the removal of the trade barriers between Russian Poland and the rest of the empire, there was a general movement toward free trade during this period. The placing of raw materials on the free lists was especially advantageous for the development of industries in the Kingdom.

This policy was continued in the tariffs of 1857 and 1868. By 1869, however, there was evidence of a reversal of the free-trade trend. The tariff of that year indicated an increase in the scale especially on machines and metallurgical products.[14] By 1877, the empire, including Russian Poland, had frankly espoused the idea of protectionism—a development which was especially auspicious for the growth of the industries of Russian Poland, predicated as they were almost exclusively on the Russian market. As one author put it, while the period 1860–1877 created all the chief conditions necessary for industrial growth—markets, communications and reserve labor force—the protective tariff policy inaugurated in 1877 created conditions of "an Eldorado for capital accumulations and industrialization."[15] Thereafter, in 1881, 1882, 1884, 1885, 1887 and 1891, the protective principle was progressively extended until the tariff of 1891 was avowedly and blatantly protectionist.[16]

By 1887, however, a new tendency was already apparent insofar as it pertained to Russian Poland. The tariff of that year placed tariff schedules on a number of raw materials upon which the industries of Russian Poland were dependent. Thereafter, the manufacturing enterprises of Russian Poland became increasingly dependent upon the raw materials from Russia proper.[17] The commercial treaty between Russia and Germany in 1894 further inhibited the industrial development of Russian Poland.[18] Thereafter, voices were increasingly raised in the councils of the Russian government deploring the preferential status of Polish industries at the expense of the incipient Russian enterprises. Witte, as Minister of Finance (1892–1900), successfully resisted the pressures of exclusively Russian industrial interests, concerned as he was primarily with the Russian treasury.[19] His political demise, however, marked a milestone in the industrial development of Russian Poland. A selective tariff policy, combined with a new policy of railroad construction and preferential freight rates favored exclusively Russian enterprises and militated against their counterparts in Russian Poland. These factors, combined with the natural advantages of closer proximity to her own raw materials and markets, tended progressively to push the products of Russian Poland from her former outlets within the empire.[20]

Thus, up to more or less the turn of the century, the industries of Russian Poland developed faster and showed greater vigor than the industries of Russia proper. Thereafter, however, the trend of development was reversed and the ratio of development changed in favor of the latter.[21] The more favorable conditions for profitable investment in Russia caused a much higher proportion of foreign capital, on which the industrial growth of Russian Poland was almost exclusively based, to flow into Russian industries.[22] The growth of relatively large scale industrial enterprises in Russia inevitably tended to attract industrial workers as immigrants, especially skilled workers from Russian Poland.

The liberal policy of the first half of the nineteenth century toward industrial immigration into Russian Poland was, to a lesser degree, applicable to agricultural immigration. It was during this period of a liberal immigration policy that considerable numbers of the so-called Lippowaners and German Mennonites settled within the borders of the empire. As an inducement, they were exempt from military conscription.[23] Within the borders of the Kingdom numerous foreign elements were settled on favorable terms by the Russian authorities on lands confiscated after the successive uprisings.[24]

Following the peasant land reforms of 1863, some of the Polish landed gentry were obliged to grant leaseholds to German and other foreign migrants. The decree of 1861, applied in the Kingdom in 1863, had likewise deprived them of their free labor supply. Many of the gentry, unable to enter into a capitalistic relationship with the local labor supply, were faced with the alternative of disposing of their landholds, selling parts of them to launch them into the new economy, or granting leaseholds. Since the indigenous peasantry was entirely lacking in capital accumulations, the landed proprietors were sometimes obliged to turn to foreigners. It was during this period that there developed a sizable German colonization in Volhynia province. Predominantly from Russian Poland, they were settled by Polish large landholders on leaseholds, principally along the central horizontal strip of that province between Wlodzimierz and Luck, on the one side, and Zwiahel and Zytomierz, on the other.[25]

The imperial decree of March 14 [26], 1887, signalized a radical departure of the government from its former liberal policy of agricultural immigration into Russian Poland and its domestic agricultural policy toward resident foreigners. Henceforth, all foreigners were deprived of the right to acquire, lease or inherit land outside the ports and cities of Russian Poland. This restriction applied also to the provinces of Vilno, Vitebsk, Volhynia, Kiev, Kovno, Courland, Livonia, Minsk, Podolia and Bessarabia.[26] It was greeted with qualms by the Polish gentry since it had the effect of throwing more land on the market and at the same time reducing the number of potential buyers, all of which inevitably tended to depress land prices.[27] Furthermore, as a reprisal against the Prussian policy of removals adopted in the Eastern Marches in 1885, it was suspect since it did not include the central Russian provinces. According to one contemporary observer, the proscriptions it imposed on land ownership in Russian Poland would tend to "make timid" existing capital investments in land and discourage new ones—all to the advantage of the central Russian provinces.[28]

But the most dramatic shifts of population within the borders of Russian Poland were those resulting from the unsuccessful Polish uprisings against the Russian authorities in the nineteenth century. The reprisals against the insurgent Polish elements resulted in widespread dislocations of that population. Some succeeded in escaping abroad while others, apprehended by the Russian authorities, were subjected to varying reprisals. Some were put to death, others had their property confiscated, others still were sentenced to various periods of confinement. Of interest here, from the standpoint of population movements, was that group of political prisoners which was transported into the interior of the empire. According to one estimate, about sixty thousand Poles from Russian Poland were transported to the interior of the Russian empire following the November Uprising (1831). Of these, ten thousand were confined in European Russia and about fifty thousand were sent to Siberia. Of the latter, thirty thousand were military personnel who were largely incorporated into the Russian armies and dispersed throughout the empire, while the remaining twenty thousand were sentenced to varying periods and types of confinement in Siberia.[29]

The dislocation of population following the January Uprising (1863) was, if anything, even more considerable. The death sentences, arrests, banishments into the interior of the empire, combined to effect a mass displacement of population in Russian Poland. The volume of these displacements has been variously estimated. Maksimov estimated that a total of 18,623 Poles were deported to Siberia up to 1866.[30] Prince Kropotkin put his estimate at 18,672 for the same period.[31] An anonymous writer, Z. O., claiming access to the prisoner registers of Tobolsk, through which almost all Siberian deportees had to pass, said that by October, 1866, their number was approaching 80,000.[32] Another writer, Jozef Ignacy Kraszewski, estimated there were over 150,000 Polish prisoners of all types sent to Siberia up to and including 1869.[33] The Englishman, William A. Whyte, recorded in his travel journal that there were between thirty and forty thousand Poles living in eastern Siberia alone at about that time.[34] Another English traveller, Henry Lansdell, considered most of the above estimates too high.[35] According to data in the Czartoryski Manuscripts, said to be based on the statistics of the Ministry of War in St. Petersburg, 31,573 Poles were deported into the depths of Russia and Siberia during the period from February 1, 1863 to January 1, 1864 from Russian Poland. Total deportations from Russian Poland up to 1867 were estimated between 250,000 and 300,000 population.[36]

Thus, estimates of total deportations vary considerably—from a few thousand to a quarter million. These deportations, already begun in 1860, took on mass proportions after 1863 and lasted until 1866.[37]

Concomitant with the deportations and as an aspect of its rigid policy of Russification of Russian Poland, the governmental authorities closed the institutions of higher learning and adopted a program of transferring Polish personnel in government employment beyond the borders of Russian Poland. In this way, many careers heretofore available in Russian Poland were eliminated. Those seeking such employment were obliged to take it in the interior of Russia. Military conscripts, after the termination of their tours of duty, not infrequently remained in Russia. Others still, educated in Russian schools, found themselves best suited to enter into some form of Russian employment. Skilled technicians and mechanics as well as ordinary factory workers, impelled by the recurring periods of economic recession in Russian Poland, were able to find suitable employment in the growing industrial centers of central Russia.

Thus, to the volume of involuntary migrants following the Uprisings, there was added a current of voluntary migrants, usually composed of a high percentage of skilled workers, teachers, engineers, doctors and lawyers trained in Russian universities but lacking career opportunities in Russian Poland; merchants and traders engaged in exploiting the vast Russian markets; and domestic artisans, craftsmen and small manufacturers displaced by the factory system of Russian Poland.[38] Even among the involuntary migrants, dispersed throughout European Russia and Siberia, a notable proportion settled there permanently after the conclusion of their confinement. They had established themselves in business, acquired families and, faced with the unencouraging alternative of returning home, decided to make their life there. In this way, they contributed to the settlement of the vast reaches of Siberia.[39]

These, like some of the discharged conscripts, not only declined repatriation to Russian Poland but frequently encouraged their friends, relatives and acquaintances to join them. Those seeking careers in industries, domestic service and the professional occupations, as well as estate managers and administrators, gravitated toward European Russia. Those seeking land, because of administrative restraints and lack of cheap land in European Russia, gravitated beyond the Urals.[40]

Thus, by the 1880's, the pressure of rural population in the Kingdom was forcing an increasing volume of peasants beyond the Urals. According to the newspaper *Sibir,* published in Irkutsk, 4,955 emigrants came to Siberia in 1881 from Russian Poland, by way of the Ural railroad, and their number increased to 5,708 in 1882[41] — this in spite of the fact that the policy toward settlement there was, if anything, restrictive. Further evidence of this eastward movement of peasant population was noted by the periodical *Przeglad Katolicki* in 1886. According to that publication there had developed a considerable volume of peasant emigration from the Russian Poland province of

Radom to Tomsk. These peasants, having liquidated their assets in Radom, hoped to get cheap land in Siberia.[42] The beginning of the construction of the Trans-Siberian railroad in 1891 not only opened opportunity for employment but also new lands.[43] In 1903, the government liberalized its passport regulations to facilitate travel within the empire.[44]

By 1906 the government embarked upon a policy of aid to the peasant population. One of the means adopted toward this end was an accelerated program of colonization and settlement in Siberia. It allocated 4,938,633 rubles for the relocation of settlers into Siberia and increased this fund to 11,000,000 in 1907. Of this latter figure, 4,865,880 rubles was earmarked for aid to emigrants. These sections were increased in subsequent budgets. In 1910 a fund of 25,000,000 rubles was established for the settlement of Siberia.[45]

While the main purpose of this program was to populate the vast reaches of Siberia, the strategic dispersal of national elements was given consideration. The western areas of Siberia were designated exclusively for settlers from the central governments of Russia. Emigrant-settlers from Russian Poland qualified for land only in the provinces of Irkutsk and Jeniseisk. Each settler was to receive 15 *dziesiatin* (approximately 30 *morgs*) for each male in the family and an interest-free government loan of 100 rubles to be repaid in ten years. Also they were to be exempt from taxation for a certain period.[46]

In 1909, Russian statistics indicate that 782 persons with migration certificates and 885 without them emigrated to Siberia from Lublin province of Russian Poland.[47] During that same year, as a result of repressive measures taken by the employers in the Dabrowa Basin, several thousand workers registered for settlement in Irkutsk and Jeniseisk.[48]

In the several years immediately preceding the war, there likewise developed a current of seasonal agricultural migrants from the eastern and northern districts of Russian Poland to the western and central Russian provinces. It corresponded to the seasonal migration from the western districts of Russian Poland to Prussia and Germany, though it never approached the volume of that migration. According to one estimate, it averaged about 5,000 migrants annually.[49]

Thus, the incorporation of Russian Poland into the Russian empire, begun with increased intensity after 1863, effected considerable shifts among its population. To the large numbers of involuntary migrants who not infrequently remained there permanently were added those seeking cheaper lands and those seeking careers in the expanding economy of Russia. The progressively increasing demographic dis-equilibrium in Russian Poland which was forcing large volumes of population to the westward was likewise intensifying the movement to the eastward. To these results of the demographic disparity the gov-ernmental authorities contributed by, on the one hand, adopting a program of industrialization of the central Russian provinces at the expense of Russian Poland, and, on the other hand, opening the vast Siberian domain to the land-hungry Polish peasants.

In a like manner, its program of restricting government employment and closing of the universities in the Kingdom as well as its Jewish residence laws in Russia, tended to favor the central Russian prov-inces. The industrial establishments of Russian Poland, at first favored by a protective tariff, later, in competition with Russian industries, found themselves progressively at a disadvantage, especially so since their production had been almost exclusively predicated on the Russian markets. The investment capital that had formerly flowed into Russian Poland was increasingly diverted into Russia.

Nor was the position of the large landholders any better. As grain producers, they were caught between the millstones of Russian and American competition. This disadvantage was but intensified when both began to draw off its cheap labor supply. The Russian govern-ment yet further intensified this disadvantage by promulgating rail-road freight rates in such a way as to favor east to west shipments of agricultural produce over west to east.[50]

All these factors combined to make Russia attractive in comparison to Russian Poland. For the peasant, this attraction was intensified when the government adopted a policy of subsidizing colonization and settlement in Siberia. But long before this policy was adopted, the pressure of economic circumstances was forcing these rural elements outward from Russian Poland. The government's program only facili-tated the choice of direction for this emigrating tide.

The urban elements of the population in Russian Poland found themselves in a correspondingly declining situation. The progress of industrial capitalism in Russia exercised a powerful force of attrac-tion, while the more advanced mass-production techniques of Russian Poland made the labor market for the skilled technician increasingly "tight." As elsewhere in the more industrially advanced countries of western Europe and in the United States, the primary demand was for the unskilled, physically-durable laborer. In Russia, however, because of its earlier stages of industrial development, the professionally and industrially skilled were in demand.[51] Since the ruling authorities, after the turn of the century, had adopted a policy which seemed to be calculated to arrest the further industrial expansion of Russian Poland, its future seemed to be lacking in promise. For these reasons, in counterdistinction to the westward emigration which was composed overwhelmingly of peasantry and unskilled workers, the emigration to European Russia was composed of a large proportion of skilled workers and professionals. Many of the latter were trained in Russian universities. Furthermore, even the unskilled Polish laborer could not compete with his Russian counterpart whose acceptable standard of living, if anything, was lower than his own.[52]

This outflow of population to Russia did not escape the attention of a number of Polish commentators. They perceived that this emigration, usually undertaken as a temporary expedient, quite frequently became permanent and therefore represented an irretrievable loss to the national cause. From this point of view, peasant emigration to Siberia was a total loss. They were least likely to return because of their attachment to the land on which they settled; they were least likely to accumulate savings which might flow back to the motherland; and finally, they seemed to be, in time, thoroughly assimilated.

The Polish emigrants that settled in the urban centers of European Russia were equally susceptible to assimilation. Since positions for skilled workers were always limited in any locality, widespread dispersion of these Polish elements usually resulted. Dispersion in turn facilitated assimilation into the new cultural environment.[53] The fact that these elements were preponderantly composed of unmarried males added to the likelihood of assimilation, since they were most likely to take Russian wives.[54] Furthermore, the Russian authorities seemed to take a jaundiced attitude toward the establishment of Polish societies and associations—organizations that generally impeded assimilatory tendencies. The few philanthropic Polish organizations that survived maintained an anemic existence. What Polish solidarity there existed was based on a common background of Polish language and Roman Catholic religion, while the most effective anti-assimilation organizations, fundamentally based on economic self-interest, like those in the United States, were almost entirely lacking.[55]

The drain that this emigration caused upon the Polish intellectual resources represented an especially serious loss to those who looked to the national interests. The intelligentsia, least disposed toward emigration in the other sectors of Poland, showed a comparatively remarkable disposition to seek careers in the empire — in effect, to come to terms with the usurper. Doctors, lawyers, teachers, engineers and skilled craftsmen — the intellectual life-blood of a nation — were being drained off to augment the resources of that traditional and dedicated enemy of Poland.[56] Emigration to other countries, though representing a loss, had some compensating features and, in some cases, was a categorical imperative of existence. Emigration to Russia had few redeeming qualifications and was probably the most widely deplored.[57] To a few, this emigration of Christian elements to the interior of Russia was all the more painful because it was, to a degree, concomitantly being replaced by an immigration of Jewish population from Russia, especially the Western Governments, as a result of the changing policy of the Russian government toward its Jewish subjects.[58]

The Russian policy toward its Jewish subjects underwent a thorough transformation after the assassination of Czar Alexander II in 1881. Up to that time, the reign of Alexander II (1855–1881) was characterized by a comparatively liberal policy toward the Jewish population in the empire. In those circumstances, many of the more ambitious of them left their shops and workbenches in Russian Poland and migrated to Russian cities. Concurrently with this outgoing movement was some migration of Jewish population from the Western Governments to Russian Poland. The laws forbidding the migration of Jewish population into the cities of Russian Poland were abolished in 1861. Long before this, however, many cities in Russian Poland permitted Jewish residents.[59]

The Land Law of May 24, 1862, removed further restraints on the Jewish population in Russian Poland. Prior to this decree, with very few exceptions, the Jewish population had no right to own land within the boundaries of Russian Poland.[60] The Reform Law of 1863 which enabled the peasantry of Russian Poland to acquire land likewise benefitted the Jewish Poles though with a significant reservation.[61] By a law of 1868, they were given the right to freedom of movement between the Western Governments and Russian Poland. Though this resulted in some migration of Jewish population from the Western Governments to Russian Poland, this movement did not assume any considerable volume until the 1880's when the rights of residence formerly granted the Jewish population in European Russia were revoked. Those that had migrated into the interior of Russia and settled either in cities or on farms were ordered to return at once to their former places of legal residence in the crowded towns of the Pale.[62]

These decrees, especially as they related to Jewish subjects whose

legal residence was in the Western Governments, resulted in a sudden
deterioration of an already declining situation of demographic disequilibrium in that area. Their situation was rendered impossible by
the supplementary decrees which forced their removal, within their
already confined areas in the Western Governments, from the rural
communities into the towns and cities of that area.[63] The series of
popular outrages on the Jewish population that coincided with this
period of repressive legislation—outrages made possible by tacit concurrence of government officials—provided only the final impulse to
migration. The pogroms of the early 1880's as well as the later ones
only gave the "signal" for a mass exodus. As one writer put it: "Even
without the Russian pogrom wave of 1881, emigration . . . would have
been inevitable."[64] The compulsion of economic necessity resulting
from an explosive demographic situation drove them out of the Western Governments. Thus, while as late as 1870 there was still some
migration of Jewish population from the Lithuanian provinces into
the interior of European Russia, a decade later this movement of
population was almost exclusively to the westward and remained so to
the outbreak of World War I.[65] Some fled to England and others to
Germany—usually the first leg of a journey to the United States.
Others still emigrated directly to the United States.[66] A considerable
volume, however, migrated to Russian Poland.[67]

Numerous other factors probably contributed to making Russian
Poland a sufficiently attractive alternative to emigration abroad. As
noted above, anti-Jewish restrictions on land ownership, applicable in
the Western Governments and elsewhere in the empire, did not apply
in the Kingdom. Agencies created for facilitating the emigration of
Jewish population abroad lacked sufficient resources to give the requisite financial aid to the great multitudes of population that wanted to
leave the Western Governments. Furthermore, some of the American
Jewish organizations had adopted a policy of selective aid which
excluded many hopeful emigrants from availing themselves of their
help. A Jewish Russian, finding his position in the Western Governments progressively untenable and lacking the financial resources to
undertake the journey abroad at his own expense, not infrequently
chose the only alternative open to him—migration to Russian Poland
where the demographic disequilibrium was less intense as a result of
the development of industry in the western districts. A less tangible but
possibly no less real force of attraction was that cultural proximity
born of hundreds of years of mutual co-existence with the Christian
Poles. This current of migrants to Russian Poland was further aug-

mented by those elements of Jewish population who had migrated into the interior of Russia from Russian Poland during the earlier period of comparative liberalism, but were now forced to remove themselves to their original place of legal residence.

All authorities are generally agreed that this volume of incoming migration into Russian Poland was considerable during the decades that preceded the war. However, lacking the requisite statistical data, the precise volume of this population movement can only be approximately estimated.[68] This inexactitude is further compounded by the fact that there was, concomitant with movement of Jewish Russians, a significant, though less measurable, return migration into Russian Poland of Christian Poles as well as German colonists who had formerly lived in Russian Poland.

Thus, while the Russian policy of favoring the industrialization of its central provinces contributed indirectly to the migration of population in Russian Poland, its policy of political and economic reprisals after the Polish uprisings, its policy of colonization and settlement of the Siberian reaches and its anti-Jewish policy in the Western Governments, represented a more direct influence on the movement of its subject populations.

In a like manner, the mortgage credit facilities which were made available to the peasants of the Kingdom in the last quarter of the nineteenth century can also be directly related to the movement of that segment of the population in the several decades preceding the war. Those elements of the peasant population which lacked either a sufficiency of land to support themselves or the credit facilities to acquire such holdings were, quite logically, the most susceptible candidates for emigration. The Russian authorities, cognizant of this fact, and consistently with their policy of widening the breach between that class of the population and the Polish landed gentry, strove in various ways to win the support of the peasants. The Land Reform Law of 1863 in Russian Poland was, to a degree, an expression of this policy. Such also was the establishment of the Peasant Bank.

Called into existence by the law of May 30, 1882, it confined its operations to facilitating parcelation of the declining landed estates among the peasantry, by providing its offices for the mediation of the sales as well as its credit facilities to make the peasant purchases possible.[69] By 1890 it had extended its area of operation to Russian Poland. A supplementary law of November 27, 1895, authorized the bank to purchase land on its own initiative and then to sell it to the peasantry. In this way, it had transformed itself from a parcelation agency to a colonization agency.[70]

By the terms of the law of 1882, the Peasant Bank was authorized to grant loans to that segment of the population that had a right to acquire so-called "Ukase lands" as defined by the Decree of 1863. This included rural and urban peasants and those engaged in employment directly associated with agriculture.[71] Its policy, as adopted in Russian Poland, authorized the bank to provide loans up to 90 percent of the total assessed valuation of the land to be purchased by the peasants.[72] The amortization of these loans was originally arranged at 8½ percent over a 24½ year period or 7½ percent over a period of 37½ years. These rates included all administrative costs and carrying charges. Before a loan was approved, the local branch of the bank reserved the right to investigate the transaction. If the directors adjudged the terms of the transaction to be disadvantageous to the peasant purchaser— that the price was too high or the terms of payment too short—it could negate the transaction by denying its loan. In this way it exercised wide discretionary powers.[73]

The advantages accruing to the peasants from these operations were many. By establishing itself as a parcelation agency, the Peasant Bank was able to limit considerably the operations of land speculators who bought up declining estates and sold them in small parcels to the peasantry at extravagant prices. Its liberal credit policy, for practical purposes, had a tendency to put private parceling enterprises out of operation.[74] As a source of long term mortgage credit for the peasants, it represented the only agency of its kind in Russian Poland. The Polish Land Credit Association *(Towarzystwo Kredytu Ziemskiego w Krolestwie Polskiem)*, though authorized by its charter to provide mortgage credit facilities to all landholders, largely restricted its credit to large landholders. As a result of this restrictive policy and prior to the establishment of the Peasant Bank, the only recourse the peasant had in seeking loans was private agencies which usually charged usurious rates.[75]

By progressively extending its area of competence, the Peasant Bank was further enabled to grant loans for operational expenses to the peasants. This was especially felicitous since the peasants, after acquiring the land through the instrumentality of the bank, frequently found themselves without the necessary capital to purchase the live-stock, seed and equipment imperative for the effective operation of their newly acquired landholds.[76] By the law of 1895, the bank was authorized to purchase large landholds, put on the market and make them available in parcels to the peasant class. This aspect of its operations offered many advantages to the peasants. Formerly such estates were usually acquired by land speculators who then sold them in parcels at inflated prices.[77]

Helpful as it was for the peasantry, this government sponsored program of parcelation and internal colonization was not without a wider political and nationalistic purpose. Like the Prussian government in the Eastern Marches, the Russian government had its own "nationality" problems in the eastern districts of Russian Poland and in the Western Governments of European Russia. Shortly after the establishment of the Peasant Bank in Russia, it became evident that that organization was not calculated to facilitate the spread of non-Russian speaking population into those nationally-mixed areas.

The policy of Russification of the eastern districts of Russian Poland was anticipated in 1874 by the incorporation of the Uniate church into the Greek Orthodox fold.[78] Even before the competence of the Peasant Bank was fully extended into Russian Poland, the Governor General in Warsaw, in a decree dated April 27, 1889, had instructed the commissioners of that credit organization to deny its facilities to all Polish and Lithuanian elements in certain prescribed areas. The denial of the mortgage credit facilities to Poles and Lithuanians, for practical purposes, excluded them from settling or extending their existing holdings in those areas.[79] Witte, the Minister of Finance, quite frankly admitted this aspect of the nationalistic intent of that organization when, in advocating the extension of its competence in 1895, he stated that it would "... simultaneously fulfill the desired political task [in the Western Governments] of creating strong Russian national settlements." This policy was unequivocally demonstrated by the subsequent detachment of the Chelm district from Russian Poland and incorporating it administratively into the Western Governments.[80]

Consistent with this policy of Russification of the eastern districts of Russian Poland, the eastward press of the peasant population into the Western Governments was arrested by an administrative edict of 1892, which excluded peasants living to the west of the Bug river from acquiring land in the Western Governments.[81]

This represented a reversal of the trend of settlement operative in the past. As late as 1883 there was still no evidence of restrictions on the Polish elements in the settlement of that area. The establishment of the Peasant Bank actually facilitated the establishment of numerous Polish agricultural settlements in the western part of Volhynia province near Wlodzimierz, Luck, Wlodzimierzec and Berezin and extending southeastward toward Zwiahel, Zytomierz and Stary Konstantynow. Many of these Polish agricultural settlements, interspersed with German ones, were established on lands cleared of forests and usually remote from waterways whose shores had long ago been settled by Ukrainian population.[82]

This prohibition was modified in 1905 when, for a short time, a more liberal policy was adopted by the authorities, and Poles west of the Bug were enabled to take over the leaseholds abandoned by German settlers. The restrictions on tenant farming and on the mortgage credit facilities were again liberalized to the extent that Poles were permitted to acquire land, though only from other Polish landowners.[83] The land reform program undertaken by Stolypin in 1909 was designed primarily to satisfy the land hunger of the indigenous population. As such it continued the remaining restriction placed on the movement of population eastward from areas west of the Bug.[84]

In spite of its reservations and nationalistic bias in the eastern areas of Russian Poland and in the Western Governments of European Russia, the Russian Peasant Bank remained the foremost instrument of government parcelation and internal colonization in Russian Poland and, as such, served the invaluable function of relieving the demographic pressure that was driving an ever-increasing volume of peasants out of Russian Poland.

In the first three years of its existence in Russian Poland, that is, up to January 1, 1894, this bank was instrumental in the purchase of lands by the peasantry representing a total cost of 3,936,954 rubles of which 71 percent (2,805,667 rubles) was supplied by the bank and 29 percent (1,131,287 rubles) by the peasant purchasers themselves.[85] In 1893 alone, with only four branch banks in operation, the Peasant Bank was directly instrumental in the acquisition of 29,240 *morgs* of land by the peasant class. More than half of this land was acquired by theretofore landless peasants.[86]

By January 1, 1901, according to its report, the Peasant Bank was instrumental in the acquisition of 454,780 *morgs* of land by the peasants in Russian Poland. Toward the purchase of this land, the peasants received 24,382,319 rubles in loans. On their part, the above purchasers provided 8,223,193 rubles which represented 25.2 percent of the total cost of the above land. The bank provided the remaining 74.8 percent. According to the figures given for its first ten years of operations (1890–1900) throughout Russian Poland, the bank was able to sell land to peasants at 20 percent below the price paid by those who bought directly from the owners, not to say how much less than the price paid to land speculators. As of January 1, 1901, this bank was instrumental in the acquisition of 5.54 percent of the total amount of land owned by the peasant class at that date.[87]

By January 1, 1904, the peasants in Russian Poland acquired 688,469 *morgs* of land with the help of the Peasant Bank, which represented more than 40 percent of the total land acquired by the peasants of Russian Poland during this period (1890–1903).[88] At that date, there were 11.3 million *morgs* of land in the hands of the peasantry—an increase of almost two million *morgs* since 1890.[89]

Ten years later, up to January 1, 1914, this bank had provided 24,741 loans—including group loans—totaling 84,106,429 rubles. The number of peasants who had availed themselves of these loans totaled 132,280 and they acquired 1,190,968 *morgs* of land.[90] Thus, of the total land acquired by the peasantry of Russian Poland since 1864 (that is, excluding the land it received by the Decree of 1864) about half was acquired with the help of the bank.[91]

The magnitude of its operations in the field of peasant parcelation is apparent when it is recalled that it did not begin its operations until 1890 in Russian Poland; that its operations were even more extensive in the Western Governments[92] and that, of the land acquired by the peasants in Russian Poland since 1864 up to the time of the bank's establishment in that area, most of the increase in peasant land ownership was largely the result of adjustments made to peasants for relinquishing their traditional privileges on non-peasant lands *(serwituty)* resulting from the Decree of 1863 and not from purchases made by way of parcelation.[93] Though the prices of land increased after the turn of the century, the Peasant Bank was able to continue selling land at prices ranging from 20 to 40 percent lower than the average prices on the open market.[94]

Despite these evident services rendered the peasantry of Russian Poland, the Peasant Bank was sometimes criticized throughout its quarter century of existence. Though there was evidence that a notable proportion of the large landholds were in a near-fatal state of mortgage indebtedness and that the extension of the Peasant Bank's operations to Russian Poland would enable many of the heavily mortgaged landholders to retrench by ridding themselves of surplus parcels, one contemporary observer reported that this public credit organization had much opposition among the landed interests. "The opponents of this economic process [parcelation and favorable credit facilities for the peasants] maintain that the Peasant Bank is a revolutionary institution created for the express purpose of divesting the *szlachta* of its land by legislative methods."[95]

One isolated and apparently anonymous observer, in making the case for the extension of the operations of the Peasant Bank into

Russian Poland, pointed out that it was only a logical extension of the reform law of 1863 which placed agricultural economy into the mainstream of capitalistic economic organization. While the large landowners had succeeded in getting an organization which provided suitable long term (mortgage) credit facilities, none such had been established for the peasant class. This organization, he felt, was both logical and necessary to restore agricultural prosperity.[96]

To others, the Peasant Bank was part and parcel of a program to Russify Poland and close the traditional eastern outlets to its surplus population.[97] Its program of internal colonization was not only discriminatory in the extreme but a failure and a delusion. Its complicated bureaucratic apparatus and formalities attendant upon applications for loans served to stymie its effective operation.[98] Ostensibly intended to facilitate the acquisition of land by the landless, it only tended to make their position more hopeless by acquiring an almost exclusive monopoly in parcelation operations.[99] Furthermore, by its original policy of favoring group purchases and unlimited liability for debts incurred, it had contributed to the financial ruin of many disillusioned peasants.[100] And, finally, its nationalistic bias was not only patently apparent in the eastern districts but throughout the Kingdom in general. Though the law governing its operations specifically restricted its benefits to Russians, Poles and Lithuanians, its commissioners frequently disqualified Polish applicants while granting verifications to immigrant Germans. These settled on a wide belt along the Vistula where they constituted a threat to the national integrity of the Kingdom.[101]

IV

Polish Attitudes toward Emigration and Its Alternatives

The various measures of the Russian authorities which directly or indirectly affected the population movements in Russian Poland, obscure and changeable as they were, nevertheless could be called policies which to a greater or lesser extent influenced their volume and direction. Among its Polish subjects, however, lacking as they did the requisite political and administrative authority to put into effect any coherent program, the vying interests and ideologies found expression for their opinions on the various phases and aspects of the movements of the population in monographic publications, the public press and public forum. These expressions, lacking the machinery of enforcement, can therefore be more appropriately called attitudes, and were as varied as were the ideological and material interests represented in Russian Poland.

Probably the dominant ideology in the several decades preceding the war was the idea of national interest. It was an ideological prerequisite which could never be ignored and to which all interests had to accommodate themselves or rationalize their particular stand on all issues relating directly or indirectly to emigration. To the degree that they succeeded in accommodating or equating their particular positions with the idea of the state — albeit a non-existent state — their opinions and attitudes regarding movements of population dominated or receded into the background.

Throughout the greater part of the nineteenth century, one of the dominant ideological orientations in Russian Poland was that of the landed gentry. To a lesser degree, the middle class point of view, as expressed by the *Positivists,* insofar as it conformed to the loyalistic demands of the authorities, likewise found expression during the period, while the populist and socialistic orientations initially found little opportunity for legal expression of their attitudes. That the ideological orientation of the landowners was frequently predicated on their social and economic interests was evident in their attitudes toward migrations as well as those aspects of life in the Kingdom that brought about the mass movements of population during that period. As early as the 1870's, the *Tygodnik Ilustrowany* undertook a consideration of the subject of emigration. Its concern, however, largely devolved around the problem of supply and cost of labor for the large landowners and the fear of the increment of socialistic ideas from abroad. The editor, greeting with approval the improved economic condition of the large landholders in Prussian Poland, postulated the practicability of establishing comparable agricultural enterprises in Russian Poland. Such undertakings would offer many emoluments not the least of which would be the resolution of the problem of emigration. As he put it: "The peasants of our villages would [then] cease emigrating to the distant parts of central and northern Germany after money from which they frequently return with harmful and dangerous ideas." He expressed grave concern about ". . . the distant and threatening thunders caused by the German economists."[1] References to peasant emigration in general, whether from the Kingdom, Galicia or Prussia, were generally couched in such analogous terms as "plague" or "disease." Though the editors had expressed an awareness of the demographic factors of migration, more frequently its causes were represented as the mischievous machinations of foreigners. Thus, an editorial in 1876 observed that, ". . . the peasants, incited by the Jew and the German, cast away their own parcels [of land] and homes and only in America do they learn the whole and painful truth. Misery teaches them [there] where is [to be found] their true fortune."[2] This may be regarded as one of the earliest expressions of the "conspiracy theory" of emigration—a theory which, though challenged, was to persist throughout the nineteenth century.

It is interesting to note, however, that the same periodical took a contrary point of view of emigration from industrial and urban centers. Categorically opposed to peasant emigration, it in turn was disposed to favor emigration of the urban proletariat as a means of stemming the spread of the "social problem" and the ideas of class conflict to the rural areas. As champion of the cause of the landed gentry, the *Tygodnik Ilustrowany* also voiced its indignation on the condition of the industrial workers and even favored a program of unemployment compensation for them.[3]

By 1880, however, there was a perceptible change in its view of the causes of emigration. An editorial of that year ventured the opinion that emigration was tied in with the increase of the rural proletariat and the progressive extinction of small peasant landholds.[4] As the volume of emigration began to assume greater and more widespread proportions, the problem of emigration was bound to come under more serious consideration. As yet, however, it was not emigration as a result of the condition of the peasantry which attracted the general attention of the conservative press, but rather emigration as it was related to the deteriorating condition of the large landholder. Emigration, when considered at all, was primarily considered as an aspect of the economic decline of the gentry and an aspect of the "agrarian problem."[5]

And, indeed, it was a problem. The abolition of socage tenure had not only divested the landed gentry of a considerable portion of its land — reimbursing them chiefly by increasing their taxes — but with one stroke had also deprived them of a considerable supply of cheap labor. Thereafter, their labor force had to be hired for wages. This sudden launching of an essentially non-capitalistic agricultural economy into the current of capitalistic exchange found many landowners totally unprepared.

Subsequent developments only aggravated an already declining economic situation. By the eighth decade the steamships and railroads were carrying the vast stores of American grains abroad and forcing the European producers out of their former domestic markets. The competitive position of the Polish grain producer, because of the relatively backward stage of agricultural technology, was all the more unfavorable.[6] To make conditions worse, Russia was flooding the grain markets of Russian Poland and compounding its advantages by adopting a railroad freight rate policy which was heavily weighted in favor of the Russian grain producers. Meanwhile, the German empire had abandoned free trade and was setting up progressively higher grain tariff barriers which closed another traditional outlet.

In this configuration of domestic and international circumstances, it was not surprising that an increasing number of large landholders were forced to liquidate their holdings. Others found themselves progressively sinking in debt and rapidly approaching that level of indebtedness from which no return was possible. The alternatives that faced them were total liquidation of their holdings and removal to the cities or abroad, or partial liquidation. By the latter procedure they hoped to meet their outstanding debts and, by a program of retrenchment and improved production methods, to continue their existence. Around these two alternatives developed a large body of literature— both scholarly and polemic. The alternatives were of fundamental importance since the survival of a way of life seemed to depend upon them. The numerical decline of large landholdings was generally attended by the expansion of peasant holdings—an expansion encouraged by the Russian Peasant Bank. This trend, permitted to run its course unrestrained, could conceivably lead to the elimination of the landed gentry as a class. Its control, therefore, was imperative. Though the trend could not, in the existing political and economic circumstances, be reversed, it could be carried out in such a way as to leave the social and economic influence of the gentry unchallenged.

Such, fundamentally, were the arguments of their more progressive spokesmen. One of the earliest proponents of this view was Ludwik Gorski. In his opinion, the sale of parts of landed estates was frequently both desirable and necessary. By this means the large landholder was enabled to liquidate his outstanding debts and fund future operations. The total break-up and sale of estates, however, was generally unnecessary and always undesirable. The continued existence of large landholds was economically and socially imperative and their owners were duty bound to persevere, inasmuch as "land in the exclusive possession of peasantry, lacking responsibility and enlightenment, is a sterile field in which is nurtured wildness, egotism and superstition." The continued existence of large landholds was thus equated with the national interest. Furthermore, partial parcelation not only helped to restore the economic solvency of some large landowners, but also restrained emigration of the local peasantry. A peasant with even a fragment of land was less likely to emigrate and thereby reduce the local labor force.[7]

Jan Bloch was substantially in accord with the above views. His researches into the mortgage indebtedness of the landed estates convinced him that a substantial proportion of them were headed for bankruptcy. Such a contingency threatened to remove them entirely from the rosters of the landed property holders and thereby dangerously reduce their ranks.[8] The same alternatives, according to A. Donimirski, had confronted the Polish gentry in Prussian Poland. There, however, they had learned to accept the efficacy of partial parcelation both as an escape from imminent bankruptcy and as a restraint on the emigration of the local peasantry.[9]

A few conservative die-hards, however, remained unconvinced. Karol Filipowicz, for example, held to the view that small peasant landholds were economically impracticable. He could justify the sale of only those parts of landed estates which were superfluous to their economy. Though he agreed that a peasant with land was least likely to emigrate, this land acquired at the expense of the manor *(folwark)* was too high a price.[10] Various alternatives were posited to relieve the condition of the peasantry, since their condition could no longer be ignored. Some favored the revival of such peasant crafts and domestic industries as pottery, weaving, baskets and wood carvings. This policy, though essentially regressive, met with approval from the conservative interests. By encouraging peasant domestic manufacture and, to the degree that this policy was successful, some sought to diminish the pressure for parcelation. The support of domestic peasant crafts was a more acceptable alternative to either emigration or parcelation.[11]

With the passage of time and the progressively increasing demographic disequilibrium of the rural population, the scope of the discussion on the agrarian problem was expanded to include a consideration of the condition of the peasantry. The spokesmen of this orientation included the more progressive landed interests as well as those representing the broader national interest. As a group, they marshalled imposing data in their attempts to establish the economic feasibility of small peasant landholds. They argued that parcelation was not only expedient but necessary to the national interest in general and to the solution of the agrarian problem in particular. Marjan Kiniorski viewed parcelation as one of the most effective means of restraining the flow of emigration, which he regarded as a drain on the nation's most important resource. According to his researches, small peasant landholds showed every evidence of economic vitality and practicability.[12] Wladyslaw Grabski and Stanislaw Chelchowski concurred with this point of view. Both were favorably disposed to parcelation as a means of relieving the rural population pressure and both expressed optimism for the future of peasant landholds.[13] Grabski even went to the lengths of proposing a program of internal colonization. In essence, his proposal appears to have been similar to the operations of the Prussian Colonization Commission. Most of the land was to be purchased from private owners — government owned lands being insufficient and, in many cases, undesirable — by the exercise of a kind of right of "eminent domain," if necessary. Since land costs would be based on their assessed valuation for tax purposes, this procedure would obviate the inordinate rise in land prices resulting from land speculation. These savings would make such land more accessible to the peasant buyers.[14]

Such a program, however, was too radical a departure from the prevailing concepts of property rights. Administered by the hostile Russian authorities, it could only lead to the forcible expropriation of the Polish gentry — a Russian counterpart of the Prussian Colonization Commission as expanded by the law of 1908 in Prussian Poland. Nevertheless, down to the outbreak of the war, the idea survived that the existence of the manorial estates was essential to the national existence. If anything, this rationale seems to have gained increasing currency in the years preceding the war. The growing considerations of national interest tended to relegate the problem of rural population pressure to secondary importance. The agrarian problem, to a degree, still remained fundamentally a problem of improving the conditions of the large landowners—that traditional bulwark of Polish sovereignty and national integrity. Stanislaw Zielinski, writing in the *Gazeta Rolnicza,* in 1912, expressed the attitude of that foremost conservative agricultural publication when he stated that ". . . [I] would not have any objection to parcelation . . . if it were not for the fact that parcelation here is conjoined with outright despoliation. Parceled estates became simultaneously devastated. Orchards, wayside trees, buildings are destroyed—this sets back agricultural progress, changes the aesthetic appearance of the countryside." Furthermore, he implied, a large proportion of parceled land fell into the hands of outsiders. The peasant, lacking in enlightenment and social responsibility, needed the manor as an example of progressive agricultural productivity.[15] Maurycy Zamoyski, likewise, expressed the attitude of his class when he deplored the widespread tendency to break up manorial estates and their sale to the peasantry. This tendency, he contended, could only lead to the cultural and economic decline of Polish agriculture.[16]

This attitude corresponded to that of Adam Krasinski, his editorial predecessor, at the turn of the century. Though widespread individual land ownership was economically desirable in principle, "in the present condition of peasant enlightenment, their mass ignorance, helplessness and backwardness, [parcelation] menaces agriculture with total collapse. Progressiveness and higher culture can be effectually practiced here only on large landholds and with their break-up will disappear from the scene giving place to primitive practices."[17]

A consideration of some of the prevailing attitudes toward one of the foremost alternatives to rural emigration—parcelation and acquisition of land by the peasantry—inevitably suggests the wide range of attitudes and opinions on emigration itself. Up to the turn of the century the "conspiracy theory," already enunciated in the seventies, still persisted, albeit in an expanded form. The newer, more mischievous instrumentality was the "agent." As a general term it included those in the employ of transportation interests and foreign countries, foreign land speculators and colonizers, and, in some cases, even emigrants themselves who recruited individuals and groups for employment abroad.

Koszutski, surveying this aspect of the general scene shortly after the turn of the century, concluded that the issue still was effectively obscured by bombast and recrimination concentrated on the question of "Who was responsible for the emigration movement?" instead of "What was responsible for the emigration movement?" Since the emphasis was on the former, the answers ran as follows: agents of shipping interests, agitators and promoters working for the Brazilian government, and others. They voiced their disapproval in such phrases as "the moral degeneration of the rural populace," "the woeful bankruptcy of the country's agriculture," "the fatal depopulation of the country," and "the great losses suffered by the national community because the emigrant leaves with considerable sums of money." In general, he concluded, while the interests of the country and the interests of agriculture were considered, too few were disposed to consider the interests of the emigrants themselves. Even when they were considered, the gravest doubts were expressed concerning the material advantages to be gained from emigration. He found that these attitudes especially prevailed among those elements of the Polish population most directly affected by what appeared to be a declining surplus labor supply. They included the owners of middle and large landholds and the public press representing their interests.[18]

By the last decade of the nineteenth century, however, a Populist and Liberal oriented press began to establish itself in the Kingdom and progressively challenge the journalistic dominance heretofore held by the conservative gentry. Not only did such publications as *Glos, Przeglad Tygodniowy, Prawda, Kuryer Codzienny, Chwila,* and others represent a new focus and orientation,[19] but their existence seemed to inaugurate a more objective stage in the historiography of emigration and its related issues. Among the earliest of these writers were Stanislaw Klobukowski,[20] Stanislaw Posner,[21] Ludwik Krzywicki[22] and Roman Dmowski. The latter expressed himself thus:

> One cannot overemphasize the effects of emigration upon the country from which it issues and upon the people who remain. One must remember that the common impulse which impels people to leave their country is the hope of improving their lot. Therefore, the first and foremost effect of emigration is the improvement of the fortunes of the masses which are leaving Europe. In reality, all European countries saw and still see a considerable portion of their

emigrants returning after experiencing disenchantment abroad. In truth, under certain circumstances the emigrants leaving Europe were going to their own ruin — I refer specifically to the emigration to Brazil and Argentina during the periods of high fever brought about by conscienceless agitation at a time when an abnormally large inflow of immigrants combined with anarchic and irresponsible conditions prevailed in South America. . . . Nevertheless, the fact remains that by emigrating masses of people quickly improve their material well-being and, concomitantly, their moral and intellectual well-being.[23]

Another dissenter from the conservative attitude was Kazimierz Kasperski. According to him:

The fear of depopulation of the country because of emigration is without foundation. On the contrary, it is testimony of our racial vitality when our people prefer to undergo hardships and difficulties rather than to submit to famine in their own country.

Anticipating Koszutski, he accused the opposition of obscuring the facts because of their particular class interests. He specifically referred to large landholders and industrial interests who found it in their interest to have an ever-present surplus labor supply and who resorted to all conceivable devices, though ineffectually, to restrict emigration. The alternative he proposed was a responsible colonization policy, the aim of which would be to realize the most favorable economic benefits for all concerned.[24]

Thus, by the turn of the century, critiques of the prevailing attitudes of the gentry began to appear with increasing frequency—criticism which challenged their credibility and motivations. The last decade of the century can therefore, with some justification, be regarded as a transitional period in the Polish historiography of emigration.[25] Thereafter, the parochial attitudes expressed by the landed gentry and its spokesmen began to lose currency despite their continued reiteration.[26]

Probably no single combination of factors was more responsible for this reorientation of views than the dramatic emigration of several thousands of people to Brazil in the years between 1890 and 1892. The response that it called forth in the public press, the measures which were adopted to counteract it and the reappraisal of the factors of migration that it forced, serve to make that manifestation a case record of the evolution of ideas on emigration.

One of the impulses for this emigration was the vigorous program of subsidization of immigration undertaken by the government of Brazil after the overthrow of the emperor in 1889. This new policy of populating the vast domains of that country was officially adopted and put into operation by the provisional decree of June 28, 1890, giving far-reaching privileges to European immigrants. By its provisions, the government of Brazil agreed to provide free transportation from any European port to the place of his choice for the immigrant. It guaranteed him cost-free quarters, food and medical care during the entire journey and free choice of area of settlement upon his arrival, as well as government support until such time as the agricultural settler harvested his first crop.[27] By way of implementing this decree, the federal government entered into negotiations with private agencies and shipping concerns to promote this immigration.[28] News of this program of subsidization, already reaching Russian Poland in the later part of 1889, combined with the explosive demographic situation in that sector of Poland, resulted in a sudden mass emigration of urban and rural population of heretofore unknown proportions, especially from the western provinces of Kalisz and Plock as well as the industrial areas of Lodz and Warsaw.[29]

This sudden and unprecedented development evoked the astonishment and alarm of the public press. Following the initial shock, there developed a widespread discussion in the periodical press on the subject of emigration in general and emigration to Brazil in particular. Especially aggrieved by this development were the spokesmen for the landed gentry. Its causes, in the opinion of one of these, were the malignant operations of foreign promoters exploiting the gullible populace.[30]

A less impassioned but equally conservative appraisal was that of Ludwik Gorski. According to him, it was largely the result of a new tariff policy inaugurated by the Austrian and Prussian governments, especially as it related to alcoholic beverages. Thereafter contraband operations along the frontier of the Kingdom had ceased to be profitable and a large number of people found themselves without means of earning a livelihood. Unused to physical labor, they became auspicious prospects for promoters. The Austrian and Russian Poles who were forcibly deported from the Prussian provinces at about this time were equally susceptible to these agents.[31]

Though the causes apparently lay outside their province of competence and since the volume of emigration to Brazil appeared to continue undiminished, many thought it incumbent upon themselves to undertake measures to arrest it. Thus, throughout the winter months when the emigration temporarily abated, the alarms of the press were raised with renewed vigor. The editor Weyssenhoff reported widespread correspondence to newspapers apprising them of the "fatal depopulation" of the villages. The clergy were urged to dissuade the prospective emigrants, and the landed gentry expressed their grave concern for their fellow countrymen.[32] More directly, the administrative authorities were prevailed upon to arrest many "agents"; proclamations were issued against illegal crossing of borders; the number of border guards was increased; the clergy were instructed to restrict the issuance of baptismal certificates and restrictions regulating the sale and purchase of "Ukase land" were intensified.[33]

Numerous other countermeasures were suggested, ranging from more intensified restrictions on the sale of all categories of peasant land to a program of railroad construction. The proponents of the latter felt that such a program would, among other things, serve to restrain emigration of the peasants by providing them with means of earning some money.[34]

All these countermeasures appeared to have had some restraining effect during the winter of 1890/1891. The movement, however, showed evidence of revival with increased vigor in the spring. As a measure against this contingency, a fund-raising project was organized in Warsaw to send observers to report on the condition of the Polish emigrants in Brazil. A sufficiency of funds was also collected to return a number of emigrants, on the premise that they would present a truer picture of the condition of the Polish emigrants in Brazil.[35] The Reverend Zygmunt Chelmicki and a Milolaj Glinka were selected to execute this mission. To reinforce the mission, the publicist-writer Adolf Dygasinski was commissioned by the *Kurjer Warszawski* to accompany them for the same purpose.[36]

They apparently discharged their commission effectively and expeditiously because by spring the editor of the *Biblioteka Warszawska* was able to report that there appeared to be a noticeable decline in the "Brazilian fever." He thought that the disillusioned emigrants returned by Chelmicki were especially effective in counteracting the promotional activities of the agents.[37]

Immediately upon his arrival in Brazil, Dygasinski began to send his dispatches to the *Kurjer Warszawski,* under the byline of *Listy z Brazylii,* from where it was picked up by other papers and widely circulated. These dispatches, as well as a fictionalized treatment of his observations, were shortly thereafter published in book form under the titles *Listy z Brazylii* and *Na Zlamanie Karku,* respectively.[38] The Reverend Chelmicki equally diligently sent his reports to the newspapers and under the same byline of *Listy z Brazylii*. Shortly upon his return, the two volume work *W Brazylii* was published.[39]

Both authors left little to the imagination — their works can only be characterized as tales of horror and distress. The condition of the emigrants already in Brazil and the prospects for future emigrants there were presented in the blackest hues. Nor were the hardships experienced by the Polish emigrants peculiar to them alone. According to one editor, reports reaching him from London indicated that British emigrants in Brazil were experiencing equal hardships, and the best efforts of British consular officials were required to free some British nationals from "Brazilian slavery." Another source reported that Dygasinski's correspondence had created such an uproar in the English press as to precipitate a veritable "chaos" in the London stock exchange.[40]

To these journalistic jeremiads were added the eloquent tones of the distinguished literary figure, Marja Konopnicka. From her summer residence in Zurich, Switzerland, she was said to have had occasion to view numerous transients from Brazil through that city. She characterized them as emaciated, exhausted, tattered and, generally, in their last extremity. Without any funds, many of them were reduced to stealing from the fields. Those with sufficient funds were able to return by way of Bremen and Hamburg; those with less funds came by way of Marseilles and travelled afoot in groups through France and Switzerland. According to information reaching her, all children perished along the way.[41] The experience had such a profound effect upon her that it inspired her to write one of the foremost Polish epics of the age, *Pan Balcer w Brazylii*, which was run serially throughout that year and the next in the *Biblioteka Warszawska*. In it the writer distinguishes herself for her great sensitivity and understanding of the heroic potential of the peasant. The cumulative effect of the work, however, presented the Polish emigrants in Brazil in most woeful circumstances and in most pessimistic tones. The equally distinguished Boleslaw Prus was reported to have expressed the same pessimism in the public press. Both, expressing intense sensitivity to the sufferings of the people, were inclined to condemn all emigration, unconditionally and without reservations. Their position on the matter was so popular that those few who opposed their intemperate views lacked the courage to challenge them.[42]

This prevailing climate of opinion was reinforced by its apparently incontrovertible basis in fact. The hardships that the emigrants encountered in Brazil were very real. The promotional activities that the

Brazilian policy called forth, based as they were on *per capita* commissions, were extremely effective.[43] Their propaganda and the desperate circumstances of the population combined to create an explosive situation. As the news spread from agent to sub-agent, it tended to be progressively exaggerated. The populace, in their extremity, were not disposed to examine the claims of the promoters critically. On the contrary, the propagandized not infrequently became the most irresponsible propagandists. As the news of this heaven-sent salvation spread from peasant to peasant, it underwent fantastic transformations. One such version which reached the distinguished scholar, Ludwik Krzywicki, claimed that the Pope ". . . moved to mercy by the poverty of a Christian people, ordered the Emperor of Brazil to give the Poles as much land as they would want."[44] Thus Brazil became to them a Promised Land—a haven from their earthly vale of tears and hardships.

The Brazilian government, on its part, was unprepared to process expeditiously this extraordinary volume of immigrants. In consequence, the receiving station on the Ilha das Flores was usually overcrowded far beyond its capacity. In these circumstances and the primitive conditions of sanitation that existed there, the immigrants were frequently decimated by disease. The federal government's usual solution of this troublesome situation was to cancel abruptly the free-passage program. This worked extreme hardships upon those emigrants who had already liquidated their interests at home and were on their way to the seaports or awaiting overseas transportation. This condition was especially aggravated if most or all the Brazilian states simultaneously withdrew their free passage privileges. Of those that survived the port of entry, some were encouraged to go to the coffee plantations of Sao Paulo where the Wakefieldian policy of settlement denied them the land for which they came. Others, upon arriving at the frontier of settlement, were obliged to spend many months waiting for the government to make the necessary surveys of land. When they finally received their land, they had to clear the forest before they could plant their crops. This proved to be an arduous task under the most auspicious circumstances but doubly arduous in view of the fact that a high proportion of the emigrants were recruited from the ranks of the urban population—elements totally unprepared for the exacting and rigorous demands of frontier existence.[45]

All these circumstances and exaggerated combinations thereof were called to the attention of the prospective emigrants. The pleas for moderation, however, fell on deaf ears. Krzywicki recalled some years later that the peasant's mistrust of the intelligentsia was without bounds. In many cases, instead of changing the minds of the prospective emigrants, the injunctions against emigration only tended to reinforce their resolve. Some, meeting with difficulties in obtaining departure permits, armed themselves with scythes and forced their way across the border.[46] One such emigrant recorded in his memoirs that, having met with official impediments to his departure, he and others like him easily found guides who helped them and their families to cross the border to Prussian Poland. From there they easily made their way to the seaport.[47] Another contemporary observer writing fifty years later was still convinced that the landed gentry had bribed the border authorities to arrest all emigrants in spite of the fact that the Russian government permitted emigration.[48]

Nor were these suspicions entirely unfounded. An official directive had authorized the issuance of cost-free exit permits within ten days of application upon deposit of 75 rubles per adult and 50 rubles per non-adult emigrant with district authorities. This deposit was to be released to the designated customs station through which the emigrant indicated intention of passing. There it was to be returned to him. Some Polish newspapers chose to interpret this as official encouragement of emigration. The Russian publications, *Warszawski Dniewnik* and *Nowoje Wremie,* on their part, maintained that these rulings were calculated to legalize the heretofore large scale illegal emigration and thereby spare the emigrant from falling into the snares of unscrupulous emigrant smugglers as well as to see that he had sufficient funds to journey abroad. The latter publication saw no need for placing any artificial barriers to emigration and expressed the opinion that the funds collected to send Chelmicki and Glinka to Brazil might have been more profitably used either to relocate the emigrants who had been returned or to find them employment.[49]

These, however, were Russian publications and as such were expected to be critical of the prevailing attitude. In time, however, the picture of unrelieved hardship that had been created by Dygasinski, Chelmicki and the others came under more critical examination. One of the earliest of these revisionists was Jozef Siemiradzki. An experienced traveller, Siemiradzki, in the company of Antoni Hempel and a certain Lazniewski, undertook "to make economic and naturalistic examinations" of Brazil in 1891. Though their journey was not directly connected with the emigration movement from Russian Poland, their correspondence and reports did much to challenge the credibility of the earlier reporters. Siemiradzki, especially, exercised a widespread influence.[50] Though he reaffirmed some of the hardships that Chelmicki and Dygasinski had reported and in one case seems to have perpetuated a new one,[51] he took considerable pains to point out that the mass emigration of 1890–1892 was of an exceptional character both in its volume and in its make-up. He noted that despite the high mortality among the initial emigrants from Russian Poland, those that survived were gradually adjusting themselves to local conditions and would, in time, very likely prosper. He was especially optimistic about the prospects of the Polish emigrants in the province of Parana and regarded Chelmicki's reports on that province unwarranted by the facts. On the contrary, he thought Polish immigrant settlements in Parana had a bright future.[52] Later he argued that the unequivocal critics of all emigration failed to consider its economic and social basis.[53] At the time he noted that though Polish emigration had declined somewhat in volume in 1892, in spite of the various restraints imposed by the Brazilian authorities it still was very much in evidence. In these circumstances he thought complaints of organized agitation invalid. In his opinion, the most effective promoters of emigration to Brazil were those Polish emigrants returned by Chelmicki and Glinka.[54] In any case, both Siemradzki and Hempel viewed either legal or administrative restrictions on this emigration as morally indefensible and, probably, ineffectual.[55]

Several years later, he expressed even more serious doubt as to the credibility of the reports made by Dygasinski, Chelmicki and Glinka. Dygasinski had spent only six weeks in Santa Catharina; Glinka was only a few weeks in Rio de Janeiro and Chelmicki only a few days in Curitiba, having spent most of his visit on a coffee plantation in Sao Paulo. Such brief and limited stays, in his opinion, did not qualify them to pass on either the practicability or folly of emigration to that country.[56]

Similar doubts were expressed by Jan Poplawski, editor of *Glos,* in his reviews of the publications of Chelmicki and Dygasinski. The novelist Stefan Zeromski took issue with Boleslaw Prus who prophesied total assimilation of Polish immigrant-settlers in Brazil. Somewhat later in a letter addressed to his wife, Zeromski expressed the view that ". . . colonization of our peasants in Brazil is a highly favorable manifestation—our peasants have every chance of establishing near Curitiba a strong colony . . . [because of local circumstances] these colonies are not in danger of being lost by assimilation."[57]

On the whole, these dissenters from the prevailing climate of opinion argued that in spite of the hardships encountered by the emigrants in Brazil—hardships that were, on the one hand, to some degree unavoidable in a mass experience and, on the other, probably exaggerated by the pessimists—they were gradually being overcome. In most cases, such hardships were temporary rather than permanent in character. Furthermore, since emigration was unavoidable in the given demographic circumstances, the concentration of Polish emigrants in Parana held high promise for the future of both the emigrants and the national cause. Though not a new concept, the idea of an unassimilable national reservoir gained increasing support, especially in Galicia where it was concentrated around the Polish Commercial-Geographical Association *(Polskie Towarzystwo Handlowo-Geograficzne)* in Lwow.[58]

The conservative elements in general, however, continued to regard all emigration as an unqualified loss to the nation. To the claims of the proponents of emigration to Parana they answered with renewed cries of disaster. News of periodic attacks on Polish settlements in Brazil by Indians was diligently circulated by their press. Even greater were the depredations resulting from the periodic attacks of locusts. Those that escaped these destructive visitations were frequently ruined by the equally destructive attacks of ants.[59] Anticipating another "fever" of emigration in the spring of 1908, the dailies began to raise the alarm in the winter months of 1907. As in former years, an on-the-spot observer in the person of Ludwik Wlodek was dispatched to Brazil. His sponsor, the Central Agricultural Association *(Centralne Towarzystwo Rolnicze)* was one of the foremost organizations for large landowners in Russian Poland.[60] These observations were published by that organization in 1909. Though more restrained, they were quite as pessimistic as those of Chelmicki and Dygasinski. In some instances, he conceded, Polish emigrants in Parana had prospered. Quite apparently the former tactic of unqualified denunciation was being modified.[61]

Some of the more conservative, however, still followed the older course. Thus, when another mass emigration to Brazil showed signs of developing in 1911 from the eastern districts of Siedlce and Lublin, the editor of the conservative *Biblioteka Warszawska,* under the heading "Alarming news from Parana," included several letters of disillusionment from alleged Polish emigrants there. Likewise included was the purported testimony of Roman Jordan.[62] Another observer, Franciszek Bayer, was dispatched by the Warsaw Emigrant Protective Association *(Warszawskie Towarzyatwo Opieki nad Wychodzcami)* to the eastern districts to investigate the causes of this new outbreak.

His reports, published serially in the *Kurjer Warszawski,* and subsequently in the Galician publication *Polski Przeglad Emigracyjny,* indicated that the chief instigators of this movement were a remigrant from Parana and a clergyman, also from Parana.[63] Of the two, the latter, a Reverend Anusz, was both more purposeful and influential by way of his correspondence with former schoolmates and colleagues in the Siedlce province of Russian Poland. These letters, presenting Parana in the most favorable light, were reportedly circulated throughout the area.[64] Simultaneously, a brochure by Michal Pankiewicz, entitled *Prawda o Paranie,* was circulated in that area. Casting suspicion upon the motives of the opponents of emigration, it extolled the benefits of that country. As a result of it, a deputation from near Czermienik was sent to the editor of the newspaper *Kurjer* in Lublin to seek advice and counsel. There they were encouraged to emigrate.[65]

In a like manner, the *Zaranie,* published in Warsaw, also encouraged emigration to that country. According to one version, Pankiewicz was said to be acting as an appointed agent of the clergyman Anusz. The former was alleged to have conducted a vigorous promotional program for emigration to Parana including putting into circulation "tens of thousands of pamphlets and broadsides."[66] For his intemperate behavior, Anusz was read out of the Galician Polish Emigration Association *(Polskie Towarzystwo Emigracyjne).*[67] Thus, down to the eve of the war, a number of observers still continued to view the causes of emigration as essentially the machinations of mischievous instrumentalities.

*   *   *

Overseas emigration, whether to South America or to the United States, represented but one type of emigration from Russian Poland in the several decades preceding the war. Because of its more permanent character, its critics generally deplored it as a drain on the national strength and foremost resource—the population. Immediately after the opening of the Prussian border in 1890, however, there developed another type of emigration. This was a seasonal emigration which was directed overwhelmingly to that country and which returned at the close of the harvest season. With only infrequent exceptions, this emigration increased annually in volume and by the turn of the century reached what the conservative press considered to be "alarming proportions."[68] Up to that time it had been largely confined to the border districts. As it spread into the interior of Russian Poland, however, voices expressing grave concern were more frequently heard. This alarm, first raised by the conservative press in the provinces, was subsequently picked up by the Warsaw publications. Throughout the winter of 1898-1899 and especially during April of 1899, the subject received widespread publicity.[69]

The landed gentry especially felt this drain on their labor supply. Newspapers representing their interests generally agreed that this emigration had reached such proportions that it threatened the domestic economy.[70] As formerly, they tended to regard the manifestation as the product of external forces and viewed its results with doubts and misgivings.[71] Their solution of the problem of emigration followed logically from their analysis of its causes. Hence, they advocated the closing of the frontier and imprisonment of all "agents."[72]

By this time, however, there had developed an opposition press which, at first gingerly and later more vigorously, challenged the heretofore relatively unopposed press of the landed gentry. These more temperate voices chose to delve deeper into the problem of emigration and saw its solution in increasing the wages of agricultural workers. Thus, while the first group simply accused the people of laziness and a predisposition toward vagrancy, the second reproached the landed gentry with an excessively inequitable evaluation of the labor of the agricultural worker. These contrary points of view were expressed by Ignacy Grabowski and Antoni Donimirski representing the conservative interests and Ludwik Krzywicki and Boleslaw Koskowski representing the socialist and liberal points of view respectively. The former point of view was most volubly expressed in the Warsaw newspapers *Slowo Polskie* and *Kurjer Warszawski,* the latter by the publications *Glos* and *Gazeta Polska.*[73]

Despite considerable disparity of attitudes and remedies suggested, there was evidence of agreement in two areas. The conservative spokesmen conceded that some effort should be made by the large landowners in improving the wages of local agricultural laborers, usually by means of increased remunerations in kind. Both were also in general agreement on the need for better information on the condition and needs of the labor market.[74] The agreement on the second point, however, was more apparent than real. The landed interests were understandably interested in the condition of the domestic labor market as it related to their operational expenses while the more liberal faction, actuated by the best interests of the emigrant, in the condition of the labor market both at home and abroad. Both sought to bring the movement under some sort of organized control; both expressed their concern for the welfare of the emigrant. The exceptional laws that the Polish seasonal emigrants were subjected to in Germany received widespread publicity in the conservative and nationalistic press, though not necessarily for the same reasons.[75] The extraordinary dependence of German agriculture on Polish immigrant labor held promising prospects for the latter.[76]

In these circumstances several efforts were made to redirect the seasonal emigration elsewhere than to Germany. One such undertaking succeeded in 1899 in directing a segment of this movement from the province of Plock to the Russian Baltic provinces. The result was reported as a total fiasco and bitterness on the part of the emigrants. Its promoters had apparently failed to take into consideration the primitive level of agriculture prevailing in those provinces, as well as the exceptional climatic conditions. The former factor tended to maintain the wage scale on a level which compared unfavorably even with that in Russian Poland; the latter tended to reduce the duration of the working season considerably below that in Germany. Both factors combined to reduce the earnings of the seasonal emigrants to a level which made it economically untenable.[77]

Another argument frequently reiterated in favoring some sort of organizational control over emigration pointed to the total absence of any public employment agencies. This lack, it was argued, frequently made for situations where an agricultural worker, unable to find suitable employment in his village, migrated to Germany even though he could have found equally remunerative employment in a neighboring village or district. As a result, local agricultural employers frequently complained of the scarcity of local labor and were obliged to recruit field workers from Galicia or employ Russian soldiers on furlough from local garrisons.[78]

Several attempts were made to establish agricultural employment bureaus to serve the needs of the large landholding interests and to protect the emigrant-laborers from hardships and abuses.[79] One such, advocated by the editor of the *Biblioteka Warszawska,* was to be organized and controlled by the landed interests to provide them with necessary field labor.[80] Another, proposed by Koskowski, was to be organized and controlled by the local agricultural associations. Since these local agricultural associations were composed of peasants, the author hoped that the peasant-emigrants' interests would best be served by them. In any case, neither got beyond the stage of public discussion.[81] By 1908, however, a Mutual Aid Association of Agricultural Workers *(Towarzystwo Wzajemnej Pomocy Pracownikow*

Rolnych) was established with several provincial branches, whose purpose was to provide compensation for incapacitated and retired agricultural workers. Among its incidental functions were those of an employment agency for both specialized agricultural workers and seasonal laborers. Since it charged the employees rather than the employers for its services, it never gained any noteworthy popularity among the seasonal laborers.[82]

The revolutionary upheavals of 1905 created widespread hopes among the Poles of Russian Poland for a measure of political autonomy for that section. Within the framework of this anticipated autonomy many hoped to establish control over the emigration movement and the subject was widely discussed. As a preliminary, an Emigration Commission was created within the framework of the Polish Ethnographic Society *(Towarzystwo Krajoznawcze)* to gather data and other pertinent information on all aspects of emigration. The first step taken by this commission was to institute a general inquiry on the subject by sending out questionnaires throughout the country to informed parties. While awaiting the return of these questionnaires, the commission arranged for a series of lectures on the subject. One lecture, by Zelislaw Grotowski, was on the subject of the seasonal migrants to Germany. He recommended the creation of an independent Emigrant Welfare Society to look to their interests abroad. The Warsaw publication, *Kurjer Warszawski,* recommended its organization within the framework of the projected Department of Labor. Adam Krasinski, the editor of the conservative *Biblioteka Warszawska,* thought such an organization should be independent and its function should be ". . . to direct the tide of emigration into predetermined and healthy channels."[83] The discussion, however, remained largely academic since the anticipated autonomy was never forthcoming.

By 1910, an organization called The Emigrants Protective Association *(Towarzystwo Opieki nad Wychodzcami)* was founded in Warsaw, which, according to its charter, was to serve as an agency to "supply information to prospective emigrants; aid in finding employment for agricultural workers both at home and abroad; maintain a legal aid bureau; look to the religious-moral welfare of the emigrant; facilitate the emigrant's journey; provide medical aid and to maintain branch agencies and shelters in areas of emigrant concentration and chief ports of embarkation." Since it was a private agency without official support and since it was not permitted to engage in such functions as the sale of railroad and steamship tickets, it was basically different from its counterpart in Galicia, the Polish Emigration Association.[84] Though it survived until the outbreak of the war and briefly published a monthly called *Wychodzca Polski,* it never achieved any widespread popularity or support. On the contrary, it was under constant attack by the radical elements whose suspicions it aroused by its critical posture during the "Brazilian fever" from the eastern districts in 1911, and by the conservative elements who were disposed to regard any organization which provided prospective emigrants with authentic information as, *ipso facto,* an organization for the encouragement of emigration.[85]

* * *

The Russian authorities, on their part, showed little disposition to satisfy the growing demands for the control and regulation of the volume and direction of emigration either to Germany or overseas. Several measures were taken to control the colonization and settlement of its domains both in European Russia and Siberia and to alleviate the distress of the peasantry.[86] Following the floods and crop failures of 1892, the government undertook a program of public works to provide the local population with the means of earning money. An outlay of 613,760 rubles was apportioned to Russian Poland for road construction and improvement in the provinces of Kalisz, Kielce, Radom, Piotrkow, Plock, Lomza, Siedlce, Suwalki and Lublin.[87]

In 1895, a ministerial commission was established to look into ". . . the regulation of hired agricultural workers," with the view of improving the condition of migrant workers during their transit and in the place of their employment. Among its other interests, it deliberated on the practicability of providing seasonal emigrants with small credit facilities, reduced railroad fares, medical attention and more equitable labor contract arrangements.[88] Largely through its representations to the Russian consular officials in Breslau and Koenigsberg they succeeded in gaining some concessions from the German authorities. The most notable of these was one which excused the Polish immigrant agricultural workers from compulsory deductions from their wages toward Prussian insurance and compensation funds from which the immigrants, as aliens, could not gain any benefits.[89]

Equally piece-meal were the government's efforts to legalize seasonal emigration. In an effort to reduce illegal emigration and at the same time discourage the prevailing practice of violating passport regulations, the authorities issued a number of administrative directives at the turn of the century aimed at facilitating the acquisition of passports.[90] Several years later, in accordance with the provisions of the Russo-German trade convention of July 28, 1904, the Council of Ministers abrogated that section of the law of March 12, 1897, which permitted the issuance of free passports only to residents along the frontier adjoining Prussia. Henceforward, all pertinent government authorities were instructed to issue cost-free passports to all "Russian laborers" going to Germany for agricultural employment.[91]

Nevertheless, large numbers of seasonal emigrants as well as overseas emigrants continued to leave without benefit of passports in the years preceding the war. Prior to the liberalized policy adopted in 1904, the majority of seasonal emigration to Germany was said to have been illegal. Because of the peasant's suspicion of governmental authorities and the troublesome formalities attendant upon obtaining a passport, the majority of seasonal emigrants either availed themselves of the easily obtainable nine-day travel permit, ignoring its limitations, or dispensed with all legal formalities. Some of them, upon their return, readily admitted their illegal departure for which they were assessed a fine of nine rubles. Others simply smuggled themselves back across the border.[92] In both cases, however, their illegal status exposed them to possible intimidation and extortionate practices by unscrupulous job brokers and employers.

Passport regulations governing overseas emigration were somewhat more restrictive, since the government had due regard for its subjects as taxpayers and army recruits. Officially, the authorities tolerated overseas emigration only by way of the Baltic ports. Unofficially, however, the border authorities presented no serious obstacles. The few that could not be bribed were deceived. In the decades before the war there developed an underground movement of emigration, conducted by professional smugglers, whose operations were known throughout the land and who were always ready, for a fee, to lend their professional services.[93] Once across the border, the German authorities imposed no impediments, provided that the emigrant showed himself in possession of a *Schiffskarte* on a German ship, or was prepared to place a deposit on such a ticket.

In the years immediately preceding the war, the central government undertook the formulation of a comprehensive emigration law which was intended to cover all aspects of the overseas and continental movement. A "formulative commission" was called into existence in 1910 and was presided over by the Vice Minister of Trade and Industry.[94]

After prolonged hearings,[95] a draft of the law was presented to the

Duma for its consideration in 1913. Among its provisions was one which stipulated that all ships of Russian registry were to be given the exclusive privilege of carrying cost-free passport bearers — passengers travelling on all other ships were obliged to have regular passports. On the subject of continental agricultural emigration, the proposed law provided for the establishment of a number of government bureaus charged with drawing up individual labor contracts between authorized representatives of the employers and the emigrants. It also provided for the establishment of posts of emigrant commissioners in various Russian embassies and consulates in Europe to look after the interests of the emigrants.[96]

Although the last two provisions covered a deficiency which had been widely deplored by many writers, the proposed law met with criticism in Russian Poland. The provision favoring travel on ships of Russian registry was pronounced unworkable, because travel by way of the Russian port of Libau was too far off the convenient routes of emigration. Furthermore, there were insufficient passenger ships of Russian registry to accommodate the large volume of emigration from Russian Poland. A strict enforcement of this proviso would therefore create a large bottleneck to emigration for several years. In practical operation, these restrictions on travel would only increase the tendency toward illegal emigration. This the editor Zamoyski considered a serious matter since the technically illegal status of the emigrants was directly related to their indisposition ever to return home.[97]

The provision of the proposed law creating government agencies for drawing up individual labor contracts was regarded as equally unworkable. Strictly enforced, it would also create a hopeless bottleneck during the rush period of seasonal emigration. He suspected, probably correctly, that this provision of the proposed law was only a tactical move by the Russian government to gain concessions from the German government in the renegotiations on the trade treaty which was scheduled to expire in 1914.[98]

Like the deliberations on the control and regulation of emigration during the period of anticipated autonomy, the anxieties and criticisms called forth by this law remained academic.[99] The law was never put into effect before the outbreak of the war and, in the meantime, the movement of emigrants to Germany and abroad continued on its timeworn way. The vacillating policy of the authorities toward emigration, if anything, may be regarded as one of unpremeditated liberalism—one that put a minimum of impediments in the way of the emigrant seeking a better life.

III. Austria and the Poles

V

The Galician *Sejm* and Its Early Policy Toward Emigration— From Studied Silence to Interdiction

Galicia, the Austrian sector of pre-war Poland, enjoyed a unique political status, in comparison to the other two sectors, in that it had acquired a considerable range of political autonomy and was, as a result, to a far greater extent the master of its own historical development. While the Polish policy of Prussia seemed to be predicated on complete cultural and political assimilation and, like the Russian policy in Russian Poland, aimed at the total elimination of the Polish landed gentry from the councils of government, the Austrian government, by adopting a conciliatory policy of mutual support, gained for its Habsburg rulers the staunch support of the Galician gentry.[1]

By virtue of their complete control of the provincial government, the landed gentry were able to follow a program calculated to perpetuate their privileged status as an agricultural ruling class. Their extensive, rather than intensive, type of agricultural economy could exist only by utilizing a very low-paid agricultural labor—a labor supply at the beck and call of the manor—and the manor as its only place of employment. This form of agricultural economy required a large reservoir of cheap labor created by an economic policy which, on the one hand, was opposed to the development of industry and which, on the other hand, was calculated to restrain and impede emigration in every way.

Early in its existence, the problem of a numerous and cheap agricultural labor force came under the consideration of the Galician *sejm*. The occasion for this discussion was provided by the passage in the Austrian *Reichsrat,* in 1868, of a law which abolished the existing restraints on free disposition of land by gentry and peasants. This law, in conformity with the then prevailing temper of economic liberalism, was calculated to remove one of the restraints impeding the transition of Austrian agriculture into the framework of modern capitalistic economy.

The question of its ratification called forth a spirited discussion in the Galician *sejm*. Deputy Kabat, its chief spokesman in that body, maintained that not only would this law, by permitting peasantry to buy small parcels of land, tend to draw into circulation their small capital holdings but, by giving the peasant the right to divide his land equally among his heirs, would preclude the formation of ą class of disinherited and landless proletariat. This category of peasants, he inferred, lacking attachment to the soil, would either emigrate or create a "social problem" at home — either contingency undesirable to the existing social order.[2]

The minority in opposition to this change, on their part, argued that, on the contrary, the new law would foster a tendency toward emigration, and opposed it for that reason. Deputy Krainski remarked that in German principalities where the unlimited break-up of land-holds was permitted by law there was a concomitant mass emigration abroad.[3] Furthermore, the opposition pointed out, the adoption of such western-type legislation would doubtless be harmful to the national interest, since the peasant would be disposed to sell his land to undesirable foreign elements whose presence in Galician rural life would be inimical to the existing order of things.[4] As to the likelihood of the emigration of the disinherited, the opposition reiterated their belief that the Polish peasant would not emigrate because of his traditional attachment to his native land, even in the face of starvation.[5]

Since there was no notable amount of emigration from Galicia at that time, and since it was generally believed that the absence of entail restrictions would lead to the agglomeration of land by the more aggressive peasantry and gentry, the majority doubtless hoped in this way to create a large reservoir of labor supply dependent upon the local manor for its livelihood. Furthermore, those of the peasantry who succeeded in extending their landholds would constitute a middle group of landholders whose economic and social interests would be identified with those of the landed nobility. That being the case, they could be counted upon to give their political support to the essentially conservative program of the ruling majority.

These motives were clearly affirmed in the majority report of the special commission appointed to consider the ratification of the law in question for Galicia. The commission expressed the opinion that, among other results, the law under consideration would foster a pro-liferation of dwarf-sized landholds insufficient in themselves to sustain a peasant family. This, however, would have the redeeming feature of providing an ever-present labor supply for the large landholders.[6] The deputy Paulin Kosinski reaffirmed the point.[7]

Essentially, therefore, the discussion centered around the most effective means of creating and maintaining a surplus labor supply for the landed gentry. As Kabat pointed out, there was no question in the committee regarding the advisability of giving the manorial landlords the right to dispose of their land as they wished.[8] Any differences of opinion devolved upon the question of whether the peasant landowners should also be given this right and what effect it would have on the local labor market. The few peasant deputies were won over to the support of the majority by being told that the proposed law would legalize existing transactions. If it was not passed, land heretofore purchased from the manors was of questionable title and could conceivably revert to the manors.[9]

The expected agglomeration of peasant land by the more affluent peasants and gentry, however, did not materialize. On the contrary, within the space of a decade it was generally apparent that peasant landholds were diminishing in size though their numbers were increasing. Together with this trend toward the creation of numerous dwarf-landholds there was evidence of an even greater tendency for manorial lands to pass over into the hands of non-gentry. This transfer was especially disquieting since the ownership of "tabular lands" included a number of political privileges—privileges traditionally reserved for the gentry.[10]

In retrospect, it is evident that the causes of their declining fortunes were largely an aspect of the generally declining conditions of the Galician economy resulting from the unsettling conditions which had everywhere followed upon the progressive inroads of modern industrial civilization upon an essentially agricultural economy. As Bujak and others pointed out, the extension of railroad communication had the effect of also extending the market of the factory production of the more industrialized areas of Europe. The Galician economy, based on agriculture and domestic production, found itself unable to compete with cheaper foreign products. Local manufactories and wagon transport were the casualties in this competition.[11] The large landholders, like their counterparts in Russian and Prussian Poland, began to feel the pressure of overseas competition on the European grain market. The crescive weight of these developments was dramatically emphasized by the successive crop failures—the potato crop failure in the mountainous districts of Galicia during the 1871–1873 period and the general crop failure in 1875.[12]

Nevertheless, the fact that peasants were acquiring land that had formerly belonged to the gentry suggested that as a labor force they were acquiring a certain degree of mobility. It was generally agreed that the peasant could not accumulate the necessary capital to buy land with wages from Galician agriculture.[13] Nor was there evidence lacking that a migrational movement was developing. As early as 1871, an interpellation was addressed to the Government Commissioner complaining that the laws relating to the return and punishment of fugitive servants, that is, those who broke their contracts of employment, were not being sufficiently enforced by the provincial authorities. In his reply, the Government Commissioner reported that efforts to track down and, if necessary, forcibly return fugitive servants had been rendered especially difficult in western Galicia because many of them had fled the country — and therefore his jurisdiction — and had gone to places like Austrian Silesia and Moravia to seek better employment in the factories there. Furthermore, he complained, the authorities of the latter countries were singularly uncooperative in extraditing these fugitive-emigrants.[14] This problem of effective "regulation" of the domestic agricultural labor supply was again raised in the *sejm* in 1874 by the Galician deputy Erazm Wolanski,[15] and continued to occupy the interest of that body throughout the following decade.

There were other evidences indicating that the indigenous labor force was finding new outlets. At about that time, in the early 1870's, there had already developed a small but significant emigration of Masurian population, largely through the efforts of the clergyman Gurowski, from the district of Gorlice in central Galicia to Parana province of Brazil.[16] In 1874 there was another organized effort undertaken to promote settlement of Galicians in Parana. At that time these activities were concentrated mainly around the district of Tarnow, also in central Galicia.[17] Even more significant, however, were the non-agricultural domestic outlets provided during the mid-century by the Governor-General of Galicia, Count Goluchowski. During the period of his first administration (1849–1856), he abandoned the former policy of doling out food and seed during periods of elemental disasters and embarked upon a systematic program of public works. Though most of his projects were pigeon-holed in Vienna, he nevertheless succeeded in obtaining sizable imperial funds for his various projects which provided a notable source of non-agricultural employment and income for the people of Galicia.[18] The construction of military defenses in Krakow in 1864–1866 and in Przemysl somewhat later provided further employment and added stimuli to the mobility of population in Galicia. Dr. Bujak, reporting on this phenomenon between 1865 and 1875 found that, besides the traditional movement of seasonal migrants to Russian Poland and Hungary, there had recently developed a seasonal migration from the westernmost Galician districts to the more eastern districts on the Dunajec River and to the factories and mines of Prussian Silesia.[19] By 1880, the condition of the agricultural labor supply had changed sufficiently to warrant the mention of emigration as a specific problem before the *sejm* by Arnold Rapaport. He called upon the central government to exercise every means at its disposal to stop the developing emigration, specifically to the United States, regarding it ". . . disastrous to the social order and to the nation." He maintained that it was "artificially stimulated," since overpopulation was not a problem in Galicia.[20]

Thus, within a decade following the repeal of the old entail laws a whole new complex of circumstances was forcing a fundamental reconsideration of the prevailing policy of liberalism.[21] The dominant gentry in the *sejm* quite apparently came to realize that as an essentially conservative class its interests could not be served within the framework of a liberal economic and social policy. It was within this new complex that the property law of 1868 came under widespread criticism and attack in the *sejm*. In 1868, a number of its proponents quite candidly argued that it would assure domestic agriculture with an abundant labor force in the persons of those peasants who would be unable to sustain themselves on their diminishing parcels of land. By the early 1880's, however, a reversal of this policy began to gain increasing support, though, for some, essentially for the same reasons as formerly. An inquiry undertaken by the *sejm* had graphically demonstrated the depressed level of the Galician economy in general and its agriculture in particular. On the basis of these findings, published in 1881,[22] Zdzislaw Tyszkiewicz renewed a motion he had made in the previous session of the *sejm* to instruct the Executive Department to undertake a re-examination of the law of November 1, 1868 ". . . to ascertain to what degree it has been responsible for the progressive impoverishment of the peasant population. . ." and, on the basis of its findings, ". . . to take appropriate action toward revising it." On his request, his motion was sent to a Committee on National Culture which, in reporting favorably upon it, recommended that the Executive Department undertake an appropriate investigation into the matter and report its findings at the next session of the *sejm*.[23] This recommendation was approved by the *sejm* and the subject came under its discussion in 1883.

Proceeding from the premise that the law of 1868—which permitted the peasant class to dispose freely of its property—had led to the progressive break-up of peasant landholds to a degree which threatened their existence, the majority of the *sejm* approved a motion requesting the *Reichsrat* to submit a project of laws ". . . which would, in their aim at heading off the ruin of the peasantry as a class in our country, delimit the existing license of the peasants to partition their land and change the inheritance laws as they pertain to peasant holdings." [24] It was maintained that the unrestrained break-up of peasant landholds would ultimately reduce them to the level of a proletariat and, as such, they would constitute a threat to the existing social structure. [25] One speaker for repeal affirmed that the high hopes motivating the passage of the law of 1868 had not been realized. Its advocates in 1868 had hoped it would favor the development of a prosperous middle class of peasant landowners; that it would foster increased agricultural productivity of the country; that it would stimulate industriousness among the peasantry and that, "above all, it would prevent further emigration of the populace of this country. . . ." Having failed in its purpose, he considered it imperative either to repeal or amend the law in question. [26] The statistician, Dr. Tadeusz Pilat, chief spokesman for the repeal motion, in presenting his arguments, cited the prosperous agrarian class in the United States as testimony of the beneficence of laws restraining alienation of property. According to his researches, ". . . since 1839 there has been a trend among the individual states and, since 1862, a federal law and later amended state laws, which provide for the creation of landholds of a certain size, called 'homesteads,' and stipulate that they were to pass undivided to but one heir." [27]

There can be little doubt that the repeal of the law in question was intended to improve the condition of the peasant and to facilitate the economic recovery of agriculture in general. There is evidence, however, that egoistic motives were not altogether lacking. Abrahamowicz most nearly gave them expression when he remarked that ". . . as soon as a peasant, with help of [the law permitting] subdivision of land, becomes owner of one *morg* of land, he regards himself as a landlord and work as hired hand or servant as beneath his station." [28] This motive was further revealed by another proponent of the repeal motion, Count Henryk Wodzicki, when he vigorously denied that the repeal of the law in question would tend to increase the number of cottagers and share-croppers, that is, the semi-serf class. [29] This contention was rather remarkable since none of those who had spoken in opposition to the motion had either directly or indirectly, by implication or inference, said that the repeal of the property law of 1868 would tend to increase the numbers of this class of hired agricultural labor.

The opposition, in general, advanced the same arguments against repeal as they did for its acceptance in 1868. Deputy Lubienski, for example, maintained that all restraints calculated to keep the peasant landholds entailed would create a class of landless and disinherited. These, ". . . without inheritance, hearth or country," lacking any material ties, would emigrate. As formerly, they held that the peasant with even the smallest parcel of land was always drawn back to his native land. Lacking this, those seasonal migrants who journeyed annually to Russian Poland were not likely to return and, thus, be lost to the "nation." Those of the "disinherited" who remained would constitute a true proletariat and, as such, a menace to the existing social order.[30]

The only opposing voice which departed from this point of view was Deputy Hausner who quite frankly regarded the repeal motion as part and parcel of a reactionary pattern being promulgated by the ruling majority of the *sejm,* and which included their views on public education, their efforts to revive the guild system to protect the old domestic system of manufacture against the modern factory system of production, and, in general, their ". . . contemptuous regard of Manchesterian economics — a disdain that has become fashionable in the higher [political and social] spheres. . . ."[31]

Although the majority was still largely concerned with the problem of domestic labor supply, some felt that its resolution dictated a newer course in the light of the developments in the seventies. Although since 1868 there had developed a significant migration of the peasantry, it was neither widespread nor numerous. Its range was still relatively local and its duration temporary. Only the most venturesome undertook to sever their domestic ties completely and betake themselves permanently overseas to the United States or Brazil. The average peasant owner of even a fragment of land, although dependent on "outside" earnings for his livelihood, was content to remain in his native village and augment his income by non-agricultural employment in nearby Russian Poland or Hungary. What distressed some of the large landholders most was this peasant's singular indisposition to indenture himself and his family to the manor. However, lacking both this particle of land and the courage and resources to venture permanently abroad, he would perforce be obliged to accept the terms of employment offered by the local manor.

Since the overseas routes of emigration had not yet become established, they thought to bind such landless local peasants to the manor. The repeal of the law of 1868, which would reimpose a system of entail upon the peasant lands, could only increase their numbers. In this light, the vigorous protests of Count Wodzicki assume greater meaning. Such, to a degree, also was the underlying motive of the special committee which took this motion under advisement. In favorably reporting upon it, the committee gave expression to this intent when it noted with some alarm ". . . that the number of peasant owners . . . is increasing and [even] exceeding the number of cottagers and share-croppers. . . ."[32]

There was apparently no thought to re-establish entail restrictions upon manorial lands. When the elections of 1883 revealed that a substantial proportion of that category of land had passed into the hands of non-gentry,[33] thereby jeopardizing the political ascendancy of the *szlachta*,[34] it was the electoral law of 1866 rather than the property law of 1868 which was subsequently changed.[35]

* * *

This attitude of the large landowners regarding a cheap and numerous supply of agricultural labor was further expressed in its deliberations on the subject of adequate credit facilities for the peasantry. One of the results of the parliamentary investigations into the causes of rural pauperization, accentuated by the cataclysmic developments in the seventies, was the realization that one of the foremost economic shortcomings of rural Galicia was the lack of favorable credit facilities. Indebtedness had been progressively accelerating, especially after the repeal of the usury laws in 1868, with the result that an increasing number of peasant landholds were being forced on the auction block.[36] The Legal Committee, which took under advisement a motion to repeal the property law of 1868, clearly recognized the relation between the high cost of credit, lack of operating and investment capital and the progressive impoverishment of the agricultural classes. It expressed its alarm at this development and noted that such a development, left unchecked, could only result in social upheaval.[37]

Nevertheless, the Executive Department which undertook an inquiry into the causes of the economic decline of Galicia in the same year found that the available credit facilities for the peasants were adequate. Dr. Tadeusz Skalkowski reported that the cost of mortgage credit for that group of the population in the Peasant Bank — the only institution which granted them that type of credit in Galicia — was rather high. In his opinion, however, this circumstance was of no great moment since the peasant did not need long-term mortgage credit. The statistician, Tadeusz Pilat, charged with an investigation into credit facilities available to the peasantry in the village banks, noted that, properly administered, they could provide adequate credit for that segment of the population.[38]

A new note, however, was sounded that same year by the deputy Rapaport. He complained that the Austrian National Bank was not fulfilling its charter obligations in Galicia. In his view, the lack of sufficient credit facilities was hampering the operation of that country's economy.[39] This contention was reiterated by Deputy Dzieduszycki during the discussion on the proposed budget for the succeeding year.[40]

This split in the ranks was reaffirmed by the Executive Department in its report to the *sejm* in 1878. Unlike the report of the previous year, it found that the progressive decline of the peasant class was the result of being suddenly thrust into the mainstream of capitalistic economy without the requisite credit facilities to facilitate this transition. As a result of these conditions, the peasants were unable to surmount the periodic set-backs occasioned by elemental disasters and were progressively falling into the fatal indebtedness of private loan sharks who were mercilessly exploiting their predicament.[41]

In its view, the Peasant Bank of Galicia was contributing to rather than alleviating this condition. The peripheral and administrative costs of contracting one of its loans, combined with its high interest rates, made its credit, in the final analysis, extremely expensive. Largely as a result of its operations, there had been a rapid increase in number of peasant and small town property put up for public auction.[42]

The other institutions of credit for the peasantry, the county loan banks and loan associations, were both suffering from inadequate access to operating capital which restricted their volume of operations in the rural areas.[43] The village loan banks, in the opinion of this report, were quite useless. They were suffering, on the one hand, from poor administration and, on the other, from the rapacity of the village officials.[44] In any case, none of them offered mortgage loans.

As a result of these credit conditions, poverty and pauperism were spreading at an alarming rate in the peasant villages. This progressive material decline left its mark on the physical character of the Galician population. In the previous year, 849 out of every thousand males of conscription age were found to be unfit for military duty.[45]

This report elicited a lengthy discussion on the floor of the *sejm* on the subject of the credit needs of the peasant class and a motion accepting the report's recommendation to pump 10,000,000 crowns into the existing local institutions was carried and sent to a special commission on loans. There, however, the allotment was reduced to 1,000,000 crowns and this recommendation was finally accepted by the *sejm* on October 9, 1878.[46] It authorized the Executive Department, the administrative arm of the *sejm,* to negotiate a loan for that sum, and ". . . to take under its consideration if, in view of the inauguration of mortgage registers [for the peasants], it would be desirable at this time to establish a mortgage institution for peasant landholds."[47]

On the basis of these instructions, the Executive Department summoned a body of experts to hold hearings on the subject. The conclusion reached by that body affirmed the need of such a public institution. On the basis of this recommendation, the Executive Department drew up a statute of such a mortgage bank for the approval of the *sejm.*[48] No action, however, was ever taken to establish such a credit institution for the peasants.

Instead, the energies of that body were redirected to the establishment of a Provincial Bank for Galicia, which would provide the credit facilities necessary for the general economic development of Galicia. As formerly, the impoverished condition of the peasant class was advanced by its proponents. One of its earliest supporters, Leon Bilinski, proclaimed in the *sejm* in 1878 the crying need of favorable mortgage credits by the peasants. In his view, the Provincial Bank would primarily serve this function thereby rescuing that class ". . . from the usurers who were reducing them to poverty."[49] The deputy Krukowiecki concurred with this opinion.[50]

The segment of the conservative gentry, however, which defeated the previous efforts to provide peasant credit facilities, again imposed its opposition. Erazm Wolanski, for example, speaking in opposition to the proposed bank, probably expressed the attitude of that group when he stated:

> I am convinced from long association with the peasantry that they do not need [such] a bank—that banks are the ruination of the peasantry. For what does he need capital? His best capital are his hands which are with him always and for which he is not obliged to pay interest. Let him only work—estates are suffering from a lack of labor supply—they can supply the capital he may need in return for his work if only there is an honest desire for employment. Loans [from banks] induce laziness, for why should he work if he can borrow. . . .

Consonant with this logic, Wolanski went on to say that he would not be a party to a project which would promote laziness among the peasantry. His specific remedy for any credit needs of the peasantry would be a mutual agreement between peasant and landlord in which, for capital loaned to the peasant, the landlord would receive repayment in the form of specified work until the debt was paid up in full. In such a way the landlord would be assured of an adequate labor supply.[51]

This was not a new idea among the landed class. It had gained popularity among them, especially in eastern Galicia, since the abolition of feudal obligations in 1848. In 1874, during the debate on the motion to "regulate the control of farm servants," it was argued that such a mutual contractual arrangement between employer and employee was the means of acquiring capital by the latter—that it would solve the problem of peasant credit facilities and save him from the fatal grasp of usury.[52]

Stanislaw Tarnowski, however, had exposed that practice for what it was in the publication, *Przeglad Polski,* in 1874. He called it a refined type of economic serfdom that had gained widespread acceptance by the landed classes throughout Galicia as a means of binding the peasant to the manor and providing them with a cheap labor supply. This practice, according to the author, was by no means exceptional but rather was the established practice throughout a large part of the Galician counties.[53]

During the debates on the proposed Provincial Bank, Tadeusz Skalkowski pointed out that political enfranchisement without the concomitant economic enfranchisement of the peasant class was an empty gesture. He reminded the assembled body that from the time of the abolition of serfdom (1848) to the establishment of the privately operated Peasant Bank in 1868, no organized institution for mortgage credit was available to that class and, hence, the field was open to a host of private speculators preying upon the financial needs of the peasants. The establishment of the Peasant Bank, in his view, only aggravated their condition since its operations were predicated on a conscienceless agitation to ensnare peasant landowners. Because of its extremely generous charter privileges, it was able to charge an average of 12 percent interest on the principal and 15 percent on delinquent debts.[54]

Since the emphasis on peasant welfare appeared to be alienating the support of the moderate conservatives, the proponents of the proposed bank expanded their arguments to embrace the total welfare of the Galician economy. Dr. Jozef Wereszczynski pointed out to them that since thirty years agriculture had ceased to be a profitable operation and examples of either farmer, industrialist or artisan achieving independent success were very few. Capital alone was creating fortunes. Several thousands of crowns on loan in a few years produced fortunes. In this way present fortunes, property and otherwise, had been recently achieved. "Banks and financial institutions do not turn to productive enterprises—they almost without exception limit themselves to lending money because loans bring highest returns." Thus, according to that observer, capital enjoyed a privileged status in Galicia as a result of the fact that there was so little of it available.[55]

Despite this general expansion of the function of a bank which was originally proposed to fill the long term credit needs of the peasants, some continued to impose their objections to its establishment. One such, David Abrahamowicz, specifically opposed the entire proposal precisely because of this one area of its competence. It was his considered judgment that to provide long-term credit facilities to peasants was to contribute to their total economic collapse. To illustrate his point, he called the attention of the *sejm* to the operations of the Peasant Bank. In his view, their impoverishment was not because the cost of its credit was exhorbitantly high or otherwise unfavorable, but for the simple reason that it made any credit available to that class — a class he regarded as "fiscally immature." Their incompetence in such matters, conjoined with a total lack of responsibility was apparent from the well-known fact that such loans were willfully dissipated.[56]

Nevertheless, by extending the functional base of the originally projected credit institution, a sufficient number of the membership were won to its support and in 1883 it was chartered as the officially sponsored discount bank for Galicia. The high promise that it held for the peasants, however, was never fully realized. A complex of factors seemed to frustrate its original intent.

As a matter of policy, all applicants were required to have their property engrossed either in the manorial land registers[57] or comparable registries of deeds and mortgages for non-manorial property. Though a law of 1874 provided for the establishment of the latter, a lack of personnel and funds impeded their expeditious establishment.[58] Thus, only three years after its establishment, the Reverend Sicznyski called the attention of the *sejm* to the fact that though the Provincial Bank had given out 8,633,000 zl. r. in mortgage loans during the first three years of its existence, 57 percent of this amount went to owners of landed estates and only 4.95 percent to the peasant landowners.[59]

When he remarked that its original proponents used the argument that it was to provide favorable mortgage credit facilities for the peasants, the Count Golejski replied that ". . . small [peasant] landowners should be happy they got fewer loans because such loans are not gifts. . . ."[60] His colleague, Count Lubienski, endorsed this view and added that the disproportion was simply due to the fact that fewer peasants applied for them.[61]

Such complaints against its "tight" policy continued to be raised thereafter in the *sejm*.[62] As late as 1908, on the occasion of a motion to liberalize the charter of the Provincial Bank, the peasant deputy, Franciszek Stefczyk, complained that the Provincial Bank was not discharging its primary commission. He pointed out that during its twenty-four years of existence 53½ percent of its mortgage loans went for urban mortgages, 34 percent for mortgages on landed estates and only 12½ percent for peasants. As a result of its rigid policy toward peasant mortgage loans, the peasant farmer was perforce obliged to avail himself of primarily short-term credits for mortgage purposes. The pressure to meet these short-term obligations, in his view, had a disruptive influence since it tended to force the peasant-debtor to betake himself, or send members of his family, abroad to earn the requisite funds.[63]

For those peasants who failed to meet the qualifications of the Provincial Bank no legitimate sources of mortgage credit were available other than those provided by the privately owned Peasant Bank of Galicia. Established during Galicia's brief experiment in economic liberalism, a period which saw the abolition of former usury laws, it entered upon a career which was to bring it widespread notoriety and economic ruin for many peasant landowners. The peasant class, newly enfranchised and as yet untutored in the ways of modern capitalistic relationships, was encouraged by a widespread promotional program to avail itself of what appeared to be a very liberal loan policy. Its agents, working on a commission basis, exploited the prevailing credit needs of the peasants to the fullest.[64] Those of the peasants who undertook such loans were soon rudely awakened. Not only were they charged a minimum of 12 percent interest on their loans but, upon falling in arrears on these payments, the rate of interest was increased to approximately 15 percent. These costs did not include the original administrative charges made for negotiating the loan.[65]

As early as 1869, petitions of grievances and memorials began to flood the Galician parliament, imploring that body for redress and relief. They continued to do so throughout the period of that bank's existence, but to no avail.[66] Teofil Merunowicz, in a pamphlet entitled *Zaklad kredytu wloscianskiego,* published in 1878, noted that at that time there were 58,140 peasant landholds in that bank's debt, about half of which were in a position of being unable to pay.[67]

A special commission appointed by the *sejm* in 1880 to make inquiries into the operations and influences of the Peasant Bank reported that a considerable number of peasant holdings were being forced on the auction block. It noted that while only 164 peasant landholds were put on public auction in 1867, in 1877 their number increased to 2,139 and, in 1879, totalled 3,164. Of these, the Peasant Bank alone was responsible for issuance of 4,877 notices of foreclosure during the 1868–1879 period.[68] By 1883 it was instrumental in putting on the auction block 6,572 farmsteads. This total did not include the number of peasant landholders forced to liquidate their holdings by other means. During the period 1895–1897, while that bank was liquidating its holdings, about 500 peasant farmsteads were forced to be put up for auction.[69]

Despite the fact that the *Reichsrat* attempted to impose certain restraints on loan operations by a law passed in 1881, Leopold Caro, writing in the last decade of the century, still maintained that the operations of loan sharks were progressively impoverishing the peasantry. The Austrian law of 1881, while defining certain credit and loan practices as illegal, was couched ambiguously and lacked comprehension. If anything, it served only to refine and make more devious the practices of the loan sharks.[70] Its lack of comprehensiveness, combined with the "Manchesterian predelictions" of the courts had the effect of negating its avowed purpose. As a result of these factors, convictions under it were very few in number and light in sentence.[71]

The *sejm* also came under Caro's criticism. Though careful in his terminology, he strongly scored "those elements of Galician society who hold that by making credit facilities relatively inaccessible to the peasant class thought they would be able to prevent them from falling into debt." On the contrary, he pointed out, such impediments only tended to drive them into the snares of usurers and other money speculators.[72]

Despite these exposures, Dr. Bujak found that the chief sources of credit of the peasant class in 1904 were still private individuals rather than banks,[73] and the historian, Jan Rutkowski, on the eve of the war, found that the increase of public auctions of peasant landholds was not only absolute but also relative. These findings led him to the conclusion that the development of healthy credit facilities had progressed at a slower pace than the need for them warranted.[74]

* * *

The policy of the Galician parliament toward mortgage credit facilities for the peasants appears to have been analogous to the policy it adopted toward its obverse aspect, parcelation. The only concession that the ruling gentry made toward the establishment of an officially sponsored parcelation program which would relieve the pressure of rural overpopulation was the passage of the land law of 1904 for the creation of leaseholds *(wlosci rentowe)*. By this act, a public fund was established to provide credit for the creation of a middle group of farmsteads or for improving or extending old ones. Those availing themselves of these credit facilities were, however, required to submit to certain restraints. Among others, these included the entailment of their land unless otherwise authorized by the lending agency and accepting certain limitations on other debts incurred against the land.[75]

This law, supported by the controlling gentry, also won the support of the representatives of the peasants, but was vigorously opposed by the Ukrainian deputies. This latter group saw in it, among other things, a Polish counterpart of the German colonization program operative in Prussian Poland — in the case of Galicia, to displace Ukrainians from an area which they claimed as traditionally their own and to relieve the pressure of population in western Galicia at the expense of the Ukrainian people in eastern Galicia.[76]

Though regarded by the parliamentary majority and their nationalistic allies as a typical example of Ukrainian obstructionism, the suspicions of the Ukrainians were not without foundation. Throughout most of the second half of the nineteenth century evidence of an eastward settlement of Polish peasants from western Galicia was apparent. Many of them, having saved some money abroad and unable to locate it in land in western Galicia — both because of its scarcity and its high price — were increasingly tending to establish themselves more to the eastward.[77] The closing of the credit facilities of the Parcelation Bank to Ukrainian peasants in 1905 only confirmed their suspicions.

At any rate, the achievements of this program were inconsequential. During its seven years of operation, a total of only 815 farmsteads were created — in 426 communities in seven eastern districts. These landholds, ranging from five to fifty hectares, totalled 9,250 hectares and represented a total value of 15,613,261 kr. Their total indebtedness at the outbreak of the war was 7,881,550 kr. It was abandoned after the war.[78]

Outside the chambers of parliament, however, the subject of parcelation came under considerable discussion and the attitudes expressed by commentators were as varied — and corresponded to — those expressed in the other sectors of partitioned Poland. The older, more conservative point of view which found expression in the defeat of the effort to decentralize the manorial land registers in 1873[79] continued to be voiced at the turn of the century, though with decreasing frequency and authority. Jozef Milewski and Wlodzimierz Czerkawski, for example, continued to caution the large landowners against "the temptation of parcelation."[80] At the other extreme were social democrats like Zofia Daszynska-Golinska who at that time advocated unrestricted parcelation of large landholds and, if necessary, their total elimination from the Galician economy.[81]

The majority, both spokesmen of the peasant class and, increasingly, those of the conservative classes, occupied a middle ground between these extremes. Franciszek Bujak, perhaps the most informed researcher into the condition of the peasant class, favored a "rational" policy of parcelation because, in the existing world economic condition, he considered the resulting small peasant landholds both vital and economically practicable. His intensive researches into the economic conditions of nineteenth and early twentieth century Galicia convinced him of the progressive improvement of peasant economy. This improvement he attributed to the felicitous configuration of western European economic factors — factors which he felt were of a relatively permanent character. The foremost of these was the prevailing policy of free immigration.[82]

On the other hand, Jan Rozwadowski, although representing the conservative orientation of the enlightened gentry, likewise supported a "rational" policy of parcelation but for wholly different reasons than did Bujak. In his view, parcelation was both socially and economically advisable but only when the landlord found himself in a position verging on bankruptcy. In such circumstances, by liquidating some of his land holdings, he would be able to meet his most pressing obligations and, by consolidating his remaining debts, escape from the precipice of bankruptcy. Though in reduced circumstances, such a manorial landowner could still remain as such and, by doing so, would not deplete the ranks of that class and therefore their political and social ascendancy. Such a program of partial parcelation had also the effect of relieving the "social danger" resulting from the presence of an increasing number of landless rural population. Under no circumstances, however, was the total break-up of manorial establishments either socially or economically desirable, advisable or even necessary. Total parcelation was akin to desertion from the field and ultimately could only lead to reducing the nation to the level of the peasant — a prospect which could only be viewed with alarm. Nevertheless, like Bujak, he saw the integral correlation between parcelation and emigration.[83]

In the intra-conservative debate on the issue of parcelation, to the ultra-conservative contention that dwarf-peasant landholds were not economically feasible and only tended to decrease the labor supply of the manor, the younger conservatives answered that such was not the case. Stanislaw Hupka, for example, maintained that a peasant with even a fragment of land remained a peasant. If he emigrated, it was only temporarily and he returned with his savings to buy up more land — a factor which only enhanced the value of manorial lands. As to the question of the economic feasibility of these small acquisitions, they had shown a greater economic vitality than those of the larger peasant landholders. This, in their view, was because the larger peasant landowner, finding it necessary to utilize the labor of others besides himself and his family, was dependent upon the condition of the local labor market — a market which was becoming increasingly weighted in favor of the agricultural laborers because of the development of other outlets through emigration. Furthermore, Hupka argued, with the development of emigration there was a growing tendency among the peasants to "pay off" all but one heir and to keep the farmhold intact. Not infrequently, peasant-emigrants completely renounced all claims to their inheritance of land when the farmhold was very small. This new practice contributed considerably to removing some of the more undesirable results of the former practice of progressive sub-division of peasant landholds.[84]

A number of circumstances and developments contributed to this changed attitude of the conservative classes. The foremost of these was the factor of their political control of the Galician government. Lacking the requisite capital accumulations to participate fully in the modern system of agricultural economy, they denied the peasant population access to favorable credit which would have facilitated their fuller participation. The Polish peasant in Prussian Poland had the alternative of satisfying his needs, if necessary, in the industrial establishments of Western Germany. Though to a lesser extent, such an outlet also existed in the growing industrial concentrations of western and southwestern Russian Poland. Furthermore, the existence of a government-sponsored parcelation bank in Russian Poland and the program of the Colonization Commission in Prussian Poland had a tendency to restrain excessive inflation of land prices. Though the Colonization Commission had been criticized as being instrumental in artificially enhancing the land values of the large landowners of Poznan and West Prussia, by their very operations they forced their Polish counterparts, the private parcelation agencies and cooperatives, to gain land for the Polish peasant at more moderate costs. The nationalistic bias of both the Colonization Commission and its private Polish counterparts had the effect of narrowing their market, thereby precluding excessive inflation of land prices.

In Galicia, the contrary was the case. The landed gentry, as a result of their political monopoly, were able to restrain effectively, on the one hand, the development of industry and, on the other, to deny the credit facilities and parcelation organizations which would have restrained the extraordinary increases in land values which followed after the development of emigration.

Contributing to this exceptional condition in Galicia was the fact that mass emigration to Germany and abroad had developed at a later date — at a time when modern communications had developed to a point where it was increasingly possible to sojourn abroad only temporarily. To a far greater extent than in either of the other two sectors of pre-war Poland, emigration from Galicia, even that segment of it which ventured abroad, returned or intended to return originally. In either case, the funds from abroad that flowed back to Galicia exceeded by far those that flowed back into either Russian or Prussian Poland. And, finally, the pressure of rural over-population in Galicia— and therefore, the hunger for land—by far exceeded that in the other sectors.

In this configuration of circumstances, the dominant class of Galicia found itself in the felicitous condition of having its most marketable commodity—its land—at a premium price. Untutored in the ways of modern agricultural economy, the peasant-emigrant was willing to pay a price which was entirely out of proportion to its real value as an investment or a productive enterprise.[85] By 1911, Bujak could logically maintain that, "the high prices of land make their sale [by large landowners] more profitable than their cultivation." The validity of this contention is reaffirmed by the fact that these conditions developed at a time when the large landowners, as producers for the export market, found themselves in a situation of declining profits resulting from the challenge of overseas grain production in the European markets— markets upon which they formerly based their economic existence.[86]

This new orientation of the landed classes toward parcelation was already evident in the parliamentary deliberations on the effects of the land law of 1868 on the political status of the gentry in the election of 1883. It was suddenly discovered that the process of the break-up of manorial lands had progressed to such a degree that, in conjunction with the election law of 1866, a privileged class of non-aristocratic political "virilists" was in the making — a class with political and social views oftentimes antithetical to those of the gentry. That, in resolving this threat, the ruling class in the parliament chose to amend the election law of 1866 rather than the inheritance and property law of 1868, as it pertained to them, suggests that already at that time they had no intention of reversing the process of parcelation, a process which, in the given circumstances, was becoming increasingly profit- able for them.

This decision also brought to light another dilemma which was to trouble them and other nationalistic elements later. As an economic group whose solvency was predicated on the existence of a cheap and numerous supply of local agricultural labor, they were unequivocally opposed to any developments which would tend to reduce or other- wise disrupt it. Emigration had a tendency to accomplish both.

With the development of cheap and speedy transport facilities, however, their economic solvency had been undermined by the com- petition of the overseas grain producing countries. In this declining economic situation, the large landowners were falling increasingly in debt and were threatened with ultimate ruin.[87] However, with the increased mobility of the peasant labor force, begun in the mid- century and reaching mass proportions in the ninth and tenth decades, there was an increasing inflow of capital. These capital accumulations were at first so small that most of them were utilized for the most basic needs like food and clothing. As the volume of emigration increased, so did the capital accumulations of the peasant-emigrants. Having satisfied their most elemental needs, in the absence of other areas of investment, these funds sought location in land. The greater the volume of emigration, the greater were the capital holdings of the emigrants. The result was a greater demand for land. This demand for land, in the absence of any restraints by the government, pushed the price of land to an unprecedented level. The large landowners of Galicia, faced with economic ruin from without, found themselves in the happy position of being able to dispose of parts of their holdings at prices heretofore unknown. A prohibitive policy of emigration, even if it were possible, would only diminish this inflow of capital, reduce the demand for land and thereby decrease its sale value. This dilemma, at least theoretically, was never quite resolved. It produced a rationale which regarded emigration as undesirable but, in the given circumstances, a necessity.

Though some writers continued to ignore the obvious relation between parcelation and emigration,[88] by the turn of the century most observers appeared to recognize it. As early as 1887, at the first meeting of the Association of Polish Jurists and Economists, Antoni Donimirski openly advocated a program of partial parcelation because he felt the increment of emigrants' earnings from abroad made it feasible.[89] The statistician, Jozef Kleczynski, at a similar meeting in 1893, reported that some village post offices were receiving annually remittances from the United States reaching twenty and thirty thousand crowns. With these savings many emigrants had managed to repay their debts, buy up land and, in general, improve the welfare of the rural communities.[90]

The Austrian authorities were also manifesting a growing interest in the material effects of this movement. In 1894 the postal authorities were instructed to compile a complete report of the total postal transmittals arriving in Galicia from North America. At the close of that year, it was found that the total receipts were 5,313,966 crowns arriving in 43,365 consignments. Since there was no commercial exchange between the United States and Galicia at that time worth mentioning, this money almost exclusively represented emigrant remittances. Perhaps the most surprising information brought out by this survey was the fact that of the 74 counties comprising Galicia, there was not even one which did not receive money from the United States by way of the mails. Since this report did not include remittances transmitted by banks and since the survey was conducted at a time when there was an economic recession in the United States, the total capital receipts from emigration abroad, without considering those accruing from continental emigration, could have only been imagined.[91]

The editor of the liberal publication *Kurjer Lwowski,* noting in 1899 that the district of Jaslo alone had received a total of 1,100,000 crowns from North America in that year, challenged the members of the "Polish Club" in the Austrian *Reichsrat* and other public dignitaries to name another comparable source of income for the people of Galicia.[92]

On the floor of the *sejm* the peasant representative, Jan Stapinski, likewise stressed the important bearing emigrant earnings, especially from the United States, had upon a multitude of the social and economic problems of Galicia and pointed out how intimately these conditions were related. It was his opinion that in a great number of Galician communities the people lived more from money and other help from the United States than from whatever they might have earned in Galicia. A dramatic illustration of this was the relief funds that came to the rescue of districts suffering from floods in that year. In closing, he remarked: "It is a well known fact that a large proportion of the churches [in Galicia] are either built or renovated with money received from emigrant-parishioners in the United States."[93] The same speaker again made the point a few years later when he affirmed that the increased economic solvency of the peasant class was largely the result of income from emigration and not domestic economic conditions. Not only did the small peasant landholds owe their continued existence to money from abroad but also the middle group of peasant farmers. This latter group, composed of peasants owning as much as 25 morgs of land, frequently sent their sons abroad to earn the necessary money to keep their holdings intact, and got "local simpletons" to work for them for 80 crowns per year, while their sons were earning up to a thousand dollars per year in the United States.[94]

The socialist representative, Ignacy Daszynski, reminded that body that despite the opposition of the ruling gentry, peasant emigration had developed to a point where it represented a powerful economic factor in the life of the country. It "enabled the peasant of western Galicia to buy out the manorial holdings of the middle gentry and, more than that, sends to this country about 50,000,000 crowns each year. The labor of the peasant in foreign lands has saved the country from abject poverty. . . ."[95]

Another spokesman for the peasants in the *sejm,* Wiktor Skolyszewski, concurred with that view. In his judgment, the peasant agriculture of Galicia at that time (1907) was sustained almost exclusively by money coming from abroad. Furthermore, the fiscal solvency of that country's budget itself was maintained by the earnings coming from abroad.[96] Should that income for some reason be cut off, the country's agriculture would suffer ". . . a basic depression of incalculable extent and consequences" — economic and social consequences which could very well be "catastrophic."[97] The deputy, Henryk Kolischer, substantially agreed with his colleague's analysis and added that ". . . our population is entirely dependent upon the economy of another nation . . . upon the American economy."[98]

As the volume of emigration increased, so did the capital that flowed back into Galicia. On the eve of the war, the historian Bujak estimated that the total sum of money from United States emigrants in the several years preceding the war averaged at least 160,000,000 crowns each year.[99] An equally competent contemporary observer, Wilhelm Feldman, concurred with this estimate and concluded that this income ". . . redeemed Galicia from certain bankruptcy."[100] The socialist, Wladyslaw Gumplowicz, could only marvel at the "extraordinary phenomenon" that was taking place in Galicia — ". . . it is not the bourgeoisie which is accumulating the capital but rather the peasant worker."[101]

VI

The Galician *Sejm* and Its Later Policy Toward Emigration— From Interdiction to Regulation and Control

The last decade of the nineteenth century may quite properly be regarded as a period of transition in the history and historiography of emigration in Galicia. From that time until the outbreak of the war there is evidence of a progressive awareness of the increasingly significant role emigration was playing in the economic and social life of that area.

Prior to then, when emigration was considered at all,[1] it was almost exclusively as an aspect of the agrarian policy followed by the *sejm*. The deliberations on the property law of 1868 and the attempts to repeal it indicated a preoccupation with the question of domestic agricultural labor supply.[2] To a degree, the credit policy adopted by the *sejm* suggests similar motivation.[3] This concern for a sufficient labor force, however, was even more explicitly expressed by the efforts to establish a more effective control over fugitive servants and laborers in those decades.

Though measures for the apprehension of fugitive servants and the regulation of agricultural labor had been suggested in the seventies,[4] the issue was not given a full discussion until the following decade. In 1882 it reappeared on the floor, at which time the *sejm* approved a motion instructing the Executive Department to prepare and submit any requisite regulations it might find necessary regarding "the control of servants" and requesting the central government to enforce existing ones more diligently. As formerly, this motion resulted from widespread complaints that manor employees failed to comply with their agreements — that they accepted advances in wages and departed for parts unknown — and that regulations requiring them to have "servant books" were not being adequately enforced by their new employers. Hence, there was an increasing lack of sufficient control over them. These developments moved the deputy Gorayski to remark that there was "a disposition toward vagabondage abroad in the land."[5]

In compliance with these instructions, the Executive Department undertook a study of the existing regulations with the view of strengthening them and eliminating the existing conflict of administrative competence in their enforcement. On the basis of its investigations, it presented a detailed series of regulations on the subject for the approval of the *sejm*. It was the considered judgment of that body that ". . . the disintegration of the conditions of employment of agricultural laborers and servants has reached such a point that it may be reckoned among the economic disasters of the country. . ." — that the ineffectiveness of the existing regulations "threatened the national economy."[6]

For minor technical reasons and the awareness that it would fail to meet the approval of the central government, the Administrative Commission, to which it was sent, declined to endorse the project of laws as they stood. These technical difficulties were of sufficient gravity to stymie the proposed legislation for the next several sessions.[7] In 1889 it again appeared on the floor of the *sejm* and provoked a prolonged debate. By that time there had developed an eloquent opposition in the persons of the Polish deputies Hausner and Romanowicz and the Ukrainian deputies led by the Reverend Siczynski. Hausner, the deputy from Brody, called it "discriminatory" and ". . . not so much a law governing the conditions of servants but a law by employers, for employers, against servants." He regarded it as an attempt to "reverse the social currents of the nineteenth century," a statement which the proponents of the law chose to interpret as his advocacy of socialism. Especially bitter was his attack on those provisions which sanctioned corporal punishment of employees.[8]

Though the opposition lacked sufficient numbers either to amend or to vote down the law, by their strategy of prolonged debates and postponements they succeeded in accomplishing its final defeat. Time ran out and the subject remained unsettled in that session. Since the question of the reimbursal of the gentry for their traditional liquor privileges *(wykup propinacji)* was scheduled for the next session and since it occupied that body for several of the succeeding sessions, the law "to regulate the employment of servants and agricultural workers" remained in abeyance.[9]

The provincial elections of 1889 marked the advent of a new period in the political history of Galicia. The increased number of peasant representatives that were returned in that and the succeeding elections of 1895 indicated the emergence of a peasant party of opposition. This group, together with the national democratic, social democratic and socialist orientations which were developing, increasingly challenged the political hegemony that the landed gentry had heretofore exercised.[10]

A number of other developments, both in Galicia and in the adjacent sectors of Poland, contributed to a reorientation on the problem of emigration. The foremost of these was the development of the "Brazilian Fever" in Russian Poland in the beginning of the last decade of the century. The concern that it called forth in all the ranks of the population of that sector had its counterparts in Galicia. The opening of the Prussian borders at the same time to seasonal agricultural workers and the news of a Russian colonization program which evoked an emigration of several thousand peasants from the eastern Podolian districts in 1892 equally focused attention upon the problem.[11] A series of sensational lawsuits — especially the so-called "Wadowice Trial" — brought to light the widespread promotional operations of the *Hamburg-Amerika Paketfahrt Actiengesellschaft (Hapag)* and the subterfuge, deceit and criminal frauds practiced by its agents, their tie-ins with public officials and the astonishing profits that were being made from the transport of emigrants.[12] These circumstances, together with the growing consciousness of the dependence of the Galician economy upon the emigrant remittances, called forth a growing demand for encompassing that movement in such a way as to control it in the best national interest.

These demands were not necessarily inconsistent with the labor policy of the *sejm* though they represented a broader approach to the problem by interposing a greater recognition of the emigrants. This new temper represented a growing recognition of the fact that emigration, for good or ill, was an unavoidable concomitant of the contemporary scene and that the interests of the landed gentry and the peasantry could be reconciled with the broader national interest.

Lacking sufficient competence in this area and faced with either the inability or indisposition of the central government to contain this movement, the Galician *sejm* contented itself, for a time, with impeding its development by administrative action. It was therefore private organizations which gave expression to this new orientation.

The first upon the scene was The Polish Commercial-Geographical Association *(Polskie Towarzystwo Handlowo-Geograficzne)* established in Lwow on April 15, 1894. The final impulse to its establishment was the investigative efforts undertaken by Jozef Siemiradzki into the condition of the Polish emigrants to Brazil from Russian

Poland in the early 1890's. Contrary to the black picture drawn by such subsidized reporters as Dygasinski, Chelmicki and Glinka, Siemiradzki reported that, under controlled conditions, emigration and colonization in Brazil — specifically in the province of Parana where already numerous colonies of Polish emigrants had established themselves — had infinite possibilities both from the view of national interest and commercial profit.[13] As a result of these and other findings, a resolution was passed by the third meeting of The Association of Polish Jurists and Economists held in Poznan in 1893 ". . . to encourage the economic development of Galicia by fostering its trade and industry. . . ."[14]

The aims of this organization, according to its charter, were ". . . to support the economic interests of the country primarily by discovering new markets for Polish industry and new commercial outlets, by collecting and disseminating accurate information on the economic conditions of various countries and by establishing direct commercial relations with them." It hoped to accomplish its task with the help of Polish emigrants abroad by initiating and maintaining ties with them.[15] Its publication, the *Gazeta Handlowo-Geograficzna,* edited by Wiktor Ungar, began publication in 1895 and lasted until 1903, at first as a bimonthly and later as a monthly. In a way, it represented a continuation of the publication *Przeglad Emigracyjny,* which was inaugurated in 1892 in Lwow by Roman Dmowski and Jan Poplawski and was published as a supplement to their *Przeglad Wszechpolski* which subsequently became the official organ of the National Democratic *(Endek)* political orientation.[16]

The Polish Commercial-Geographical Association applied its entire attention to emigration and its foremost project was the concentration of permanent emigrants abroad in Parana. Deploring the rapid assimilation of Polish immigrant settlers dispersed throughout the non-Polish settlements, it undertook a program of their settlement or resettlement in compact, homogeneous groups. This idea was vigorously propagated in its organ, the *Gazeta Handlowo-Geograficzna.*[17] Under its sponsorship, various delegates were sent to the United States and South America to promote its projects — including Emil Dunikowski,[18] Stanislaw Klobukowski[19] and, later, Jozef Okolowicz.

In the course of its operations, it accumulated a sizable body of information on the conditions of emigration abroad and especially the province of Parana in Brazil. Thus, when the Brazilian government entered upon another program of populating its domains in 1896 by subsidizing immigration, that organization was in a position to exercise considerable influence in the movement.

The first news of an "emigration fever" was raised in the periodical press of Galicia in January, 1895. It began from the rural districts around Lwow and progressively spread to Kamionka, Brody, Zloczow, Przemysl, Bobrka, Kolkiew and, to a lesser extent, into the nine adjacent counties. Kolbuszowa was the only western district affected by this emigration.[20] Upon receipt of information on these developments, the Polish Commercial-Geographical Association addressed a petition to the *sejm* to institute inquiries into the authenticity of the claims made by the promoters. On the basis of this petition, the deputy Teofil Merunowicz, on February 5, 1895, raised a motion that the Executive Department take under consideration the "emigration problem" in general and emigration to Brazil in particular. Though the Executive Department failed to undertake to comply with these instructions, it did recommend that Jozef Siemiradzki and the Ukrainian clergyman, Wolanski, be commissioned by that body to journey to Brazil to conduct a personal investigation into the emigration problem. Simultaneously, Dr. Stanislaw Klobukowski was sent by the Commercial-Geographical Association.[21]

Siemiradzki's investigations only confirmed the position he had formerly taken in the case of the "Brazilian Fever" from Russian Poland in 1890–1892: that overseas emigration, directed to Parana, had a promising future.[22] In the course of his investigations, he found that the two chief agencies which promoted emigration from eastern Galicia were those of one Silvio Nodari and one Gergoleta, both with offices in Udine, Italy. Somehow they managed to compile—or acquire—a mailing list of many eastern Galician villages and in that way succeeded in reaching the peasants directly with their prospecti. For a nominal fee, they promised to send them free steamship tickets from Genoa to Rio de Janeiro.[23] Siemiradzki soon established that indeed they did provide free steamship tickets, but that certain extravagant practices frequently attended their promotional activities. For one, it was discovered that when the promotional propaganda had aroused widespread decision for emigration — and after many peasant landholders had liquidated their properties — some agents were extorting payments for the available tickets provided by the shipping companies.[24] Others, in their enthusiasm to recruit as many emigrants as possible, were spreading the rumor that the Brazilian government was also providing free land — a claim which the Commercial-Geographical Association of Lwow took pains to correct.[25]

Throughout these developments that organization endeavored to remain scrupulously free from any activity which could be construed as encouraging emigration. Upon Siemiradzki's recommendation, the Austrian branch of the German Catholic organization, the St. Raphael Society, rather than the Polish Commercial-Geographical Association, was entrusted with the disbursal of the free steamship tickets provided by the shipping companies. The latter organization was ready to impart information to prospective emigrants, but was not prepared to go to the length of being the instrument of providing their transportation.[26]

In an informational handbook for prospective emigrants to Brazil, the Polish organization advised them against ". . . ill-considered departure from the land of your fathers. . ." and enjoined them to ". . . consider well if you can not, with diligence and enterprise, here in your country, achieve a tolerable existence."[27] However, if after sober deliberation, emigration was definitely decided upon, it offered them various counsel and warnings in undertaking the journey to Brazil. Among these the prospective emigrants were warned against availing themselves of free transportation provided by such Brazilian states as Sao Paulo and Espirito Santo, which needed workers on their coffee and sugar plantations, since both the climate and the labor were unsuited for Europeans. Having availed themselves of their free transportation, the immigrants could not leave and go elsewhere unless they either reimbursed them the costs or worked the debt off in some way. Pointedly the prospective emigrant was advised ". . . not to be tempted into such emigration because he will pay dearly for it—perhaps even with his life."[28]

The province of Parana, on the other hand, offered many advantages:

> Without doubt there are not, in the whole territorial expanse of the state of Brazil, more favorable conditions for European immigrants than in the state of Parana. Its healthy and temperate climate, the condition of its soil [and] its present state of development give the European immigrants a guarantee of peaceful and profitable conditions for work.[29]

For these reasons, the Polish emigrant to Brazil was advised that, immediately upon his arrival in Rio, he should ask the colonization authorities there to send him to Parana. Failing this, he should choose Santa Catharina or Rio Grande do Sul, that is, areas where there were other Polish immigrant concentrations.[30] In closing, the emigrants were advised that:

Only through enlightenment, concord and hard work will the Polish element succeed in perpetuating its national existence and preserving the faith of their fathers. Build then, fellow countrymen, Polish churches and schools, establish societies and libraries, venture into commerce and industry, increase your crop yields with attention and diligence, maintain close spiritual and economic ties with Poland — and God will bless your work.[31]

The St. Raphael Society, on its part, likewise appeared to have made sincere efforts to explode the over-blown claims made by promotional propaganda and to provide the emigrants who had irrevocably decided upon emigration to Brazil with valid information. Both organizations, however, came under severe criticism in the conservative press. In its view, the dissemination of such information was tantamount to encouragement of emigration. The German organization especially was accused, on the one hand, of stimulating emigration and, on the other, of unwarranted intrusion upon the commercial interests of Trieste. Not infrequently, it was accused of nationalistic bias.[32]

As in the case of the "Brazilian Fever" in Russian Poland, when the Austrian authorities tried to contain the movement by denying exit to those with insufficient funds, their efforts proved unavailing.[33] According to a contemporary observer, this policy seemed to have the contrary effect of stimulating emigration.[34] And, again as in the case of Russian Poland, numerous "letters from Brazil" deploring conditions there made their appearance in the conservative press. To these were added the personal testimonies of disillusioned emigrants who had returned to Galicia. As counter-propaganda their efforts proved largely ineffectual inasmuch as the promoters of emigration succeeded in casting suspicion on their validity.[35] Siemiradzki, writing a few years later, was convinced that such efforts succeeded only ". . . to undermine completely the already badly undermined trust of the peasants toward the intelligentsia." Only when the Brazilian government ceased to subsidize transportation in the spring of 1896 did the movement cease.[36]

Varying estimates have been made to establish the volume of this movement to Brazil, ranging from about nineteen to thirty-two thousand Galicians. That the greater part of it, estimated at from three-fourths to four-fifths, settled in Parana, was regarded as testimony of the effectiveness of the activities of the Polish Commercial-Geographical Association and its supporters.[37] On the basis of this success, it was about this time that the idea of Parana as an exclusively Polish colony abroad gained increasing currency and support. The Galician periodical *Gazeta Handlowo-Geograficzna,* taking its cue from the Viennese *Kolonial-Zeitung,* affixed it with the title "New Poland."[38] This concept had been systematically reiterated by numerous publicists and literary figures, including Okolowicz, Klobukowski,[39] Janina Krakow, Kazimierz Warchalowski,[40] Marian Bielicki, Korcjusz,[41] and others.[42]

Despite its apparent success in its mission to concentrate Polish emigrants to South America in the province of Parana, the Polish Commercial-Geographical Association failed in its concomitant mission of establishing sufficiently remunerative commercial relations with the Polish emigrants either there or elsewhere abroad. That, combined with the continued hostility and mistrust that its operations engendered in the conservative circles, caused it to cease its operations in 1897.[43] When a corresponding "fever" of emigration to Argentina appeared to be developing in that year from the easternmost counties of Galicia and Bukovina, it remained aloof from the proceedings.[44]

On the basis of its accumulated information, however, an organization called The Polish Colonization and Commercial Association *(Polskie Towarzystwo Kolonizacyjno-Handlowe)* was established in Lwow that same year, as a limited liability corporation.[45] Going a step further than the former organization for the concentration of Polish-speaking elements in Parana, it proposed to colonize that province and, to this end, dispatched its emissary, Zenon Lewandowski,[46] with instructions for contracting to buy up large tracts of land from the provincial government for that purpose. This project, though it promised opulent returns, never passed beyond the preparatory stages because of its failure to raise even a tenth part of its proposed capitalization.[47]

A similar enterprise, The Colonial Publications Export Association *(Zwiazek Kolonialny Wydawniczo-Wywozowy),* established two years later, in 1899, through the initiative of Stanislaw Downarowicz, Waclaw Zmudzki and Ernest Lillien, likewise failed and apparently for the same reasons. It also sought to establish commercial relations with the Polish settlements in Parana and to promote education. Toward that end, it maintained an agency and bookstore in Curitiba for almost two years. It also issued a popular publication called *Prawda* which was edited by Jozef Okolowicz who, in 1908, was to be instrumental in the establishment of the Polish Emigration Association.[48]

In the meanwhile, the progressive increase of emigration impelled the Galician *sejm* to undertake further measures to assure domestic agriculture a sufficient labor force, and corresponded with the growing tendency toward regulation and control of the movement of population. This movement found its expression in the passage of the law of March 16, 1904, which provided for the establishment of public employment agencies throughout Galicia.

A number of recent developments conspired to cause that body to depart from its traditional policy of studied silence on emigration and unequivocal opposition to disseminating information on the condition of the European labor market. One was the growing consciousness that the emigration movement, heretofore confined largely to the western part of Galicia, was beginning to sweep over the eastern part— that foremost stronghold of Polish landed conservatism. The inertia having been overcome by the "Brazilian Fever" of 1895-1896, emigration to North America gained popularity when the Brazilian outlet was closed. Among the Greek Catholic Galicians, the Canadian homestead policy gained increasing popularity.[49] In 1902, Deputy Merunowicz informed the *sejm* that a large scale emigration of Ukrainian peasants was in evidence in the eastern districts of Husiatyn, Sniatyn and Borszczow.[50] Also at about this time, the Prussian *Arbeiterzentrale* entered into negotiations with the leaders of Ukrainian nationalists to encourage seasonal emigration to Prussia and with money earned abroad to return and buy up land — preferably parceled Polish estates.[51]

The second, and even more alarming, development was the series of agricultural strikes that swept over eastern Galicia in 1902 and 1903, and shook the agrarian economy and its privileged gentry to the core. According to a contemporary observer, the Polish press, both conservative and nationalistic, raised the alarm as if in one voice. With the exception of the socialist (P.P.S.) publication *Naprzod,* all chose to regard the strike as an instrumentality of the Ukrainian nationalists and an effort by the Ukrainians to ". . . inundate and despoil the Polish race." Represented as such, even though a sizable proportion of the peasants involved were in fact Poles, the Galician authorities were unopposed in the repressive policy they adopted.[52]

Nevertheless, the eastern Galician agricultural laborers succeeded in gaining some increases in wages as a result of these strikes. The increased wages, the prospect of a recurrence of such strikes in the future, and the increasing volume of both seasonal-continental and permanent-overseas emigration caused the conservative elements to change their stand.[53]

Although the Marshall of the *sejm,* Count Andrzej Potocki, in his opening address to the *sejm,* commended to their attention the need for an employment bureau in the spring of 1902,[54] because of the persisting reluctance of the Podolian gentry, no action was taken in that session. After the agricultural labor upheavals in eastern Galicia of that year, it was subsequently passed in the succeeding session, this time, however, over the opposition of the Ukrainian deputies.[55] The justification for its passage was based on the contention that, lacking information on the local labor market, the peasant frequently ventured abroad while the adjoining manor, ready to pay comparable wages, was suffering from the lack of field hands. Others justified it on the grounds that it would protect the peasant against the exploitative tactics of German employment agencies.[56]

The employment bureaus established by the law of 1904 showed considerable vigor in developing their operations as labor brokerages. The direction of their development, however, began to cause grave concern among the original proponents of the law. It was early discovered that, while the peasants were reasonably willing to avail themselves of their offices as intermediaries for employment abroad, they showed themselves singularly reluctant in applying for available employment in Galicia. When these information bureaus, by direction of the *sejm,* undertook to administer the law in such a way as to encourage domestic employment, the peasants refused to patronize them.

Because of these tendencies, there developed a movement in the *sejm* to amend the law in question. Zdzislaw Tarnowski, a proponent of the original law, in 1907 frankly stated that it had been expressly passed to regulate the supply of domestic agricultural labor in such a way as to assure domestic agriculture an adequate supply.[57] Prince Czartoryski, a hereditary member of that body, also frankly stated that the law of 1904 should be administered in such a way as to, first, assure a sufficient labor force for the county; second, to assure a sufficient labor force for the country, and third, only the remaining surplus should be sent abroad by the agencies. As to the interest of the workers, he felt that ". . . if they chose to work as diligently here [in Galicia] as they do abroad, they would earn just as much money. . . ."[58]

Stanislaw Dambski, chief of the department in which the operations of the employment bureaus were concentrated, quite unequivocally expressed his alarm at the growing tendency of the peasantry to seek employment abroad rather than at home. In his view, ". . . the consequences of such a development would be terrible for the country," and unless it was somehow restrained it could only lead to the ". . . complete decline of native agriculture and, therefore, the complete decline of our country's affluence and strength."[59]

Commenting upon their declining influence, Dambski felt that it was largely due to the mistrust with which the employment bureaus were regarded by the peasants. This mistrust, according to him, was due to the activity of private agents who strove to put the government agencies in the worst light. To correct this misconception and mistrust he invited all interests, including the clergy in church and the teachers in school, to break down this mistrust.[60]

The Reverend Stojalowski likewise expressed his awareness of the peasant mistrust toward these government informational agencies — a mistrust which was incomprehensible to him. He suspected that it was so because the peasants were unused to getting such service from the government free of any charges to them.[61] Jozef Huryk, spokesman for the Ukrainian deputies, expressed the opinion that the employment agencies established by the government were quite simply designed to put impediments in the way of seasonal emigrants, to protect the Polish landlords in the event of strikes, and that the ostensible solicitude for the welfare of the emigrant was really a desire to care for the interests of the large landowners. In his opinion, only an increase in wages in Galicia to the level paid abroad would effectively stem the tide of emigration.[62]

The Executive Department, in reporting on the above motion, recommended a law to reorganize the existing employment agencies and reaffirmed that the chief purpose of the new law would be to establish a more centralized control over that network to the end that it would correct some of the incapacities of the existing organization. Chief of these was their inability to provide "sufficient numbers of workers needed in the country." The proposed reorganization would have the following end in view: "The satisfaction of all the needs of domestic production in all its aspects — these [labor] needs must be satisfied regardless of any difficulties."[63]

This represented an overt statement of a policy which already had been put into effect in eastern Galicia when the emigration movement first became evident. As early as 1903, the Ukrainian deputy, Dr. Eugeniusz Olesnickyj, addressed an interpellation to the Imperial Commissioner *(Komisarz Rzadowy)* calling his attention to certain extra-legal restraining practices of some of the district administrative officials *(starostas)* in several of the eastern districts. These officials, as, for example, the *starostas* of Kalusz, Rohatyn, Husiatyn and

Horodenka, in the face of the law which permitted such emigration, denied "work books" to Ukrainian applicants and, in some cases, caused the seasonal emigrants to be unwarrantably interrogated and harassed — said interrogations not being recorded in the police protocols.[64]

In 1904, the Ukrainian deputy, Teodor Bobachieskyj addressed a similar interpellation to the same executive official on behalf of the peasants of the village of Koropce in the district of Buczacz, who were denied their "work books" — in effect, passports — to go to Germany for seasonal work in spite of the fact that they had each paid 10 crowns for them. He complained that various impediments were imposed by the *starosta* of that district despite the fact that their issuance was outside his competence.[65]

Thereafter, until the outbreak of the war, similar interrogations and complaints were addressed to that official. Those seeking passports to go abroad not infrequently met with the same official impediments. To these were added the obstructive tactics of railroad officials who cooperated with the district officials. Others, when pressed for "work books," issued only "servant books" which prevented seasonal emigrants from qualifying for the discount rates provided by the Austrian railroads. Still others were charged with being in collusion with private emigration agencies and denied exit permits to those who refused to patronize the agency they designated.[66] To all such interpellations the Imperial Commissioner declined either explanation or reply.

With the Polish-speaking Galician peasants, represented as they were by increasingly vocal and numerous spokesmen in the *sejm*, the ruling authorities were obliged to adopt a less heavy-handed policy. The government labor bureaus having failed in their purpose and the combined efforts of all the ruling strata being unable to dispel the suspicion that attached to them, the Galician *sejm* adopted a policy of subsidizing a private organization whose avowed purpose was to "organize, insofar as possible, the many-sided protection of the emigrant, normalizing emigration and initiating a policy of emigration in the best national interest."[67] As a private organization with only a limited subsidization of the Galician *sejm*, it presumably would escape the suspicion that blighted the same efforts of the Galician Employment Bureau. This organization, The Polish Emigration Association *(Polskie Towarzystwo Emigracyjne)*, established in Lwow in 1908 and later transferring its seat of operations to Krakow, was in effect a semi-official arm of the Galician emigration policy.[68] Many of its initiators were formerly associated with the Polish Commercial-Geographical

Association and, to some extent, it represented a policy of emigration which was a logical extension of that of the former organization supplemented by that of the government employment bureaus established throughout Galicia by the law of 1904. This policy, according to one of its spokesmen, was to restrain and discourage all emigration insofar as possible by finding local employment for prospective emigrants. This failing and the prospective emigrants being unshakably resolved to emigrate, the P.T.E. tried to direct seasonal emigration to France, Denmark, Bohemia, Sweden and, lastly, to southern Germany — pointedly boycotting Prussia.[69] Emigrants decided upon permanent overseas emigration were encouraged to go to Parana where, in concentrated and homogeneous Polish-immigrant settlements, they would be least exposed to assimilation.[70] Those whose avowed purpose was to emigrate overseas, but only temporarily, were advised to go to the United States.[71] That its function was substantially in accord with that of the Galician employment bureaus was substantiated by one of its founders who maintained that the chief impulse to emigration was the lack of adequate employment agencies. This lack substantially impeded "internal migration" of agricultural workers, that is, filling the demand for agricultural workers in the more removed localities of Galicia. That the emigrant could have, in many cases, found profitable employment in the neighboring county, he had no way of knowing. This condition, according to Okolowicz, often resulted in a situation where there was widespread emigration abroad from one locality because of a poor agricultural labor market there, while in another locality, oftentimes not far removed, large agricultural landholders complained of the lack of a labor supply.[72]

Like the Galician Employment Bureau, the P.T.E. organized a network of employment agencies and information centers. Unlike the former, however, it included a steamship ticket service to operate in areas in which the emigrant was most subject to the extortionate practices of private agents, and an emigrant shelter in Krakow. It also published a bi-monthly periodical *Polski Przeglad Emigracyjny* and a popular illustrated weekly called *Praca.*[73]

Nevertheless, as a semi-official expression of the Galician emigration policy, it represented a considerable change from the prevailing policy of the past. It recognized the existence of rural emigration and attempted to control and regulate it in the best interests of the emigrant and the country. As such it represented a wide ranging complex of motivations. Doubtless some nationalists saw in the regulation and control of the movement potential diplomatic counters to be exploited in the national interest. Others saw in its operations openings for careers and profit. Others still, however, saw it as an organization to protect the emigrants against extravagant practices of employers and officials.

The scope of its operations also represented a considerable expansion over the operations of the Galician Employment Bureau and its privately operated predecessors. Not only did it undertake to divert the migration to Prussia into other countries but, as a concomitant of this enterprise, endeavored to find new markets for emigrant labor. Largely upon its initiative, pilot groups of seasonal emigrants were sent to France, Bohemia, Moravia, German Austria and Switzerland while investigations into the feasibility of similar projects to other countries were undertaken.[74]

Measured by its original ambitions, its achievements were inconsiderable. The achievements in themselves, however, were not inconsiderable. From the pilot group of 800 agricultural laborers which was dispatched to France in 1908, the movement grew to an estimated 10,000 in the years immediately preceding the war.[75] Similar undertakings with non-agricultural workers, usually miners, were less successful.[76] Though on a smaller scale than France, several thousand of agricultural workers were annually venturing into Bohemia, Moravia and other Austrian provinces in the years before the war.[77] The seasonal migrations to Switzerland,[78] Denmark,[79] and Sweden,[80] though some developed independently of the P.T.E., also came under its attention.[81]

Consistent with the policy enunciated by its precursors, the P.T.E. sought to maintain and extend cultural and material ties with the Polish emigrants in Parana and, toward this end, sought to extend its competence into the area of education and fostering commercial relations.[82]

Almost all phases of its operations met with some criticism from the extreme points of view, both at home and abroad. Okolowicz, one of its directors, reported hostility on the part of French employers who complained against the interference of foreign agencies. At home it encountered similar criticism. One clerical newspaper in Galicia, *Glos narodu,* criticized its program in France because it saw in it an increased religious indifferentism among the Polish emigrants in that country. A Populist newspaper, *Kurjer codzienny,* accused it of supporting Polish emigration to France in order to save tottering French clericalism from bankruptcy.[83] The reaction of the public press to its operations in behalf of Parana also frequently varied in the extreme.

In 1913, Okolowicz reported, while one daily vigorously criticized it in a series of articles for propagandizing in behalf of emigration to Parana, two others were simultaneously attacking it for restraining emigration to that country.[84]

Despite the concerted efforts of the P.T.E., the Galician employment bureaus, the pronouncements of the conservative and nationalistic periodical press to contain emigration and divert it from Prussia, the movement to that country continued undiminished until the outbreak of the war. Some proponents of controlled emigration cited the statistical data of the *Arbeiterzentrale* as substantiation of the effectiveness of their efforts.[85] Indeed, these statistics, based on the number of *Legitimationskarten* issued by that agency to the various nationality groups do indicate that from a high point in the season of 1908–1909, when 86,050 registration papers were issued to Polish-speaking Galicians, the number declined the following season to 83,447 and thereafter, up to the outbreak of the war, maintained itself at a fairly stable level of about 75 thousand per year.[86]

This success, limited though it was, was more than cancelled by the increase in seasonal migration to Germany of Ukrainian Galicians. Up to the season of 1909–1910 they still represented a numerical minority of the total seasonal migrants from Galicia to Germany. Thereafter, however, their total steadily exceeded that of the Polish-speaking elements until, in the last season before the war, their number exceeded the Polish Galicians by almost 39 thousand emigrants. Considering this increase in the migration of Ukrainian Galicians to Germany, the total number of migrants from Galicia to that country, with minor setbacks in 1910–1911 and 1911–1912, increased progressively in the years preceding the war.[87] Even this minor success of the nationalistic elements comes under suspicion when consideration is given to such factors as the likelihood of many Polish Galicians, for reasons of convenience, registering themselves as Ukrainian at the border stations to escape the onerous restraints imposed upon the Poles, and the likelihood of the *Arbeiterzentrale* officials themselves, though not encouraging this tactic, at least not discouraging (or overlooking) it, because of their nationalistic assignment to diminish the dependence of Prussian agriculture upon Polish-speaking elements by displacing them with laborers of other nationalities. For that matter, the spokesmen for the P.T.E. and other like-minded organizations appear to have failed to take into consideration those Polish-speaking Galicians, said to be "numerous," who managed to cross the border and find employment without identification papers; those who extended their stay from previous years in provinces of the Reich where neither "legitimatization" nor prohibition against year-around employment were compulsory (e.g., Baden, Wirtenberg, Bavaria); those who having discharged (or fled from) their contractual commitments in France, Sweden and Denmark went to work directly in Germany.[88]

The main current of Galician emigration continued to be directed to Prussia with a minor movement going to Saxony, Hanover, Westphalia, Baden, Wirtenberg and, to a much lesser extent, Bavaria.[89] A few writers on the subject were discerning enough to note the powerful forces that favored seasonal emigration to Germany over elsewhere on the continent; such factors as geographical proximity, the ease of obtaining employment because of the large demand, the greater acquaintance of the Polish elements with the German language as against other non-Slavic European languages, and, most important of all, the comparative wage scale.

Franciszek Bujak, one of the most astute observers of the contemporary scene, probably touched upon a fundamental reason for the failure of these diversionary efforts when he noted, in his detailed study of the village of Maszkienice, that new seasonal migrants tended to follow the traces of their predecessors. Older seasonal emigrants frequently had neither cause nor desire to change their usual destination as long as wages and working conditions remained satisfactory. Finding new places entailed a certain amount of adjustment and additional expense. Changes in direction and destination did occur because of changing conditions of the labor market, but these changes came about gradually. Though unaware of the imposing statistical tables of comparative wage scales compiled by the exponents of emigration to elsewhere than Prussia, Bujak testified to the sensitivity and response of the migrant workers to the conditions of the labor market. Though not a professional, the peasant migrant showed remarkable intelligence in choice of direction. This direction, according to Bujak, ". . . is the best indicator of the largest differential between the local wage scale and the comparative wage scale abroad."[90]

The final judgment of Okolowicz, one of the founders and directors of the P.T.E., may be regarded as an epitaph to this aspect of their enterprise. Writing at a later date, he concluded that in spite of some isolated cases of abuse and even brutality, the living and working conditions as well as the administrative organization on the German estates were much better than in Poland.

These conditions, together with higher wages, ease of obtaining employment, the propaganda activities of the recruitment agencies and the duration of the working season resulted in mass migrations to Germany every year in spite of repeated efforts of the Polish press to boycott the Prussian Junkers.[91]

VII

Vienna and Galician Emigration — From Passive Liberalism to "Nationalization" in the Imperial Interest

At approximately the same time that scattered voices were being heard in Galicia for the organization and control of emigration, a similar transformation was taking place in the councils of the central government in Vienna. Heretofore, the central government was content to remain steadfast in its relatively liberal attitude toward the emigration of its subjects. This attitude was largely expressed by Article IV of the Constitution of 1867 which stated that the government reserved the right to restrict emigration of its subjects only on the ground of the subject's duty to fulfill his military obligations. Failure to discharge this duty as a result of emigration resulted in the loss of citizenship. In a word, freedom of emigration was limited only by the liability to do military service.[1]

Subsequent ministerial directives had a tendency to liberalize even this restriction. Thus, according to the order of the Minister of War, dated May 10, 1867, the civil authorities could not deny passports abroad to those who were not under investigation or with criminal records. This same order abolished the former visa and other documentary requirements at Austrian border stations.[2]

The Army Law of 1889, an order of the Minister of Defense, dated November 7, 1889, and a ministerial rescript of that official in 1890, tended to further modify the fundamental law insofar as it pertained to the emigration of conscripts. Thus, while the Army Law of 1889 authorized the Minister of War to issue emigration permits to army reservists who had completed their line duty, the order of the Minister of Defense of 1889 authorized that official to issue exit permits even to those who had not completed their tour of duty, those conscripts who had not yet been called to duty and those who had not yet reached conscription age, provided they could show that they were emigrating with their parent or parents. Section 8 of the same official's rescript of

1890 instructed the civil authorities to issue passports to those who had completed their line duty.[3]

Nevertheless, while the Austrian government did not put any great impediments to emigration, neither did it in any way try to facilitate or encourage emigration. The official policy throughout most of the second half of the nineteenth century concerning prospective emigrants was to regard it as *gemeinnützige Unternehmungen*, that is, to supply only generally useful information from time to time in the public press. This information, vague and sparse as it was, was accorded little weight. Formerly, to give information on prospects abroad for the emigrants was generally regarded as incitement to emigration.[4] In line with that policy, laws regulating the establishment of emigration agencies,[5] laws regulating prospectuses and periodical advertisements[6] and laws regulating the confiscation of pamphlets and brochures inciting emigration[7] were placed on the books.

The early regulations, especially the ministerial directive of 1852, which categorically prohibited emigration agencies, were still consistent with the older policy of prohibition of all emigration. The net result was that these prohibited agencies continued their operations clandestinely and the regulations, as such, had no success in stemming the tide of emigration which developed later.[8] Since the volume of emigration continued to increase despite the restraints upon agents and since these emigration and shipping agencies continued their operations without legal concessions from the government, later regulations had a tendency to be more in line with economic realities and gradually adapted themselves to the principle of regulation rather than the principle of prohibition. Such already was the temper of the directive of November 29, 1863, which was supplemented by those of November 27, 1873; July 1, 1876; October 13, 1887; May 29, 1888; June 18, 1888; December 20, 1892; 1895, 1904 and 1908, as well as by the commercial laws of January 27, 1897 and February 5, 1907.[9] In any case, even the prohibitive laws of the earlier period were regarded as dead letters by Polish writers on the subject because, in the absence of adequate enforcement by the administrative authorities in Galicia, they were generally honored more in their breach than in their observance.[10]

Likewise of little effect were administrative rulings which established minimums on financial resources for emigration. According to observations made in the Galician *sejm* as early as 1880, a decree that the emigrant had to be in possession of at least 320 crowns was in effect at that time. Railroad authorities were instructed to turn back those who did not meet this minimum cash requirement. The speaker noted, however, that even when this regulation was rigidly enforced by the railroad officials, the prospective emigrants merely resorted to crossing the Prussian border clandestinely.[11] In a paper read by Kleczynski at the Third Congress of Polish Jurists and Economists in Poznan in 1893, he remarked that transportation costs to the United States amounted to about 240 crowns but inasmuch as Austrian authorities did not permit emigrants to leave the country with less than 500 crowns, the emigrant usually borrowed the difference and mailed it back from Hamburg.[12]

By the turn of the century, however, evidences of a changing attitude began to be more and more apparent. In the Galician *sejm,* Teofil Merunowicz, a deputy from the district of Lwow, moved for the passage of the following resolutions:

> 1. that the Galician *sejm* petition the central government to take up the subject of emigration as soon as possible with the view of assuring for its emigrants, as citizens, its protection abroad and, for the country, all possible profits to be obtained therefrom;
>
> 2. that the central government establish an advisory institution— as has already been done in other countries of emigration—with the requisite executive authority, to watch over emigration, and
>
> 3. that the Galician *sejm* instruct its Administrative Department to examine into the causes, direction and particulars of emigration in the various localities of the country and to formulate appropriate recommendations to regulate it in the best economic and national interest. . . .[13]

He further requested that its report and recommendations be tendered to the *sejm* and, insofar as it was necessary, to the central government and to the Galician representatives in it, with the view of ultimate regulation of the problem by appropriate legislation by the central government.[14]

In elaborating on this motion a few days later, the speaker remarked that he did not share the general opinion that regarded all emigration as an unmitigated misfortune. On the contrary, properly regulated and controlled, emigration offered many mitigating advantages both for the emigrant, in particular, and for the country, in general.[15] Quite likely this motion had the protection of the emigrant in mind and, for this reason, was couched in such terms as to make it acceptable to the largest possible segment of the central body. This coincided with a point of view which was gaining support in Vienna and was referred to as "the nationalization of emigration," that is, enacting such laws and establishing such administrative procedures whereby the profits from transport, housing, feeding, and all other expenditures attending emigration would accrue to Austrian interests. He reaffirmed this feature of his motion by citing the excellence of Prussian and German laws which restricted the transportation of emigrants to the German transportation interests; which reserved for the German agents and agencies the expedition of all emigration and which, in general, looked to providing German investments with the highest possible profits.[16] He further remarked that it was incumbent upon the central government to undertake, by appropriate legislation, to regulate emigration in such a way as to establish emigrants abroad in concentrated settlements or groups which would remain in close relationship with the mother country.[17]

Upon the request of Merunowicz and with the approval of the *sejm,* his motion was remanded to the special Committee on Employment Bureaus which was deliberating an appropriate measure to regulate the supply of the domestic labor force.[18] That body took no action on the motion at that time.[19]

Nevertheless, in the succeeding sessions of that body, which met in the fall of 1904, a similarly motivated motion was made by Jerzy Baworowski. He moved that the Galician *sejm* petition the central government:

1. to pass appropriate legislation to regulate overseas emigration which would assure the emigrants all legal protection from their place of departure at home to their place of arrival abroad;

2. to regulate this emigration in such a way that all Austrian emigration, especially from Galicia, be channeled onto Austrian railroads via Vienna to Trieste and onto ships which were authorized for such traffic by government concession;

3. that there be sufficient ships in Trieste to transport these emigrants;

4. that the operations of Cunard and "Austricana," which have the government concessions for this traffic, be closely scrutinized and supervised, and

5. that the central government undertake the immediate establishment of an emigrants' shelter in New York to look to the interests of Austrian subjects and thereby to counteract "the capricious deportment of the United States' immigration commissioner."[20]

After enumerating the hardships and indignities that the emigrant was subjected to by agents and foreign (i.e., German) railroad and shipping agencies, the speaker remarked that the Austrian government had made itself a party to these malpractices by not effectively directing this flow to Trieste. By this oversight, the central government was delinquent in the protection of its national, economic and financial interests. The millions of crowns to be realized from the transport of emigrants, he remarked, should cease to be "stuffed into the pockets of Germans and Prussians." It was his patriotic observation that "this money should remain in Austria."[21] Like Merunowicz before him, the speaker, in elaborating on his motion several days later, expressed the opinion that it was the duty of the central government to direct the flow of emigration to such areas where it could be concentrated into a homogeneous body, thereby averting their loss by assimilation.[22]

This motion was approved and remanded to the Commission on Agricultural Reforms for further study and recommendations. When that body made its report to the *sejm* several days later, it recognized its lack of competence to recommend any specific details of an emigration law, but recommended that the Galician *sejm* pass a resolution urging the central government to do everything in its power, by way of laws and administrative disposition, to direct all emigration from Galicia to the Austrian port of Trieste.[23]

This recommendation, as well as a rider attached by Merunowicz requesting the central government to establish consular officials in areas where seasonal emigrants to Germany were concentrated, was passed by the *sejm* shortly thereafter.[24] The only dissenting voice that was raised against Baworowski's motion was that of Henryk Kolischer. This speaker recognized the need to safeguard the interests of the emigrants but felt that Baworowski's motion, as recommended by the Commission on Agricultural Reforms, if acted upon by the central government would tend to place artificial restraints upon emigration, render inoperative the tendency toward reduced transportation rates because of the competition between the shipping interests, to the detriment of the best interests of the emigrants. In general, it would increase rather than decrease the hardships of emigration. In closing he called Baworowski's motion "less a motion on emigration, for their protection, than the settlement of what is commonly referred to in Vienna as the 'Trieste Question'."[25]

Underlying this changing orientation and coinciding with it chronologically was the growing recognition that emigrant earnings abroad were looming increasingly more important in the fiscal balance of

Galicia.[26] This tendency was manifested in the provincial *sejm* on December 29, 1902, when Deputy Jan Stapinski made a motion either to liberalize or completely suspend the law relating to military deserters insofar as it applied to returned emigrants who had emigrated before fulfilling their military duties. In his view, the rigid application of the law in question tended to discourage many emigrants from returning home with the sizable savings they had accumulated in the United States.[27]

This motion was shelved for several months and it was not until September 15 in the following year that Stapinski further elaborated upon it. At that time, its author stated that his motion resulted from his personal observations and interviews among Polish emigrants in the United States on his trip to that country.[28] He took the opportunity to read the personal testimonies of several Galician emigrants he met there, to prove that many would-be remigrants failed to return because of their fear of punishment as deserters. All testified that they would have liked to return and settle in Poland with their substantial savings but the fear of imprisonment deterred them. These, he said, were only a few of the hundreds whose similar testimonies he had in his possession.[29] He also took this opportunity to place into the protocol testimonies of some returned emigrants who had originally emigrated before fulfilling their military obligations and the hardships they were made to suffer upon their return. According to his observations, the Przemysl Command was especially severe in that respect.[30]

Furthermore, the law in question itself was inequitable in its application. County officials charged with the administration of the law governing military conscripts varied considerably in its interpretation and application, insofar as it pertained to applicants for passports. Thus, while the *starostas* of Sanok and Brzozow issued passports to male applicants in the 16–19 age group, the *starosta* of Jaslo continued to regard all male children, whatever their age, as potential conscripts—thereby refusing them passports.[31] In his view, it was not the fourteen to seventeen-year-olds who were given passports to go abroad who never returned, but rather those who were forced to leave without passports, because of fear of prosecution as deserters.[32] Though the *starostas* of Galicia exempted Polish emigrants with United States citizenship from its stipulations, Stapinski affirmed that precisely for this reason he advocated the suspension of the law in question. Such a recourse he viewed as an irrevocable step toward permanent separation from the mother country.[33]

Whatever may have been its sentiment on the subject, the committee which passed upon it did not approve his suggested course of action. In its opinion, Stapinski's motion had widespread ramifications since it challenged an exclusive prerogative of the Crown — amnesty. It made the observation that any legislative changes of laws, whether civil or military, pertaining to military obligations would have a disorganizing influence upon the army. The only corrective that was possible, in the opinion of the committee, was to appeal to the central government to regulate emigration by passing appropriate laws and establishing appropriate administrative agencies.[34]

Stapinski took vigorous exception to this report and its recommendations, charging that the committee had misunderstood his motives from beginning to end. He called the attention of the *sejm* to some of the committee's errors of fact and remarked upon the impossibility of solving the problem in question by individual petitions for amnesty. Put to a vote, the report of the Legal Commission was nevertheless approved by the *sejm* assembled.[35]

Though the *sejm* at this time indicated its incompetence to deal with the subject of facilitating the remigration of "illegal" emigrants, similar motions expressing their concern over the problem of remigration continued to make their appearance before that body. Thus, in the following session of the provincial parliament, Baworowski was moved to remark that the government's efforts to impede the acquisition of passports had failed to stem the tide of emigration. As a result of this policy, two-thirds to three-fourths of the emigrants from some districts were "illegal" and were forced to avail themselves of the services of emigrant smugglers.[36]

This subject was again raised at a still later date when Wiktor Skolyszewski remarked that the *Einzelarrest* and enforced fulfillment of military obligations — usually with about a year added to the regular period of enlistment for desertion — caused many would-be remigrants, ". . . with their considerable savings. . . ," to decide against returning to Galicia. For this reason, the speaker moved that the *sejm,* as a body, implore His Imperial Majesty, the Emperor Franz-Joseph, to extend to all illegal emigrants his benevolent protection from the military courts by issuing a general amnesty on their behalf — this as a paternal gesture on the occasion of the sixtieth anniversary of his reign.[37]

These and other aspects of the central government's relatively passive policy relating to emigration were criticized both within and outside the halls of the *sejm.* Caro and others pointed out that because of the stringent Austrian military law concerning the emigration of

AUSTRIA AND THE POLES

people of conscription age, many of them emigrated via German ports since German authorities never abided by the stipulations of the Austro-Prussian commercial convention of February 10, 1831 (especially articles 13, 14 and 17) which, theoretically at least, was still binding upon the signatories. According to this convention, desertion and its encouragement or abetment were made punishable by law even in Germany. German officials who were obliged to return deserters and prosecute those who had encouraged them in this enterprise did not enforce it. As a matter of fact, according to informed testimony, it was flagrantly disregarded even in Vienna where several agencies made expeditious arrangements for the emigration of draft-age youths their specialized enterprise. To all this the Austrian authorities, in the view of some writers, were indifferent.[38]

This indifferentism, in Caro's view, was reflected in the official attitude toward emigration statistics. He pointed to the apparent disposition of the government to use foreign statistics rather than to compile more dependable ones at the source of emigration.[39] Another complained that the lack of registers of population as well as the lack of requirements for compulsory passports rendered impossible the control of emigration at its source.[40]

The Austrian government's consular service came under special criticism of others. This arm of the government abroad, in comparison to that of other countries of emigration, was represented as poorly developed. About two-thirds of its consular establishments abroad were said to be conducted by local merchants who regarded their office as honorary, thereby enhancing their social prestige. According to Bujak, there were only four consulates represented by official government employees (Berlin, Hamburg, Breslau and Cologne) in all of Germany; the remaining fifteen were "honorary."[41] Caro, citing the *Almanach da Gotha* for 1909, noted that while Austria-Hungary had twenty-two consulates and one consular agency in the United States in that year, only the consuls in Chicago, New York, Philadelphia and Pittsburgh, the vice-consuls in Charleston and Cleveland and the consular agent in Hazleton, Pennsylvania, were professional careerists. The remaining posts were occupied by "honorary" appointments. In New Orleans, for example, the Austro-Hungarian consul was neither an Austrian nor a Hungarian subject but a "foreigner." Care for the best interests of the Austrian subjects abroad was therefore very negligible.[42]

Others pointed out that there were comparatively too few consular officials in areas of immigrant concentration; that these officials, almost without exception, were ignorant of any of the Slavic languages — a circumstance which made them practically useless in understanding the grievances brought before them by those most numerous immigrant Austrian nationals. The result of this situation was that the consular officials remained largely indifferent to the legitimate needs of the emigrants, confining their activity almost exclusively to fostering Austro-American commercial ties, while the emigrants were exposed to a long list of hardships and injustices — grievances which they were reluctant to bring before their country's representatives abroad.[43]

Probably, with only the exception of Russia, no country was more indifferent to the needs of its emigrants or was less able to retain its control over them. In comparison to the widespread contacts maintained by the Italian consular service with its emigrant nationals in the United States, the activities of the Austro-Hungarian consular service were negligible. In Brazil, the situation was likewise represented as deplorable. There the close relationships maintained by both the German and Italian governments with their emigrants was regarded as worthy of emulation. Those governments maintained close ties with their emigrants by subsidizing schools, teachers, and by maintaining widespread consular networks ever ready to intercede with the Brazilian government in questions concerning the interests of their subjects. The governments of both Austria and Russia, however, had shown themselves singularly negligent in maintaining cultural, social and economic ties with their emigrant-nationals. Hence, the resulting large degree of assimilation into the culture of their new country and, in their view, their loss to the fatherland.[44]

* * *

Though accused of both negligence and indifferentism in its policy toward emigration, the central government in Vienna was not entirely unresponsive to the changing attitudes toward emigration. As a result of these importunities and memorials addressed to it, the government undertook to put forth a project for a comprehensive emigration law. Such a law was presented to the parliament by Kaltenbrunn, an official *(Hofrath)* in the Ministry of Internal Affairs, in 1904. By way of further deliberation on "the emigration question," that ministry invited the participation of all informed persons on the subject in an extra-parliamentary inquiry which it convened on June 26, 27 and 28 of the following year.[45]

Though these hearings failed to produce any concrete results which could have been embodied in the proposed law, the testimony of the participants throws much light upon the complex of motivations and attitudes prevailing on the subject of emigration. According to one reporter, the body of experts which participated in these hearings was comprised of persons chiefly "interested in the emigration problem" but few who were sufficiently objective. Frequently the hearings degenerated into "a stubborn altercation" between the representatives of German shipping interests and Austro-Americana *(Allgemeine öster-reichische Schiffahrtsgesellschaft)*. Since the hearings were not organized for the systematic exploration and commentary upon the specific details of the proposed law, those who participated generally spoke in broad generalizations.[46]

Though the hearings brought out a variety of conflicting testimonies on the causes and conditions of emigration, the question of "nationalization" of emigration seemed to dominate. Quite simply this represented a movement to write into the proposed law such provisions which would tend to direct what emigration was authorized on Austrian railroads, to Austrian ports (Trieste) and on to Austrian ships (Austro-Americana). This was to be a large source of national income otherwise exported to Germany and German interests. Only incidentally it was hoped that the law would correct some of the more flagrant frauds practiced upon Austrian emigrants in Germany. Also, it would facilitate the control of emigration. Some proponents of this program even sought to write into this law the exclusive monopoly of all Austrian overseas emigration for Trieste. Besides such overt representatives of Austro-Americana as Kalmus and Cosulich, most other Austrian experts supported this movement. Those representing the German interests quite naturally opposed it very strongly.[47]

Since the body of experts did not submit a report of its findings as a body but rather each announced his own findings, the results of the hearings were, for practical purposes, indeterminate. When the projected law was shelved, it was with the great satisfaction of numerous Galicians, Austrians and, especially, the representatives of the German shipping interests.[48]

The issue of a comprehensive law "for the protection and control of emigration" could not be dismissed or completely ignored. Because of the continued pressure the government again sponsored a project for an emigration law in 1908 and again in 1912.[49] Again hearings were held upon the laws in question. These hearings, like those which preceded them, contributed not at all to the passage of the laws in question, which remained buried in the archives of the Austrian parliament.[50]

Though the comprehensive law for the control of emigration failed to be passed, the hearings on the proposed laws afforded the interested spokesmen a chance to advance many arguments for their passage. These arguments, in themselves, throw much light on the prevailing attitudes toward many of the aspects of emigration. Thus, "subsidized emigration" came under widespread attack. Though the proposed laws of 1904 and 1908 authorized responsible authorities to restrict recruitment to such countries where, in the opinion of such authorities, the life, health, morality and/or economic security of the emigrants were endangered, the critics of this provision pointed to the stipulation of the German, Italian and Hungarian laws which practically prohibited such activities.[51] The provision for the control of the emigration of minors came under criticism as did those for the regulation of informational agencies.[52] On one occasion the Austrian authorities were strongly criticized for their apparent inability to protect their emigrant nationals in transit through Germany — this despite the fact that *Freizugigkeit* had been guaranteed to Austrian citizens by commercial treaties[53] — and, on another occasion, an expert took the opportunity to exhibit transmittal forms of several private banks in the United States, couched in the various Austrian languages but bearing varying fraudulent exchange rates for United States dollars.[54]

A variety of reasons for the failure of its passage was advanced by writers on the subject. One, noting that a certain amount of emigration by way of Trieste had begun in 1903, with the establishment of Austro-Americana, grieved the fact that its operations in the transport of emigrants never became extensive. This, in his view, was because of that organization's lack of either extensive capital resources or the requisite governmental support for such an enterprise.[55] Another, citing the transcript of the hearings on the law of 1912 as his authority, concluded that the government was unable to oppose the German *Schiffahrtspool* because of that organization's unlimited capital resources, its exceptionally efficient and widespread organization, its unequalled fleet of ships and its unequivocal support by the German government.[56]

Even among the Galician "experts" a diversity of opinion and views was manifest not only as to the details of the law in question but even its advisability. These differences surfaced during the Fourth Congress of Polish Jurists and Economists in 1906 when something like a confrontation developed over this issue between Artur Benis and Leopold Caro. The former argued that the Austrian Ministry of Interior conceived the proposed law of 1904 in typical bureaucratic fashion — without any knowledge of Galician circumstances and without the participation of informed elements. As if purposely, it had created a law for the protection of German economic interests insofar as it pertained to both seasonal and overseas emigration.[57] He was essentially supported in his views by the Galician deputy to the Reichstag, Baron Battaglia, who argued that the issue of emigration, in all of its manifold influences and consequences, should be the preserve of provincial (i.e., Galician) authorities inasmuch as the interests and concerns of the federal government were not always consistent and compatible with the interests and concerns of Galicia which, incidentally, provided 80 percent of the emigration from the empire.[58]

Caro, on his part, challenged the statistical data on which Benis based his position, reaffirmed the widespread operations of recruiting agents and, while admitting that the proposed law was imperfect, strongly supported it on the grounds that once it was passed its inadequacies could subsequently be amended.[59]

Generally speaking, the Galician critics of the law, then and later, expressed concern over the possibility of centralized bureaucracy which such a law might foster — a bureaucracy which might be responsive to the needs and interests of Austria but not necessarily the needs and interests of the Galician emigrants or Galicia.[60]

With the passage of time, even the foremost proponents of a federal emigration law began to lose heart. Caro, for example, concluded that Austria's policy was one of vacillation caused by its conflicting desire to serve the interests of domestic employers demanding all possible restrictions on emigration and Austrian and German transport interests, with the best interests of the emigrants regarded as inconsequential. That being the case, — and until such a comprehensive and all-embracing emigration law could be passed — Caro advocated ameliorative treaty arrangements with such countries as Germany through which the main tide of overseas emigration passed.[61]

By 1912, Okolowicz expressed similar disillusionment over the law's prospects in Vienna. In his view, the chief stumbling block was the Austrian government's indisposition to provoke the antagonism of Germany which benefited from the existing uncontrolled situation. By this time he had come to regard the repeated — and unavailing — "hearings" as of a pattern of Vienna's procrastination on the subject. This procrastination was the consequence of the federal government's attempt "to ride two horses," i.e., serve the best interests of its subjects — specifically, the emigrants — and the interests of its political allies — specifically, Germany.[62]

Stanislaw Lazarski, speaking in the Galician *sejm* in 1905, probably approached the facts as closely as anyone when he prophesied that such a law had little likelihood of passage in the near future because of the administrative areas of competence which it would inevitably cut across — areas of competence zealously guarded by the various government agencies and ministries in Vienna. Insofar as such a law would have to do with emigration abroad, it would intrude upon the heretofore province of the Ministry of Foreign Affairs; insofar as it would pertain to emigrants in transit, it would collide with the area of competence of the Ministry of Trade; insofar as the law would deal with the operations of steamship agents and other promoters, it would intrude upon an area traditionally reserved for the Ministry of Internal Affairs; insofar as it had to do with the regulation of freedom of movement, it would encroach upon the preserve of the Ministry of War. On the basis of his experience with Austrian bureaucracy, he was disposed to conclude that while it was extremely difficult to enlist the cooperation of one agency in the drafting of any laws, the likelihood of all four cooperating on a comprehensive emigration law seemed hardly possible.[63]

The nationalistic proponents of rigid control over emigration chose to interpret these failures to pass an emigration law as another case of the central government's indifference to the hardships of the Polish emigrants — hardships which could only be overcome by an independent nation looking to the best interests of its nationals.

IV. The Poles on Emigration

VIII

Attitudes and Opinions on "Causes" of Emigration

Whether in Prussian, Russian or Austrian Poland, the prevailing attitudes toward emigration underwent similar transformation and reorientation. These changes are most apparent upon an examination of the causes and effects attributed to the phenomenon of emigration by both publicists, polemicists and writers in the academic vein.

Thus, throughout the early periods of emigration from these respective areas, the departure of the population most frequently was regarded as actuated from without — by factors outside the control or influence of the ruling classes which predominated. When emigration became more manifest, it was regarded as a "fever" — a sort of a mass hysteria, a mob action, in which the individual participants were incapable of rational consideration or appraisal of the realities of their existence. The intelligentsia, the clergy and the gentry regarded it as their sacred duty to break the "spell," to arrest the "stampede," to dispel the "collective illusion" to which the ignorant peasants, because of their drab and monotonous existence, were especially susceptible. The emigrants were regarded as victims of mass suggestibility. They were motivated by emotion rather than rational self-interest. The prime mover of emigration, in this view, was the "agent" — a malignant instigator — a "Pied Piper" who was leading the ignorant masses to their inevitable doom.[1]

As late as 1893, at the meeting of the Polish Jurists and Economists in Poznan, Maksymilian Jackowski, the venerable patron of the Polish agricultural organizations of Prussian Poland, saw the cause of emigration not to lie in the desire to earn money by the emigrants, but rather in the incitement of unscrupulous "agents" and the not infrequent disposition of the populace toward vagrancy and vagabondage.[2]

A change, however, in the analysis of the causal factors of emigration was then already apparent. Klobukowski and Kleczynski, who read papers on emigration from Russian Poland and Galicia respectively, felt impelled to give more realistic appraisals. Klobukowski saw the causes of emigration in the material poverty of the people. Therefore, the only means of dealing with it would be to improve their material position. In his view, the remedy to the "problem" lay in improving the economic level of the country. Short-term first-aid methods would prove unavailing.[3]

Nevertheless, the "agent-demon" was never completely expurgated from the texts dealing with causes of emigration. Siemiradzki, reporting on the "Brazilian Fever" from Russian Poland in 1892 still held that the agency of Bendaszewski and Co. was almost exclusively responsible. This agency, established by one Bendaszewski, a merchant in Curitiba, included the Brazilian Jose dos Santos of Lisbon and, "it was said," the Catholic clergyman Gurowski. According to the author, this organization entered into contract with the federal government of Brazil to supply that country with 50,000 farmers from Germany and Poland. To this end, Bendaszewski established residence in Hamburg but, inasmuch as emigrant recruitment activities were strictly regulated in Germany, was obliged to carry on his agitation via Lisbon where his partner, Jose dos Santos, was established. Their agitation proved to be so effective that instead of 50,000 farmers from Germany and Poland about 100,000 Poles alone were sent via Bremen to Brazil in a few months. As a result of these malignant activities at least four of the border counties of Russian Poland were threatened with depopulation.[4]

The culpability of the agents in that fever of emigration continued to be reiterated by even the most informed writers ever afterward.[5] The economist, Zofia Daszynska-Golinska, noted several years later that, ". . . in the three-year period of the feverishly aroused tendency to wander to Brazil, a conspicuous part of the emigration from Russian Poland was the work of agents." However, she did append the qualification that: "Naturally, the promises of the agents must fall on the auspicious soil of discontent with the existing conditions and poverty . . . possessing nothing, they have nothing to lose." Discontent with the existing conditions of living must be manifest and this can be done either as a result of a higher level of education, which permits the individual to depart from the established ways in the direction of his destiny, or as the result of agents and entrepreneurs who draw profits from the emigrants. The alternative is positive action by the government or the society.[6]

In her qualifications and recommendations, she was in harmony with the changing attitude toward emigration which was taking place at approximately that very time. Nevertheless, the castigation and exposure of "agents" continued to be a dominating topic of interest and outstanding preoccupation for many writers on the subject. One of the most prolific, perhaps the most eloquent, certainly the most dedicated, was the Galician lawyer, Leopold Caro. Writing in German, Austrian and Polish publications, he made the exposure of the malevolent operations of the "agents" one of his central themes — his special cause.[7] His works, to many, represented an indictment of not only numerous private "agencies"[8] but also the governments of Brazil, Canada, Texas, Louisiana, South Carolina and others.[9] They were accused of everything from subterfuges and deceit to runs on the banks of Galicia in 1909 and 1913.[10] He became one of the foremost advocates of legislative restraint upon emigration, in general, and the complete suppression of private informational or promotional agencies, in particular.[11] When Dr. Benis suggested that perhaps these so-called "agents" were serving a useful function — that all were not reprehensible exploiters of the emigrants — Caro, publicly and in print, suggested that such studies as Benis', "sympathetic to agents," should be ignored.[12]

Successive writers on emigration, though with more restraint, continued to reiterate the charges against the "agent." As late as 1914, Helena Landau felt justified in taking to task the periodical press and even "the heavier book publications," specifically Caro, for their continued and indiscriminate belaboring of "the agent" without adequately considering the fundamental socio-economic factors that were the real causes. She noted that those who maintained that Galicia was not overpopulated, that is, its density of population was not equal to the industrialized countries of western Europe, were quick to raise the hue and cry against the agent and to see him as the chief causal factor of emigration.[13]

Implicit in the arguments of those who held the agent primarily responsible for emigration was that the peasant-emigrant was ignorant and illiterate.[14] How else explain his disposition to accept the promotional propaganda of the "agent"? How else to explain the astonishing success of the "agent"?

Caro, in his time one of the most widely recognized authorities on emigration, as late as 1914 still argued that although the cause of emigration was the poor material condition of peasant agriculture in Galicia, this was largely the result of "the lack of the most elementary of education." The author based his statement on the apparent fact that when mass education was at a comparatively primitive stage in Germany, prior to the middle of the nineteenth century, as it was in

Austrian Poland in the immediate pre-war period, the emigration agents also found fertile fields for their operations in that country. Subsequent progress in public education in Germany resulted in the decline of emigration.[15]

Caro seemed to argue that emigration was particularly attractive to the illiterate elements of the population. Thus, using United States statistics, he showed that the illiteracy rate among the Polish immigrants in the 1901–1905 period averaged 27.5 percent, and 32 percent in the period between 1905–1908. Of the total immigrants to the United States during these two periods, 19 percent and 19.8 percent were laborers, 31.6 percent and 40.6 percent were farmers, 24.4 percent and 22.2 percent were women and children, while skilled artisans and people with higher education comprised only 6.9 percent and 3.3 percent of the total.[16]

Using the same statistics, the author emphasized his point by graphically illustrating the responsiveness to changing economic conditions in the United States by various language groups. Thus, the Hungarians, Poles, Croats and Slovaks responded immediately to economic recession by a decline in emigration, while Germans, Jews, Czechs, Roumanians and others responded more slowly. Furthermore, while the first group resumed emigration before the recession had completed its course, the second group showed a reluctance to emigrate for a longer period. According to his interpretation of this statistical data, this phenomenon was due to the higher intellectual level of the second group and their greater resistance to the flowery promises of the agents.[17]

The second cause of the material decline of the rural Galician population — and therefore their disposition toward emigration — was the contemporary widespread alcoholism "not only among the peasants in eastern Galicia and in Bukowina but also among the [Polish] Masurians." The author substantiated this thesis by quoting statistics of the disproportionately large number of arrests for drunkenness in Galicia. In a like manner, the author regarded the excessive litigiousness of the peasants as a primary cause of their depressed material level and, hence, their willingness to emigrate. Again comparative statistics were used to establish his argument.[18]

By this device of confusing causes with effects, the author sought to establish that ignorance and emigration were obverse aspects of the same coin. Proceeding from these premises the author went on to affirm that the break-up of peasant landholds was similarly the result of the peasant's own shortcomings.[19]

No less a commentator than the reputable economic historian, Jan Rutkowski, reiterated this theory. Though relegating them to secondary status as causes of emigration, he affirmed that lack of education, litigiousness and alcoholism — which caused turmoil and increased the failure of peasant economy — as important contributory factors fostering emigration.[20]

By the turn of the century, however, even the advocates of rigidly controlled emigration found such arguments difficult to accept. Daszynska-Golinska, for example, pointed out that, of the several factors which promoted emigration, the economic ones occupied the first place. Her obvious implication was that emigration was, on the contrary, a manifestation of dissatisfaction with the prevailing conditions of existence. This expression of dissatisfaction need not necessarily follow from the existence of over-population, but it was proof that among the masses of the populace there were those whose needs and expectations were not satisfied.[21]

Landau-Bauer again took particular exception to the contention of Caro and his school. Among others, she pointed to the fact that despite the high level of public education in Germany in the period immediately preceding the war, there was a continued emigration of German rural population — to the German industrial centers. As for Caro's analysis of the Galician level of education, she quite unequivocally stated that the low level of education was the result rather than the cause of their poverty and, therefore, their disposition to emigration. She held that if by some magic the number of public schools in Galicia were doubled, the result would be a doubled volume of emigration.[22]

Buzek, also representing the new orientation, substantially reaffirmed this contention. Using the same nationality groups as Caro, he was able to maintain that in spite of the higher degree of rural poverty in Galicia, mass emigration did not develop until the early 1880's *because* of the lower level of mass education. To the degree that their intellectual horizons were broadened, emigration continued to develop thereafter.[23] Subsequent writers, after Buzek, generally accepted this more obvious correlation between enlightenment and emigration. They noted that the apparent proportional relation between the degree of poverty and intensity of emigration was not always constant. That is to say, those habituated to the most abject poverty were not likely to emigrate as readily as those elements of the population who possessed enough to keep from starving but not enough to satisfy their wants. Since abjectest poverty was found to be frequently a correlate of illiteracy and social backwardness, these elements of the population frequently lacked even sufficient initiative to flee from starvation.[24]

The fact that the educated middle and upper classes of Polish society contributed an exceedingly small proportion in the total volume of emigration seemed to give support to those who saw a direct relation between illiteracy and emigration. Since the peasant-emigrants did not engage in periodical polemics or academic discourse upon the primary causes for their emigration, it was perhaps inevitable that those to whom the task fell should entertain such notions. Those who were sufficiently candid, however, analyzed this phenomenon more realistically. Thus, Szawleski, in analyzing the apparent reluctance of Polish intellectuals to emigrate, noted:

> . . . The indisposition [of Polish intellectuals] to emigrate to America was well established because the humanistically educated European, lacking acquaintance with the English language, was consigned to a hard battle for existence for which he was neither intellectually nor physically prepared. Areas for intellectual enterprise among the Polish [American] communities were few and for even those there was a bitter competition. The way into American business enterprises was restricted — the American [businessman] was loath to accept an intelligent foreigner who, to tell the truth, was little prepared for the hard school of American life. Thus, when the only available employment in the factory was either too difficult or uncongenial, and when the educated emigrant failed to have American connections, he usually sought employment in various individual combinations or went into the services of various speculative enterprises having as their aim the exploitation of his own naive co-nationals.[25]

Still another ostensible cause of emigration which was frequently reiterated was the political and religious disabilities imposed by the partitioning authorities. As an outside "cause" this point of view was popular with many of the conservative landed gentry. Its currency persisted much longer than the other "outside" causes because it was readily adopted by the growing nationalistic movement in the decades preceding the war and, as such, became one of the rallying cries of the apostles of "regulation and control" of emigration. Agaton Giller, one of the guiding spirits behind the movement to organize the emigrants for the national cause, gave early expression to this point of view when he wrote:

> The emigration of the Polish people is the inevitable consequence of their miserable condition to which they were driven by the exterminating system of the government on behalf of the Germans on our land.[26]

Though he conceded that a significant proportion of the Polish emigrants from Prussian Poland in the United States emigrated of their own free will, the next largest proportion, however, were driven to this expedient by the religious persecutions of the authorities. These ". . . were forced to depart from Polish land remaining under the domination of the Germans because of the persecution of the Church called forth by the May laws of Bismarck. . . ."[27]

Nor did the other sections of Poland lack similar *bête noire.* Thus, as late as 1924, Szawleski affirmed that:

> An auspicious basis for emigration from Polish lands was the systematic destruction of Polish initiative toward industrializing and commercializing Prussian and Austrian Poland and treating these areas as markets for unloading German manufacture as well as the calculated neglect of all needs for the normal economic development of Russian Poland.[28]

Isolated individuals, however, came to be heard more frequently voicing opinions to the contrary. Thus, by 1910, Szukiewicz, writing in the consistently conservative *Biblioteka Warszawska,* could remark that in spite of the "political persecution" of Polish elements in Prussian Poland there was very little evidence of overseas emigration among them. On the contrary, though there was a tide of emigration in existence, it was directed to the western industrial centers of Germany. This, among other observations, led him to minimize "political elements" as causal factors of Polish emigration in general. As for "religious persecution" as a factor in emigration, he observed that probably only a small fraction of Uniates in Russian Poland left their homes because of "religious" factors. As for the Mariavite movement and its attendant "fratricidal battles," he judged that it had practically no effect on emigration.[29]

The importance of "emigrant letters" as primary causes of emigration was early realized though, for various reasons, caution in their criticism was indicated. Siemiradzki, in his investigations into the causes of the first "Brazilian Fever" from Russian Poland found that a large number of letters from Polish immigrants in Parana, praising local conditions and prospects, were sent by the Brazilian authorities to their embassy in St. Petersburg and, from there, ". . . despite the vigilance of the authorities. . . ," successfully tendered to the addressees "where they had the desired effects."[30]

By 1910, Szukiewicz was convinced that the promotional activities of the so-called "agents" was secondary to "emigrant letters" from friends and relatives abroad. Furthermore, by that time there were so many "Americans" (returned emigrants) living in Poland that "agents" as primary sources of emigration information were of secondary importance. In his view, the role of these letters as causal factors of emigration could not be overemphasized, especially when they were accompanied by "prepaids," that is, the requisite funds and steamship tickets for emigration. This latter practice, he felt, made the United States accessible even to the most destitute elements who otherwise could not have gone to that country.[31]

To clamor for restraints upon emigrant correspondence, however, was both impolitic, from the nationalistic point of view, and uneconomical, from even the traditionally conservative point of view. Ignorance or malicious intent, however, could be ascribed to the authors of the letters without compunction. Thus, Okolowicz could write, in 1920, that though these letters were frequently objective and in good faith — "to the best knowledge of the sender" — many were motivated by a promised commission from the steamship ticket agent, a favor from their employers, and other material emoluments. Still others, according to his observations, were deliberately falsified by scribes writing for the illiterate peasant-emigrant. Thus, unintentionally, the United States Postal Service became one of the most effective agencies for the encouragement of emigration.[32]

Interestingly enough, it was the economists and economic historians who first began to uncover the more fundamental factors underlying emigration. From them the facts of emigration gradually filtered down to the more responsible periodical press and even the general public.

Probably no single publication issued in Poland in the nineteenth century had more far-reaching repercussions than Szczepanowski's *Nedza Galicji (Galician Misery)* published in 1888.[33] Its publication caused widespread realization of the material poverty of that sector of Poland and called forth much periodical literature. Though his methods were criticized by such statisticians as Pilat and Kleczynski, few could gainsay his conclusions.[34] This dedicated advocate of industrialization estimated that as late as the date of his publication about 50,000 people perished annually as a result of poverty and hunger. It was he who coined the popular aphorisms: "Each Galician produces the equivalent of one fourth person and consumes the equivalent of one half person. . ." and ". . . the Galician works poorly (i.e., produces poorly) because he eats poorly (i.e., consumes insufficiently) and he cannot feed himself better because he works (i.e., produces) too little."[35]

Shortly thereafter the newly established Association of Polish Jurists and Economists took the subject of emigration from the three sectors of Poland under discussion. Succeeding meetings dealt with such topics as the economic conditions of peasant agriculture and economic conditions in Galicia in general.[36]

Equally important in establishing the underlying causes of emigration, in particular, and the economic conditions of Galician peasantry, were the painstaking studies of Bujak which began to appear at the turn of the century and continued regularly thereafter up to the outbreak of the war. His studies of the rural peasant communities of Zmiaca,[37] Limanowa[38] and Maszkienice[39] attracted widespread attention. The latter study especially won wide esteem and authority. Among the more significant findings of that more or less representative village in western Galicia was that of the 236 family units which comprised that village eleven families were adjudged to be in "good" economic condition; thirty families in "fair" condition; sixty-five families in "marginal" condition; 105 families in "insufficient" condition; and twenty-five families were living in "poverty." Since these conditions were established according to their own estimates of "a tolerable standard of living," the author concluded that 130 families could not possibly sustain themselves at a "tolerable living standard" or "minimum standard of living." A considerable proportion of the remaining families, better situated, likewise could not manage to sustain themselves from the soil. Hence, a high proportion of the population was obliged to work elsewhere than in the village.[40]

According to his investigations, emigration from that village traced back to the late 1850's. By 1863 about forty men went to work on the railroad bed of the Przemysl-Lwow line. They earned about 55 cents per day — 20 cents of which was used for rations. Annually thereafter, groups of men from Maszkienice went eastward *(na Rus)* to work on railroad construction gangs until 1887 when they discovered and continued the periodic journey to the Ostrawa-Karwin industrial basin in Austrian Silesia.[41]

This local study also tended to reveal the progress of one of the blights upon peasant agriculture — the progressive splintering of their landholds. In 1873, the land in Maszkienice was already divided into 4,209 parcels and by 1899 their number had increased to 5,036. In the latter year each peasant farmhold was composed of, more or less, nine parcels. The average width of each parcel of land was about six meters though quite a number of them were of about 1.5 meters, or about five furrows wide. He was one of the earliest to popularize the term "checkerboard" *(szachownica — Gemenglage)* as the outstanding characteristic of peasant agriculture in Galicia.[42] Nor was this a reflection of some inherent peculiarity of the Galician peasant. Quite the contrary, this was the result of the laws regulating the distribution of land through inheritance as they were applied by the district courts. These courts preferred to apportion the land to the surviving heirs by dividing the landhold lengthwise, thereby largely precluding any injury to the parties concerned as far as land of varying fertility was in question. This adjudication was entered into the court records and the surveyors' maps of the recorder of deeds. This latter official sometimes found his task impossible because the extremely narrow strip was illegible on the scale of his map.[43]

Bujak was one of the earliest to point out that while the wage scale of Galician agricultural workers during the second half of the nineteenth century maintained a fairly even level, this, in view of the continually increasing grain prices and other consumer goods, must have resulted in a decline of real wages during that period.[44] This progressive pauperization was reflected in the changing ages among the newly married young men of that village. Formerly, before military conscription was compulsory, people entered upon marriage when they were about 20 years old. By 1899 only the more opulent could marry immediately after concluding their military service, i.e., at about 24 years of age. The majority, less favorably situated, were obliged to work several years. By that year, marriage was rarely entered upon at an earlier age than 28.[45] Furthermore, in 1899 as well as later, the direction and destination of the seasonal migrations was not determined by the workings of some malignant and mischievous forces but rather the response of a particular occupation group to the changing relative wage scale.[46]

In Russian Poland the statistical publications of the Warsaw Statistical Committee and the comprehensive historical researches of Stanislaw Koszutski began to explore systematically into the economic conditions of that sector of Poland.

While it was the Warsaw Statistical Committee and such private enquiries as that conducted by the *Kurjer Warszawski* in 1901 which began to collect the basic data for economic research, it was scholars like Koszutski who, exploiting this data, interpreted it and established the meaningful relationships between population, industrial development, labor market, comparative wage scales and emigration.[47] Using the compilations of the Warsaw Statistical Committee, he pointed out that the excessively large proportion of potential hired workers —

about one-third of the total rural population in Russian Poland —
caused a record decline in the industrial and agricultural wage scale.
By an analysis of the available data on agricultural employment, he
reached the conclusion that the average day's wage of the agricultural
laborer in 1890 was 36 kopeks — a scale one-third of that in France,
one-half of that paid in the Prussian provinces and only three-fourths
of the average wage scale for comparative employment in the fifty
provinces of the Russian Empire.[48] Citing the findings of the investigations conducted by Filipowicz for the *Kurjer Warszawski,* he noted
that, almost without exception, all those who answered the questionnaires concerning wages in America testified that in comparison with
the wages in Russian Poland the emigrant in the United States earned
more money and sooner.[49]

On the basis of his extensive researches he was able to establish that
the chief cause of the movement of the rural population was the
unsatisfactory living conditions prevailing among them and that the
chief causes contributing to their emigration were such factors as the
density of the population and its progressive rate of increase, and the
relationship between wage levels and living costs.[50]

Once a critical examination into the economic conditions of the pre-
war sectors of Poland was initiated, the causal factors of emigration
began to assume more realistic character. Later writers, taking the
available census schedules as a point of departure, were able to point to
the extraordinary growth of the rural population in the second half of
the nineteenth century.[51] Lacking sufficient outlets in domestic agriculture or industry, this increment of rural population contributed to a
demographic disequilibrium in the country. This was especially apparent in Galicia where, as a result of the increasing population, the
number and proportion of "dwarf" landholds was increasing alarm-
ingly. Ludkiewicz found that of the total rural landholds in 1859, 35.6
percent were less than two hectares. By 1902 their number had increased to 42.3 percent of the total agricultural landholds.[52] Grabski
established that while in 1859, of the total rural landholds, 60 percent
represented landholds of less than five hectares, by 1902 their proportion had increased to almost 80 percent.[53]

Still another researcher found that there were, in 1902, about
444,000 peasant landholds so small — less than two hectares — that
they could assure a food supply for an average family for only three
months of the year, and another 369,000 were of such size that they
could assure a supply of food for the average family for eight months
of the year at most.[54] According to the estimates of the Galician

Executive Department, the average peasant landhold in 1892 was five *morgs,* in 1896 it was 4.2 *morgs,* and by 1910 it was only 3.6 *morgs.*[55]

Not only were the peasant landholds diminishing in size but apparently, because of a configuration of factors, these dwarf-holdings were splintered into a multiplicity of parcels so as to make their efficient utilization impossible. Thus, Ludkiewicz noted that at the time of his writing (c. 1909) there were 18 million parcels of land belonging to about one million owners, that is, each farmhold was composed of about eighteen separate and frequently non-contiguous pieces of land.[56] Another researcher, Wladyslaw Grabski, found that toward the end of 1911 there were 19,340,341 parcels of taxable land. Furthermore, he estimated that there were as many more parcels of land not in this taxable category. With somewhat less than a million independent landholders in Galicia at that time, the separate parcels for each landholder amounted to about thirty-five pieces of land. These, he found, were usually in narrow, widely scattered strips. Each strip necessitated the keeping of a boundary-strip which remained uncultivated and was an everlasting source of conflict and litigation between neighbors.[57]

In density of population, predominantly agricultural Galicia was found to exceed even some of the more industrialized areas of Europe. Thus, Ludkiewicz noted that, since Galicia had a density of population approximating seventy people per square kilometer while Germany had only twenty-five per square kilometer, almost all of Galicia, with the exception of the suburban or industrial areas and the less densely populated mountainous districts of eastern Galicia, could, without hardship, qualify as providers of emigration.[58]

Bujak estimated that in the years immediately preceding the war there was an excess of about 1,200,000 of agricultural population in Galicia, that is, over and above those necessary to till the available soil effectively. For these people, therefore, there was no employment in that country and, it followed, no means of livelihood.[59] It was no accident, in the view of another, that the emigration tide most strongly affected those districts bounded by the rivers Dunajec, Vistula, Dolny San and Wisloka. These were the most densely populated districts in the country.[60]

The statistics for the other sectors of Poland were no less revealing. Because of the rapid increment of rural population in Russian Poland, Szawleski found that while in 1891, of the total rural population, 13 percent were landless, by 1907 their proportion had reached to 31 percent of the total rural population.[61] Zalecki, quoting the statistical researches of Willcox, estimated that there was an excess of 3,776,055 adult (16 to 59 years of age) rural population in Poland within the boundaries established after the war.[62] The effect of this condition of population on the wages of the country was, to some, logically obvious.

In time, moreover, the wage scale for comparable employment abroad received more attention as a factor determining not only emigration but also its direction. Thus, despite the persistent fiction that wages in domestic agriculture were approximating or equalling wages for comparable employment abroad, the compilations of the Warsaw Statistical Committee unequivocally disproved such claims.[63] More careful observers, in time, were bound to admit that though in isolated cases domestic agricultural wages approximated those paid abroad, these wages were for a brief period of time rather than for an entire season. Though the wage of an agricultural worker in Russian Poland might compare favorably with the average wage reckoned over the entire season abroad, this wage approximation lasted for but a few weeks at most. The rest of the season the domestic worker had to settle for a fraction of the wages paid abroad.[64] Others took care to note that "piece work," with its opportunity for greater earnings, was widely available in Germany, while in Poland it was largely lacking.[65] Still others found that though the wages of agricultural workers increased as much as 30 percent in Russian Poland in the decade before the war, they were, in general, considerably lower than those paid abroad. Piltz, for example, found that the average day's wage in 1912 in Russian Poland for an adult male agricultural laborer was between 1.59 and 2.38 francs. This corresponded to 3.97 francs in Germany. The adult female agricultural worker in Russian Poland received an average day's wage ranging from 1.06 to 1.46 francs. For comparable employment in Germany, she received 2.65 francs per day.[66]

In Galicia, where the demographic disequilibrium was even greater, the wage levels were found to be correspondingly lower. This went a long way toward explaining the extraordinary phenomenon of the existence of seasonal migration from that sector of Poland to Russian Poland in the years before seasonal employment in Germany became available.[67] Importation of seasonal workers into Galicia, itself glutted with an excess of agricultural manpower, therefore seemed out of the question. As Bujak observed, probably nowhere in Europe could field workers be hired more cheaply than in Galicia. Nevertheless, the periodical *Rolnik,* the organ of the Economic Association of Lwow, continued to publish articles on the advisability and economic feasibility of importing Chinese "coolies"![68]

Saryusz-Zaleski found that the condition of the industrial workers of Galicia was little better than that of the agricultural workers and, over a period of years, seemed to be deteriorating. On the basis of the wage statistics of the Lwow Chamber of Commerce and Industry, he found that, using prevailing cost of rye as an index, the unskilled industrial worker in Galicia earned on the average 7.3 kilograms of rye per day in the 1861–1870 period and only 5.7 kilograms during the 1876–1880 period.[69]

Though wages for agricultural workers increased somewhat after the agricultural strikes in 1902 in eastern Galicia, wages were found to be still but a fraction of those paid abroad. The fact that the volume of emigration increased rather than decreased in the decade before the war was attributed, by Landau, not only to the wage differential but to the growing consciousness of personal worth and, therefore, increasing dissatisfaction with prevailing living and working conditions.[70]

Closer attention to wage differentials went a long way toward explaining the phenomena of changing "character" and direction of emigration. Buzek, among others, found that, since the improvement of material well-being was the prime impulse of emigration, given equal opportunity to improve their material status in nearby areas or overseas, the migrating population mostly chose the former. The changing direction of emigration from Prussian Poland confirmed him in his judgment. Until the early 1890's, this migration was directed chiefly overseas. From that time, however, with the rapid industrial growth of western Germany, greater masses of emigrants were diverted to areas like Rhineland, Westphalia and Brandenburg. Such, he found, was the case in the other sectors of Poland. Up to the 1890's emigration from Russian and Austrian Poland was directed chiefly abroad, especially to the United States. Since that time, however, there developed a mass seasonal and temporary migration to Prussia and the German provinces, as well as to Scandinavia, the Czech lands, France and elsewhere in Europe.[71]

On the eve of the war, the more objective observers, speaking of Poland as a whole, were willing to concede that the wages paid in western Europe — to say nothing of those in the United States — were, in general, two or three times higher than at home.[72] Others agreed that the landless peasant had little hope of acquiring his own land by his labors in Poland. He and numerous small landholders who wished to extend their meager holdings could only accomplish it by money earned abroad.[73]

In time the correlation between density of population and economic development became more established as factors of emigration. The idea of "economic density" of a population — an idea widely accepted by modern demographers[74] — as against the relatively meaningless concept of "territorial density" of population acquired more currency as a fundamental factor of emigration. This idea was inherent in the causal relationships of some earlier investigators of emigration, though it was not until the years preceding the war that it gained more general acceptance. By that time Rutkowski could hold that the most general, primary cause of emigration was the more rapid growth of rural population than the progress in the intensification of agriculture[75] — which could employ greater numbers on smaller areas — and, especially, the insufficient development of industry. It was these circumstances, in his judgment, which resulted in the surpluses of rural population, the break-up of peasant landholds and the continually increasing labor supply with its attendant decline of wage scale. Thus, while the rapid growth of industry in the United States and Europe, especially in western Germany, was creating a great demand for working hands, Poland was suffering from a surplus of population. Polish emigration to the United States was but one branch of a general European movement. It manifested itself later in Poland than in western Europe because of Poland's geographical remoteness from the main European ports of embarkation.[76]

Zaleski, especially, stressed the difference between geographical density of population and economic density of population. He noted that certain districts in Upper Silesia, such as Bytom, Katowice, and Zabrze, with over 2,589 inhabitants to the square mile still had room for an increase of population, whereas several purely agricultural districts of Galicia, with only 207.2 or 233.1 inhabitants to the square mile must be regarded as over-populated. "Economic saturation" being an accomplished fact, "nothing but the rapid development of industry and, consequently, urban resettlement, can preserve the country from a general exodus. . . ." To him, migration of population was a natural and logical remedy to an adverse economic density of population.[77]

Others, at a later date, enunciated the same idea. Papieski concluded that the cause of seasonal emigration was entirely the result of the disproportion between the growth of the population and the economic development of the country.[78] Szawleski, in his broadcast fashion, also touched upon this idea when he noted that a "contributing" factor to the volume of emigration in the pre-war years was ". . . the fact of the extraordinary over-population of the Polish village with rural proletariat because of the strong natural increase of the population and the break-up of peasant landholds. [This] surplus of rural population could find no employment in industry which was either neglected or did not develop at a sufficient pace to utilize all of this labor supply."[79] Elsewhere he noted that the tempo of economic development was much more gradual than the tempo of population increase.[80]

In an equally broadcast fashion, another chronicler of emigration, Jozef Okolowicz, concluded that it was the over-abundance of rural proletariat, an excess of dwarf landholds incapable of sustaining the livelihood of their owners, the low level of agrarian economic culture and the low productivity of the soil which combined to make the rural areas "a vast reservoir of unemployed labor which, unable to find employment in Poland neither in agriculture nor in industry, was forced to venture abroad to places which promised employment."[81] He specifically cautioned against perceiving the idea of over-population in the limited, geographical-territorial sense as a cause of emigration. Thus, while Galicia and Russian Poland were among the more densely populated areas in Europe, there were other areas which were even more densely populated and yet the volume of emigration from the latter was negligible and, in some cases, as for example, Saxony, there was an excess of immigration over emigration. Lacking urban-industrial outlets, the process of rural "proletarization," that is, the tendency toward landlessness, was rapid and intensive, especially in Galicia. These conditions existed throughout the nineteenth century.[82]

With a greater comprehension of the economic factors of emigration and the requisite statistical data for analysis of the conditions prevailing in Poland, some writers were moved to conclude that while the quantitative and qualitative make-up of a population movement as well as its direction was contingent upon a multiplicity of factors, the primary, decisive causal factors, however, were the socio-economic conditions in the country or area from which emigration originated, as well as these conditions in the country or area toward which migration was directed.[83] Thus, in time, the "push and pull" theory of emigration gained increasing acceptance over the former tendency to attribute the cause of emigration to "outside" factors exclusively.

A few observers were disposed, in the case of Poland, to go even a step further. For example, Jan Bloch, a writer of wide ranging intellectual and business interests, speaking specifically of the emigration to Brazil in 1890-1891, felt constrained to remark that, in his opinion, it was primarily a desperate flight from poverty predominantly by people who felt that they had nothing to lose.[84] Still another, on the basis of an examination of the letters of prospective emigrants to the Galician P.T.E., concluded that the chief reason for emigration to "America" was not the hope to "earn their fortune" but rather to escape the poverty and even stark starvation that threatened their immediate existence at home.[85] Bujak, probably the most thoroughly informed scholar on the subject, concluded that the primary and direct causes of emigration are the conditions prevailing in the given country of emigration. Conditions abroad, that is, in the countries of immigration, do not cause emigration from a given country but rather determine, to a large extent, its *direction*.[86]

IX

Attitudes and Opinions on "Effects" of Emigration

That there would be evidence of a remarkable degree of correlation, both in point of time and individual orientation, between "causes" of emigration and "effects" of emigration seems perhaps obvious. As long as, and by whomever, emigration was attributed to the "demon-agent," the consequences, or effects, of emigration were logically, at least, of an equally malignant nature. Thus, as late as 1912, one observer, writing in one of the official periodicals of the P.T.E., deplored the moral decline in the land as a result of loosened social strictures abroad, especially among the women and girls. To him, a sojourn abroad as a seasonal worker was sufficient to hopelessly compromise any young woman.[1] Another, writing at about the same time, deplored the effects of emigration on the growth and development of the population at home. In his view, emigration, by delaying marriages and causing widespread illness among women because of over-work, contributed significantly to the decline in birth-rate as well as to the higher incidence of social disease, tuberculosis and other debilitating diseases.[2] Especially heavy was the price exacted by the mining and manufacturing industries of the United States. These casualties of American industrial society, according to another observer, amounted to tens of thousands — all, as alien immigrants, without hope of just compensation.[3] Those who escaped being maimed physically were driven to insanity — ". . . an offering on the altar of American industrial civilization. . ." — victims of cultural maladjustment. Both were subject to final deportation where they became life-long burdens upon the community and, presumably, a testimony of the futility of emigration.[4]

The economy of their own country, on the other hand, suffered from the lack of a sufficient labor force. Because of the volume of emigration, there was a frequent necessity of leaving crops unharvested in the fields and marked decreases in livestock production. The result was an insufficiency of livestock for slaughter to supply the urban centers and the inordinately high prices for meat.[5] An especially popular preoccupation of some economists was the painfully statistical estimates of the economic losses sustained by the departure of the emigrant as a potentially productive individual who departed at the height of his productive potential without remitting to the society the expenses it bore rearing him. Still others made equally detailed estimates of the amounts of capital that the emigrant departed with from his mother country.[6] Although observers like Klobukowski had challenged this mercantilistic view of population, in general, and emigration, in particular,[7] it continued to maintain a singular currency even after the turn of the century. Indeed, it seemed to gain a renewed vitality as the pressure for industrialization accumulated in the decade preceding the war.[8]

Not only did the economy suffer, but the cultural effects of emigration were equally deleterious. Instead of acquiring the best features of foreign culture, frequently they acquired the worst and, returning to their native villages, frequently were the cause of "demoralization."[9] Equally deleterious, from the cultural-lingual point of view, was the apparent disposition of emigrants to "Polonize" foreign words and expressions thereby debasing the language.[10]

To be sure, some seasonal emigrants succeeded in returning home with some money, but these savings were inconsiderable and inconsequential to the total economic picture.[11] As late as 1902, the editor of the publication *Biblioteka Warszawska* contended that evidence indicated no direct relationship between the volume of emigration and the tempo of peasant acquisition of land via "parcelation."[12]

By this time, however, these views represented isolated vestiges of a passing generation. Already at that time the Warsaw Statistical Committee was publishing its surveys indicating that the seasonal emigrants to Germany alone were returning with 7,928,000 rubles in 1900; 9,032,000 rubles in 1901 and 8,575,000 rubles in 1902.[13] By 1904 the total savings from that country increased to 11,425,174 rubles and, with the growing volume of emigration, was bound to increase in the years to come.[14] Simultaneously with this influx of capital it was estimated that "several" million rubles were being transmitted annually to that sector of Poland from the United States.[15] In Prussian Poland where the remittances from "America" were relatively negligible, one author estimated in 1901 that about five million marks came into Poznan province alone each year from emigrants in the interior of Germany.[16]

In Galicia, also at the turn of the century, the researches of Bujak were bringing to light some rather revealing information. In 1899 the author estimated that the capital brought home by the male seasonal emigrants to the village of Maszkienice amounted to more than 24,000 crowns. This amount did not include the earnings of sixteen girls and women who had worked in Germany and Denmark. Furthermore, according to his careful estimate, the total net income from local farming of the village — crops, animals, animal products, etc. — did not exceed 20,000 crowns. Since the greater part of the income of this representative western Galician village came from the "outside" and since approximately one-half of all its family units participated in seasonal emigration, the income could hardly be called "additional" or "supplementary." Rather, he thought it should be regarded, in the least, of equal rank with the income from its total economy.[17] Hupka, investigating into the economic conditions of several villages in the central Galician county of Ropczyce, found that the average annual income per family as a result of migrant labor, during the period 1902–1907, was as follows in the following villages: Brzeziny — 1,477 crowns; Niedzwiada — 624 crowns; Mala — 360 crowns; Glinnik — 831 crowns; Laczki — 614 crowns; Broniszow — 595 crowns; and Lopuchowa — 432 crowns. The total sum of savings accruing to these seven villages during the 1902–1907 period was 1,695,651 crowns.[18]

Erazm Piltz estimated that during the period 1908–1911 the amount of money either sent back or brought back to Galicia from "North America" averaged annually about 141,750,000 francs.[19] During the same period, the seasonal emigrants to Germany, Denmark and elsewhere on the continent brought back, on the average, about 30,000,000 francs each year.[20] Bujak, on the basis of sixty dollars per seasonal and temporary emigrant, estimated that the annual inflow into Galicia during the years immediately preceding the war was between twenty-four and thirty million dollars.[21]

A more venturesome writer estimated that in the pre-war years the average seasonal emigrant to Germany saved and returned home with 120 marks. Estimating the total annual emigration of "Polish elements" to Germany in those years to be about one-half million, the net capital savings returned to the three sectors of Poland would amount to about 60 million marks or not quite 15 million dollars. The inflow of capital from the United States to the three sectors of pre-war Poland in the years immediately preceding the war, "when Polish emigration to the United States took on a more temporary character," he estimated at 45 million dollars annually. This amount included transmittals by the mails and banks as well as money brought back by remigrants.

Allowing for an estimated five million dollars from seasonal emigration from elsewhere than Germany and the United States, the author came to the conclusion that an estimated total of about 65 million dollars of capital accumulations flowed into pre-war Poland each year in the years immediately preceding the war. Deducting 10 million dollars for travel costs and money taken abroad by the emigrants, the annual net income for the three sectors of Poland was about 55 million dollars annually.[22]

More cautious observers, while conceding that it was impossible to estimate the steady inflow of marks and dollars from emigrants' earnings abroad, concluded that it grew to multi-million dollar proportions and, as such, ". . . represented a very important factor in the fiscal solvency of Russian Poland and Galicia."[23]

With the passage of time, the far-reaching effects of these annual increments of capital from abroad were gradually recognized. One of the more apparent results was the progressive improvement of credit facilities. The peasant-emigrant, having accumulated some capital holdings, not infrequently became the village capitalist in competition with other loan agencies.[24] Although these loans were largely restricted to short term loans,[25] the increment of capital into the relatively "tight" economy of Galicia tended to bring down the costs of even the long-term mortgage credit. Already in 1900 Bujak noted a decline in mortgage credit costs as compared to 1870, ranging from one and one-half percent to as much as 20 percent. Even the widely criticized Peasant Bank reduced its mortgage credit rates from 12 percent to ten percent.[26]

Moreover, because of the greater availability of capital to the peasants, many of the former practices of "working off" personal and private debts had fallen into disuse. Sometimes the peasant-debtor still pledged his work but usually only for a certain amount of days during harvest season. More frequently, having other and more remunerative outlets for his labor, the peasant-debtor preferred to repay his debts in coin.[27] By 1911 Bujak saw evidence of greater peasant participation in the *Reiffeisenkassen* where his deposits brought a return of about eight percent and in turn further augmented local credit facilities.[28]

Generally, however, it was found that he preferred to locate his capital in land. During the period between 1873 and 1914, more than two and one-half million *morgs* of land were acquired by way of parcellation in Russian Poland. The buyers, predominantly small landholders, were able to wage this campaign against the progressively dwindling area of their landholds almost exclusively by means of money earned abroad.[29] In Galicia a similar process was in evidence. While the amount of peasant land was 4,500,000 *morgs* in 1859, by 1889 it had increased to 4,800,000 *morgs;* by 1902 to 4,900,000 *morgs,* and in 1912 it amounted to 5,200,000 *morgs.*[30]

In Prussian Poland, many of the seasonal and temporary emigrants returned and purchased lands or otherwise improved their holdings with savings earned in German factories and mines. Most land purchases were made from large landholders. From the turn of the century until the outbreak of the war, it was recognized that this increment of funds was largely responsible for changing the tide in favor of the Polish-speaking elements in their battle against German colonization.[31] Numerous writers began to acknowledge the fact that this phenomenon was largely the result of emigration. Many of these contended that all financial resources necessary for the acquisition of land via parcelation by the peasant class came from outside earnings. Rarely, if ever, was the peasant able to accumulate such capital resources from profit from his own land.[32]

This phenomenon, for numerous reasons and from several points of view, was regarded as a singular boon. From a demographic point of view, the acquisition of peasant holdings was regarded as a very effective corrective for the rural disequilibrium that existed, especially in Russian Poland and Galicia. The "Populist" elements, considering its political and social ramifications, applauded the increase of peasant land holdings. They regarded these capital increments as a valuable instrumentality in changing the balance between large and peasant landholds. The landed gentry, finding themselves in a position of being "land poor" in a situation of growing indebtedness, could now effectively liquidate all or part of their debts by selling some of their surplus holdings.[33]

There were, however, several qualifying circumstances which attended these developments. For one thing, the landless class of peasantry were found to be only infrequent participants in this phenomenon, lacking as they did both the requisite capital holdings or other assets necessary as security for loans. As a group, they suffered twofold losses: the inability to acquire land, and the loss of employment with the progressive break-up of large estates.[34]

Still another tendency soon became apparent which tended to negate, to a degree, the efforts of the peasants to acquire land. As a result of the influx of money, the disposition of the peasants to locate it in land and the lack of properly controlled parcelling agencies, especially in Galicia, the speculation in land that developed had a tendency to raise the prices to unprecedented levels.[35]

Bujak, for instance, found that the prices of land in Maszkienice in 1900 ranged from 200 to 1200 crowns per *morg* — the average about 700 to 800 crowns. These prices represented an increase of about 50 percent over those in 1875.[36] A decade later he found that the average price for an average *morg* of land had increased about 100 percent.[37] Small parcels tended to bring a comparatively higher price than larger parcels because more people could afford to purchase them, and therefore, more bidders for them tended to raise their comparative price.[38] These inflated prices, especially apparent in Galicia, were likewise evident in all sectors of Poland already in the eighth decade of the nineteenth century.[39] The conservative peasant, imbued with the idea of the sanctity of the soil and lacking other outlets for his capital resources, was apparently willing to buy land at prices not commensurate with its possible economic returns. In some cases, the alternative seized upon was to purchase land to the eastward. Since the land costs tended to be generally cheaper in the eastward direction, some peasants found it economically expedient to remove themselves to eastern Galicia where land prices were less inflated.[40] This, in view of the Polish nationalistic elements there, already fighting "the battle of numbers," was an exceedingly felicitous development. When, on the other hand, a few were impelled by the runaway prices to relocate themselves outside the borders of historical Poland, the tendency was widely deplored.[41]

To a degree, the result of these developments was the pathetic phenomenon of the ambition for land being frustrated by the inflationary price spiral. Not infrequently the peasant undertook seasonal emigration as a temporary expedient to acquire land, but was obliged to extend the practice until, in some cases, it became a permanent way of life.[42]

This development led some observers to draw a distinction on the economic feasibility of the various types of migrations. While earnings from temporary emigration in the United States contributed to the extension of peasant landholds, those from seasonal emigration to Germany did not, since the latter savings were largely consumed during the winter months of inactivity. This distinction was especially popular with those elements who advocated the regulation of emigration in order to bypass Prussia, as well as those who were disposed to see little or no good accruing from emigration in general.[43]

This distinction persisted well into the postwar period even though Bujak, as early as 1900, had rejected it as both invalid and meaningless by showing that more than half of the participants in the parcelation of an estate in the village of Maszkienice were workers who earned their chief, if not sole, livelihood from seasonal migrant labor.[44] He was among the few who noted that while in some cases the money earned from seasonal emigration was consumed during the winter months of inactivity, it was not dissipated or otherwise consumed by choice, but rather because there was absolutely no employment to be had during that period of the year in Poland.[45]

Whether favorably or unfavorably disposed to emigration, most observers and commentators were agreed that emigration tended to raise the level of the domestic wages.[46] Whether this fact was "good" or "bad," of course, depended largely upon their respective points of view. The conservative elements tended inevitably to regard it as increasing domestic production costs and thereby threatening domestic production with total collapse on the world market. As on other aspects of emigration, it fell to a few like Koszutski and Bujak to set the pattern for the investigation of this far-reaching effect of emigration.

Using the data provided by the Warsaw Statistical Committee, Koszutski found that during the period 1890–1900 the average day's wage for men engaged in field work in Russian Poland increased from 28 to 32.1 kopeks, and for women from 20 to 22.8 kopeks. These represented average day wages for field workers employed for the entire year.[47] The most noteworthy rises in the wage scale for agricultural workers were to be seen in the provinces of Kalisz, Suwalki and Plock — provinces from which the volume and proportion of emigration to Prussia and America were largest. Of these, the highest scale for a day's wages was evident in Kalisz where it was about double the scale in the rest of the country. This was the case in wages for field work for both men and women. His conclusion: it was no coincidence that the amount of seasonal emigration to Germany was higher from that province than any other one.[48]

Bujak's investigations were more painstaking and detailed. While the average day's wages in about 1880 for male field workers ranged from 0.60 to 0.80 crowns, by the period 1901–1905 the wages had gradually increased to the point that they ranged from 0.80 to 1.15 crowns per day. In those areas where migrant workers were used, the wage scale ranged from 1.07 to 1.30 crowns per day.[49]

The period 1899–1911 saw a considerable increase in the wages paid for local agricultural labor in the village of Maszkienice: the day's wage of the harvest field worker increased 80 percent; that of reapers increased 115 percent; that of threshers increased 125 percent, and that of teamsters increased 50 percent.[50] Though the wages of the seasonal migrants from that village increased only 57 percent (carpenters) and 100 percent (pick and shovel construction workers) during those eleven years, while the costs for local job services increased at a somewhat higher ratio, the net wages abroad still remained considerably higher — a disequilibrium which encouraged an ever increasing volume of seasonal emigration.[51]

The development of the practice of seasonal emigration also brought about changes in the comparative advantages of various job functions on the local labor market. Thus, prior to the development of seasonal emigration, the teamster, invariably the more affluent farmer, enjoyed the comparative advantage in the exchange of services. With the development of seasonal emigration, the poor peasant-farmers and the agricultural laborers became increasingly aware of the value of their services on the world labor market. Consequently, the wages for their services became increasingly contingent upon wages paid on the western European labor market, while the job services of the more affluent peasant-farmer, the teamster, remained a local service which could not be profitably sold beyond a five to six kilometer radius and therefore remained contingent upon a more restricted, local labor market. Thus, to a large extent, the positions of advantage between the poor peasant and the well-to-do peasant were reversed.[52]

As early as 1899 youthful farm "help" was extremely hard to get for the middle and upper group of peasant landholders because they could earn at least twice as much "out in the world." The increased volume of emigration in the following decade intensified this situation.[53] In 1899 there were 30 persons in the status of "farm servants" and only nine of them were in the 12 to 16 age group. None were younger. They earned between 16 to 28 crowns per year including the usual emoluments. By 1911, however, there were only 12 farmholds employing "farm servants." With the exception of one, none could really be called "agricultural" servants because they were composed of seven children in the 8 to 13 age group, while, of the older ones, four were cripples who were unable to work in the fields and were employed solely in pasturing livestock or fulfilling simple household tasks. Actually, only six of the above could be regarded as "hired" servants, the remainder were from kindred families. These servants received from 26 to 36 crowns per year, including the usual emoluments. A comparison of the age composition and wages showed some notable changes in the 12-year period. Fourteen and fifteen-year-olds could go abroad and realize net earnings from five to seven times higher than in their native village.[54]

Because of the larger volume of seasonal emigration — especially its increased proportion to total population — Bujak found that even the smallest farmsteads, operated by the wife and small children, found it necessary at times to hire help, especially during the rush periods. Despite this apparent shortage of farm labor, however, Bujak found that there was never a lack for hired help during the periods of their imperative need. All field work was completed at the appointed time; no crop harvest was wasted; no land lay fallow. As a matter of fact, agricultural productivity had increased over the 12-year period and the amount of fallow land had decreased.[55]

The author explained this apparent impossibility quite simply. Though the rural economy had entered, to a degree, into the framework of capitalistic economic organization, vestigial remnants of the old exchange economy survived and, with the development of intensified seasonal emigration and the resultant decrease of labor supply, even tended to revive. Thus, the practice of assuring for themselves a supply of labor when it was imperative revived the practice of "working off" debts and obligations accrued for other services. This repayment "in kind" for certain job services — "beholden work" — was scrupulously detailed and standardized by local custom. Thus, a teamster could exchange one day of his services for three days of labor of an ordinary field hand. A teamster, on his way to the market, might carry another peasant going to the market with his produce, in exchange for the latter's manual labor at a later date or season. Services rather than cash were exchanged and all necessary work was accomplished at its appointed time.[56]

For this reason, the author took issue with the widely quoted statement by Stefan Schmidt that as a result of the large volume of seasonal emigration the peasants in western Galicia not infrequently left half of their land fallow.[57] To such statements of those who maintained that local agriculture suffered as a result of the large volume of seasonal migration, the author pointed out that if such were the case, the peasant-farmers of Maszkienice and environs would not participate so extensively in leasing additional land to put under cultivation — a system widely practiced in Maszkienice and in the neighboring localities.[58]

Not only was more land put under cultivation, but the author saw positive evidence of increased productivity of each labor unit engaged in local agriculture. Without decreasing the crop yield per unit, a smaller number of population cultivated a larger amount of land than they did in 1899. This, to him, suggested that less time was lost on unproductive activity and that the non-emigrating population was more fully and profitably utilizing their productive potential than they were 12 years before.[59]

"The longstanding and widespread complaint that there is a lack of agricultural labor," he remarked in 1911, "is voiced now, as formerly, by local residents." In reality, he found that there was not so much a "lack" of agricultural labor but, rather, that it cost more. Thus, he frequently observed the "natural inconsistency" of a local peasant-farmer who emigrated abroad each year as a laborer, considering the increasingly higher wages he was paid abroad as only just, while complaining bitterly of the increased wages he was asked to pay for farm help hired by his wife during the harvest period when he was absent abroad. His views changed accordingly, if he was speaking as an employee or an employer.[60] His conclusion:

> The cost of labor in Maszkienice must of necessity tend to equate itself with the wages paid for agricultural labor on the western European labor market insofar as the village remains in commerce with that labor market. It appears, however, that these costs [of local labor] have a sufficient basis in the increase in the value of the agricultural produce . . . complaints about the exhorbitant cost of labor have no more validity or basis in fact than they had formerly.[61]

These were some of the economic effects of emigration which Bujak saw in Maszkienice in his second study. This greater economic solvency of the peasant was especially apparent in the material conditions of his life.[62] There were, however, but few improvements in the cultivation of the soil. Though he saw evidences, since 1875, of new and improved varieties of wheat, rye and potatoes being gradually accepted by the peasants of western Galicia — usually introduced by peasants from distant localities — the effects of emigration upon the agricultural practices of the Galician peasant were apparently inconsiderable. This Bujak attributed to the quite considerable disparity between the two worlds of the emigrant — especially the disparity between technical productivity, on the one hand, and the cramping restraints of tradition at home, on the other. The latter, in his opinion, tended to discourage any innovations in the time-established agricultural practices and methods.[63]

The many who concerned themselves with a resolution of the agrarian problem, both in Russian and Austrian Poland, tacitly took the factor of emigrant earnings into consideration. Not infrequently they were occupied with estimating the minimum size for self-sufficient, economically feasible peasant farmholds. Biegeleisen[64] and Hupka[65] held that in "favorable circumstances" holdings between two and five hectares in western Galicia were economically feasible, that is, economically healthy and capable of "rational" existence. This, in itself, was a recognition of the economic progress achieved by the peasant economy in the several decades preceding the war.

Though the integral correlation between emigration and parcelation was generally recognized by the turn of the century, the consequences of parcelation were debated by both the progressives and conservatives down to the outbreak of the war. One reporter, summarizing the deliberations on the subject at the Fourth Congress of Polish Jurists and Economists in 1906, concluded that although none of the participants any longer voiced the old argument that "parcelation represented the fourth partitioning of Poland," the overwhelming majority appeared to justify the existence of the manorial estates on social, political, economic, cultural and, indeed, on grounds of national interest. Only the most radical — and those only peripherally and indirectly — suggested the prospect of forcing their removal by a system of graduated taxation and/or legislation which defined their maximum size — an idea that was summarily dismissed as unworthy of consideration by the participants.[66] That view had been expressed in the clerically oriented *Przeglad Powszechny* in 1904, when Juliusz Makarewicz had expressed his regrets on the apparent break-up of manorial estates *(dwor, folwark)* — ". . . a centrum of radiating culture in their locality." Nevertheless he saw that as an ineluctable alternative to massive and permanent peasant emigration.[67]

The progressive elements of Polish society were equally divided on the consequences of parcelation. The social-democratic periodical *Krytyka,* throughout 1912, carried a forensic exchange on the subject between Helena Landau and Edward Maurizio. The former seemed to advocate the complete proletarization of the surplus peasantry and their absorption by indigenous industry; the latter sharply challenged the thesis of the economically debilitating influences of parcelation and, its corollary, the economic impracticability of small peasant landholds. Maurizio held that Landau's was the viewpoint of an urban intellectual; that in recent years, when the process of parcelation was most intense, certain areas of agricultural productivity had, in fact, been more intensively and successfully produced on small rather than large landholds; that the proliferation of producer cooperatives and Reiffeisen-type of credit unions were a testimony of the rapidly improving cultural-economic level of the peasant villages and, that the peasant quest for economic self-sufficiency, albeit "impoverished self-sufficiency," should not be despised.[68]

If there was a lack of agreement upon the economic effects of emigration, the less measurable and more intangible moral, cultural, political and other effects caused even a wider divergence of opinion. Here again, however, Bujak provided a valuable corrective. On the basis of his investigations, he was able to report that he found no evidence of promiscuity among the female migrants to Germany. Even if they were so disposed, the collective character of their work and life minimized the opportunity. On the contrary, he thought that there was more such opportunity in the native village than among the seasonal agricultural workers in Germany.[69] Neither did emigration, in his judgment, have any noticeable effect on the incidence of social disease nor, as some claimed, on the number of illegitimate children.[70] As far as the general health level of the community was concerned, the author concluded that seasonal emigration, generally speaking, had no adverse effects. On the contrary, the improved living conditions which followed upon emigration brought about a marked improvement in the general health level.[71] Others, while not specifically mentioning emigration as a cause, nevertheless noted remarkable declines in infant and adult mortality rates in the period between 1870 and 1910, especially in Russian Poland and Galicia.[72]

Though of small practical profit in his domestic life and environment, the cultural and intellectual horizons of the emigrant were considerably widened by his experiences. These advances were evident to Bujak already in 1899. The seasonal migrants manifested these advances in their dress, their eating habits and even in their manners and general level of enlightenment. These changes came about as a result of their visual and aural experiences, without their conscious effort and, frequently, in spite of their wills. This, in his opinion, was because of the wide disparity between their cultural level at home and that which they found abroad.[73]

Since they most generally journeyed together, worked together, lived together and fraternized almost exclusively with one another, the "social" influence they exerted upon their domestic environment was negligible.[74] Nevertheless, ". . . the old peasant type, sometimes rowdy, but generally awkward and docile, has slowly passed out of existence. . . . Spiritual independence and self assurance develop as a result of great exertions, painful experiences and strong impressions. . . . In a word, through emigration our people acquire an auspicious basis for their spiritual development . . . their impressions make up, in a

measure, for their lack of 'book learning'."[75] This experience combined with the increased activity of various political parties had
combined to make the peasant increasingly politically conscious.
There was a greater tendency to hold elective officials accountable for
any fiscal irregularities or misappropriations of public funds though,
regrettably, these malpractices were still not accorded equal gravity
with violations of private property rights.[76]

Janik, an equally sympathetic observer, noted some remarkable
changes in the traditional deportment of the Polish peasant in the
United States. He found the old-country submissiveness and groveling
behavior especially less apparent. While the peasant remained a diligent churchgoer, he no longer indulged in the more demonstrative
manifestations induced by religious experience.[77] Another observer
concluded that despite the considerable deficiencies in the cultural
make-up of the emigrant in the United States he nevertheless stood
decidedly above the level of the environment from which he issued.[78]

X

Summarization: Persistence of Prewar Attitudes in Postwar Poland

Thus, in the several decades preceding the war, the attitudes and policies toward emigration underwent substantial transformations. Inevitably they were conditioned by the transformations taking place in the social, political and economic life in their respective areas as well as in the western world in general.

Though the various problems that actuated the policies of the respective authorities were unique and indigenous to the Polish sectors of the pre-war countries concerned, the economic impulses to emigration were common to all. The German policy to retain control over the Eastern Marches by a continued program of German colonization doubtless facilitated, as it was intended to, the emigration of some of the Polish-speaking elements in that area. At the least, it had the advantage of not interposing any impediments to their emigration while encouraging, in every way, the immigration of Germans. That this policy was not decisive in the emigration of Poles from Greater Poland was attested by the growing volume of German emigration that called it into existence. Polish emigration was inevitably destined to, and did, follow German emigration first to America and, by the turn of the century, into the industrial interior of Germany.

The Kingdom, as a section of pre-war Poland, had the advantage of having attained a comparatively higher degree of industrial development within its confines. Nevertheless, even its higher level of economic development was insufficient to overcome the demographic disequilibrium induced by the natural increases of rural population and the refugee-immigrants from the Western Governments. In consequence of this, it became and remained essentially an area of both temporary and permanent emigration in the several decades before the war.

Of the three, however, Galicia suffered most from a demographic imbalance. Its industrial development was largely frustrated by the combined policies of the authorities in Vienna and the landed gentry in

Lwow. This combined with an almost explosive natural increase in the second half of the nineteenth century made it an auspicious area for the development of emigration.

Thus, despite the particular identities of each of the sectors, all could validly be termed depressed areas, insufficient to support their masses of population in the period under discussion. When the demographic pressures found outlets abroad, all contributed substantially to the growing tide of emigration from that general area of central Europe.

The general attitudes of the more representative segments of Polish society toward this phenomenon likewise followed a parallel evolution during those years. Prior to the development of an outspoken middle class, the dominant attitude was that of the landed gentry. It was an attitude conditioned largely by both their patriotic hopes and their economic interests and ranged from studied silence to vigorous opposition and forcible restraint. The last decade of the nineteenth century, however, witnessed a growing challenge to the social and intellectual monopoly of those elements of population. By that time a more numerous urban population was establishing itself in the cities and towns of Greater Poland. In the Kingdom, the election of middle class representatives to the first *Duma* testified to the growing influence of that class while, in Galicia, that decade saw the progressive assertion of peasant interests in the *sejm* at Lwow.

The several years preceding the war, however, witnessed the resurgence of Polish nationalism. Though not lacking in the other sectors, this development was especially apparent in Galicia which, because of its greater degree of political autonomy, became a rallying ground — a Polish Piedmont — for these revived currents which cut across former groupings and included the socialist, populist, national democrats as well as the older, conservative orientations.[1] This temper combined with the realization that emigration, in one form or another, could not be contained. Even if its total confinement was possible, it was more generally recognized as inadvisable in view of the growing dependence of the rural economy in particular and the general fiscal solvency of the areas concerned on emigrant earnings abroad. These factors were the motor forces behind the movement for regulation and control after the turn of the century. Parallel and equally operative with these was the hope that more effective control would circumvent mass fevers induced by the misrepresentations of agents;[2] would guard against the undue exploitation and swindling of emigrants; would provide public information bureaus with the actual conditions of labor, wages and transportation and would provide the emigrant with proper consular protection abroad.

One of the more striking corollaries of this tendency was the emergence of what could be appropriately called "a politics of emigration" in the early years of the twentieth century. It seemed to be a justified response to the ever-expanding efforts of the German authorities to establish their total control over the seasonal emigrants from the Kingdom and Galicia.[3] More especially, it appeared to be a promising means for the nationalists-irredentists to organize and control this emigration as an effective political-economic counter for the realization of their concept of national interest. They were doubtless sustained by the knowledge that the politics of "national unity" in the Eastern Marches was successfully countervailing the policy of Germanization in that area.[4] Equally sustaining was their feeling that the country supplying labor had an effective bargaining counter against the country importing labor. Leopold Caro, for example, citing German economists like Sering and Brentano as his authorities, frequently affirmed the imperative dependence of German agriculture on Polish immigrant labor. From this, he seemed to assume that in a Polish-German confrontation the bargaining advantage would be on the side of the Poles — if they were properly organized.[5] Among others, such was the motive of the advocates of a comprehensive federal emigration law from 1904 until the outbreak of the war. In the interim, many of its proponents favored an extended network of public labor bureaus which would have as their priority the supplying of Galicia's labor needs and interests.[6] Until such laws were passed, the authorities in Vienna were urged to negotiate ameliorative treaty arrangements with countries like Germany to provide a modicum of equity for the Polish emigrant workers.

It was in this climate of intensified nationalism that the P.T.E. was organized in 1908 with the explicit function of redirecting seasonal emigration away from Germany.[7] The most militant expression of this sensibility was an effort to extend this boycott into the arena of German consumer goods, a strategem which apparently enjoyed some success in Prussian Poland. Localized in an organization called Polish Watch *(Straz Polska)* and originally intended as a counter-effort to the Prussian removal policies and discriminatory school laws in the Eastern Marches, its operations were extended to the other sectors of pre-war Poland as a result of a convocation *(wiec)* held in April, 1908 in Krakow.[8]

In these circumstances, the "indifferentism" of the partitioning powers, especially Russia and Austria, came under increasing criticism.[9] Szawleski, for example, maintained that:

... the partitioning powers looked upon the emigration fever which was weakening the Polish people with either indifference or satisfaction . . . limiting their control to ineffectual military and police regulations. . . . The consular protection of the partitioning powers limited itself to matters of loyalty to the crown, military service and the receipt of inheritances after deceased emigrants.[10]

The disposition to place the blame on the partitioning powers had the advantage of being consistent with both the older practice of emphasizing the external causes of emigration and the new nationalistic-irredentist tendencies. This latter represented a noteworthy innovation insofar as Galicia was concerned. Heretofore, the landed gentry and their spokesmen generally followed a policy of uncritical loyalty to the crown.[11] These criticisms of the central government represented a divergency from that policy and orientation. As a result, not only was there a greater tendency to blame the partitioning authorities but, with the growth of middle-class opposition, to venture some criticism of ". . . the egoistic interests of the proprietary classes," who were unequivocally opposed to any and all emigration.[12]

This change in attitude had the added advantage of presenting the advocates of regulation and control as the champions of the best interests of the total population in an attempt to overcome the general mistrust with which the gentry were regarded by the peasant classes. The suspicion with which the landed gentry was regarded was understandable in view of the long-standing historical tradition of that class. Early in the period of Galician autonomy, when the *sejm* sought to pass a memorial to the Crown in support of a federalistic policy — a policy which would have given them even greater autonomy in Galicia — the peasant deputies through their spokesman, Laskorz, expressed themselves as follows:

> We will not vote in favor of this address because you, My Lords, say that you want autonomy. . . . We are afraid of autonomy because it has not been long since our backs have healed [from the effects of such autonomy] and we still remember it well and have no desire for it a second time. . . . You, My Lords, want it in order that you may again do as you please. We stand behind our Most Illustrious Lord.[13]

To a considerable extent, the same suspicion and mistrust was attached to the clergy. Many writers on the subject, at that time and since then, have observed this phenomenon. Bujak, as early as 1899, observed that since the earnings accrued abroad by the seasonal emigrants were imperative to their very existence, it was ". . . small wonder, then, that the people chose to ignore the injunctions of the clergy against these 'excursions,' chiefly because of their fear for their salvation, the decline of their morality and piety and, especially, their fear of socialism." [14]

Ignacy Daszynski, writing in his memoirs in the postwar period, bitterly remarked that:

> . . . it was interesting to observe how the ruling gentry deported itself in the face of this imperative manifestation. Frightened with the loss of the world's cheapest workers . . . the *szlachta* thrust upon the clergy especially the duty of restraining emigration by frightening the village folk from the pulpit with the greatest tales of horror which awaited the emigrants. . . . And when . . . there developed a variety of protective associations (St. Raphael and others) it was the clergyman-politician who alone profited from them. . . . [15]

Since the appointment to a position in the village parish was controlled, to a degree, by the manor, it was small wonder that only the more refractory elements among the clergy came out openly for emigration. Znaniecki found that the Catholic church unhesitatingly declared itself in favor of preserving the old traditions and against any innovations whatever: ". . . even when it has to yield, it yields only in the last extremity [and] fights for tradition as long as it can without impairing its influence. . . ." [16]

The older intelligentsia, to a degree also the retainers of the gentry, enjoyed little confidence in the eyes of the peasantry. Boleslaw Prus, writing in the periodical *Tygodnik Ilustrowany* in 1886, noted that:

> It is an undeniable fact, pitiable beyond expression, that the intelligentsia has no common unity with the peasant; it knows him not; does not understand him; does not see and does not influence him. The Jewish innkeeper, the loan-shark, the clandestine advisor, even the thief . . . [sometimes impelled by the exigencies of his calling to seek rural residence] possess greater trust and confidence among the peasantry than does the intelligentsia which styles itself as leader of society. There is nothing more grievous, nothing more shameful, than to become an alien among your own and toward your own. Nevertheless, this is the point we have already reached. [17]

Still another observer, commenting upon the prevailing intellectual climate at the turn of the century, concluded that:

The intelligentsia not only lost its ties with the whole of society . . . but enclosed itself in a kind of a caste which is called Society, a caste not actually closed and not hereditary . . . but nonetheless a caste, possessing its separate egoistic interests which it jealously guards. . . . We see in this social group tendencies directly antagonistic to the intellectual interests of the whole of society and directed toward the conservation of a separate, privileged status of those who succeeded in one way or another to this status . . . the boundaries between the intelligentsia and the other privileged classes tend to be obscured completely. . . . The concept of "intelligentsia" and "Society" fuses into one . . . the intelligentsia, having lost its sense of duty to the whole of society, preserved only the desire to maintain its privileges . . . zealously opposing everything which threatens to curtail these privileges while at the same time feeling its solidarity with all those groups . . . who have a privileged status. . . .[18]

Count Dzieduszycki, himself an heir of a noble lineage, reproached his people when he wrote that:

. . . a veritable social chasm separates the higher social stratum from the more numerous lower ones: the peasantry, the petit bourgeois and the Jewish community. We have become so accustomed to the extreme oriental humility of our people that it does not surprise us that the peasant does not dare to sit down in the presence of gentry though he may not be in his employ — that he remains with his head bared before him in the most inclement weather — that he kneels before him. The aristocracy of our country, that is, *the gentry, the clergy, the higher intelligentsia and those who aspire to one of those aristocratic groups,* take great care to differentiate themselves [from the lower class] by their manners, their customs and usages, their dress and even their speech. . . .[19]

The new nationalism, by ostensibly incorporating the peasant into its purview, had the advantage of obscuring traditional class antipathies. In this intensified climate of nationalism the prevailing attitudes toward overseas emigration, *i.e.,* emigration of a more permanent character, were accordingly subjected to modification and reappraisal. By the last years of the nineteenth century all but the most unreconstructed reactionaries had become generally reconciled to the fact of that emigration. A variety of arguments had been advanced to tolerate it. As regards emigration to the United States, the chief rationale of the more liberal elements was that it, in fact, was of a temporary character *(wychodztwo zarobkowe).* Peasants who had formerly settled, to a notable degree, on the farms — and were thereby permanently rooted there — were, in the closing decades of the nineteenth century, increasingly gravitating to the urban-industrial centers. Modern industrial processes were able to effectively utilize even the most unskilled workers. Accordingly, the Polish immigrant's attachment to his new environment was becoming increasingly tenuous and largely contingent upon his employment. If, as it happened in the early 1890's, he found himself a casualty of the periodically recurring recessions, the inevitable impulse was to return home rather than watch his limited savings dwindle away. Though poverty was not unknown to him, urban poverty had an intensity and depth peculiar to itself and unknown to rural poverty. The availability of relatively cheap and rapid transportation facilities doubtless facilitated his decision.

Equally important in this relatively liberal view of emigration to the United States was the growing awareness of the substantial remittances that were forthcoming from it. Furthermore, the geographic remoteness of the United States was counterbalanced by the widespread organizational network of Polish American societies,[20] Polish-American press,[21] Polish-American parishes,[22] Polish-American schools[23] and Polish-American communities — all of which constituted a formidable counterbalance to the assimilatory tendencies of the urban-industrial environment in which they lived. Through the combined efforts of these instrumentalities, the peasant emigrant, a passive political element at home, was increasingly developing a national consciousness and creating a permanent reservoir of national strength.[24] There were a few in Poland who saw in the Polish emigrants in the United States potential legions of Fennianists ready to do battle in the cause of Polonia Restituta.[25]

There were some, to be sure, who had expressed doubts regarding the permanence of those ghetto-like concentrations and, with them, the religious, educational, social and organizational networks. Still others expressed their qualms concerning the ultimate effect of the urban-industrial milieu in the United States upon the peasant-emigrant. These inclined to emphasize the greater permanence and greater resistance to assimilatory forces of agricultural rather than urban concentrations. Taking a page from Friedrich List and other like-minded economists, they maintained that only by concentrating lingual and national elements could they successfully overcome assimilation in a foreign country. An ideal alternative to the broadcast scattering of Polish elements abroad would be a program of controlled, regulated and directed emigration to a predetermined area where even the most distant generations would not fall victims to national or cultural assimilation; where they would be established into compact homogeneous settlements which could be extended and augmented by further Polish emigration. Such emigration would then be "an instrument of national expansion, a means of peaceful extension of the national frontiers," instead of "a shrinkage of the motherland, denuding her of her citizens." Rural concentrations had the added advantage of sheltering the emigrant from the deleterious influences of an industrial society.[26]

To these, Parana seemed to be ideally suited for such an enterprise. That country, "with comparatively small effort and means, could become the basis of Polish colonial expansion" through "peaceful annexation, since it was a country of vast natural and mineral resources, with an [indigenous] population of low cultural level and lacking in assimilatory vigor."[27]

Not infrequently, they went to some lengths to establish that the United States, with its glutted labor market and minimum quotas of financial resources for admission, was outside the purview of a large proportion of emigrants from Poland. Siemiradzki, for example, as early as 1892, had maintained that ". . . that way is today closed for that segment of prospective emigrants which is without sizable resources, that is to say, the largest segment. . . . " Not only was the barrier into the United States apparently insuperable but the promise of its economic prospects rather doubtful as the considerable proportion of remigrants from that country testified.[28]

The Fourth Congress of Polish Jurists and Economists held in 1906 signalized, in some ways, a new militancy and a retreat from the comparative liberalism that characterized the last years of the nineteenth century. Increasingly more voices were raised against overseas emigration to the United States. When Benis expressed the view that approximately 75 percent of the emigrants to that country returned to their homeland—and returned with a substantial quota of savings[29] — he was extensively challenged by many of his auditors at the conference. Caro, a widely recognized authority on the subject, vigorously cast doubt on his statistics on the volume of remigrants, his data on the money they brought back into the country and his methodology in general. Despite Benis' disclaimer to the contrary, he reaffirmed that United States industrial and mining interests frequently resorted to contracting labor in Poland despite the federal law which prohibited such practices.[30] Roman Dmowski, an equally recognized authority on emigration and the emerging spokesman of the National Democratic *(endek)* party, concurred with Caro and adjudged the emigration to the United States, from the view of national interest, a total loss because of the uncompromisingly assimilative character of Anglo-Saxon culture.[31] Kazimierz Warchalowski likewise questioned Benis' statistics on remigration and concluded that many more emigrants to the United States remained there permanently than was generally admitted.[32] Dr. Kumaniecki,[33] Wlodzimierz Czerkawski,[34] Wladyslaw Zukowski,[35] and Delegate Buynowski, to a greater or lesser extent, were generally in accord with those views. Buynowski, for example, was convinced that if the Polish laborer worked as hard in his native land as he did in the United States, he would earn twice as much money.[36] Delegate Slupski serously questioned the former justification of emigration to the United States that saw the Polish-American remigrant as a reservoir of technological know-how facilitating the industrial development of Poland.[37] Stanislaw Koszutski, a respected economic historian, generally deplored all emigration and went so far as to question the subject as within the legitimate purview of discussion for the congress. In the most general terms, his alternative was the industrial development of all sectors, which would obviate the need for emigration.[38]

Those that still sanctioned emigration to the United States continued, as formerly, to rationalize it as temporary in character *(wychodztwo zarobkowe).* Delegate Wysocki probably was correct in assuming the sentiments of that body when he affirmed that "all assembled are agreed that emigration to the United States, to the degree that it is temporary — and to the degree that the emigrant returns with his savings — is advantageous both to the emigrant and the greater national interest."[39] He was essentially seconded in this view by Roger Battaglia,[40] Czerkawski,[41] Buynowski[42] and, of course, Benis. In time, even the long-accepted idea of "New Poland" in Parana came under more extended challenge.[43]

In this framework of thought, the attitude toward "subsidized emigration" underwent some change. As formerly, some continued to maintain a critical attitude toward the immigration policy of countries like Brazil and the homestead policy of Canada on the ground that they stimulated and encouraged unnecessary emigration.[44] The Canadian homestead policy was admittedly liberal. In spite of its liberality, however, when the total expenditures for transportation from Europe, purchase of land, building of homes and purchase of the requisite farm equipment were tallied, they often proved insurmountable to precisely those elements of the population who needed help most. For these reasons, such destitute elements of the population were advised that they had better and quicker opportunities in Parana.[45] American "prepaids" as a type of subsidies for emigration still came under some criticism but usually in connection with the hardships to which they exposed the recipient in his journey abroad. This "dark page in the history of Polish emigration" was facilitated by the "prepaids" which, lacking precise schedules of departures and name of ship, permitted the shipping companies to cram the emigrants on ships that were old, unseaworthy and of insufficient capacity.[46]

Since this new orientation was contemporaneous with, and, to a degree, a product of the growing movement of nationalism, it was probably inevitable that its basic aspects were consistent with the prevailing ideas of nationalism. This is evident from the way the Polish writers distinguished between "emigration" and "migration." They invariably referred to population movements within "historical Poland" as migration or internal migration. Thus population movement from Poznan province to Westphalia, for instance, was called "emigration" by the Polish writers of the period, though it was "internal migration" *(Binnenwanderungen)* from the German point of view. Likewise, the movement of population from Russian Poland to the interior of Russia was referred to as "emigration." Population movement from Galicia to Russian Poland or Prussian Poland, however, was referred to as "internal migration" by Polish writers though, strictly speaking, it crossed the then existing national boundaries.[47]

To the degree that the temper of nationalism gained wider acceptance in pre-war Poland, the consciousness of manpower became increasingly prominent.[48] Insofar as the various political orientations became more nationalistic, they espoused the idea of regulation and control. Thus, for example, while the program of the Socialist party in 1881 only mentioned emigration as one of the manifestations of the "preponderance of capitalism" and made no specific mention of a policy in dealing with this phenomenon,[49] by 1907, one of the foremost spokesmen of socialist revisionism was referring to it as a "necessary evil," "a regrettable blood-letting," and deploring the departure of "the most vigorous and enterprising elements of the population," — attributes from which the country of emigration failed to profit.[50] As early as 1895 the spokesmen of the crystallizing Peasant Party were already expressing their solicitude over this loss of population.[51]

Within the prevailing context, "Polish emigration" was likewise invariably understood to mean Polish-speaking, Christian elements, rather than all people living within historical Poland. Much of the concern and solicitude that attached to Polish emigration was generally not in evidence where other ethnic, lingual or religious minorities were concerned. In Russian Poland, already by the last decades of the nineteenth century, this parochialism was increasingly in evidence. There it represented, to a degree, a reaction against the moderately assimilatory tendencies of the Positivists, on the one hand, and, more especially, against the influx of Jewish population from the "Western Lands" after the promulgation of the restrictive May Laws. Although propagated among the peasantry by journalists like Jan Jelenski, the editor of the periodical *Rola,* the chief antagonism emanated from the urban classes who found in the immigrants competitors in employment and business enterprise. This antagonism was apparently magnified by the economic recession which developed in that sector of Poland in 1882. Thereafter this attitude gained increasing popularity among both the National Democratic, Populist and clerical spokesmen.[52] By the last decade of the nineteenth century, the Populist publication *Glos,* despite its progressive anti-clerical and humanitarian position, had abandoned its hope for the resolution of the "Jewish Question" by way of progressive and enlightened assimilation and came out for supporting Jewish emigration to whatever parts of the world where their national ambitions could be realized.[53] To the degree that total assimilation met with resistance, the rhetoric of some nationalists began to assume decidedly Hakatist overtones.[54] The establishment of an information bureau for Jewish emigrants in Warsaw was greeted with approbation by the editor of the *Biblioteka Warszawska* in 1906. While taking care to let it be known that he was not an exponent of unlimited emigration, either Christian or Jewish, he concluded that Jewish emigration would be for the best in view of the conflict that was likely to develop within the country between "antagonistic elements — fundamentally antagonistic because of race, temperament and political ambitions." The editor, like many of the intelligentsia of the day, was expecting widespread political reforms which would have given Russian Poland far-reaching autonomy and self-government as a result of the revolutionary upheavals in Russia. In these circumstances, "the normalization of the steady outflow of surplus Jewish population" was to be desired — it would be "in the best interest of the country," etc. — the whole editorial expressing an ill-concealed elation on the subject of mass emigration of the Jewish population.[55]

In Galicia, parallel attitudes had been developing and became increasingly apparent and compounded by the presence of a numerous

Ukrainian-speaking population. Already in 1891, Weyssenhoff, the editor of the widely read conservative publication *Biblioteka Warszawska,* voiced his approbation of a contemplated project of Baron Hirsch to colonize Jewish Russians abroad. However, when a rumor developed that Hirsch intended to allocate eight million francs for the purchase of land in Galicia for their resettlement, the editor reported that this news "appalled local circles . . . called forth alarms cautioning against the loss of the country." He concluded that all of Hirsch's resources would be unable to undo the hostility such a project would create.[56] At the same time the editor of the conservative *Kuryjer Polski* was frequently inveighing against the "aggressively entrepreneurial Armenians, Germans and Jews" who were "divesting the knightly descendants of noble past of their patrimony," simultaneously expressing his willingness to expedite their emigration to the United States.[57] By the turn of the century, the Reverend Stojalowski, after a brief, inaugural venture into Christian Socialism, was emerging as the self-appointed spokesman of the peasant party *(Partja Ludowa)* in the Galician *sejm.* When a speaker on the floor noted that, among others, about 16,000 Jewish Galicians had emigrated that year (1901), he interposed the remark: "A pity there were not three times as many."[58] At about the same time the Galician socialist, Ignacy Daszynski, was being charged with "Judophilism" because of his intemperate criticism (in the *Reichsrat*) of Christian-clerical and National Democrat policies in Galicia. The author, writing in the *Niwa Polska,* construed this as the basest betrayal by Daszynski.[59] A few years later, the deputy from Brody, Naton Loewenstein, apparently caused the assembled *sejm* some restless moments when he enumerated some of the causes of the progressive pauperization of the Jewish Galicians and the social, political and economic dangers to which they were leading. That body subsequently approved his motion instructing the Executive Department to undertake an inquiry into the subject.[60] When no report was forthcoming, the same deputy again raised the question a year and a half later.[61] He was then informed by a spokesman for that department that "the extensive character of its investigations precluded an early report" but assured him that its findings would be submitted to the *sejm* in due course.[62] Nevertheless, there is no evidence that such a report was ever submitted prior to the outbreak of the war. On the eve of that war, the editor of the P.T.E. publication, the *Polski Przeglad Emigracyjny,* while expressing the intention of that organization to expand its function to include "care and protection over Jewish emigration," generally tended to regard it as desirable from the social, political and economic point of view inasmuch as they represented an over-populated element in Galicia.[63]

As far as the Ukrainian Galicians were concerned, Leopold Caro, a more or less representative spokesman of the new nationalism in the several years before the war, was expressing the general disquiet over the continually spreading tide of emigration into eastern Galicia. There, in his view, "the [Polish-speaking] emigration disease takes on truly catastrophic proportions." Like a number of his contemporaries, he felt that the continued rate of Polish-speaking emigration from that area would in time result in Galicia becoming a Ukrainian country.[64]

In this climate of opinion, Polish historians and statisticians, like their German counterparts in the Eastern Marches, increasingly became manpower conscious when considering the problem of emigration.[65] The case of Wladyslaw Studnicki may serve as an example of a social democrat become nationalist. He saw the national strength and the possibility of regaining independence directly contingent upon the quantity of its citizens.

> . . . as long as western Galicia and the Kingdom are more densely populated than Prussian Poland, any efforts to annex them to Prussia, wholly or in part, must result only in the de-Germanization of Prussian Poland because of the latter's lesser density of population. . . .

At the same time, the greater density of population in Russian and Austrian Poland ". . . precludes their undermining by way of German colonization." Finally, ". . . when we think of armed conflict [in the cause of national independence] in the near or more distant future, it is important for us to consider how many hands the Polish people have . . . their potential strength."[66] In this general atmosphere, increasingly voices were raised advocating a revival of the historical direction of colonization and resettlement of Polish-speaking elements: "internal colonization" into the ethnically mixed eastern districts of both Russian Poland and Galicia.[67] Unwittingly perhaps, the rhetoric of the *Hakata* was being assimilated into the ideology of the new nationalism.

To the degree that these currents of nationalism were conjoined with the increasing momentum for industrialization, the former mercantilistic views of population gained renewed currency in the years immediately preceding the war. The emigrant was again regarded as an economic unit of value lost to the national economy and the existence of a surplus of population as auspicious factors for the industrial development of the country. The discussions and deliberations of the Fifth Congress of Polish Jurists and Economists in 1912, to a degree, seem to sustain this view. Where the subject of emigration loomed large on the agenda of their deliberations in the past, the congress of 1912 was exclusively concerned with industrialization. The only discussions approaching the subject of emigration had to do primarily with the question of labor supply as it related to the main concern of industrial development. Because the subject of industrialization preempted all other discussions, even the question of labor supply was insufficiently discussed — in the view of some participants. In summary, emigration was only peripherally mentioned in conjunction with the domestic labor supply which, in turn, was only discussed in conjunction with their main preoccupation: industrialization.[68] It would seem that a full circle had been completed. Like the ruling gentry in the initial stages of emigration in the second half of the nineteenth century, emigration when considered at all, was considered within the context of the main concern: a cheap and abundant supply of labor. As in the past, the aggressive bourgeois used the dogma of "national interest" as their rationale.

Polish emigrants abroad, within the parochial definition of nationality, were generally regarded in a rather paternalistic manner as the "enormous proportion of Poles who live in the 'diaspora' outside the territory of ancient Poland," — a national calamity directly resulting from the political violation of Poland by the partitioning powers. These causes would inevitably be removed by a politically independent Poland.[69] Usually circumspect scholars, drawn into the spirit of the crusade, tended to invest national self-determination with millennial promise.[70]

*   *   *

To a degree, these attitudes on emigration and population carried over into the post-war period and continued to involve writers in apparent contradictions. Szawleski, in a sense, represented an example of the post-war scholarship on emigration. Though he could not have been unaware of the importance of the world-wide immigration restrictions on the economy of Poland,[71] he continued to affirm that the passive policy of the partitioning powers toward pre-war emigration contributed to the economic and national debilitation of Poland:

... [The] advantageous aspects of emigration balance only slightly as against the losses. ... In the light of historical and statistical data it is an indisputable fact that the planless pre-war emigration is one of the reasons why the Second Republic today [1927] is not yet a sufficiently vigorous organism. ... .[72]

Despite his apparent concurrence with the representations his government was making on behalf of revising its quota allotments upwards,[73] he continued to deplore the economic loss sustained by the country by the loss of its most vigorous elements — a loss attributed to the delinquency of the partitioning powers[74] — though he conceded elsewhere that the postwar Franco-Polish immigration convention was essentially a "paper document" and that the Germans continued to recruit Polish workers freely while the Polish authorities satisfied themselves by pronouncing it illegal.[75]

Elsewhere he reiterated the delinquency of the consular establishments of the German, Russian and Austrian authorities in their responsibilities to the pre-war Polish emigrants.[76] By 1927, however, himself a one-time vice-consul in New York, he was moved to conclude that:

Today our "eyes and ears" abroad are predominantly blind and deaf. We still have an abundance of paper dignitaries, full of concern about automobiles, fashionably cut clothes . . . , hiding behind this facade their lack of knowledge. . . .[77]

His interest in the changing demographic configuration of the country, as before the war, continued to be primarily directed at the changing proportion of lingual or "ethnic" components of the country. Thus, he continued to deplore permanent overseas emigration as a fatal blood-letting which would ultimately sap the national vigor of the country. In line with this point of view, he continued to express approbation of the comparatively high fecundity ratio of Polish women — a phenomenon which was exalted as "a physiological characteristic of the Polish race,"[78] in spite of the generally accepted agreement on that country's demographic disequilibrium, especially in the rural districts.

Others more or less shared the same views. Okolowicz continued to criticize the lack of control over emigration prior to the war.[79] Caro, writing in the 1920's, reiterated his position before the war when he stated:

We should not permit emigration, especially permanent emigration, from our country. When, before the great war, masses of our peasants were forced to emigrate to other parts of the world and place their labors and efforts at the disposal of foreign countries — this was the shame of our people.[80]

Daszynska-Golinska still spoke of the pre-war migration to Germany as "strengthening the economic force of the enemy"[81] and, citing the researches of German economists like Wilhelm Roscher, maintained that a strict correlation existed between the declining rate of natural increases of the population and the decline and fall of nations.[82]

The deepening depression of the thirties, however, had a salutary effect on the thinking of a number of writers on the subject of emigration. Not only were the restricted postwar outlets further delimited but a number of emigrant-aliens abroad, especially in France, were forced to return to Poland.[83] In these circumstances, the economics of emigration were exposed to closer scrutiny. The *Peasant Memoirs* published by The Institute for Social Studies *(Instytut Gospodarstwa Spolecznego)* in 1935 unequivocally proclaimed the progressive decline in the material conditions of the peasantry as compared to the progressive improvement of their conditions in the pre-war years.[84] Others saw a similar decline of the material condition of the Jewish population in the inter-war period.[85] At least one historian of the industrial development of Galicia stated that the comparatively rapid industrial development of that part of Poland in the decade before the war was in a large measure due to the increased purchasing power of the rural population which, in turn, was largely the result of the inflow of capital resulting from emigration.[86]

Still another perceived the relation between the growth of rightist and leftist political currents, the economically deteriorating conditions in inter-war Poland and the absence of emigration outlets for the surplus population. Upon examining and analyzing an imposing volume of writings and studies of pre-war and inter-war rural life, Zabko-Potopowicz found that, as regards political ideology, the peasants, as a social and economic group, were disposed to enter into harmonious political cooperation with the gentry and clergy in the years preceding the war when their material conditions were progressively improving. This ideological-politial rapport, however, was shattered in the inter-war period which marked their progressive material decline. As a result, a variety of radical political orientations became increasingly manifest.[87]

Jozef Poniatowski, more than any other, vigorously criticized the older, nationalistic rationale on emigration. On the basis of rather involved and complicated premises, that author estimated that between eight and nine million of the total population engaged in agriculture in 1935 could be regarded as surplus. Over and above this, there was also a surplus of rural population not actively engaged in agriculture, though their number was impossible to estimate.[88] This, in his opinion, represented between a third and a half of the total productive labor potential in agriculture which was not necessary to the effective exploitation of the agricultural resources available in that country. Moreover, this segment of the rural population not only did not contribute to the increase of the aggregate income of the nation but, by contributing to the consumption of the total income, was reducing the total product of the nation.[89]

The ideal alternative, he conceded, would have been to incorporate this surplus population into an expanding economy. Such an expanding economy would have included the intensification of agriculture and the industrialization of the country as a whole. Optimum intensification of agriculture, however, was especially contingent upon surplus productivity and the availability of capital. The former was negated by the surplus population and, in turn, the decline in agricultural profits impeded capital accumulation and, therefore, intensification.[90]

The same sort of process was militating against the industrialization of the country. The capitalization of industry could have as its source either foreign increment or domestic accumulations. The former, however, inevitably entailed a sacrifice in national integrity and the latter was almost impossible as long as the per capita income of the nation barely permitted marginal existence.[91]

The alternative then, as he saw it, was either emigration or reduction of the accelerating natural increases of the population. As a means of resolving the problem of overpopulation, Poniatowski conceded that a case could be made for the exponents of birth control[92] as against emigration — an economic argument — or those who hold that economic development is possible in spite of overpopulation. However, those authorities who regarded emigration as both harmful to the nation and necessary, that is to say, a "necessary evil," appeared to be lacking in consistency:

> I judge, that they mean to say that they would rather that there was neither emigration nor the unfavorable conditions that are the cause of it. Actually, however, such a position says nothing. The wringing of

hands over an imagined "loss" would be superfluous if we took under consideration the fact that emigration only replaced another regulator of overpopulation — an increased rate of mortality.[93]

Basing his findings upon the statistical compilations of Buzek, Grabowski and others, he reiterated the thesis that pre-war emigration increased rather than decreased the natural increase of the population — not because of increased birth rate but rather because of the decline in mortality.[94] To him, the correlation between emigration and the decline in mortality seemed as unquestionable as the direct correlation between overpopulation and the lack of credit facilities for economic expansion.[95] He was one of the earliest to realize the futility of regulating the volume and direction of emigration as an instrument of politics. Speaking of the experience of postwar Poland, he concluded that in the exchange of population, as in the exchange of goods, the advantage normally lay with the importing rather than the exporting nation.[96]

Notes

INTRODUCTION

1. Though either the terms "historical Poland" or "ethnographic Poland" can be said to be of questionable validity and exactitude, they are intended to correspond generally with territorial boundaries of Poland after the first partitioning in 1772. The territorial delineations of this study were dictated by political-administrative organization that prevailed during the period covered.
2. Appendix A.
3. Appendix C.
4. Appendix B.

CHAPTER ONE

1. Jozef Feldman, in his comprehensive study of the influence of the "Polish Question" on the diplomatic policy of Bismarck, first published in 1937, is one of the principal exponents of this point of view. I have leaned heavily on this work both as a source and guide in the historical evolution of German nationalism which expressed itself in the immigration and emigration policy of that government in the second half of the nineteenth and the early twentieth century. I have used the second, revised edition, *Bismarck a Polska* (Krakow: 1947).
2. *Ibid.,* 49, 50, 51, 54–55, 80, 81, 302, in particular, and the first six sections, in general.
3. Already in 1854 Bismarck was aware of the fact that the reestablishment of an independent Polish state was less important to Austria than either to Prussia or Russia. Galicia, outside the natural frontiers of Austria, was not as crucial to Austria as Poznan to Prussia. Hans Rothfels, *Bismarck und der Osten. Eine Studie zum Problem des Nationalstaates* (Leipzig: 1934), 42.
4. Georg Heinrich Pertz and Hans Delbruck, *Das Leben des Feldmarschalls Grafen Neithardt von Gneisenau* (Berlin: 1880), Vol. V, 17 and ff.; Karl von Clausewitz, *Politische Schriften und Briefe* (München: 1922), 233 and ff.; Leopold Gerlach, *Denkwürdigkeiten* (Berlin: 1891–1892), 11, 201; and others, cited in Feldman, *op. cit.,* 52–53, 86, 105 ff. See also, Rothfels, *op. cit.,* 20.
5. Ryszard Spazier, *Historja powstania narodu polskiego w r. 1830 i 1831* (Krakow: 1833), tom. 1; Jozef Feldman, *Sprawa polska w roku 1848* (Krakow: 1933), rozdz. 1–2; Heinrich von Poschinger, *Preussens auswärtige*

Politik, 1850–1858 (Berlin: 1902), Vol. II, 152, 317; R. H. Lord, "Bismarck and Russia in 1863," *The American Historical Review* (October, 1923), Vol. XXIX, No. 1, 24–48; Jozef Feldman, *Mocarstwa wobec powstania styczniowego* (Krakow: 1929), passim.

6. Richard Wonser Tims, *Germanizing Prussian Poland* (New York: 1941), 17.

7. Johannes Behrendt, *Die polnische Frage und das oesterreichische-deutsche Bündnis 1885 bis 1887* (Berlin: 1927), 26; Alfred von Waldersee, *Denkwürdigkeiten.* . . (Berlin: 1923), 1, 219, 223, 301, 303; Pawel Popiel, *Pamietniki* (Krakow: 1927), 247 ff.; Boleslaw Limanowski, *Szermierze wolnosci* (Krakow: 1911), 274.

8. Chlodwig von Hohenlohe-Schillingsfürst, *Denkwürdigkeiten* . . . (Leipzig: 1906), II, 343. (English translation edited by George W. Chrystal, 1906, 2 vols.).

9. Feldman, *Bismarck a Polska,* sect. 7, 268 ff. Rothfels emphasizes this community of interest by correlating the *Kulturkampf* with its Russian counterpart against the Polish Catholic Church in general and the Uniate clergy in particular. *Op. cit.,* 44. In his memoirs the Chancellor explicitly affirmed the essentially anti-Polish intent of the *Kulturkampf:* "The inauguration of the *Kulturkampf* was predominantly motivated, as far as I was concerned, by its Polish aspect." Later, in Jena in 1892, he remarked ". . . we could have dispensed with the *Kulturkampf* if it was not for the Polish Question which was intimately tied with it." Manfred Laubert, *Die preussische Polenpolitik von 1772–1914* (Krakau: 1942), 142. That the lingual assimilation, implicit in the school law of 1873 was primarily dictated by considerations of national security is manifest by his corresponding attitude toward the lingual assimilation of the Alsatians in 1870 at which time he called the strong emphasis on the use of the German language by the Alsatians a "professorial idea" calculated to impose a glaze of Germanism on that population. Rothfels, *op. cit.,* 19–20.

10. Feldman, *op. cit.,* 61 ff. See also Lillian Parker Wallace, *The Papacy and European Diplomacy, 1869–1878* (Chapel Hill: 1948), 189, 204, 212, 231 and chapters 6 and 7.

11. Kazimierz Zimmermann, *Frederyk Wielki i jego kolonizacja rolna na ziemiach polskich* (Poznan: 1915), I, p. viii, et seq.; Max Bär, *Westpreussen unter Friedrich dem Grossen* (Leipzig: 1909), II, 50, 54, 76, 339, 508, 591; Max Lehmann, *Preussen und die katholische Kirche* (Leipzig: 1893), VI, 349. Flottwell's nationality policy was one of peaceful coexistence. When the government sponsored a program of parcelation it was, with minor exceptions, predicated on the participation of both the German and Polish-speaking elements, though it was very restrictive as far as the Polish *Grossgrundbesitzer* was concerned. Laubert, *op. cit.,* 74–76. It is noteworthy that after the revolutionary upheavals in Krakow and Poznan in 1846 the Russian ambassador in Berlin expressed regrets that Frederick William IV apparently was unaware of the nationalistic implications of the upheavals. Rather than the comparatively liberal policies of Frederick William IV he would have preferred a more stringent policy of Germanization. Rothfels, *op. cit.,* 43.

12. For evidences of departure from cosmopolitan-idealistic concept of state from 1815 and thereafter, see Heinrich L. Koppelmann, *Nation, Sprache und Nationalismus* (Leiden: 1956), 210 ff.

13. Although the expulsion order was construed by the Polish elements as levelled exclusively against them, Richard Blanke, basing his conclusions on findings of Helmut Neubach's *Die Ausweisungen von Polen und Juden aus Preussen, 1885–1886* (Wiesbaden, 1967) argues that the expulsions were not exclusively motivated by anti-Polish considerations inasmuch as approximately 30% of the expellees were Jewish and that the chief popular pressure for it came from urban, petit-bourgeois interests resentful mainly of alien-Jewish economic competition and that "many local and provincial administrators in the east . . . were enthusiastic proponents of expulsion because they expected that this would rid them of politically-active, left-leaning Jewish traders and artisans." Richard Blanke, "Bismarck and the Prussian Polish Policies of 1886," *Journal of Modern History* (Chicago), Vol. 45, no. 2, June 1973, 215–216.

14. Heinrich von Treitschke, *Politics* (New York: 1916), I, 269 ff. (Translated from the German by Blanche Dugdale and Torben de Bille, 1916) 2 vols. See also: Moritz Busch, *Our Chancellor* (London: 1884), II, 160 ff.

15. *Stenographische Berichte über die Verhandlungen des Haus der Abgeordneten.* Landtag (Berlin: 1882), 7 February 1882, and *ibid.,* 8 March 1883.

16. Eduard von Hartmann, "Der Ruckgang des Deutschtums," *Die Gegenwart* (Berlin: 1885), Nos. 1 and 2.

17. Friedrich J. Neumann, "Germanisierung oder Polonisierung?" *Jahrbucher fur Nationaloekonomie und Statistik* (Jena: 1883), N.F., VII Band, 457 ff.

18. Albert von Randow, "Die Landesverweisungen aus Preussen und die Erhaltung des Deutschtums an der Ostgrenze," *Jahrbuch fur Gesetzgebung, Verwaltung und Volkswirtschaft im Deutschen Reiche* (Leipzig: 1886), X, 91. On political impact of Randow's demographic researches see: St. Klobukowski, "Roczna emigracja polska," *Ekonomista Polski* (Lwow: 1890), T. I, 215–216. Ludwik Krzywicki likewise recognized the ethnographic significance of the predominantly westward press of emigration and population shifts in central and eastern Europe which were reversing the historic Teutonic press toward the East — into ethnographic boundaries of historical Poland. See his, "Nasze wychodztwo," *Ateneum* (Warszawa: 1901), T. CI, 434–5.

19. Otto von Bismarck, *Die Gesammelten Werke* (Berlin: 1929), XIII, 67, 68. Speeches in Reichstag on March 14, 16, 1885, accusing Polish elements at home and abroad with fomenting "preventive war" with Russia. See also, Feldman, *op. cit.,* 322 ff., 335, 357. In the past he had favored a *Kleindeutschen* point of view because he wanted to preserve Austria-Hungary as a big power in the interest of European equilibrium. Koppelmann, *op. cit.,* 220. Blanke, *op. cit.,* 212–215, seriously questions the pro-Russian motivation of the removal decree, i.e., its *diplomatic* motivation.

20. As early as December 31, 1871, Bismarck had recommended to the Minister of the Interior, Graf zu Eulenburg, the removal of alien Polish elements from the Prussian provinces and especially Poznan charging them with fomenting revolutionary sentiments. This measure, however, was to have been directed against ultramontanist elements: "Jesuits who were drifting around in the province. . . ." Some correspondence from Bismarck to Count Eulenburg in 1872 in *Das neue Deutschland* (Berlin: 1912), cited by Laubert, *op. cit.,* 138 and Feldman, *op. cit.,* 289–290.

21. Tims, *op. cit.,* 116–117. See also, *infra,* ch. I, fn. 60, and ch. II, 25.
22. For public explanation of his action, see Puttkamer's speech in Landtag, on May 6, 1885. *Stenog. Berichte . . . Haus der Abgeordneten. Landtag.,* 1756–1761.
23. Tims, *loc. cit.;* Laubert, *op. cit.,* 143–144; Feldman, *op. cit.,* 322–323; Jozef Buzek, *Historja polityki narodowosciowej rzadu pruskiego wobec polakow* (Lwow: 1909), 188–189, 407–408; Leon Wasilewski, *Nationalities in Pomerania* (Torun: 1934), 27; Stanislaw A. Kempner, *Rozwoj gospodarczy Polski* (Warszawa: 1924), 223, 253; Jozef Okolowicz, *Wychodztwo i osadnictwo polskie przed wojna swiatowa* (Warszawa: 1920), 255; Jan Rutkowski, *Historia gospodarcza Polski* (Poznan: 1950), II, 241; Deputy Jazdzewski in Reichstag, *Stenog. Berichte . . . des Reichstages,* VI per. II sess., 15 January 1886, 526; and Windthorst, *ibid.,* 552. An editorial article in the Krakow publication *Przeglad Powszechny* reported that the proscriptive edict elicited outraged response in large areas of the Polish press there and that, although it was originally aimed at Russian subjects, it soon was applied to Austrian subjects and, indeed, all alien elements. In his view, it was the laboring classes that suffered most grievously since neither long residence nor, even, Prussian military service provided exemption from its strictures. These hardships were magnified when Russian border authorities refused to permit the return of subjects who had been abroad for ten years or more. Apparently, however, some exceptions were made in areas where removals threatened to dangerously diminish local agricultural labor supply. ____, "Z Poznania. Jeszcze o wydaleniach," *op. cit.,* listopad 1885, t. VIII, nr. 23, 304–309. Stanislaw Klobukowski, somewhat later, saw a possible correlation between the removal policy and the emigration fever to Brazil in 1891 which was especially intense from such border areas of Russian Poland as, e.g., Plock province. Since many of the removal victims were originally from those areas and, forced to return there, found themselves landless and without means of support, these circumstances made them particularly susceptible to the promise of free transportation and land in Brazil. See his, "Nowy exodus," *Ateneum* (Warszawa, 1891), t. LXI, 5.
24. *Stenog. Berichte . . . des Reichstages,* 1885–1886, January 15, 1886, 525ff. See also, Laubert, *op. cit.,* 143–144; and Chorazy, "Interpelacja polska w parlamencie niemieckiem," *Niwa* (Warszawa: 1885), R. XIV, t. XXVIII, zesz. 264, 923–934. Blanke makes a telling case for the idea that Bismarck, from the beginning, knew that he was not doing Russia a favor by his removal policy because ". . . long negotiations had been necessary to get even the reluctant approval of the Russian government for his expulsion measures." *Op. cit.,* 213. Blanke's thesis seems to be reinforced by the fact that Bismarck's protectionist policy on cereal grains, begun in 1879 and augmented in 1885, was viewed as having grievous consequences on the agricultural economy of Russian Poland, and, as such, could hardly be regarded as an amicable gesture to the Russian government. See, for example, Ch., "Za pol miesiaca. Przeglad polityczny," *Niwa* (Warszawa: 1885), R. XIV, t. XXVII, zesz. 256, 295–307; *ibid.,* zesz. 257, 385–389.
25. Buzek, *op. cit.,* 188; Feldman, *loc. cit.;* Laubert, *op. cit.,* 144, and Julian B. Marchlewski, *Stosunki spoleczno-ekonomiczne pod panowaniem pruskiem* (Warszawa: 1903), 325 and fn. The editor of the Warsaw publication *Niwa* remarked upon the unanimity of outrage of both Polish and Russian

press to this cavalier procedure and clamored for appropriate reprisals. When the imperial *ukaz* of 12 (24) May 1887, which prohibited foreigners to buy, lease or operate rural land *(nieruchomosc wiejska)*, was published it was construed by Polish press as being among its other motives, a Russian response to the Prussian removal policy. *Chorazy,* "Sprawy biezace," *op. cit.,* R. XIV (1885), t. XXVIII, 463–467, 527–529; *ibid.,* R. XV (1886), t. XXIX, 273–275 and *ibid.,* R. XVI (1887), t. XXXI, 941–947. For pertinent remarks by Heinrich Rickert, deputy from Danzig, in the lower house of the Prussian parliament, see *Stenog. Berichte . . . Haus der Abgeordneten Landtag.,* 1886, III Band, 1360. See also, *infra,* 40.

26. Feldman, *op. cit.,* 327–329.

27. *Ibid.,* 324–325. Blanke, exploring new Prussian archival sources, especially the records of the meetings of the Prussian Council of Ministers, presents a well-documented and well-reasoned case for the thesis that the opposition coalition which had developed in the *Reichstag* against Bismarck on the issue of the expulsion directive of 1885 was the chief motivating reason for his embarkation on the more militantly nationalistic course which led to the *Ansiedlungsgesetz* of 1886. See his *op. cit.,* 211–239.

28. Ludwig Bernhard, *Die Polenfrage* (Munich and Leipzig: 1920), 116. Witold Lewicki reported that at the conference of "der Verein fur Socialpolitik" held in Frankfurt a. M. in Sept. 24–25, 1886, Sombart, Schmoller and others close to the National Liberals enthusiastically endorsed a government subsidized policy for the colonization of Germans on lands bought up from Poles in the Eastern Marches. See his, "Parcelacya w Galicyi jako objaw spoleczny," *Ekonomista Polski* (Lwow: 1890), T. I, 120–121. As a party, the National Liberals favored the establishment of medium-sized landholds (Rentenguter) as against the creation of dwarf-sized landholds — the *Erbpacht* idea. Blanke, *op. cit.,* 227ff.

29. *Verein für Forderung des Deutschtum in den Ostmarken,* founded in November 3, 1894, for the relocation in Prussia of Germans living abroad. Laubert, *op. cit.,* 155. See, *infra,* 20ff.

30. Randow, *loc. cit.*

31. *Stenog. Berichte . . . Haus der Abgeordneten. Landtag.,* 22 February 1886, 686ff.

32. Laubert, *op. cit.,* 136.

33. Excerpt from Tiedemann's diary in Bernhard, *op. cit.,* 118.

34. *Stenog. Berichte . . . Haus der Abgeordneten. Landtag.,* January 14, 1886, 3–4.

35. Bernhard, *loc. cit.;* Laubert, *op. cit.,* 144–145.

36. *Stenog. Berichte . . . Haus der Abgeordneten. Landtag.,* 28 January 1886, 159–163.

37. *Ibid.,* 29 January 1886, 197–205.

38. *Ibid.,* 28 January 1886, 186. See also, *ibid.,* 182–187, 189, 190; 29 January 1886, 223; and 30 January 1886, 259.

39. *Ibid.,* 30 January 1886, 225–228.

40. *Ibid.,* 29 January 1886, 213–216.

41. *Stenographische Berichte über die Verhandlungen des Haus der Abgeordneten. Herrenhaus* (Berlin: 1886), 27 February 1886, 80–81.

42. *Ibid.,* 27 February 1886, 81–83, 98.

43. *Ibid.,* 27 February 1886, 86–89. A representative of the new currents in

that body was Hans Hugo von Kleist-Retzow who maintained that "... there is likely no other nationality that possesses the colonizing abilities of the Germans. The whole of northern Germany in which we now live was thus acquired. I and my forefathers, of Slavic antecedents, became German and we owe all this to such a colonization." *Ibid.,* 27 February 1886, 92.

44. *Stenog. Berichte . . . Haus der Abgeordneten. Landtag,* 28 January 1886, 164–175; 29 January 1886, 206–212.

45. Lucius von Ballhausen, *Bismarck-Erinnerungen* (Stuttgart and Berlin: 1920), 336, 341, 347, 349, 393 ff. Here again Blanke points out the disparity between Bismarck's public utterances and his private commitments. Though publicly he seemed to favor the creation of medium-sized, independent farmholds out of estates as embodied in the *Rentenguter* idea of the National Liberals, in private correspondence and conversations, he seemed, in fact, to favor the *Erbpacht* idea of creation of small-holding tenant farmers — an idea congenial to the interests of estate owners in their growing need of a cheap, resident supply of agricultural labor. See his, *op. cit.,* 227 ff.

46. Feldman, *op. cit.,* 350–352; Laubert, *op. cit.,* 135–136; Hans Rothfels, "Bismarck, das Ansiedlungsgesetz und die deutsch-polonische Gegenwartslage," in his *Ostraum, Preussentum und Reichsgedanke* (Leipzig: 1935), 95.

47. Johannes Penzler, *Fürst Bismarck nach seiner Entlassung* (Leipzig: 1898), VI, 476. See also, Feldman, *op. cit.,* 354–355. Blanke contends that despite Bismarck's public statements to the contrary, he had the *total* Polish population in mind throughout the deliberations on the *Ansiedlungsgesetz* of 1886, i.e., including the peasantry; that his strong support of Kulturminister Gossler's supplementary anti-Polish measures — aimed at gentry, clergy and peasants alike — place Bismarck in the camp of the Treitschkes, Hartmanns, *et al.* Blanke, *op. cit.,* 234–236.

48. Marchlewski, *op. cit.,* 314 and Rutkowski, *op. cit.,* II, 309. For complete text of the law of 1886 see, Prussia. *Gesetz-Sammlung für die königliche preussischen Staaten, 1806 bis 1886* (Berlin: 1887), 197.

49. Marchlewski, *op. cit.,* 314–315 and Rutkowski, *op. cit.,* II, 310.

50. Marchlewski, *op. cit.,* 318. See also, Laubert, *op. cit.,* 146; Tims, *op. cit.,* 54, 154. By 1913 the average price per hectare was 1820 M. Rutkowski, *op. cit.,* II, 310.

51. That the policies of removal and German colonization in the Eastern Marches, initiated and implemented by Bismarck, were responsible for creating a counter-nationalism which, for the first time began to reach down to the masses of the Polish-speaking elements, does not seem to have occurred to the former Chancellor. Indeed, the impact of his measures in all sectors of pre-war Poland was so intense that it may well have prompted the first challenges to the prevailing idea of "organic work" and accommodation with the partitioning powers. See, for example, T. J. Choinski, "Ze stosunkow Poznanskich," *Niwa* (Warszawa: 1885), Rok. XIV, Tom XXVIII, zesz. 264, 877–884, and Ch., "Sprawy biezace," *Niwa* (Warszawa: 1886), R. XV, T. XXIX, zesz. 268, 273–275.

52. Kempner, *op. cit.,* 222–223, 245; Tims, *op. cit.,* 14–15; A. Donimirski, "Parcelacya," *Biblioteka Warszawska* (1895), T. 220, 319–320; Marchlewski, *op. cit.,* 341, 343, 344, 345–346; Rutkowski, *op. cit.,* II, 311–312; Laubert, *op. cit.,* 148–150. In this nationalistic confrontation among the serious debits (on the Polish side) some writers considered peasant emigration to the United

States and the emigration of intelligentsia to other sectors of historical Poland as an unwarrantable "blood letting" which was weakening the national effort in Prussian Poland. See, for example, Jozef Milewski, "Ze stosunkow poznanskich," *Niwa* (Warszawa: 1886), R. XV, t. XXIX, zesz. 273, 621.

53. Marchlewski, *op. cit.,* 341.

54. Tims, *op. cit.,* 111–112, 113. See Appendix A.

55. Marchlewski, *op. cit.,* 343; Kempner, *op. cit.,* 245. Up to 1892, many Polish gentry availed themselves of the offices of the *Ansiedlungskommission* to dispose of their land. After that, progressively more land was bought by that agency from German landowners. Laubert, *op. cit.,* 145. The Polish landed gentry frequently came under criticism, especially from the Socialist and Populist press. The former held that, as in the days of the Franco-Prussian war when the Polish gentry encouraged the peasants to join the Prussian ranks — and march off to battle against democratic France to the martial notes of "Jeszcze Polska nie zginela" —, so the gentry availed themselves of the bounties and emoluments provided by the colonization fund and, like their equally politically privileged Junker counterparts, both were equal beneficiaries of those government subsidies. While the Polish gentry addressed themselves vehemently to the "national cause" and enjoined "national unity" in Poznan province, they manifested a singular disinclination to support like activities in Silesia. This, in the author's view, was largely because the national issue in Silesia was parallel and identifiable with the class issue — German land and mine owners versus Polish peasants and workers — a parallel and identification that the Polish estate owners had no wish to "import" into Poznan province. ____, "Polska polityka w zaborze pruskim," *Przedswit* (Geneva), R. VII, nr. 22, 23, 24, 31 grudnia 1888, 1–4. A. W. Warski, writing somewhat later in the Populist publication *Glos,* bitterly indicted the Polish gentry which dominated the Polish caucus in both the Reich and the Prussian parliaments. In spite of their professed mandate to stand guard over its "thousand year culture," they generally aligned themselves with the conservative Junker parties in both houses. He called them "Polish Junkers" who traumatically resisted any political alliances with the leftists in either the cause of social justice or ethnic equity. A. W. [Warski], "Hakatyzm i solidarnosc polsko-pruska," *Glos* (Warszawa), R. XVI, nr. 7, 3 (16) luty 1901, 89–90. He reiterated the same charges subsequently when he adjudged the call of the Polish gentry in Prussian Poland for "national unity" as part and parcel of their duplicity and cynicism. He held that the Prussian politics of Hakatism redounded to the economic interests of all Junkers — Prussian and Polish alike. He cautioned that, to the degree the populist *(ludowce)* press in Poznan concurred with this spurious politics of "national unity," they were playing into the hands of the Polish gentry. A. W. [Warski], "Tryumfy hakatyzmu i szlachty polskiej," *op. cit.,* R. XVII, nr. 38, 7 (20) wrzes. 1902, 580–581. Jozef Milewski, neither a populist nor socialist, had earlier said that the Polish population in the Eastern Marches, confronted with "the storm clouds of aggressive Teutonism" found themselves without vigorous or effective spokesmen or champions in the Reich parliament. See his, "Ze stosunkow poznanskich," *Niwa* (Warszawa: 1886), R. XV, t. XXIX, zesz. 273, 605ff. As late as 1911, Jozef Frejlich, addressing himself to the political orientation of the Polish emigrant concentrations in Rhineland-Westphalia, maintained that because of the religious or semi-religious structure and leadership of their

organizations, their political weight inclined heavily toward the Catholic Centrum. Since the Centrists, as a party, followed a policy that accorded with the German policy of Germanization and assimilation, it worked, in fact, against the interests of the Poles. Also, they (the Poles) were thereby recruited into the Centrist's campaign against the German socialist movement and parties. In the home province of Poznan this had the effect of strengthening the conservative politics of the Polish large landowners against the growing currents of peasant populism. See his, "Polskie wychodztwo zarobkowe w obwodzie przemyslowem westfalsko-nadrenskiem," *Czasopismo prawnicze i ekonomiczne* (Krakow: 1911), R. XII, 60–65, 86.

56. Marchlewski, *op. cit.,* 347–350; A. Donimirski, "Kolonizacja i spolki rolnicze," *Niwa* (Warszawa: 1888), R. XVII, t. XXXIV, zesz. 328, 241–252.

57. A. Donimirski, "Parcelacya," *Biblioteka Warszawska* (1895), T. 220, 315–316.

58. Laubert, *op. cit.,* 144.

59. Donimirski, *op. cit.,* 315.

60. Tims, *op. cit.,* 16–20, 111–112, 116–117; Buzek, *op. cit.,* 189. Although the removal policy inaugurated in 1885 was not abrogated to the degree of permitting the permanent settlement of alien Polish elements in Prussia, for practical purposes, the expulsion of these elements ceased in 1891. Laubert, *op. cit.,* 152.

61. For complete text of the law see: Prussia. *Übersicht über die Geschäftstätigkeit des preussischen Hauses der Abgeordneten in der III. Session der 17. Legislaturperiode vom 12/XI/1890 bis zum 20/VI/1891* (Berlin: 1891), 592–613.

62. Donimirski, *op. cit.,* 314; Tims, *op. cit.,* 111–112; Rutkowski, *op. cit.,* II, 310–311.

63. Tims, *op. cit.,* 54.

64. Rutkowski, *op. cit.,* II, 311.

65. Zdzislaw Ludkiewicz, "Ziemia i ludnosc rolnicza," in Stanislaw A. Kempner (ed.), *Dzieje gospodarcze Polski porozbiorowej* (Warszawa: 1920), II, 102; Rutkowski, *op. cit.,* II, 311. In connection with the *Rentengutsgesetzgebung* of June 27, 1890 and July 7, 1891, a measure of cooperation was affected by the Polish *Bank Ziemski* and the General Commission. The former received government credits and sold about 40,000 hectares of its properties to the latter. This collaboration was terminated shortly thereafter when the General Commission refused to acquiesce to the formation of smaller farmsteads which, presumably, would be more accessible to Polish settlers. Laubert, *op. cit.,* 153. For a complete table by provinces and sizes of leaseholds established annually by the General Commission under the provisions of this law during the period 1891–1911, see: Prussia. *Verhandlungen des königlichen Landes-Ökonomie-Kollegiums* (Berlin: 1913), III Tagund der XII Sitzungsperiode, 168.

66. *Berliner Neuste Nachrichten,* October 2, 1894, cited by Tims, *op. cit.,* 30.

67. *Ibid.,* 16–29.

68. *Ibid.,* 56.

69. *Ibid.,* 44–45.

70. *Ibid.,* 250–251.

71. *Ibid.,* 55–56. Though the larger part of the German population was

probably not interested in this organization — its foremost basis of support being the large landowners, officials, teachers and clergy — it nevertheless helped considerably in creating a united German front in the Eastern Marches. Laubert, *op. cit.*, 155.
72. Tims, *op. cit.*, 57.
73. *Ibid.*, 62.
74. *Ibid.*, 256-260.
75. F. S. Krysiak, *Hinter den Kulissen des Ostmarken-Vereins* (Posen: 1919), 159-164, cited by Tims, *op. cit.*, fn. p. 152. That the Polish emigrant earnings from abroad — but especially from the Rhineland-Westphalia industrial areas — were to become the determining economic factor in "the conflict for the land" in the Eastern Marches was apparently unanticipated by these elements. See *infra*, 151 and 154 ff.
76. Richard Böckh, "Die Verschiebung der Sprachverhältnisse in Posen und Westpreussen," *Preussische Jahrbucher* (Berlin: 1894), LXXVII Band, 424-436.
77. Marchlewski, *op. cit.*, 314-315.
78. For text of this supplement to the law of 1886 see: Prussia. *Gesetz-Sammlung fur die königlichen preussischen Staaten*, 1898 (Berlin: 1899), 63. For a discussion of the criticism against the colonization program by Delbruck and Stumpfe, see Laubert, *op. cit.*, 147.
79. Marchlewski, *op. cit.*, 317-318; Tims, *op. cit.*, 123-124. For text of supplementary law of 1902 see: Prussia. *Gesetz-Sammlung fur die königlichen preussischen Staaten, 1902* (Berlin: 1903), 234.
80. Tims, *op. cit.*, 124-128.
81. *Ibid.*, 128. For text of supplementary law of 1904 see: Prussia. *Gesetz-Sammlung für die königlichen preussischen Staaten, 1904* (Berlin: 1905), 227-234.
82. Tims, *op. cit.*, 128-129.
83. *Ibid.*, 129-130.
84. *Ibid.*, 131, 155-166.
85. *Ibid.*, 163.
86. For text of law of 1908 see: Prussia. *Preussische Gesetzsammlung, 1908* (Berlin: 1909), 29-34.
87. Feldman, *op. cit.*, 345, 352; Tims, *op. cit.*, 166-179.

CHAPTER TWO

1. See *supra*, 9.
2. Tims, *op. cit.*, 115. The number of people residing in Westphalia province at various times who were born in Poznan province were: 1,007 in 1871; 4,225 in 1880; 13,875 in 1890; 57,347 in 1900 and 83,873 in 1907. Those born in Poznan and living in Rheinland province numbered: 1,535 in 1871; 3,244 in 1880; 7,562 in 1890; 28,269 in 1900 and 46,915 in 1907. Those born in West Prussia but living in Westphalia were: 5,405 in 1880; 14,569 in 1890; 33,832 in 1900 and 43,551 in 1907. Residents of Rheinland province, born in West Prussia, numbered: 4,450 in 1880; 9,717 in 1890; 22,248 in 1900 and 35,736 in 1907. A comparable volume of emigration from the two eastern provinces was also apparent during the periods mentioned to the province of

Brandenburg and to the *Stadtkreis* Berlin. The volume of emigration from the two eastern provinces to the two western provinces was exceeded only by the emigrants from East Prussia which almost equalled the combined total of emigration from the two former provinces. *Zeitschrift des königlichen preussischen statistischen Landesamtes* (Berlin: 1907), Jahrgang XLVII, 38–39 and *Statistik des deutschen Reiches* (Berlin: 1910), Band 210, Abt. IX, Teil I, 68 ff.

For other and more detailed statistical compilations on the various movements of population in the eastern districts see: Heinz Rogmann, *Die Bevölkerungsentwicklung im preussischen Osten in den letzten hundert Jahren* (Berlin: 1937), *passim*. See Appendix A.

3. Several critics of Puttkamer's removal directive of 1885 based their arguments on precisely these economic grounds. See, for example, Spahn, Windthorst, Lyskowski, *et al.,* in *Stenog. Berichte . . . Haus der Abgeordneten. Landtag,* 6 May 1885, 1752 ff., and Jazdzewski, Liebkrecht, *et al.,* in *Stenog. Berichte . . . des Reichstag,* 15–16 January 1886, 525 ff. See also, Laubert, *op. cit.,* 144.

4. See *supra,* ch. 1, fn. 21 and fn. 60. The newspaper *Kurjer Warszawski* (nr. 3, sobota, 3 styczen 1891, p. 3), under the rubric "Opening of the Border for Workers" reported a telegraphic communique from Berlin that the *Reichsanzeiger* reported that the presidents of the eastern provinces were instructed, via ministerial rescript, to permit the transit of immigrants from the Kingdom and Galicia — especially rural and industrial workers of both sexes and single persons. Families weighted down with children were permitted entry only in exceptional circumstances.

5. Buzek, *op. cit.,* 215; Tims, *op. cit.,* 119. Daszynska-Golinska has the periods of arrival and departure confused in her *Land Reform in Poland* (London: 1921), 16.

6. Tims, *op. cit.,* 116.

7. Okolowicz, *op. cit.,* 255.

8. Georg von Mayr, "Statistik der deutschen Binnenwanderungen," *Schriften des Vereins für Sozialpolitik* (Leipzig: 1893), Bd. 58.

9. Buzek, *op. cit.,* 215; Tims, *op. cit.,* 185.

10. Buzek, *op. cit.,* 408–409.

11. *Ibid.,* 410 ff.; Daszynska-Golinska, *op. cit.,* 16.

12. Buzek, *op. cit.,* 408–409.

13. *Ibid.,* 407–408; Rutkowski, *op. cit.,* II, 241.

14. Tims, *op. cit.,* 121; Szawleski, *Kwestja emigracji w Polsce* (Warszawa: 1927), 54. Okolowicz mistakenly dates its origin to 1902. See his *Wychodztwo. . . ,* 264 and "Wychodztwo" in St. Janicki (ed.), *Stosunki rolnicze Krolestwa Kongresowego* (Warszawa: 1918), 112. For details of operations and activities of this organization, including some statistical data, see Leopold Caro and Karl Englisch, *Emigracja i polityka emigracyjna* (Poznan: 1914), 279–294.

15. Tims, *op. cit.,* 117, 122–123; Buzek, *op. cit.,* 410; Marya Balsiger, "Polskie wychodztwo sezonowe do Niemiec," *Srodkowo-europejski zwiazek gospodarczy a Polska* (Krakow: 1916), 97. This aspect of its activities received widespread attention by the nationalistic elements in Poland where it was accused of spreading anti-Polish propaganda and sentiments among the Ukrainian Galicians. See, *e.g.,* F. S. Krysiak, *Hinter den Kulissen des Ostmarken-Vereins* (Posen: 1919), *passim; Polski przeglad emigracyjny* (Kra-

kow: 1911), Nos. 22, 23; *ibid.,* 1914, zesz. 1; an article entitled "Na uslugach Hakaty" in *Gazeta poranna* (Krakow: April 18, 1914); an article entitled "Akcya Ruska przeciw P.T.E.," in *Wiek Nowy* (Krakow: January 22, 1914); an article entitled "Wplywy Pruskie" in *Slowo Polskie* (Warszawa: February 1, 1914); *Czas* (Warszawa: November 20, 1913), and *Kurjer Warszawski* (Warszawa: March 31, 1914). Tims came to the conclusion that this phase of H.K.T. activity "did not bulk large in the whole. . . ." *Op. cit.,* 123.

16. Bronislaw Potocki, writing in the social democratic publication *Krytyka,* urged that if the Polish-speaking elements in Prussian Poland were to benefit from world opinion — because of the forcible policies of Germanization and expropriation — the Poles had better put their own house in order as far as the Ukrainian elements were concerned in Galicia, where the nationalistic discord was sharpening dangerously. See his, "Kwestja ruska w Galicyi i projekt jej zalatwienia," *op. cit.* (Krakow: 1908), R. X, t. I, 129–139.

17. Okolowicz, *Wychodztwo.* . . , 265; Okolowicz, "Wychodztwo" in Janicki (ed.), *op. cit.,* 112; Szawleski, *op. cit.,* 54.

18. Okolowicz, "Wychodztwo," in Janicki (ed.), *op. cit.,* 112.

19. *Die Ostmark* (1900), 46–47, 111 ff., cited by Tims, *op. cit.,* 119 fn. This concern about the "national character" was reiterated by Rudolf von Bitter in his *Handwörterbuch der preussischen Verwaltung* (Leipzig: 1906) in an article entitled "Ausländischer Arbeiter."

20. Tims, *op. cit.,* 119.

21. Buzek, *op. cit.,* 411.

22. Karl Englisch, "Die oesterreichische Auswanderungstatistik," *Statistische Monatsschrift* (Wien: February–March 1914), 130. See also, Balsiger, *op. cit.,* 98.

23. Szawleski, *op. cit.,* 54–55; Balsiger, *op. cit.,* 95–96; Caro and Englisch, *op. cit.,* 262; Okolowicz, *Wychodztwo.* . . , 271–272. It was not until the outbreak of the war that the Prussian government authorized the *Arbeiterzentrale* as sole agency for this purpose. See Okolowicz, "Wychodztwo" in Janicki (ed.), *op. cit.,* 113.

24. Rutkowski, *op. cit.,* II, 238; Balsiger, *op. cit.,* 97–98; Okolowicz, *Wychodztwo.* . . , 268; Caro and Englisch, *op. cit.,* 279–280 and fn. 2, 301, 355. According to its own statistics, it succeeded in lowering the wage scale of male agricultural workers during the 1907–1911 period. See Okolowicz, *op. cit.,* 271. Similar expressions of opinion were made by Anton Knoke, *Ausländische Wanderarbeiter in Deutschland* (Leipzig: 1911), *passim* and by Drs. Schmidt and Luppe in *Der Arbeitsmarkt* (Berlin: October, 1910). Dr. Luppe expressed the opinion that it had long ceased to be an employment agency and had become an institution for the importation of foreign labor, thus serving exclusively the interests of German employers. In the industries and trades where there was no general lack of labor, it had become an instrument for bringing down the wage scale. Likewise it served to depress wages for agricultural workers by establishing a pattern for low-wage agricultural labor contracts without legal guarantees for the workers.

25. Caro and Englisch, *op. cit.,* 279, 282, 283; Balsiger, *op. cit.,* 91; Buzek, *op. cit.,* 413–414; Okolowicz, *op. cit.,* 255–256, 267. Despite this rigid control, some writers maintained that there was a good deal of traffic in false documents. Caro found that during the two-year period of 1908 and 1909 the German authorities succeeded in seizing about 5,000 false *Legitimationskarte.* Caro and Englisch, *op. cit.,* 267, 286. See also Okolowicz, *op. cit.,* 259.

26. *Ibid.,* 266; Szawleski, *op. cit., 55.*
27. Caro and Englisch, *op. cit., 286.*
28. Daszynska-Golinska, *op. cit., 16.*
29. Jozef Buzek, *Poglad na wzrost ludnosci ziem Polskich w wieku 19-tym* (Krakow: 1915), 48.
30. Caro and Englisch, *op. cit.,* 284; Balsiger, *op. cit., 99.*
31. Caro and Englisch, *op. cit.,* 275; Balsiger, *op. cit.,* 99, 102–103; Rutkowski, *op. cit.,* II, 238–239; Okolowicz, *op. cit., 257.* For a reproduction of a typical agricultural labor contract issued by the *Arbeiterzentrale,* see Okolowicz, *op. cit.,* 275–278. To encourage the acquisition of the *Legitimationskarte* at the border station, the charge was two marks at the stations and increased to five marks in the interior of Germany. Caro and Englisch, *op. cit.,* 269.
32. See, for example, petition No. 63 and comments on the subject by Baron Heereman von Zuydwyk, Dr. Ritter (Breslau), Schultz (Lipitz), Richard Vopelius (Sulzbach), *Landgerichtsrath* Schmieding (Dortmund) and Count von Berlepsch in the lower house of the Landtag, 29 April 1891, 2016–2020, and 30 April 1891, 2025 ff., and Karl Gottlieb von Wiedebach and Count Emil von Hohenthal in the upper house, 18 June 1891, 394 ff.
33. Caro and Englisch, *op. cit.,* 275–276; Balsiger, *op. cit.,* 99, 101–102.
34. Aleksander Woycicki, *Dzieje robotnikow przemyslowych w Polsce* (Warszawa: 1929), 178–179; Caro and Englisch, *op. cit.,* 274, 356. Franz Schlegelberger, *Das Landarbeiterrecht* (Berlin: 1907), *passim,* and Edgar Loening, "Das Vereins- und Koalitions-recht der Arbeiter im deutschen Reich," *Verhandlungen der Verein für Sozialpolitik* (Leipzig: 1897), treat the subject quite thoroughly. This factor combined with prevailing lower wages paid agricultural workers was sufficient to dissuade many German industrial workers from augmenting the labor forces in the Eastern Marches. Though the idea of recruiting unemployed industrial workers into the agricultural labor force won some popularity among the conservative gentry, the fear of infiltration of "socialistic ideology" via such workers was sufficient to cause them to abandon it. See Caro and Englisch, *op. cit.,* 261.
35. Leon Papieski, *Emigracya i kolonizacya oraz zadanie polskiej polityki emigracyjnej* (Warszawa: 1918), 68–69; Balsiger, *op. cit.,* 103; Okolowicz, *Wychodztwo. . . ,* 256–257 and fn. 1.
36. See *infra,* 115 ff.
37. The popular term for seasonal immigrants, *Sachsengangerei,* was apparently taken from a monograph of that title by Karl Kaerger published in Berlin in 1890. Its Polish equivalent was *Obiezysasi.*
There are no comprehensive statistics available for the annual migrations from the Kingdom and Galicia to Germany during the period under discussion. The most creditable data, that compiled by the German *Feldarbeiterzentrale,* did not begin until 1907. Even these, however, are not completely accurate since, on the one hand, identification papers were not compulsory in all provinces of the German empire and, on the other, "considerable" numbers of migrants were said to have by-passed these requirements where they were compulsory. Szawleski, *op. cit.,* 53; Okolowicz, *op. cit.,* 257–259; Balsiger, *op. cit.,* 91–92. Prior to that time, statistical estimates were based on the compilations of various agencies of the countries of emigration. The earliest of these were the annual statements of seasonal emigration from Galicia compiled by

local government officials from 1896 until the turn of the century. These, according to creditable evaluations, have been adjudged as decidedly too low because of the disposition of emigrants to leave without notifying local authorities. Buzek, *op. cit.*, 42. Thereafter figures for temporary emigration are available for the Kingdom from statistics compiled by the Warsaw Statistical Committee and the statistical adjunct of the Russian customs bureau. The considerable variance between the comparative data of these two sources renders them both extremely questionable. In any case, they apparently included "temporary" emigrants to all European countries and America as well as those "permanent" emigrants who, for reasons of expediency, classified themselves as "temporary" emigrants. Not included in either category were the sizable numbers of both types of emigrants who departed without notifying the authorities.

The emigration statistics compiled by the Austrian border commissioners at the main border stations in Bogumin, Oswiecim, Szczakow and Cieszyn, beginning in 1902, indicate the same shortcomings and for apparently the same reasons. These discrepancies are especially apparent when they are compared with the statistical data made available by the *Arbeiterzentrale* after 1907. Thus, for example, while 139,953 Galicians were issued *Legitimationskarte* by the German agency, the Austrian border commissioners reported 157,669 "seasonal" emigrants from Galicia that year. Thereafter the disparity increases until in the season 1909/10 the former listed 165,403 immigrants and the latter 309,029; in 1910/11, the former listed 160,285 while the latter set the figure at 330,520 "seasonal" emigrants. Okolowicz, *op. cit.*, fn. 1, p. 258; Balsiger, *op. cit.*, 93; Szawleski, *op. cit.*, 52; Englisch, *op. cit.*, February–March 1913, 144. For statistical compilations, from both the Kingdom and Galicia, broken down into lingual groups, based on the data made available by the *Arbeiterzentrale* from 1907 until the outbreak of the war, see: Okolowicz, *op. cit.*, 260–262; Caro and Englisch, *op. cit.*, 285; Buzek, *op. cit.*, 47; Szawleski, *op. cit.*, 53; Balsiger, *op. cit.*, 92; Jacob Lestschinsky, "National Groups in Polish Emigration," *Jewish Social Studies*, Vol. V, No. 2 (April 1943), 102; Zdzislaw Ludkiewicz, *Zagadnienia programu agrarnego a emigracja* (Warszawa: 1929), 7.

CHAPTER THREE

1. Aleksander Woycicki, *Dzieje robotnikow przemyslowych w Polsce* (Warszawa: 1929), 78–79.
2. *Ibid.;* Eugeniusz Boss, "Sprawa robotnicza w Krolestwie Polskiem w okresie Paszkiewiczowskim, 1831–1855," *Rozprawy Historyczne* (Warszawa: 1931), t. X, zesz. 1, 15.
3. Woycicki, *op. cit.*, 79–80.
4. Stanislaw Koszutski, *Rozwoj ekonomiczny Krolestwa Polskiego w ostatniem trzydziestoleciu, 1870–1900* (Warszawa: 1905), 15; Stanislaw A. Kempner, *Rozwoj gospodarczy Polski* (Warszawa: 1924), 109; Feliks Gross, *The Polish Worker; A Study of a Social Stratum* (New York: 1945), 21–22.
5. See, Stanislaw Smolka, *Polityka Lubeckiego przed powstaniem listopadowym* (Krakow: 1907), 2 vols., especially I, 173–214; Jan Zdzitowiecki, *Xiaze-minister Franciszek Xawery Drucki-Lubecki, 1778–1846* (Warszawa:

1948), 307–488, and Edward Strasburger, *Stan rolnictwa polskiego w dobie powojennej, a program ekonomiczny Lubeckiego* (Warszawa: 1915), passim.
6. Woycicki, *op. cit.,* 80. The Prince Minister Lubecki reported in May, 1824, that about 150,000 "pairs of working hands" had arrived from Germany in recent years. Smolka, *op. cit.,* I, 194.
7. Boss, *loc. cit.;* Mieczyslaw Ajzen, "Polityka gospodarcza Lubeckiego," *Rozprawy Historyczne* (Warszawa: 1931), t. X, zesz. 2, 26–27.
8. Woycicki, *op. cit.,* 147–148.
9. Aleksander Woycicki, "Historja rozwoju warstwy robotniczej w czasach nowszych" in Stanislaw A. Kempner (ed.), *Dzieje gospodarcze Polski porozbiorowej w zarysie* (Warszawa: 1920), II, 147.
10. Woycicki, *loc. cit.* See also, J. Weyssenhoff, "Kronika Miesieczna," *Biblioteka Warszawska* (1892), t. 208, 603.
11. Woycicki, *loc. cit.* See also, Leo Klimecki, "Kingdom of Poland," *Polish Encyclopedia* (Fribourg: 1922), Vol. III, Part III, 532, and Gross, *loc. cit.*
12. *Koszutski, op. cit.,* 15–16.
13. *Ibid.,* 18; Jozef Buzek, *Poglad na wzrost ludnosci ziem Polskich w wieku 19-tym* (Krakow: 1915), 19. For concise history of Russian tariff policy from 1850, including the earlier policy which was exceptionally favorable for the growth of industry in Russian Poland, see Marceli Lewy, *Wzajemny stosunek przemyslu Krolestwa Polskiego i Cesarstwa Rosyjskiego przed wojna wszechswiatowa* (Warszawa: 1921), 108–130.
14. Koszutski, *op. cit.,* 19; Kempner, *op. cit.,* 84.
15. Rosa Luxemburg, *Die industrielle Entwicklung Polens* (Leipzig: 1898), 20. See also, Koszutski, *op. cit.,* 121–122; Buzek, *op. cit.,* 19; Kempner, *op. cit.,* 100–102, and Jan Bobrzynski, *Na przelomie Polskiego przemyslu* (Warszawa: 1919), 15ff.
16. Koszutski, *op. cit.,* 111–116, 118–119; Kempner, *op. cit.,* 102.
17. Koszutski, *op. cit.,* 112–116.
18. *Ibid.,* 117–118, 124–128, 129; Kempner, *op. cit.,* 108.
19. Kempner, *op. cit.,* 105.
20. Lewy, *op. cit.,* 107ff., 131–135.
21. For statistical evidence showing the steady proportional development of Russian Poland's industry within the Russian empire and its marked decline after 1900, see *ibid.,* 3–59.
22. *Ibid.,* 60, 61, 62–91, 91–107.
23. Martin Schrag, "The Swiss-Volhynian Mennonite Background," *Mennonite Life* (North Newton, Kansas), October, 1954, IX, no. 4, 158–161. See also, *The Congressional Debates on the Mennonite Immigration from Russia, 1873–1874,* 4, edited by Ernst Correll, a reprint from *Mennonite Quarterly Review,* July, 1946.
24. Henry Maruszczak, "Zmiany w zaludnieniu wojewodztwa lubelskiego w latach 1822–1946," *Annales Universitatis Mariae Curie-Sklodowska* (Lublin: 1949), Sectio B, t. IV, nr. 5, 82, 101, 115.
25. J. Wasowicz, "Z geografji osiedli wiejskich na Wolyniu," *Czasopismo Geograficzne* (Warszawa: 1934), t. XII, zesz. 3–4, 287; Maruszczak, *loc. cit.* See also, J. Wasowicz, "O Polskiej wyspie etnograficznej kolo Zytomierza," *Polski Przeglad Kartograficzny* (Warszawa: grudzien 1926), t. II, nr. 15–16, 186–191.

26. J. K. Plebanski, "Kronika miesieczna," *Biblioteka Warszawska* (1887), t. 187, 113–116. See also *supra*, ch. 1, fn. 25.

27. Jan Bloch, "Ziemia i jej obdluzenie," *Biblioteka Warszawska* (1891), t. 203, 335. Aliens could, of course, become Russian citizens quite easily if they felt that their property holdings made that alternative preferable to, for example, the sale of their landholdings at what they might have considered inequitable prices.

28. Plebanski, *loc. cit.* See also, Chorazy, "Sprawy biezace," *Niwa* (Warszawa: 1887), R. XVI, t. XXXI, zesz. 300, 941–947.

29. Michal Janik, *Dzieje Polakow na Syberii* (Krakow: 1928), 114–115. For the various categories and types of confinement, see Zygmunt Librowicz, *Polacy w Syberii* (Krakow: 1884), 114 ff.

30. Sergiei Maksimov, *Sibir i katorga* (St. Petersburg: 1871), III, 80.

31. Petr Kropotkin, *Memoirs of a Revolutionist* (Boston: 1899), 179.

32. Z. O., *Powstanie Polskie nad Bajkalem i sprawa Kazanska* (Lwow: 1868), cited in Janik, *loc. cit.*

33. Boleslawita [pseud. for Jozef Ignacy Kraszewski], *Tulacze, opowiadania historyczne* (Warszawa: 1897), I, 109.

34. William A. Whyte, *Land Journal from Asia to Europe* (London: 1871), 284.

35. Henry Lansdell, *Through Siberia* (London: 1882), II, 18 ff.

36. Prince Czartoryski, "Les deportations en Siberie, le nombre des deportes et leurs sort dans l'exil," in his *Rekopisma Czartoryskich*, Nr. 5577, cited in Janik, *op. cit.,* 307. Kempner, *op. cit.,* 83, estimates a loss of about 150,000 of the Kingdom's most vigorous citizens as a result of the January Uprising. Szawleski, *op. cit.,* 32, repeats this estimate.

37. By succeeding edicts of the Czar Alexander II in 1865, 1867, 1868, 1871, 1874, 1876 and Czar Alexander III on May 27, 1883, the sentences and types of confinement were progressively reduced until the latter edict which granted complete amnesty. See Janik, *op. cit.,* 307, 397 ff.

38. Gustaw L. Zalecki, *Studja kolonjalne* (Warszawa: 1928), II, Cz. 1, 55; Szawleski, *op. cit.,* 41; Jozef Okolowicz, *Wychodztwo i osadnictwo polskie przed wojna swiatowa* (Warszawa: 1920), 366–368; Librowicz, *op. cit.,* 265, 267; Janik, *op. cit.,* VIII.

39. An article entitled "Poljaki w Sibiri" in the Irkutsk newspaper *Sibir,* 1883, nr. 31, cited by Janik, *op. cit.,* 7, 116, 397, 398; Okolowicz, *op. cit.,* 366.

40. Zalecki, *loc. cit.;* Librowicz, *op. cit.,* 267. Jan Rozwadowski, *Emigracja polska we Francji* (La Madelaine-les-Lille: 1927), 74, briefly touches on this subject. See also: Leopold Caro and Karol Englisch, *Emigracya i polityka emigracyjna* (Poznan: 1914), 254–255, and Wojciech Szukiewicz, "Wychodztwo na Syberje," *Biuletyn P.T.E.* (Krakow: 1910), 237 ff.

41. Cited by Librowicz, *op. cit.,* 265.

42. *Przeglad Katolicki* (Warszawa: 1886), nr. 43, discussed by J. K. Plebanski, "Kronika miesieczna," *Biblioteka Warszawska* (1886), t. 184, 292.

43. Gerard Piotrkowski, *Syberja pod wzgledem religijnem* (Warszawa: 1926), and the same author's articles on the same subject in the periodical *Glos Narodu* (Warszawa: 1927), nr. 22–26, cited by Janik, *op. cit.,* 428–429. Zenon Pietkiewicz in his "Ruch przesiedlenczy w Rosyi z przemyslem rolnem," *Ekonomista Polski* (Lwow: 1890), T. III, 236, 241, estimated that, up to that time, emigration from European Russia to the trans-Ural regions did not

exceed 3,000 families (*i.e.,* approximately 18,000 individuals) annually. He noted that the government adopted a policy facilitating this emigration in 1889.
On the basis of information provided by the St. Petersburg *Kraj* and other Russian newspapers, the editors of the *Przeglad Emigracyjny* of June 1894 reported the growing manifestations of peasant emigration to Siberia from the Kingdom. Committed as they were to the concentration of overseas emigrants in Parana (Brazil), the editors were very critical of this trend, especially from the "national" point of view. See *op. cit.* (Lwow), R. III, nr. 12, 15 czerwiec 1894, 111–112.
44. Adam Krasinski, "Kronika miesieczna," *Biblioteka Warszawska* (1903), t. 249, 206–207.
45. Wladyslaw Grabski, *Materialy w sprawie wloscianskiej* (Warszawa: 1907/1919), II, 132–133.
46. Maurycy Zamoyski, "Kronika miesieczna," *Biblioteka Warszawska* (1910), t. 278, 593; Okolowicz, *op. cit.,* 376.
47. Caro and Englisch, *op. cit.,* 254; Jozef Okolowicz, "Wychodztwo" in Stanislaw Janicki (ed.), *Stosunki rolnicze Krolestwa Kongresowego* (Warszawa: 1918), 116, and Jozef Okolowicz, *Wychodztwo i osadnictwo...,* 375.
48. According to the newspaper *Iskra,* published in Sosnowiec, emigration to Siberia was inaugurated by two political exiles who were acquainted with that country and as a result of their "agitation" deputations were sent from several villages to St. Petersburg to learn the details of colonization in Siberia. As a result of these inquiries, several hundred families registered for emigration — this despite the fact that the Russian committee for the resettlement of Siberia, located in St. Petersburg, did not actively agitate for settlement there. On the contrary, their informational handbook specifically stated that resettlement in Siberia was one of the most difficult ways to improve oneself materially. Caro and Englisch, *op. cit.,* 254–255; Okolowicz, *Wychodztwo i osadnictwo...,* 375; Zamoyski, *op. cit.,* 592–594. Lest the migration to Siberia take on "feverish" proportions, an "on-the-spot investigator," one Aleksander Borowinski, was sent there by the *Warszawskie Towarzystwo nad Wychodzcami* to make a report on the condition of the Polish settlers there. His findings published in their periodical *Wychodzca Polski* (Warszawa: 1912), czerwiec, gave a picture of unrelieved hardship and disillusionment.
49. Szawleski, *op. cit.,* 41. Grabski, *op. cit.,* III, 76, citing the *Trudy* of the Warsaw Statistical Committee as his source, noted that this emigration numbered 13,551 in 1908 and declined to 5,293 in 1912. Jan Rutkowski, *Historja gospodarcza Polski* (Poznan: 1950), II, 239, only noted that it existed.
50. An editorial entitled, "Wychodztwo wiejskie" in the newspaper *Glos* (Warszawa), R. XVI, nr. 12, 10 (23) marzec 1901, 165–166, referred to an article issued by the Russian ministry of foreign affairs which touched upon the subject of the seasonal emigration to Germany. Reflecting on the tariff crisis that was developing between Russia and the Reich, it threatened the latter with a stoppage of this imperatively needed supply of agricultural labor if the Germans continued to restrict access of Russian cereal grains to the Reich's market. This politics, strongly supported by the gentry of Russian Poland — themselves suffering from competition of Russian grain — must, in the view of the editor, prove to be futile. He doubted if that tide of emigration

could be effectively brought under administrative control or restraint. He remarked that even in the 18th century, when the peasants were *glebae adscripti,* they managed to flee. This may be regarded as one of the earlier but, subsequently, more recurrent manifestations of what may be called "the politics of emigration."

51. Caro and Englisch, *op. cit.,* 256; Okolowicz, *Wychodztwo i osadnictwo....,* 366–367.

52. Szawleski, *op. cit.,* 41.

53. Caro and Englisch, *op. cit.,* 253, 258.

54. *Ibid.,* 255. This, according to Okolowicz, was allegedly the case with government workers especially, since success in their occupations was largely dependent upon the degree of their assimilation. They often put such extravagant emphasis on their loyalism and zeal that they alienated even the Russians. This type of Russianized Polish functionary succeeded even in gaining recognition in Russian literature — "sketched by the genial pen of Szczedryn in the person of Krzepczesiulski." See his, *Wychodztwo i osadnictwo....,* 373–374.

55. Caro and Englisch, *op. cit.,* 258; Okolowicz, *Wychodztwo i osadnictwo....,* 371–372. Though vehemently opposed to emigration to Russia, and indeed emigration anywhere, Caro was disposed to take a kindlier view of the Polish-speaking emigrants living in the Caucasus area since "the old and subtle Georgian culture" was not sufficiently vigorous. In any case, in the event of mixed marriages between Poles and Georgians, neither regarded themselves as Russian. *Op. cit.,* 256.

56. Caro and Englisch, *op. cit.,* 254, 257, 258; Rutkowski, *op. cit.,* II, 237; Okolowicz, *Wychodztwo osadnictwo....,* 369–371; Okolowicz, "Wychodztwo" in Janicki (ed.), *op. cit.,* 115.

57. As one writer eloquently expressed it, Russia was "a Danaidian cistern [which] surreptitiously consumed hecatombs of Polish intellect and labor." Szawleski, *op. cit.,* 15. The various numerical estimates of the total emigration from Russian Poland to districts of the Russian empire indicate a disparity as wide as those made for the political deportees following the uprisings and, in some cases, are compounded by them. One source places his estimate at half a million population for the period 1863–1916. Kempner (ed.), *Dzieje gospodarcze Polski porozbiorowej,* 11. Another estimated that about 600,000 emigrants from Russian Poland settled elsewhere in the Russian empire prior to 1914. Szawleski, *op. cit.,* 41. The *Dziennik Peterburski,* published in St. Petersburg, estimated that approximately 600,000 Poles, almost exclusively from Russian Poland, were living within the Russian empire but outside the boundaries of Russian Poland in 1910. This estimate was based on Catholic diocesan registers. Another estimate, based on the same sources, places their number at approximately 400,000. J. Grabiec [pseud. for Jozef Dabrowski], *Wspolczesna Polska w cyfrach i faktach* (New York: 1911), 140–141 and fn. 1. The former figure was more widely accepted though possibly because it was more frequently reiterated. See, for example, several articles on the subject by Waclaw Sieroszewski in the publications *Biuletyn Polskiego Towarzystwa Emigracyjnego* (Krakow: 1910), nr. 5 and 7, as well as in the *Polski Przeglad Emigracyjny* (Krakow: 1911), R. V, nr. 11 and 12 and Caro and Englisch, *op. cit.,* 252–253. An inquiry into the passport permits granted for this travel is likely to be even less accurate since many, if not a majority, of the migrants apparently made the journey without these passport papers.

58. See, for example, the attitude expressed by Adam Krasinski, "Kronika miesieczna," *Biblioteka Warszawska* (1906), t. 264, 600–605 and Adam Skierko, "The Jews in Poland," *Polish Encyclopaedia* (Geneva: 1921), Vol. II, No. 5, 941. Wilhelm Feldman felt that the Russian government's Jewish policy, which was forcing their migration into the Kingdom, was deliberately designed to arouse hostility between Christian and Jewish Poles. See his, *Dzieje polskiej mysli politycznej, 1864–1914* (Warszawa: 1933), 368.

59. Bohdan Wasiutynski, *Ludnosc Zydowska w Krolestwie Polskiem* (Warszawa: 1911), 49. See also, Lewis Browne, *Stranger than Fiction* (New York: 1925), 332–333. Because of the almost unrelieved series of repressive laws during the reign of Nicholas (1825–1855) insofar as they related to the Jewish population in the Western Governments *(Ziemie Zachodnie)*, a very strong current of migration developed from that area into Russian Poland — this, in spite of the almost equally repressive measures promulgated by the then Russian Governor of Russian Poland, Paskiewicz (1832–1856). David Kandel, "Zydzi w Krolestwie Polskiem po 1831 r.," *Biblioteka Warszawska* (1910), t. 279, 546.

60. Jan Bloch, "Ziemia i jej obdluzenie," *Biblioteka Warszawska* (1891), t. 203, 338. By 1885, Bloch estimated that there were 500,530 *morgs* of land in Russian Poland in their possession. *Ibid.*

61. The Jewish population living within the framework of peasant villages at the time of issuance of this Ukase were likewise the recipients of the land that they had previously cultivated as well as the other land privileges *(Serwituty)* granted the peasants. They, however, were denied the right to deed their holdings and privileges thus acquired to their heirs. Thus, rights and guarantees granted by that law could not be of profit to their children and as "Ukase lands" they could be sold only to other peasants. Bernard Bobrzynski, "Zydzi w rolnictwie na terenie bylej Kongresowki i Kresow Wschodnich" in Ignacy Schiper, *et al., Zydzi w Polsce odrodzonej* (Warszawa: 1933), II, 410.

62. The Pale legally included the ten governments which constituted the Kingdom. S. Hirszhorn, "Dzieje Zydow w Krolestwie Polskiem od 1864 do 1918," in Schiper, *et al., op. cit.,* I, 472–474.

63. Eugene M. Kulischer, *Jewish Migrations; Past Experiences and Post-War Prospects* (New York: 1943), 23.

64. Salo W. Baron, *A Social and Religious History of the Jews* (New York: 1937), I, 264. See also, Kulischer, *loc. cit.* Hans Rogger, in a paper delivered at the American Historical Association meeting in San Francisco in December, 1973, suggests some new and interesting motivations behind both the anti-Jewish outrages of the 1880's and the policies of the Russian authorities. From a typescript of that paper provided by the author.

65. The periodical, *Die Deborah,* Vol. XVI, No. 6, August 5, 1870, noted a steady stream of impoverished Jewish emigration abroad from the Lithuanian provinces. Permission was granted without any restrictions. It noted, however, that the trend to emigration to Russia was more favored by the Jewish population in spite of the fact that a guarantee of the possession of at least 175 rubles plus a five ruble fee for a passport was required of each head of a family migrating to Russia. The writer explained this phenomenon by stating that ". . . the ordinary Jew in Lithuania feels rather keenly that he is unfit to achieve anything in a more highly cultured land and that it is, at all events, better for him here where he still stands to a certain degree above the general level of the culture." Furthermore, the local citizens' committees established to lend aid to

the migrating Jewish population seemed to have been more favorably disposed toward helping emigrants who wanted to go to Russia rather than those who wanted to emigrate abroad. Quoted in Rudolf Glanz, "Source Materials on the History of Jewish Immigration to the United States," *Yivo Annual of Jewish Social Science* (New York: 1951), Vol. VI, 116.

66. Kulischer, *op. cit.*, 21–24.

67. See statistical study of Wasiutynski, *op. cit.*, passim.

68. Wasiutynski attributed the proportionate increase of the Jewish population in Russian Poland from 13.9 percent of the total population in 1893 to 14.64 percent in 1909 not to natural increases but largely to immigration from the Lithuanian and Byelorussian provinces. This seems to be borne out by the rather sizable proportionate decreases of the Jewish population in those areas during that period. With due consideration of the untrustworthiness of the available Russian statistical data, he estimates that about 100,000 Jewish Russians migrated to Russian Poland during that period. Wasiutynski, *op. cit.*, 7, 99. Skierko, using Wasiutynski's sources, but dismissing his reservations, estimated that the number of Jewish immigrants during the same period was about 140,000. Adam Skierko, "The Jews in Poland," *Polish Encyclopaedia,* Vol. II, No. 5, 934–935. Kaplun-Kogan and Tartakower estimate that the volume of Jewish immigration into Russian Poland during the period 1897–1913 was 226,000 and 300,000 respectively. See Arjeh Tartakower, "Stan liczebny i rozwoj naturalny ludnosci Zydowskiej w Polsce," in Schiper, *et al., op. cit.,* II, 188 and Wladimir W. Kaplun-Kogan, "Die Judische Sprache- und Kulturgemeinschaft in Polen," *Zeitschrift fur Demographie und Statistik der Juden,* July, August, September, 1915. Numerous other writers, without venturing any estimates of its volume, make mention of "a considerable" amount of emigration of Jewish Russians into Russian Poland in the pre-war years. See, for example, Jan Rutkowski, *Historia Gospodarcza Polski* (Poznan: 1950), II, 241; Stefan L. Zaleski, "General Demography of Poland," *Polish Encyclopaedia* (Geneva: 1921), Vol. II, No. 2, 151; Max J. Kohler, *Immigration and the Alien in the United States* (New York: 1936), 238.

69. F. Fendi, "Z ekonomiki, IX," *Biblioteka Warszawska* (1886), t. 177 [181], 85.

70. L. Kotowicz, "Bankowosc i kredyt w Polsce" in Stanislaw Kempner (ed.), *Dzieje gospodarcze Polski porozbiorowej w zarysie* (Warszawa: 1920), I, 180; Z. Ludkiewicz, "Ziemia i ludnosc rolnicza," in *ibid.,* II, 102.

71. The Jewish population was largely excluded. F. Brodowski, "Rosyjski Bank Wloscianski. . . , " *Sprawa Rolna* (grudzien 1920), zesz. 5/7, 35.

72. C. Reklewski, "O znaczeniu podstawowych reform. . . ," *Biblioteka Warszawska* (1888), t. 187, 215. See also, Witold Kula, *Historia gospodarcza Polski, 1864–1918* (Warszawa: 1947), 24. This, in effect, represented a more liberal policy than that which was adopted in the rest of the empire where it set a ceiling of 75 percent of the total valuation of the land to be purchased. Reklewski, *loc. cit.*

73. Reklewski, *op. cit.*, 217–218; Kotowicz, *loc. cit.* Prior to the extension of its operations in Russian Poland, the going interest rates for purchase of land by the peasants, available from private sources, averaged out between 30 and 36 percent per annum. H. Wiercienski, "Proletaryat wiejski i zapowiedziane pozyczki dla wloscian," *Ateneum* (Warszawa: 1886), t. XLIV, 197.

74. Bloch, on the basis of his statistical studies of the mortgage indebted-

ness of the landed gentry in Russian Poland, found that both the volume of parcelation and the average price of the land purchased via parcelation during the 1885–1890 period had declined radically. This he attributed to "a certain restraint and watchful expectancy" caused by an announcement of the Russian authorities that branches of the Peasant Bank would be established in Russian Poland. This may contribute somewhat to an understanding of the generally critical view the landed gentry took of the operations of that bank. Jan Bloch, "Ziemia i jej obdluzenie," *Biblioteka Warszawska* (1891), t. 203, 142–143, 147, 149. For an earlier but similar view on peasant mortgage credit facilities, see Anastazy Kwiryn, "Stopa procentowa," *Ateneum* (Warszawa: 1877), t. IV, 531–553.

75. Reklewski, *op. cit.*, 224; J. Weyssenhoff, "Kronika Miesieczna," *Biblioteka Warszawska* (1894), t. 213, 616. When a proposal was made to create a "general use fund" *(fundusz uzytecznosci ogolnej)* from the savings of the Polish Land Credit Association, amounting to about 3 million rubles, for mortgage credit facilities for the peasants in 1886, it apparently created a good deal of anxiety among the landed elements. H. Wiercienski, *op. cit.*, 193–200.

76. Kula, *op. cit.*, 24.

77. Brodowski, *op. cit.*, 47–48.

78. Stanislaw A. Kempner, *Rozwoj gospodarczy Polski* (Warszawa: 1924), 96. Despite its widespread publicity in the Polish press, this policy apparently did not evoke any noteworthy shift of population. According to a petition for aid addressed to the Galician *sejm* in their behalf, there were 55 refugee Uniate clergymen from the Chelm district living in Galicia in 1875. These together with their families totalled 208 people. Their total increased to 247 by 1876. *Stenograficzne Sprawozdanie sejmu galicyjskiego . . .*, VI ses., III per., 22 pos. (20 maj 1875), 504–509; *ibid.*, VII ses., III per., 12 pos. (28 marzec 1876), 251. See also, *Alegata do sprawozdan stenograficznych . . . sejmu krajowego . . . z r. 1875*, Alegat LXXXVII.

79. They included the eastern and northern districts of Chelm, Hrubieszow, Tomaszow, Bilgoraj, Zamojsk and parts of Janow, Krasnostaw and Lubartow in the province of Lublin; Bielsk, Wladowa, Radzyn, Konstantynow and parts of Siedlce and Sokolow in the province of Siedlce, as well as six communities in the Augustow district of the province of Suwalki. Brodowski, *op. cit.*, 36. See also, Wladyslaw Wroblewski, "Dzialalnosc parcelacyjna Banku Wloscianskiego," in Stanislaw Janicki (ed.), *Stosunki rolnicze Krolestwa Kongresowego* (Warszawa: 1918), 64.

80. Wroblewski, *op. cit.*, 68.

81. J. Wasowicz, "Z geografji osiedli wiejskich na Wolyniu," *Czasopismo Geograficzne* (1934), t. XII, zesz. 3–4, 287–288.

82. J. Wasowicz, "O Polskiej wyspie etnograficznej kolo Zytomierza," *Polski Przeglad Kartograficzny* (grudzien 1926), t. II, nr. 15–16, 186–187, 190.

83. Wasowicz in *Czasopismo Geograficzne* (1934), t. XII, zesz. 3–4, 287–288. See also, Stefan L. Zaleski, "General Demography of Poland," *Polish Encyclopaedia* (Geneva: 1921), Vol. II, no. 2, 203 and fn. 1.

84. Wasowicz in *Polski Przeglad Kartograficzny* (grudzien 1926), t. II, nr. 15–16, 186–187.

85. A. Donimirski, "Parcelacya," *Biblioteka Warszawska* (1895), t. 220, 310, citing an article by Jan Bloch entitled "Bank Wlosciania parcelacya" in the periodical *Gazeta Rolnicza*, 1895, as his source.

86. Donimirski, *op. cit.*, 309, 314. To maintain uniformity and to facilitate comparison, land measures have been reduced to their equivalents in *morgs* whenever they were cited in terms of either *hectares* or *dziesiatins*, with one *dziesiatina* equivalent to 1.09 *hectares* and one Polish *morg* equivalent to .56 *hectares*. For other equivalents, including currency and avoirdupois weights, see "Vie economique de la Pologne," *Encyclopedie Polonaise* (Geneva: 1921), Vol. III, XII.

87. Brodowski, *op. cit.*, 50–51; Stanislaw Dzierzbicki, "Sprawozdanie z dzialalnosci Banku Wloscianskiego," *Gazeta Rolnicza* (Warszawa: 1902), nr. 23, cited by A. Krasinski, "Kronika Miesieczna," *Biblioteka Warszawska* (1902), t. 247, 186, 187. For extensive statistical data on impressive operations of this peasant credit facility since its inauguration in 1883 through 1899, throughout the empire and including Russian Poland, see: St. Dzierzbicki, "Dzialalnosc banku wloscianskiego," *Ekonomista* (Warszawa: 1901), R. I, t. II, 336–378. Koszutski appears to be in error when he mentions that by 1900 this bank had advanced five million rubles in loans for the purchase of 90,000 *morgs* of land in Russian Poland. See his *Rozwoj ekonomiczny Krolestwa Polskiego...* (Warszawa: 1905), 106.

88. Wladyslaw Studnicki, "Problemat agrarny," *Biblioteka Warszawska* (1906), t. 264, 23.

89. Kula, *op. cit.*, 25.

90. Ludkiewicz, *op. cit.*, II, 102; Stanislaw Roslaniec, *Samorzutne scalenie gruntow* (Warszawa: 1928), 79.

91. Kula, *op. cit.*, 24. See also, Wladyslaw Grabski, *Rocznik statystyczny Krolestwa Polskiego*. Rok. 1914. (Warszawa: 1915), 63.

92. Ludkiewicz, *loc. cit.*

93. Kula, *op. cit.*, 25. In Lublin province alone this bank was instrumental in the parcelation of 163,538.5 *morgs* of land to peasants during the period 1892–1911. During the preceding 30 years (1864–1893), i.e., prior to the establishment of that bank, only 31,516 *morgs* of land were bought by the peasants of that province. Brodowski, *op. cit.*, 28.

94. Grabski, *op. cit.*, 69.

95. F. Fendi, *op. cit.*, 95. For statistical compilations of growing mortgage indebtedness of landed gentry in 1882 see, R. Buczynski, "Nasza wlasnosc ziemska," *Biblioteka Warszawska* (1882), t. 168, 358–361; for 1890 see, Jan Bloch, "Ziemia i jej obdluzenie w Krolestwie Polskiem," *Biblioteka Warszawska* (1891), t. 202, 219–270, 549–587. For a more polemic treatment of the same subject, as of 1903, see, Kazimierz Rakowski, "Gospodarcze niedobory naszego kraju," *Biblioteka Warszawska* (1906), t. 263, 125–164. In Rakowski's view all the economic, social and political shortcomings of the Kingdom are due to Russia. The solution: autonomy or independence for Russian Poland.

96. Fendi, *op. cit.*, 95–96.

97. Kotowicz, *op. cit.*, I, 180; Zaleski, *op. cit.*, 203 and fn. 1; Adam Krasinski, "Kronika miesieczna," *Biblioteka Warszawska* (1907), t. 266, 604.

98. J. Weyssenhoff, "Kronika miesieczna," *Biblioteka Warszawska* (1891), t. 202, 423–424 and *ibid.* (1892), t. 208, 410–411; S. Krzeczkowski, "Wychodztwo wloscian z Krolestwa na zarobki," *Biblioteka Warszawska* (1901), t. 243, 54. The so-called "petit-gentry" were especially aggrieved because they were excluded from the credit facilities of the Peasant Bank and, simultaneously, failed to meet the minimum requirements established by the

Towarzystwo Kredytu Ziemskiego, as a consequence of which they were also excluded from the favorable mortgage credit facilities provided by the latter organization for the landed gentry. Krasinski, *op. cit.* (1902), t. 247, 183–184.
99. Krasinski, *op. cit.* (1902), t. 247, 186.
100. A. Donimirski, *op. cit., * 310. The socialist *Przedswit,* perhaps predictably, criticized the Peasant Bank for the above reasons adding that, since most agricultural communes and associations were made up generally of well-to-do rather than poor peasants, the only recourse that remained for the latter was still the usurer. N., "Lichwa, jej przyczynki i skutki," *op. cit.* (Londyn), Ser. III, nr. 9, wrzesien 1896, 3.
101. Brodowski, *op. cit., * 35–36 and fn.

CHAPTER FOUR

1. "Kronika tygodniowa," *Tygodnik Ilustrowany* (1876), cz. 2, 196, quoted by Barbara Michalowska, "Sprawy ziemstwa i wsi," *Przeglad Nauk Historycznych i Spolecznych* (Lodz: 1954), t. IV, 219.
2. *Ibid.;* "Kronika tygodniowa," *Tygodnik Ilustrowany* (1876), cz. 2, 130ff.; "Kronika tygodniowa," *ibid.* (1877), cz. 2, 54; "Kronika tygodniowa," *ibid.* (1880), cz. 1, 136, 143, in Michalowska, *op. cit., * 218–219.
3. "Wiazanka nowosci," *Tygodnik Ilustrowany* (1870), t. VI, 59, in *ibid.,* 225–226.
4. "Korespondencya z Poznania," *Tygodnik Ilustrowany* (1880), cz. 2, in *ibid.*
5. The editor of the conservative publication *Biblioteka Warszawska,* reporting on the petition for aid made by 72 large landholders to the *Towarzystwo Kredytu Ziemskiego,* noted that an important cause of their calamitous condition was the emigration of peasants. J. Weyssenhoff, "Kronika miesieczna," *Biblioteka Warszawska* (1891), t. 203, 608–609.
6. One writer considered the agricultural crisis precipitated by the American grain exports in the 1880's as the most significant factor influencing the structure of the rural economy of Poland since the land reform law of 1863. In this way, United States agricultural production was influential, indirectly at least, in creating a situation conducive to emigration. Roman Jablonowski, "Wiejska ludnosc bezrolna," *Roczniki Socjologii Wsi* (1938), t. III, 130.
7. Ludwik Gorski, *Znaczenie wiekszej wlasnosci i obowiazki wiekszych wlascicieli ziemskich* (Warszawa: 1883), 183ff. Also issued serially in the monthly publication *Niwa* (Warszawa) throughout 1882 and 1883. The author was a long-time chairman of the executive committee of the *Towarzystwo Kredytu Ziemskiego.* For other details on the author, see memorial essay by Adam Krasinski, "Ludwik Gorski," *Biblioteka Warszawska* (1902), t. 248, 209–233. When denounced for his espousal of the idea of parcelation, the editor of the periodical *Niwa* went to great lengths, in his own defense, explaining that he advocated only partial parcelation of large estates and only to financially facilitate their survival as social, political and economic bastions of a way of life. Ch., "Sprawy biezace," *Niwa* (Warszawa: 1886), R. XV, t. XXIX, zesz. 275, 814–817.
8. Jan Bloch, "Ziemia i jej obdluzenie," *Biblioteka Warszawska* (1891), t. 204, 68–69, 125.

9. A. Donimirski, "Parcelacya w Poznanskiem," *Biblioteka Warszawska* (1893), t. 209, 161, 163, 164, 169. The author noted that the Polish Congress of Jurists and Economists, at its first convention in Krakow in 1887, passed a resolution on parcelation substantially in accord with his expressed views on the subject. *Ibid.*, 161–162. Actually, however, only a resolution was passed to establish a committee to undertake a study of the question of "internal colonization" and present its findings at the next meeting to be held in Lwow in 1889. See, Stanislaw Starzynski, "Pierwszy zjazd prawnikow i ekonomistow polskich," *Przewodnik naukowy i literacki* (Lwow: 1887), R. XV, 953–959. See also, Adolf Suligowski, "Pierwszy zjazd prawnikow i ekonomistow polskich," *Ateneum* (Warszawa: 1887), T. XVLIII, 308–310.

10. Karol Filipowicz, *Parcelacya jako program spoleczny* [odbitka z Gazety Rolniczej] (Warszawa: 1883), passim.

11. F. Fendi, "Z ekonomiki, IX," *Biblioteka Warszawska* (1886), t. 177 [181], 84. Later as the nationalistic temper began to assume bolder forms, some editorials favored the improvement of the lot of the peasant by establishing local retail stores. The Museum of Industry and Agriculture *(Museum przemyslu i rolnictwa)* undertook a program to establish such Christian stores to eliminate "the foreign middleman and loan-shark." J. Weyssenhoff, *op. cit.,* t. 201, 652.

12. Marjan Kiniorski, "Wieksza i mniejsza wlasnosc ziemska," *Ekonomista* (Warszawa: 1903), R. III, t. 1.

13. Antoni Zabko-Potopowicz, "Wies polska w swietle polskich prac naukowych i publicystycznych z okresu po uwlaszczeniu wloscian," *Roczniki Socjologii Wsi* (Warszawa: 1937), t. II, 97.

14. Wladyslaw Grabski, *Materialy w sprawie wloscianskiej* (Warszawa: 1907), I, Sect. VII, 60–74. Grabski, however, was not an unqualified advocate of parcelation especially inasmuch as he saw a direct relation between unregulated parcelation and the fragmentation of peasant landholds. He seems to have hoped, by means of controlled parcelation, to restore to existence a class of independent yeoman farmers *(kmiecie)*, occupying 60 to 100 *morg* landholds, which would be more economically viable. This view provoked a forensic exchange at the Fourth Congress of Polish Jurists and Economists in 1906. His views on parcelation and the economic viability of small peasant landholds and even on the correlation between dwarf-landholds and parcelation was challenged by a number of his fellow delegates. See, e.g., Bohdan Wasiutynski, [IV Zjazd prawnikow i ekonomistow polskich], *Czasopismo prawnicze i ekonomiczne* (Krakow: 1906), R. VII, 25ff.; Delegate Krzyzanowski, *op. cit.,* 1907, R. VII, 108–109; Delegate Lipowski, *op. cit.,* R. VIII, 111–112; Delegate Buynowski, *op. cit.,* R. VIII, 118–122; Dr. Lewicki, *op. cit.,* R. VIII, 122–125; and Dr. Gross, *op. cit.,* R. VIII, 147ff. Dr. Gross may have touched upon the basic orientation of the disputants when he argued that Grabski's thesis of the declining productivity in the various sectors of Poland due to fragmentation of landholds was based on a G.N.P.-type of measure of economic prosperity, rather than a consideration of the life-support of the people (i.e., an unwarranted emphasis on production of goods rather than the wherewithal to sustain life, albeit on a marginal level, in an expanding population).

A view similar to Grabski's, expressed earlier in the periodical *Wiek,* was attacked by a writer in the peasant-oriented *Glos.* He accused the gentry of regarding the trend toward parcelation as some sort of "Vandal incursion" which, like in Ancient Rome, was destroying the stronghold of culture and civilization. His own position, probably reflecting that of the *Glos,* favored any and all parcelation. "Every purchased *morg* [by peasant] represents not only a diminution of [the gentry's] properties but also their power." Kor., "Na widnokregach. Przed parciem Wandalow," *Glos* (Warszawa), R. XVII, no. 29, 6 (19) lipiec 1902, 463–464. This extreme view was expressed as early as 1875 by Ignacy Maciejowski [Sewer] in the Warsaw periodical *Niwa.* He argued that large landed estates had lost their economic feasibility because of their lack of capital, the conditions of the European grain markets and the increasing wages of agricultural workers. The editors of that publication explicitly disassociated themselves from that view. Witold Lewicki, "Parcelacya w Galicyi jako objaw spoleczny," *Ekonomista Polski* (Lwow: 1890), T. I, 117–118. Jan Rozwadowski in his "Znaczenie parcelacyi wiekszej wlasnosci," *Ekonomista* (Warszawa: 1901), R. I, t. I, 283–304, essentially reiterated Maciejowski's position though he apparently modified it considerably in his "Znaczenie parcelacyi wiekszej wlasnosci dla Galicyi," *Przeglad sadowy i administracyjny* (Lwow: 1901), R. XXVI, 511–529, in which he came out in favor of a "rational" and "controlled" policy of parcelation guided by economic, political and social considerations. These considerations prompted him to advocate the establishment of leaseholds *(wlosci rentowe)* on the model of the Prussian *Rentenguter* idea — leaseholds that were essentially consistent with what Grabski had in mind. For a concise distinction between the *Rentengut* and *Erbpacht* concepts of land settlement, see: Richard Blanke, "Bismarck and the Prussian Polish Policies of 1886," *Journal of Modern History,* Vol. 45, No. 2 (June 1973), 228. For more extended treatment of the subject of parcelation, see, *infra,* 160 ff.

15. Quoted by Jan Lutoslawski, *Rolnictwo Polskie przed wojna a dzisiaj* (Warszawa: 1921), 18–19.

16. Maurycy Zamoyski, "Kronika miesieczna," *Biblioteka Warszawska* (1911), t. 281, 397, 400.

17. Adam Krasinski, "Kronika miesieczna," *Biblioteka Warszawska* (1902), t. 247, 188.

18. Stanislaw Koszutski, *Rozwoj ekonomiczny Krolestwa Kongresowego w ostatniem trzydziestoleciu, 1870–1900* (Warszawa: 1905), 214–215.

19. The editor of the periodical *Niwa* probably expressed the qualms and anxieties among the older, controlling elements of the press when he vigorously deplored the anti-clerical, anti-gentry editorial policies of some of those publications, calling them and their literary sympathizers (e.g., Boleslaw Prus) advocates of "an obsolete liberalism" and Quixotic tilters at windmills. Chorazy, "Sprawy biezace," *Niwa* (Warszawa), 1886, R. XV, t. XXIX, zesz. 275, 812–814; *ibid.,* 1886, R. XV, t. XXX, zesz. 282, 467–471; *ibid.,* 1887, R. XVI, t. XXXI, zesz. 289, 66–68 and *ibid.,* 1887, t. XXXI, zesz. 292, 315–319. See also: Antoni Mazanowski, " 'Chlopi' Reymonta," *Przeglad Powszechny* (Krakow) lipiec-wrzesien 1909, t. CIII, 319.

20. See fn. 19, Ch. 6, *infra.*

21. A series of articles entitled "Rural Exodus" in the publication *Prawda* throughout 1900. See also his *Nad otchlania; w sprawie handlu zywem*

towarem [Ruch etyczny, III] (Warszawa: 1903), I, and *Drogi samopomocy spolecznej* (Plock-Warszawa: 1903).

22. For a short, but perceptive, essay on the gravity and historical significance of the developing emigration from historical Poland, its scope and varieties of direction and its paramount contemporary consequences see his [K. R. Zywicki], "Nasi wychodzcy," *Ateneum* (Warszawa: 1901), t. CI, 433-442.

23. Roman Dmowski, *Wychodztwo i osadnictwo* (Lwow: 1900), I, 90. See also review article of above publication by T. Kudelka, "Wychodztwo i osadnictwo. Roman Dmowski. Czesc pierwsza. Lwow, 1900," *Przeglad Powszechny* (Krakow), czerwiec 1900, t. LXIV, nr. 198, 442-445.

24. Kazimierz Kasperski, "Wychodztwo polskie i jego przyczyny," *Ekonomista Polski* (Lwow: 1900), nr. 39.

25. Wilhelm Feldman also regarded this as a turning point in the political history of the Kingdom — a period which saw the decline of the former loyalist orientation as well as older democratic orientations and the emergence of newer groupings more logically attuned to modern circumstances. These groupings included the National Democrats, socialists as well as the intermediate groupings in the political spectrum. See his, *Dzieje polskiej mysli politycznej, 1864-1914* (Warszawa: 1933), 211 ff. For evidence of the 1890's as a turning point in the economic history of the Kingdom, see, Marceli Lewy, *Wzajemny stosunek przemyslu Krolestwa Polskiego i Cesarstwa Rosyjskiego przed wojna wszechswiatowa* (Warszawa: 1921), 108-130.

26. As late as 1910, Wojciech Szukiewicz felt it necessary to preface his essay on "the problem of emigration" in a liberal publication by discountenancing "the still prevailing tendency among homegrown economists" to attribute emigration to "artificial and artificially nurtured" causes and, for those reasons, should be constrained and discouraged. See his: "Z zagadnien emigracyjnych," *Ekonomista* (Warszawa: 1910), R. X, t. II, 78-79.

27. Manoel F. Ferreira-Correia and Serro Azul, *Opis stanu Parana w Brazylii* (Lwow: 1896), 51ff., an informational handbook for prospective emigrants, translated from the English by Jozef Siemiradzki, was first published in Portuguese in 1893.

28. Caro and Englisch, *Emigracja i polityka emigracyjna* (Poznan: 1914), 217.

29. During its short duration it has been estimated that approximately 30,000 people emigrated to Brazil from Russian Poland. Okolowicz, *Wychodztwo i osadnictwo. . . ,* 198; Okolowicz, "Wychodztwo" in Stanislaw Janicki (ed.), *Stosunki rolnicze Krolestwa Kongresowego* (Warszawa: 1918), 107; J. Siemiradzki, "W sprawie emigracji. . . ," *Biblioteka Warszawska* (1900), t. 236, 144.

30. Weyssenhoff, *op. cit.,* t. 201, 427-428, 429, 430. The author did, however, concede that the promotional activities would have been largely ineffectual were it not for the economic and social conditions prevailing in the land. *Ibid.,* 430; *ibid.,* t. 202, 198-201.

31. Ludwik Gorski, *Poglad na stan i ekonomiczne potrzeby malej wlasnosci ziemskiej w Krolestwie Polskiem* (Warszawa: 1891), quoted in Grabski, *op. cit.,* III, 124. The author also published a series of essays on the "Brazilian Fever" in the bi-monthly *Niwa* throughout 1891, wherein he expressed the judgment that false hopes rather than the pressure of economic circumstances

in Russian Poland were the real causes of this emigration. See also K. [Klobu-kowski], fn. 23, Ch. 1, *supra.*
32. Weyssenhoff, *op. cit.,* t. 201, 429–432. Even the relatively liberal *Kurjer Warszawski,* under the rubric "Letter from Brazil," reprinted a letter from a Jozef Piaskowski originally written to the provincial newspaper *Kaliszanin* wherein he [Piaskowski] reported the receipt of a letter from a German emigrant in Brazil who wrote: "If anyone wishes to know how the Lord Jesus suffered on the cross, let him go to Brazil and he'll learn." *Kurjer Warszawski,* Nr. 3, 3 styczen 1890, 2.
33. Weyssenhoff, *op. cit.,* t. 201, 429; *ibid.,* t. 203, 417; *ibid.,* t. 204, 433.
34. *Ibid.,* t. 201, 651.
35. These resources enabled them to provide for the return passage of 232 Polish emigrants chosen on the basis of their original place of residence in such a way that there were no more than two from each district. In this way, their sponsors apparently hoped to extend as much as possible their anti-emigration testimonials. *Ibid.,* t. 202, 638–639.
36. *Ibid.,* t. 201, 652; *ibid.,* t. 202, 198, 638–639.
37. *Ibid.,* t. 203, 417.
38. The publication of his dispatches began in the *Kurjer Warszawski* (1890), nr. 224 and extended into 1891. They were reprinted in his *Listy z Brazylii specialnego delegata Kurjera Warszawskiego* (Warszawa: 1891). For a fictionalized treatment of the subject see his: *Opowiadanie Kuby Cieluchowskiego o emigracyi do Brazylii* (Warszawa: 1892) and "Na zlamanie karku" in his *Pisma wybrane* (Warszawa: 1950), t. V.
Dygasinski represents an interesting, though probably not unique, example of the transition of a Polish intellectual from radicalism to conservatism. Up to about the time of these publications he was generally reckoned among the "populists" *(ludowce)* — the proponents of a peasant democracy. These publications represented a reaction from that point of view. Thereafter the formerly "noble peasant" is repeatedly portrayed by him as a stupid, venal lout, patent thief, habitual drunkard and niggardly miser. The chief female protagonist in *Na zlamanie karku,* Maryana Grzedzianka, alone succeeded in Brazil and was apparently satisfied with her success: she became a prostitute. This literary preoccupation is manifested in numerous of his subsequent works. For a detailed study of Dygasinski as a dramatist and publicist, see: Zygmunt Szweykowski, *Dramat Dygasinskiego* (Warszawa: 1938), *passim.*
39. Zygmunt Chelmicki, *W Brazylii; notatki z podrozy* (Warszawa and Krakow: 1891), t. I–II. See also his, *O Paranie* (Warszawa: 1895). For a concurring opinion on this emigration by the editor of the Catholic-oriented publication *Przeglad Powszechny,* see: ____, "W Brazylii. Notatki z Pod-rozy," in *ibid.,* maj 1892, t. XXXIV, nr. 101, 265–267.
40. Weyssenhoff, *op. cit.* (1892), t. 207, 391; Jozef Siemiradzki, "Stosunki osadnicze w Brazylii," *Biblioteka Warszawska* (1892), t. 205, 109.
41. Weyssenhoff, *op. cit.* (1891), t. 204, 432.
42. St. Knauff, "Stefan Zeromski a sprawa emigracyjna," *Kwartalnik Naukowego Instytutu Emigracyjnego* (Warszawa: kwiecien-wrzesien 1928), R. III, t. II–III, 426. Jozef Siemiradzki, "W sprawie emigracyi wloscianskiej w Brazylii," *Biblioteka Warszawska* (1900), t. 236, 128.
43. The federal government of Brazil contracted to pay a commission of

160 francs for each immigrant supplied by several private agencies. Caro and Englisch, *op. cit.,* 217.

44. Ludwik Krzywicki in his introductory essay to the publication: *Pamietniki emigrantow: Ameryka Poludniowa* (Warszawa: 1939), VII.

45. Okolowicz, *Wychodztwo i osadnictwo . . . ,* 181 ff.; Dmowski, *op. cit.,* 100. The authors of the informational handbook for prospective emigrants to Parana in 1896 noted that of the total Polish emigrants who settled in that province in the period 1890–1892, only about 20 percent were by background farmers. The overwhelming majority were factory workers and artisans from such urban areas as Lodz, Warsaw, etc. Ferreira-Correia and Azul, *op. cit.,* 72. One of the simplest yet most powerfully eloquent testimonies of the hardships on the Brazilian frontier was recorded by a peasant-emigrant in his memoirs several decades later: "Within a week my family diminished from six souls to three. I made the coffins for my neighbor's children; he made them for mine. The graves we dug together." Memoir No. 9, "A blacksmith in Parana, son of a peasant in Opatow, born in 1862," *Pamietniki emigrantow: Ameryka Poludniowa* (Warszawa: 1939), 122.

46. Ludwik Krzywicki, *op. cit.,* VII–VIII. See also, Weyssenhoff, *op. cit.* (1892), t. 206, 365. The editor of the *Przeglad Powszechny,* reporting yet another letter on the subject of "the export of Polish white slaves" *(wywozu bialych polskich niewolnikow),* expressed the usual anguish of that publication on their misguided enterprise simultaneously deploring the unwarranted antagonism toward the gentry by the peasants. This prejudice he attributed to literary figures like Boleslaw Prus who had been systematically indicting that class. He also saw the hand of socialist malcontents in this matter. As a consequence of their activities, the pessimistic injunctions of writers like Dygasinski and others were either mistrusted or discredited and the emigrants could not be dissuaded from "their fatal enterprise." ____, "List z Antwerpi, o polskich wychodzcach do Brazylii," *Przeglad Powszechny* (Krakow), kwiecien-czerwiec 1891, t. XXX, nr. 88, 158–160. For further critical commentary on Prus' pro-populist and anti-gentry sympathies, see: Chorazy, "Sprawy biezace," *Niwa* (Warszawa: 1886), R. XV, t. XXX, zesz. 282, 467–471 and *ibid.,* R. XVI, t. XXXI, zesz. 292, 315–319.

47. Memoir No. 11, "Farmer in Parana, son of an agricultural laborer from near Kalisz, born in 1879," *Pamietniki emigrantow: Ameryka poludniowa* (Warszawa: 1939), 141.

48. Memoir No. 14, "Farmer in Santa Catarina, son of a brickmaker in former Russian Poland, born in 1878," *ibid.,* 205.

49. Weyssenhoff, *op. cit.* (1891), t. 203, 417–418.

50. Siemiradzki's earliest journey to South America was reported in his *Z Warszawy do rownika; wsponmienia z podrozy po Ameryce poludniowej, odbytej w latach 1882/1883 . . .* (Warszawa: 1885). His dispatches from Brazil during the "Brazilian fever" from Russian Poland in 1890/1892 were published as "Listy z Brazylii" in the Lwow periodical *Przewodnik naukowy i literacki,* styczen 1892, 65–83; luty 1892, 174–190; marzec 1892, 268–278; kwiecien 1892, 362–371; maj 1892, 468–475; lipiec 1892, 646–659; sierpien 1892, 738–746; wrzesien 1892, 817–822; pazdziernik 1892, 912–928; listopad 1892, 1033–1042; grudzien 1892, 1188–1202. During this period he also wrote an essay entitled "Stosunki osadnicze w Brazylii," *Biblioteka Warszawska* (1892), t. 205, 104–126 and a small book, *Za morze, szkice z wycieczki do*

Brazylii (Lwow: 1894). These were later combined into the two volume work: *Szlakiem wychodzcow; wspomnienia podrozy do Brazylii* (Warszawa: 1900).

By that time the author had become associated with the Polish Commercial-Geographical Association of Lwow which was promoting the idea of a "New Poland" in Parana. His view of the prospects of Polish emigrant settlers in that country accordingly changed as is evidenced by his subsequent publications: "Wychodztwo polskie w Brazylii," *Przeglad Powszechny* (Krakow), kwiecien 1897, t. LIV, nr. 160, 360–369; sierpien 1897, t. LV, nr. 164, 193–218; kwiecien 1898, 37–47; "Obrazki z Nowej Polski, I, Wpuszczy," *Przeglad Powszechny* (Krakow), kwiecien 1899, 38–61; "La nouvelle Pologne, etat de Parana, Brasil," *Universite nouvelle institut geographique de Bruxelles* (1899), I, II; "W sprawie emigracyi wloscianskiej w Brazylii," *Biblioteka Warszawska* (1900), t. 236, 127–154; "Pod obcem niebem, szkice i obrazki," *Biblioteka nowa uniwersalna* (Krakow: styczen 1904), R. XVIII, ser. 2, 1–32 ff.; and a booklet entitled: *Polacy za morzem* (Lwow: 1900).

Antoni Hempel published his observations in his *Polacy w Brazylii, przez ... czlonka wyprawy naukowej dra. Siemiradzkiego do Brazylii i Argentyny* (Lwow: 1893).

51. In his *Szlakiem wychodzcow* ... , I, 164, he speaks of an overland exodus of 6,000 Polish immigrants from Brazil to Argentina, ". . . along the shore of the sea. Departing from Santos, they succeeded in reaching Montevideo and Buenos Aires, where they were cared for by a group of intelligent Poles. A multitude of small children who were unable to bear the hardships of this journey were sold along the way to Negroes [in exchange] for food. . . . Nowadays one can frequently see such adopted children, wholly 'Brazilianized.'" Later observers adjudged this to be either a complete fabrication or, more likely, a reiteration of a fanciful legend current among the immigrants. See, for example, Jozef Wlodek, *Argentyna i Emigracya* (Warszawa: 1923), 361; Okolowicz, *Wychodztwo i osadnictwo* ... , fn. 1, 181–182.

52. J. Siemiradzki, "Stosunki osadnicze w Brazylii," *Biblioteka Warszawska* (1892), t. 205, 108, 111–112, 118–119 ff.

53. J. Siemiradzki, "W sprawie emigracyi ... ," *Biblioteka Warszawska* (1900), t. 236, 128.

54. *Ibid.* (1892), t. 205, 120. Kazimierz Gluchowski, a painstaking researcher, came to the conclusion that the outbreak of a federalist revolution in the southern states of Brazil in 1893 was the only effective instrumentality in breaking the "fever" from Russian Poland. See his: "Polacy w Brazylii," *Kwartalnik Instytutu Naukowego do badan emigracyi i kolonizacyi* (Warszawa: kwiecien–czerwiec 1927), R. II, nr. 2, 112. Weyssenhoff thought that the outbreak of cholera in eastern Europe and the restrictive regulations that it called forth in the countries of transit were the most effective restraints upon this emigration. J. Weyssenhoff, *op. cit.* (1892), t. 208.

55. B., "Polacy w Brazylii. Przez Antoniego Hempla," *Przeglad Powszechny* (Krakow), marzec 1894, t. XLI, nr. 123, 437–439; Jozef Siemiradzki, "Wychodztwo polskie w Brazylii," *ibid.,* kwiecien 1897, R. XIV, t. LIV, nr. 160, 361.

56. J. Siemiradzki, "W sprawie emigracyi ... ," *Biblioteka Warszawska* (1900), t. 236, 127–128.

57. For broader treatment of Zeromski's expressed views on emigration in general, see Knauff, *op. cit.,* 424–435.

58. For genesis, organization and purpose of this group see, *infra,* 103 ff. Its proponents, in their zeal, not infrequently went to the extreme of condemning all other emigration in their effort to channel all necessary emigration to this *Nowa Polonia.* One such intimated that German passenger agents, acting in conformity to German colonial policy, were disposed to encourage and direct Polish emigration to the United States rather than to the southern Brazilian states where future concentrations of Polish immigrants would obstruct German-speaking colonial projects. Gustaw L. Zalecki, *Studja kolonjalne* (Warszawa: 1925–1928), I, 89. Another made it a point to note that he had met "many Polish immigrants who came to Parana from the United States because of the widespread unemployment in the latter country." Siemiradzki, "Stosunki osadnicze w Brazylii," *Biblioteka Warszawska* (1892), t. 205, 105.

An extreme point of view was that of Wladyslaw Studnicki and in this respect represents the views of a former liberal become nationalist. According to him, an overseas emigration that did not exceed half of the natural increase of the population would not reduce the national strength. This emigration, in the given circumstances of Russian Poland, may be regarded as a "necessary evil" *(smutna koniecznosc).* However, Polish emigration to the United States should be discouraged as much as possible since Polish emigrants in the United States tended to become "nationalistically indifferent," especially the "spiritually insufficient" Polish emigrants from Prussian Poland. In his opinion, there was no future for the Polish cause in the United States and, therefore, no future for Polish emigration in that country. Since, however, territorial possession must preclude national existence and development, Polish emigrants needs must first establish their territorial existence and ". . . here our eyes turn to South America . . . a Polish Zion." Wladyslaw Studnicki, "Emigracya," *Krytyka* (Krakow: 1911), R. XIII, t. XXIX, 77 ff. For impact of militant currents of nationalism generated in the several years before the war on attitudes on emigration to the United States, see, *infra,* Ch. 10, p. 169 ff.

59. See, for example, Caro and Englisch, *op. cit.,* 228–229. At a later date, Okolowicz was disposed to conclude that the stories of Polish settlers being ravaged and killed by Indians were largely fictitious and untrustworthy. *Wychodztwo i osadnictwo . . . ,* 174. The Galician correspondent of the socialist *Przedswit,* not without some irony, reported that the gentry's opposition to any and all emigration had prompted them to view the efforts of Klobukowski, Siemiradzki and others associated with the Lwow organization, with serious qualms and to put them under suspicion of "Socialism." Socjalista, "Z Galicyi," *op. cit.,* Ser. II, t. I, nr. 14, pazdz. 1891, 1. The editor of that publication in 1894 reported that the conservative press of that date still inclined to "rend their clothes in despair, that the motherland is losing so many of its sons." He suggested that this last be understood as "the proprietary classes are losing so many of their servants." ____, "Kilka slow o emigracyi polskiej," *op. cit.,* Ser. III, nr. 10, pazdz. 1894, 21.

60. Krasinski, *op. cit.* (1907), t. 268, 378.

61. His observations were first published under the title: *Kolonie polskie w Paranie* (Krakow: 1909), later as *Polskie kolonie rolnicze w Paranie* (Warszawa: 1910) and finally as, *Polacy w Paranie* (Warszawa: 1911).

62. Zamoyski, *op. cit.* (1912), t. 287, 196–201. Jordan had actually journeyed to Argentina and his qualified reports had to do with a project to direct seasonal emigrants to that country — a project contemplated by the Galician

Polish Emigration Association (P.T.E.). Okolowicz, *op. cit.*, 244–249; Caro and Englisch, *op. cit.*, 203–204. See also, Roman Jordan, *Argentyna jako teren dla polskiego wychodztwa. Sprawozdanie z podrozy informacyjnej* (Krakow: 1912), and his, "Widoki dla wychodzcow w Argentynie," *Polski Przeglad Emigracyjny* (Krakow), R. VI, styczen 1912, 4–13; *ibid.,* luty 1912, 49–62 and *ibid.,* marzec–kwiecien 1912, 92–110. This contemplated project was apparently a feature of that organization's effort, in the years immediately before the war, to redirect the seasonal emigration tide away from Germany. Theoretically, it offered sanguine prospects — the profitable employment of migrants during the winter months (in the southern latitudes) and their return to Poland during the spring and harvest seasons there. The idea was apparently suggested by the successful seasonal emigration to that country from Italy and Spain.

   63. According to him, a certain woman returned at the beginning of 1911 to the village of Branica near Radzyn to claim an inheritance. She had been living for a number of years on a farm in one of the older agricultural settlements in Parana and had improved her condition markedly. Her apparent prosperity attracted the attention of the townspeople who queried her for details of living conditions there — as an eye-witness. While she did not engage in any wide-scale agitation, yet the fact that when she departed for Parana she took all her relatives with her had such an effect in the locality that the people were ready to believe anything good that was said about Parana and to be indifferent to critics. Very shortly thereafter, a mass movement to Parana began near Radzyn — first the landless and then even small landholders. *Kurjer Warszawski,* n.d., cited by Okolowicz, *Wychodztwo i osadnictwo . . . ;* 200–201. See also, Franciszek Bayer, "Sprawozdanie delegata Warszawskiego Towarzystwa Opieki nad Wychodzcami, Franciszka Bayera, z podrozy informacyjnej po Podlasiu," *Polski Przeglad Emigracyjny* (Krakow: 1911), R. V, nr. 17.

   64. Okolowicz, *op. cit.,* 200.

   65. *Ibid.* See also, Michal Pankiewicz, *Z Parany i o Paranie* (Warszawa: 1916). Pankiewicz later published a work entitled: *W sprawie wychodztwa do Sao Paulo* (Warszawa: 1926).

   66. Zamoyski, *op. cit.,* 197. Commenting on these developments, the editor of the socialist *Przedswit* reported that the conservative organ of the large landowners, *Slowo,* was raising a hue and cry about this "disaster" and was being joined by like-minded conservative-clerical journals. In his view, they saw this development as a consequence of "radical intrigue," represented by the newspaper *Zaranie* and the clergyman, Anusz, who were suspected of not only "hurting the interests of the country," but also intriguing to create a "Polish Republic" in Parana. St. Os . . . arz, "Z calego kraju," *op. cit.,* R. XXX, nr. 4, 1911, 183–184.

   67. Okolowicz, *op. cit.,* 201–202. Bayer, *loc. cit.,* was convinced that Anusz, et al., were acting in good faith since they could not have profited in any way from this emigration. Though representatives of shipping interests, etc., may have been secretly active, he felt that their influence was negligible and much exaggerated by the critics of the "New Poland" idea in Parana. The editors of the P.T.E. journal, the *Polski Przeglad Emigracyjny,* reported, in 1912, that the efforts to renew this tide of emigration to Brazil (via Hamburg) were largely unsuccessful due, in part, "to the cautionary efforts of the P.T.E.

and its kindred organization [in Russian Poland], the Warsaw Emigrants Protective Association *(Towarzystwo Opieki nad Wychodzcami),"* as well as the disillusioning reports of some of the returned emigrants themselves.____, "Rozmaitosc," *Polski Przeglad Emigracyjny* (Krakow), R. VI, luty 1912, 75 and *ibid.,* R. VI, maj–czerwiec 1912, 249–252. This posture of the P.T.E. in this matter is particularly noteworthy because it seems to represent a departure from the position it — and its antecedent, the Polish Commercial-Geographical Association — adhered to regarding Parana as an area of colonization. See *infra,* 103 ff. That this departure — and the subsequent dissolution — of the P.T.E. was dictated by the pressures of nationalism in the years immediately preceding the war is explored, *infra,* ch. 6, p. 115 and fn. 84.

68. Michal Radziwill, "Kronika miesieczna," *Biblioteka Warszawska* (1899), t. 233, 173.

69. *Ibid.*

70. *Ibid.*

71. Koszutski, *op. cit.,* 217. The editor of the *Biblioteka Warszawska* represented it as largely the product of promotional agencies operating among a gullible populace and the prevailing tendency in general as "a type of moral infection." Radziwill, *loc. cit.* One contributer, Kazimierz Rakowski, saw only demoralization and degradation as its product. See his, "Wychodztwo polskie w Niemczech," *Biblioteka Warszawska* (1902), t. 248, 75–77.

72. This was substantially the attitude the landed gentry took toward the emigration of the peasants to the urban and industrial centers of Russian Poland. Weyssenhoff deplored this tendency: ". . . in the last years the population of the larger cities, especially the industrial ones, has increased considerably while a wide radius of rural villages was devastated, totally depopulated." *Biblioteka Warszawska* (1892), t. 206, 355. Koszutski quoted another critic who came to the conclusion that ". . . the hired farmhand is a typical nomad and therefore, without just cause, he wanders from a better manor to a worse one, from the manor to the city and then back again to the manor. . . ." Koszutski, *op. cit.,* 224. An interesting polemic against urban migration is that of one Jerzy Ryx: "This desire for sensational pleasures, to shine with someone else's feathers, to live-it-up, etc. — defects which are justly condemned in intelligent circles as a danger to the differentiation of status between the manor and the peasant — are deliberately and clandestinely encouraged by scummy elements, have gained curency among the masses of the people in alarming proportion. . . . [Such] people, deluded with this false and misunderstood urban well-being and not receiving from any source truly healthy directives, cast off their former ant-like, but nevertheless steady, livelihood and hasten there where most often misery and moral degeneration awaits them. . . . I look upon these unenlightened with love, forebearance and true sadness — these who are blind to every light and deaf to any teaching; who hasten today en masse to cities, factories and abroad — and I marvel at their disdain for the healthy and sufficient piece of bread." Jerzy Ryx, "Przyczynek do kwestji robotniczej w oswietleniu cyfr rachunkowosci rolnej," *W Naszych Sprawach* (Warszawa: 1896), II, 215.

The editor of the conservative *Niwa* suggested in 1885, in view of the large-scale, urban unemployment that the government, among other alternatives, consider restricting migration from rural to urban areas. Chorazy, "Sprawy biezace," *op. cit.,* 1885, R. XIV, t. XXVIII, 529–532. The socialist Wladyslaw

Gumplowicz, for differing reasons, endorsed overseas emigration of the rural population because, "Without this outlet, the stormy influx of the emiserated agricultural proletariat would soon overwhelm and destroy the workers' organizations in the cities and, with them, the whole socialist movement." See his, "Kwestja agrarna," *Przedswit* (Londyn), Ser. III, nr. 6, czerwiec 1899, 5.

73. See, for example, Boleslaw Koskowski, *Wychodztwo zarobkowe wloscian w Krolestwie polskiem* (Warszawa: 1901), a collection of articles published in the *Gazeta Polska* during that year. For Ludwik Krzywicki, see his: "Wychodztwo za zarobkami," *Glos* (1887), nr. 14, 213–214; "Obiezysastwo," *Gazeta Polska* (1892), nr. 3; "Wedrowka ludow," *ibid.* (1892), nr. 86; "Proby Powstrzymania emigracyi," *ibid.* (1892), nr. 87; "Kontrola a sprawa emigracyi," *ibid.* (1892), nr. 88; "Obiezysasi," *ibid.* (1892), nr. 220; "Prawa przeciw wychodztwu," *ibid.* (1892), nr. 270; "Wedrowka ludow," *ibid.* (1894), nr. 158; "Wyludnienie wsi," *ibid.* (1895), nr. 13; "Obiezysastwo," *ibid.* (1899), nr. 41, 52, 200, 247; "Polacy w zachodnich dzielnicach panstwa pruskiego," *ibid.* (1899), nr. 135. For Grabowski, see his "Bogactwo narodowe," *Slowo Polskie,* 14 luty 1907. See also, *supra,* p. 160.

74. Radziwill, *op. cit.* (1899), t. 233, 174–175.

75. Leopold Caro, for example, in a paper read at a conference of the Central Agricultural Society *(Centralne Towarzystwo Rolnicze),* an organization of large landowners — and reflecting that group's apparent concerns — affirmed that emigration (and especially seasonal emigration to Germany) represented a serious loss to domestic agricultural production. To correct this flaw he recommended the establishment of a network of public agricultural labor employment bureaus to satisfy indigenous labor needs as their first priority and then to control the emigration of surplus labor going abroad. See his: "Wychodztwo polskie," *Ekonomista* (Warszawa: 1907), R. VII, t. II, 2–3. The passage of the Expropriation Law of 1908 in Prussia evoked new alarms of a German *Drang nach Osten* and the growing threat of German agricultural settlements in Russian Poland. Stefan Gorski in the periodicals *Swiat Slowianski* and *Tygodnik Ilustrowany* and Adam Krasinski in the *Biblioteka Warszawska* demanded organized action against the sale of land to German settlers who were "threatening to overrun the land." Krasinski, "though not a proponent of precipitate alarms," gave complete coverage to Gorski's articles which included numerical estimates of German residents in Russian Poland, their "strategic dispersal along areas of military importance," their "obviously subversive" organizations and activities, etc. Adam Krasinski, "Kronika miesieczna," *Biblioteka Warszawska* (1908), t. 270, 190–194, 421–431.

76. This subject, which may be called, with some justice, "the politics of emigration," is dealt with more extensively *infra,* 165ff.

77. S. Krzeczkowski, "Wychodztwo wloscian z Krolestwa na zarobki," *Biblioteka Warszawska* (1901), t. 243, 56.

78. See, for example, Jozef Okolowicz, "Wychodztwo" in Stanislaw Janicki (ed.), *Stosunki rolnicze Krolestwa Kongresowego* (Warszawa: 1918), 98. Erasmus Piltz speaks of the importation of Galician field workers as if this practice continued throughout the pre-war years. Erasmus Piltz, *et al., Poland* (London: 1918), 246. For a populist rejoinder to this argument see, Alfred Weglinski, "Rok na wsi: kwiecien," *Glos* (Warszawa), R. XVI, nr. 18, 21 kwiecien (4 maja) 1901, 265–266.

79. Michal Radziwill, "Kronika miesieczna," *Biblioteka Warszawska* (1901), t. 241, 394–397.

80. *Ibid.*

81. Koskowski, *loc. cit.* See also: J. Krzyzowski, "Biura posrednictwa pracy i obrony prawnej dla 'Obiezysasow'," *Glos* (Warszawa), R. XVI, nr. 10, 24 luty (9 marzec) 1901, 135; A. Mediksza, "Wychodztwo i posrednictwo," *ibid.,* R. XVI, nr. 15, 31 marzec (13 kwiecien) 1901, 213, and B. Wasiutynski, "Ruch wychodzcy z Krolestwa Polskiego," *Czasopismo prawnicze i ekonomiczne* (Krakow: 1906), t. VII, 32. The prospects of an expanded degree of autonomy for Russian Poland in 1906 prompted Wasiutynski to think in terms of a system of public, agricultural employment agencies which would have the effect of countervailing the exclusive monopoly of German agencies in the recruitment of emigrant labor.

82. Adam Krasinski, "Kronika miesieczna," *Biblioteka Warszawska* (1908), t. 269, 616–619.

83. *Ibid.* (1907), t. 266, 602–604. See also: _____, "Komisya emigracyjna w Warszawie," *Polski Przeglad Emigracyjny* (Lwow), R. I, nr. 1, pazdz. 1907, 5–9. At approximately the same time a group called the 'Parana' Association *(Towarzystwo 'Parana')* came into existence constituted apparently by young, professionally and technically trained, intellectuals seeking wider horizons for their careers. Prospects for their talents seemed particularly promising in Parana — at least, better than their prospects at home. Their organization, founded as a joint-stock company, was modelled somewhat on the Polish Commercial-Geographic Association in Lwow, that is, conjoining idealistic, nationalistic motives with entrepreneurial ambitions. The editor of the Galician *Polski Przeglad Emigracyjny* viewed their prospects with some pessimism but nevertheless wished them well, if only as an outlet for the surpluses of "intellectual proletariat" in Russian Poland. *Ibid.,* 9–11.

84. Wojciech Szukiewicz, "Sprawa wychodztwa," *Biblioteka Warszawska* (1910), t. 278, 123–124.

85. *Ibid.,* 105 ff.; Mieczyslaw Szawleski, *Kwestja emigracji w Polsce* (Warszawa: 1927), 67 ff.; Jozef Okolowicz, *Wychodztwo i osadnictwo polskie przed wojna swiatowa* (Warszawa: 1920), 400–402; [Ludwik Gorski], "Kronika," *Wychodzca Polski* (Warszawa), zesz. 3, grudzien 1911, 22–23, and F. Z., "Wstrzymanie kolonizacyi brazylijskiej," in *ibid.,* 3. At least one of the contributors to this periodical, quite possibly reflecting its editorial views, spoke very favorably of the possibilities of redirecting overseas emigration to Canada — into rural, agricultural enclaves, more resistant to acculturation and assimilation than the dispersed emigrants in the urban-industrial centers of the United States. See: Jozef Modlinski, "Kolonizacya polska w Ameryce Polnocnej," *ibid.,* 5–6.

Even the conservative spokesman for the landed gentry, Maurycy Zamoyski, was disposed to chide that element of the population for its tendency to raise the alarm of "depopulation of the country" and its disposition to restrain all emigration even with falsified information and/or police measures. "Kronika miesieczna," *Biblioteka Warszawska* (1912), t. 287, 200–201.

86. *Supra,* 42 ff.

87. Weyssenhoff, *op. cit.* (1892), t. 206, 161.

88. *Ibid.* (1895), t. 219, 545.

89. Krzeczkowski, *op. cit.*, 54–55. This concession seems to be at variance with point made by Papieski, Balsigerowa and Okolowicz, *supra*, fn. 35, Ch. 2.
90. *Ibid.*
91. Relatively cost-free, inasmuch as a fee of 50 kopecks was charged for the book and two 75 kopeck stamps were necessary — for the passport petition and the government's reply — making the total cost two rubles. Szukiewicz, *op. cit.*, 108–109.
92. Memoir No. 1, "A worker in the Province of Cordoba, son of a small landholder in Kielce, born in 1889," *Pamietniki emigrantow: Ameryka poludniowa* (Warszawa: 1939), 7; Radziwill, *op. cit.* (1896), t. 223, 182; Krzeczkowski, *loc. cit.* See also *supra*, fn. 37, Ch. 2.
93. Szawleski, *op. cit.*, 35; Witold Kula, *Historia gospodarcza Polski, 1864–1918* (Warszawa: 1947), 23.
94. Szukiewicz, *op. cit.*, 126–127.
95. Michal Bujanowski, a former member of the *Duma*, and the publicist Ludwik Wlodek who participated in the hearings reported that the motive of the Russian authorities was primarily to develop Russian shipping. *Ibid.* See also: Wojciech Szukiewicz, "Z zagadnien emigracyjnych," *Ekonomista* (Warszawa: 1910), R. X, t. II, 100–102; Editorial, "Rozmaitosc," *Polski Przeglad Emigracyjny* (Krakow), R. IV, nr. 2, styczen 1910, 10 and Editorial, "Project Rosyjskiej ustawy emigracyjnej," *ibid.*, R. VI, nr. 7, lipiec 1912, 257–263.
96. The proposed emigration law was treated in some detail by Maurycy Zamoyski, "Kronika miesieczna," *Biblioteka Warszawska* (1914), t. 293, 387–390.
97. *Ibid.*, 389.
98. *Ibid.*, 390.
99. Marya Balsiger in *Srodkowo-europejski zwiazek gospodarczy a Polska* (Krakow: 1916), 105–106.

CHAPTER FIVE

1. For a comprehensive analysis of the political and ideological orientations in Galicia, see Wilhelm Feldman, *Stronnictwa i programy polityczne w Galicyi, 1846–1906* (Krakow: 1907) and pertinent sections of his *Dzieje polskiej mysli politycznej, 1864–1914* (Warszawa: 1933).
2. *Stenograficzne sprawozdania z drugiej sesji drugiego perjodu sejmu krajowego krolestwa Galicyi i Lodomeryi z Wielkiem Ksiestwem Krakowskiem z roku 1868* (Lwow: 1868), 302–303, hereinafter cited as *Stenog. Sprawozd.* with appropriate session, position, date and pages. *Ibid.*, 17 pos. (18 wrzesien 1868), 318–319, 324. See also, *Alegata do sprawozdan stenograficznych . . . 1868,* Alegat XXXVI, 11.
3. *Stenog. Sprawozd.*, II ses., II per., 16 pos. (17 wrzesien 1868), 296–297.
4. *Ibid.*, II ses., II per., 15 pos. (16 wrzesien 1868), 274–276; *ibid.*, 16 pos. (17 wrzesien 1868), 306–307. See also *Alegata do sprawozdan stenograficznych . . . 1868,* Alegat XXXVI a.
5. *Stenog. Sprawozd.*, II ses., II per., 16 pos. (17 wrzesien 1868), 297, 306.
6. *Alegata do sprawozdan stenograficznych . . . 1868,* Alegat XXVI, 4.
7. A peasant living on a small piece of land, insufficient to feed and clothe him and his family, must perforce augment his livelihood by outside employ-

ment. That small piece of land, according to Kosinski, by keeping him rooted to the peasant village, would assure the manor of a cheap laborer dependent upon the manor for his livelihood. *Stenog. Sprawozd.,* II ses., II per., 15 pos. (16 wrzesien 1868), 266.

8. *Ibid.,* 16 pos. (17 wrzesien 1868), 288.

9. *Ibid.,* 15 pos. (16 wrzesien 1868). According to Bujak, the repeal of the entail laws in 1868 was but a *de juris* recognition of a *de facto* practice. On the basis of his examination of the political writings in the first half of the nineteenth century, he concluded that the gentry favored and even encouraged the progressive break-up of peasant landholds contrary to the imperial patent in force at that time, because they saw their own interests best served by this process. Franciszek Bujak, "Rozwoj wsi zachodnio-galicyjskiej w drugiej polowie XIX w.," *Z odleglej i blizkiej przeszlosci. Studja historyczno-gospodarcze* (Lwow: 1924), 105. See also, A. Rembowski's review of the above essay by Bujak in *Biblioteka Warszawska* (1905), t. 259, 182.

10. The Galician law *(ustawa krajowa)* of 1 November 1868 repealed the existing entail legislation and the Austrian law *(ustawa panstwowa)* of the same year further facilitated the development of this process of alienation. Galician parcelation had its origins in these laws. Witold Lewicki, "Parcelacya w Galicyi jako objaw spoleczny," *Ekonomista Polski* (Lwow: 1890), T. I, 244–247. As early as 1874 the *sejm* was informed that the law of 1868, permitting the free disposition of land in Galicia, was having an effect which was contrary to what its supporters in 1868 had anticipated. *Stenog. Sprawozd.,* IV ses., III per., 21 pos. (14 styczen 1874), 378, 429. The designation "tabular land" or "tabular estates" was a legal distinction for manorial property registered as such because of the traditional privileges which appertained thereunto.

11. Bujak, *op. cit.,* 124–130; Bujak, *O naprawie ustroju rolnego w Polsce* (Warszawa: c. 1918), 22–23; Wojciech Saryusz-Zaleski, *Dzieje przemyslu w bylej Galicji, 1804–1929* (Krakow: 1930), 132–135; Stanislaw A. Kempner, *Rozwoj godpodarczy Polski, od rozbiorow do niepodleglosci* (Warszawa: 1919), 22; Emily Greene Balch, *Our Slavic Fellow Citizens* (New York: 1910), 47, 135–137; John Rozwadowski and Francis Bujak, "Galicia and Silesia of Cieszyn," *Polish Encyclopaedia* (Geneva: 1921), Vol. III, Pt. II, 262.

12. Bujak, "Rozwoj wsi zachodnio-galicyjskiej . . . ," *Z odleglej i blizkiej przeszlosci . . . ,* 112. The years 1872 and 1873 were also marked by the worst cholera epidemic in the recorded history of Galicia. According to official statistics, 19,667 died from that disease in 1872 and 90,802 in 1873. Because of its severity, the year 1873 represented one of the few years in the second half of the nineteenth century when the death rate exceeded the birth rate in that area. Jozef Buzek, "Rozsiedlenie ludnosci Galicyi wedlug wyznania i jezyka," *Wiadomosci Statystyczne o stosunkach krajowych [Statistischen Mitteilungen uber die Verhaltnisse Galiziens]* (Lwow: 1909), t. XXI, zesz. 2, 199; Stefan L. Zaleski, "General Demography of Poland," *Polish Encyclopaedia* (Geneva: 1921), Vol. II, No. 2, 142.

13. See interesting commentary on this situation by Dr. Jozef Wereszczynski in *Stenog. Sprawozd.,* IV ses., IV per., 22 pos. (18 pazdz. 1881), 501.

14. *Ibid.,* II ses., III per., 5 pos. (19 wrzesien 1871), 5.

15. *Ibid.,* V ses., III per., 8 pos. (28 wrzesien 1874), 96. As late as 1884, one writer, addressing himself to the need for an agricultural labor control law,

somewhat wistfully deplored the passage of the old *glebae adscripti* which constrained the peasants' predisposition to "vagrancy, vagabondage and irresponsibility." Zymunt Nawratil, "Slowo o robotnikach rolnych," *Przeglad sadowy i administracyjny* (Lwow: 1884), R. IX, 66. See also *infra,* 101 ff.

16. J. Siemiradzki, "Stosunki osadnicze w Brazylii," *Biblioteka Warszawska,* t. 205 (1892), 107.

17. The Brazilian land company which had undertaken this program to colonize the Brazilian tidewater failed in its enterprise and the emigrants they recruited in Galicia were resettled ultimately near Curitiba. K. Gluchowski, "Polacy w Brazylii," *Kwart. Inst. Nauk*... (kw.–czerw. 1927), R. II, nr. 2, 108. For further evidence of emigration from Galicia to Brazil during that decade, see letter of Rev. Anusz, dated September 29, 1908, from Araucara colony in Parana to the periodical *Polski Przeglad Emigracyjny,* reprinted in Zdzislaw Ludkiewicz, *Kwestja rolna w Galicyi* (Lwow: 1910), 267–270, and the precis of a paper on emigration delivered by Jozef Kleczynski at a meeting of the Third Congress of Polish Jurists and Economists in 1893 in Tadeusz Smarzewski, "Wiedza prawno-ekonomiczna na zjezdzie naukowym," *Biblioteka Warszawska* (1893), t. 212, 331.

18. Bronislaw Lozinski, "Agenor hr. Goluchowski w pierwszym okresie rzadow swoich," *Biblioteka Warszawska* (1900), t. 239, 89–92.

19. Franciszek Bujak, "Rozwoj wsi zachodnio-galicyjskiej w drugiej polowie XIX w.," *op. cit.,* 119–120, and his "Wychodztwo zarobkowe w Galicji," *op. cit.,* 228. The nineteenth century seasonal migrations of Carpathian harvesters to Russian Poland trace as far back as the sixteenth century. Even before that time there were migrations from Galicia to Silesia, Brandenburg and elsewhere in Prussia as is evident from the statutes of Olbracht in 1496 and the constitutional injunctions of various Polish *sejms* and *petit-sejms* against such migrations. Bujak, "Wychodztwo zarobkowe w Galicji," *loc. cit.;* Smarzewski, *op. cit.,* 331; Feliks Koneczny, "Konserwatysm chlopski," *Biblioteka Warszawska* (1903), t. 251, 579–580; Jan Stanislaw Bystron, "Szlaki migracyjne na ziemiach Polskich," *Przeglad Socjologiczny* (1936), t. III, zesz. 3–4, 124–125; J. S. Bystron, *Kultura ludowa* (Warszawa: 1936), 95, and Jan Rutkowski, *Historia Gospodarcza Polski* (Poznan: 1950), II, 15.

20. He based this statement on a comparison of the density of population in Galicia and Austrian Silesia as of the census of 1869. *Stenog. Sprawozd.,* III ses., IV per., 3 pos. (12 czerwiec 1880), 20; *ibid.,* 6 pos. (18 czerwiec 1880), 111–114; *Alegata do sprawozdan stenograficznych* ... *1880,* Alegat 42. This motion was sent to the Administrative Commission from which it was not reported.

21. Thereafter the Galician *sejm* followed a more tutelary policy, sometimes referred to as "moderate state socialism" which corresponded with that of the central government after the financial crash in 1873 and coincided with the neo-Mercantilistic tendencies in Europe in general. Eliasz Wytanowicz, "Polityka agrarna sejmu galicyjskiego w cyfrach budzetow krajowych," *Studja z historji spolecznej i gospodarczej poswiecone Franciszkowi Bujakowi* (Lwow: 1931), 281.

22. Jozef Kleczynski, "Ekomiczne stosunki Galicyi. Czesc 1. Stosunki wloscian w Galicyi," *Wiadomosci statystyczne o stosunkach krajowych* (Lwow: 1881), Rocznik VIII, zesz. 1.

23. *Stenog. Sprawozd.,* IV ses., IV per., 11 pos. (3 pazdz. 1881), 200–201; *ibid.,* 12 pos. (5 pazdz. 1881), 220 and *ibid.,* 28 pos. (23 pazdz. 1881), 815–818.
24. *Ibid.,* I ses., V per., 7 pos. (27 wrzesien 1883), 145–146; *ibid.,* 8 pos. (1 pazdz. 1883), 177–179; *ibid.,* 21 pos. (17 pazdz. 1883), 538–567.
25. *Ibid.,* 8 pos. (1 pazdz. 1883), 178–179.
26. *Ibid.,* 21 pos. (17 pazdz. 1883), 553.
27. *Ibid.,* 565.
28. *Ibid.,* 555.
29. *Ibid.,* 558.
30. *Ibid.,* 560–562.
31. *Ibid.,* 542–543.
32. *Alegata do tomu pierwszego sprawozdan stenograficznych z I ses., V per., sejmu krajowego . . . z r. 1883,* Alegat 110, 2.
33. Tadeusz Pilat, "Wybory do sejmu krajowego w r. 1883," *Wiadomosci statystyczne o stosunkach krajowych* (Lwow: 1884), Rocznik VIII, zesz. 111, 112–113, 133–136.
34. For commentary on the political and social implications of these tendencies, see *Stenog. Sprawozd.,* I ses., V per., 21 pos. (17 pazdz. 1883), 550, 566; *ibid.,* V ses., V per., 8 pos. (9 grudzien 1887), 137, 145. This tendency was first called to the attention of the *sejm* in 1874 by Deputy Baum. *Ibid.,* IV ses., III per., 21 pos. (14 styczen 1874), 374, 429.
35. *Alegata do stenograficznych sprawozdan sejmu krajowego . . . z r. 1886/1887,* t. II, Alegat 151; *ibid.,* z r. 1887/1888, t. I, Alegat 31; *ibid.,* t. II, Alegat 60. At the First Congress of Polish Jurists and Economists (Krakow, 1887), during a discussion on the advisability of reforming existing inheritance laws as they pertained to peasant landholds, it was maintained that the right of unlimited divisibility of their land resulted in a tendency toward irrational fragmentation. In Russian Poland, however, peasant landholds of less than 6 *morgs* could not be broken up via inheritance. Adolf Suligowski, "Pierwszy zjazd prawnikow i ekonomistow polskich," *Ateneum* (Warszawa: 1887), T. XLVIII, 305.
36. In 1875, Deputy Stepek, citing the findings of the Galician Statistical Bureau, noted in the *sejm* that while in 1867 only 164 peasant landholds were put up for auction to satisfy debts on their land, their number had increased to 271 in 1868, 614 in 1873 and 1,026 in 1874. *Stenog. Sprawozd.,* VI ses., III per., 14 pos. (10 maj 1875), 225.
37. *Alegata do sprawozdan stenograficznych sejmu krajowego . . . z r. 1876,* Alegat LXXIV.
38. *Ibid.,* z r. 1877, Alegat 8.
39. *Stenog. Sprawozd.,* I ses., IV per., 6 pos. (17 sierp. 1877), 152–156.
40. *Ibid.,* 14 pos. (29 sierp. 1877), 461–462.
41. *Alegata do sprawozdan stenograficznych . . . sejmu krajowego . . . z r. 1878,* Alegat 7.
42. According to the findings of its statistical bureau, these auctions had increased from 1,026 in 1874 to 1,326 in 1875, to 1,433 in 1876 and to 2,139 in 1877. *Ibid.,* 6–7.
43. Called *powiatowe kasy pozyczkowe* and *towarzystwa zaliczkowe,* respectively. *Ibid.,* 3–5.
44. *Ibid.,* 2–3.
45. *Ibid.,* 7.

46. *Stenog. Sprawozd.,* II ses., IV per., 14 pos. (8 pazdz. 1878), 351–405; *ibid.,* 15 pos. (9 pazdz. 1878), 409–434; *ibid.,* 16 pos. (10 pazdz. 1878), 409–434. See also *Alegata do sprawozdan stenograficznych . . . sejmu krajowego . . . z r. 1878,* Alegat 7 and Alegat 101.

47. *Ibid.,* z r. 1880, Alegat 28.

48. It was composed of Henryk Wodzicki, Piotr Gross, J. Pajaczkowski, W. Russocki, Arnold Rapaport, Tadeusz Pilat, H. Kieszkowski, M. Gnoinski and A. Gorajski. *Ibid.*

49. *Stenog. Sprawozd.,* II ses., IV per., 14 pos. (8 pazdz. 1878), 357–358.

50. *Ibid.,* 373–375.

51. *Ibid.,* IV ses., IV per., 21 pos. (17 pazdz. 1881), 470.

52. *Ibid.,* V ses., III per., 8 pos. (28 wrzesien 1874), 96–97.

53. Tarnowski cited a typical example. A peasant suddenly in need of 30 florin, in the absence of local credit facilities, was forced to address his plea to the lord of the manor. There he obtained the loan on the condition that he give one day of his labor each week *as interest* until the loan was *paid in full.* By reckoning the value of this labor at 25 cents per day — the total interest for 52 weeks was 13 florin, or almost 50 percent interest. Stanislaw Tarnowski, "Porcje," *Przeglad Polski* (1874), R. IX, t. X, 163–179, reprinted in *Galicja w dobie autonomicznej, 1850–1914; Wybor tekstow,* edited by Stefan Kieniewicz (Wroclaw: 1952), 209, 215. A trial case before the courts of Krakow in 1877 was otherwise unremarkable except that it brought to light the prevailing interest rates which, in this case, amounted to 3.52% interest per month, i.e., 42.24% per annum. Anastazy Kwiryn, "Stopa procentowa," *Ateneum* (Warszawa: 1877), T. IV, 533–534 and ff.

54. *Stenog. Sprawozd.,* IV ses., IV per., 22 pos. (18 pazdz. 1881), 499.

55. *Ibid.,* 501.

56. *Ibid.,* 21 pos. (17 pazdz. 1881), 476–477.

57. When an attempt was made in 1873 to make these registers *(ksiegi tabularne)* accessible to prospective purchasers without journeying to either Krakow or Lwow, the effort was defeated by those who held that decentralization would facilitate parcelation. *Ibid.,* IV ses., III per., 15 pos. (30 grudzien 1873), 230, 239, 241.

58. For numerous attempts by both public and private individuals to accelerate the establishment of these *ksiegi hipoteczne,* see *ibid.,* I ses., IV per., 5 pos. (16 sierp. 1877), 177; *ibid.,* 6 pos. (17 sierp. 1877), 151–152; *ibid.,* II ses., IV per., 2 pos. (13 wrzesien 1878), 18; *ibid.,* 4 pos. (19 wrzesien 1878), 45–46; *ibid.,* 10 pos. (2 pazdz. 1878), 213–215; *ibid.,* I ses., V per., 7 pos. (27 wrzesien 1883), 161.

59. *Ibid.,* V ses., V per., 15 pos. (20 grudzien 1887), 385–386.

60. *Ibid.,* 388.

61. *Ibid.,* 389.

62. See statements by the deputies Koziebrodzki, Struszkiewicz and Merunowicz in *ibid.,* VI ses., V per., 28 pos. (9 styczen 1889), 33–34, 36–37, 38.

63. *Ibid.,* I ses., IX per., 6 pos. (22 wrzesien 1908), 261–264; *ibid.,* 10 pos. (1 pazdz. 1908), 408; and *ibid.,* 12 pos. (8 pazdz. 1908), 513. This point was reiterated by the same speaker in *ibid.,* 53 pos. (13 pazdz. 1909), 3106.

64. Franciszek Bujak, "Maszkienice, Wies powiatu brzeskiego; Stosunki gospodarcze i spoleczne," *Rozprawy Akademji Umiejetnosci, Wydzial Historyczno-Filozoficzny* (Krakow: 1902), t. XXXI, 149–152. See also, *supra,* fn. 54, Ch. 5.

65. Bujak, "Rozwoj wsi zachodnio-galicyjskiej w drugiej polowie XIX w.," *op. cit.,* 115.

66. See, for example, *Stenog. Sprawozd.,* III ses., II per., 13 pos. (9 pazdz. 1869), 214-215; *ibid.,* II ses., III per., 23 pos. (16 pazdz. 1871), 2; *ibid.,* II ses., IV per., 24 pos. (18 pazdz. 1878), 800. One extensive petition addressed to the Legal Commission of the *sejm* by a *Towarzystwo ochrony miejscowej wlasnosci ziemskiej* of Mielec, in outlining the practices of the Peasant Bank, observed that wherever that bank extended its operations on a wider scale there was evidence of a marked economic and material decline of the general welfare and a rapid increase of emigration to the United States. *Ibid.,* V ses., IV per., 19 pos. (6 pazdz. 1882), 344-345.

67. Teofil Merunowicz, *Zaklad Kredytu Wloscianskiego* (Lwow: 1878), quoted by Wladyslaw Zawadzki, "Kronika Lwowska," *Biblioteka Warszawska* (1878), t. 152, 92-95.

68. *Alegata do sprawozdan stenograficznych sejmu galicyjskiego . . . z r. 1880,* Alegat 159, 2.

69. Bujak, *loc. cit.* See also his *Maszkienice,* I, 141.

70. Leopold Caro, "Lichwa wiejska i kredyt wloscianski," *Biblioteka Warszawska* (1896), t. 223, 477. The popular notion that Jews were the exclusive operatives in this ruinous practice was challenged by a writer in the socialist *Przedswit.* In Galicia, bankruptcy proceedings against the peasants during the period 1867-1883 were initiated: (1) in 41% of the cases by Jews, (2) in 30% by the Peasant Bank and (3) in 17% of the cases by private Christian creditors. N., "Lichwa, jej przyczyny i skutki," *ibid.,* Ser. III, nr. 9; wrzesien 1896, 2-6.

71. Caro, *op. cit.,* 481-482.

72. *Ibid.,* 487. He was one of the first to point out the direct relationship between emigration and the almost total absence of legitimate and favorable credit facilities for that class of the Galician population. In his view, it was this deficiency which forced many of the peasants to do business with usurers — an exigency which frequently reduced them to bankruptcy and, therefore, to emigration. *Ibid.,* 475, 481, 487, 489. For a short but incisive survey and evaluation of the credit facilities available to the peasant class at that date see, *ibid.,* 484-486. Dr. Wladyslaw Krainski, at the Second Congress of Polish Jurists and Economists (Lwow, 1889), in a paper entitled "On the organization of peasant credit facilities in Galicia," suggested the extension into the villages of Schultze-Delitsche and Reiffesen type of banks. The general membership of that body was reported to have voiced its approbation of this suggestion. D., "Drugi zjazd prawnikow i ekonomistow polskich," *Przewodnik naukowy i literacki* (Lwow: 1889), R. XVII, 954-955.

73. Bujak, *op. cit.,* 116.

74. Jan Rutkowski, "Licytacje sadowe posiadlosci wloscianskich i malomiejskich, zarzadzone w latach 1910-1912 z uwzglednieniem lat dawniejszych," *Wiadomosci statystyczne o stosunkach krajowych* (Lwow: 1914), t. XXV, zesz. 1, 1-17. For the condition of peasant credit facilities in pre-war Russian Poland, see *supra,* 48ff.

75. Zdzislaw Ludkiewicz, "Ziemia i ludnosc rolnicza," in Stanislaw A. Kempner (ed.), *Dzieje gospodarcze Polski porozbiorowej w zarysie* (Warszawa: 1920), II, 102. In its stipulations and intent the law providing for the establishment of *wlosci rentowe* seems to have been modeled after the *Rentenguter* legislation of 1890-1891 in Prussia. See *supra,* 19ff.

76. *Stenog. Sprawozd.,* II ses., VIII per. (1904), 18, 824–895, 905–937. For the contending views on this subject see: A. Warski, "Z nedzy Galicyjskiej," *Glos* (Warszawa), R. XVI, nr. 26, 16 (29) czerwiec 1901, 389–390, representing the earlier, populist view and H. Wielowiejski, "Kolonizacja wewnetrzna i metoda jej przeprowadzenia," *Przeglad Powszechny* (Krakow), marzec 1914, t. CXXI, nr. 363, 305–315, representing the conservative-nationalistic point of view.

77. Jozef Kleczynski, "Stosunki ekonomiczne w Galicyi," *Wiadomosci statystyczne* (Lwow: 1881), R. VII, zesz. 1, 71; R. Buczynski, "Nasza wlasnosc ziemska . . . ," *Biblioteka Warszawska* (1882), t. 167, fn. 1, p. 348; Fr. Morawski, "Przesiedlenie sie ludnosci z Galicyi zachodniej do wschodniej," *Wiadomosci statystyczne* (Lwow: 1890), R. XV, zesz. III, 43, 45, 50; U., "Kronika galicyjska," *Biblioteka Warszawska* (1892), t. 208, 58–59; *ibid.* (1893), t. 209, 124; *ibid.* (1895), t. 218, 117; Jozef Buzek, "Rozsiedlenie ludnosci Galicyi wedlug wyznania i jezyka," *Wiadomosci statystyczne* (Lwow: 1909), t. XXI, zesz. II, 190–196, 200, 201–202; Leon Wasilewski, "Ze stosunkow polsko-ruskich w Galicyi wschodniej," *Biblioteka Warszawska* (1911), t. 283, 455–464; Wlodzimierz Wakar, "Territorial Development of the Polish Nation," *Polish Encyclopaedia* (Fribourg: 1921), Vol. II, No. 3, 517–531, 532, 533 and fn. 2, 553.

78. Wytanowicz, *op. cit.,* 278–279; Wilhelm Feldman, "Unarodowienie ziemi," *Krytyka* (Krakow: 15 kwiecien 1914), R. XVI, nr. VIII, 66.

79. See, *supra,* fn. 57.

80. Jozef Milewski, *W sprawie utrzymaniu ziemi w naszym reku* [odbitka z *Ziemianina*] (Poznan: 1884), 73; Jozef Milewski, "O kwestji socjalnej, mowa na wiecu lwowskim," *Przeglad powszechny* (Krakow: sierpien 1896), 244–260; Jozef Milewski, "Kwestja robotnikow rolnych," *Przeglad Polski* (Krakow), marzec 1906; Wlodzimierz Czerkawski, "Wielkie gospodarstwa, ich istota i znaczenie," *Rozprawy Akademii Umiejetnosci,* Wydzial Historyczno-Filozoficzny (Krakow: 1896), t. XXXIV; and their collaborative work, *Polityka ekonomiczna* (Krakow: 1905), 2 vols.

81. Zofia Daszynska-Golinska, "Ze statystyki rolniczej," *Ateneum* (Warszawa), sierpien 1892; "Z demografii wspolczesnej," *ibid.,* kwiecien 1894, 103–116; "Wlasnosc rolna w Galicyi," *ibid.,* lipiec 1899, 72–108; *ibid.,* sierpien 1899, 315–339; "Badania nad wsia polska," *Krytyka* (Krakow: pazdziernik 1903), R. V., zesz. 10; "Wlasnosc rolna w krajach Austryi," *Ekonomista* (Warszawa: 1904), R. IV, t. I, zesz. 1; *Wlasnosc rolna w Galicyi, studyum statystyczno-spoleczne* (Warszawa: 1900); *Alkoholizm jako objaw choroby spolecznej* (Krakow: 1905); *Zarys ekonomii spolecznej* (Lwow: 1898).

82. Franciszek Bujak, "Rozwoj wsi zachodnio galicyjskiej w drugiej polowie XIX w.," *Z odleglej i blizkiej przeszlosci. Studja historyczno-gospodarcze* (Lwow: 1924); "Kilka przyczynkow i sprostowan do pracy Dra. Hupki . . . ," *op. cit.,* 160–162; *Uwagi spoleczno-gospodarcze dla wloscian* (Lwow: 1916), 7.

83. Jan Rozwadowski, *Parcelacya wielkiej wlasnosci w swietle postepowania pruskich instytucyj posredniczacych* (Lwow: 1903), 359–360. See also his: "Znaczenie parcelacyj wiekszej wlasnosci w Galicyi," *Przeglad sadowy i administracyjny* (Lwow), lipiec 1901, R. XXVI, 511–529. For a short discussion of Rozwadowski's brief venture into economic radicalism, see *supra,* fn. 14, Ch. 4.

84. Stanislaw Hupka, *Stan wspolczesny i metoda badan wsi polskiej w Galicyi Zachodniej* (Krakow: 1912), 16; his, *Uber die Entwicklung der westgalizischen Dorfzustande in der zweite Halfte des 19 Jahrhunderts* (Teschen: 1910), 273–274. Substantially the same point of view was expressed by Leon W. Biegeleisen in his: *Rozwoj gospodarczy nowoczesnej wsi polskiej* (Krakow: 1916–1917), 2 vols., and *Przewod spadkowo-opiekunczy a ustroj wlasnosci chlopskiej. Studyum z zakresu gospodarczo-sprawnych stosunkow ludnosci wloscianskiej w Galicyi* (Lwow: 1914). Not infrequently the family remaining in Poland found itself in the ambiguous position of desiring to retain contacts with the member abroad, for material and other reasons, but at the same time discouraging his return if his presence would cut off their receipts from abroad and possibly prove a hardship for others of his family at home as, for example, the claiming of his rightful legacy which in the meantime had become a sole source of livelihood for other members of his family. See, for example, Nos. 283, 310 and 619 of the peasant correspondence in William I. Thomas and Floryan Znaniecki, *The Polish Peasant in Europe and America* (Chicago: 1918–1920), Vol. I.

85. The Galician correspondent of the *Biblioteka Warszawska,* as early as 1893, noted the tendency of the emigrant-peasants to locate their savings almost exclusively in land and thereby contributing to inflated prices. U., "Kronika galicyjska," *op. cit.* (1893), t. 211, 88. The Galician deputy, Wiktor Skolyszewski, reminded the provincial *sejm* in 1907 that emigration was almost exclusively responsible for the tremendous increases in land prices and creating a situation which was especially auspicious for those who owned land. *Stenog. Sprawozd.,* III ses., VIII per., 28 pos. (26 wrzesien 1907), 1833. For the peasants' social concept of land ownership see, Thomas and Znaniecki, *op. cit.,* I, 190.

86. Franciszek Bujak, "Maszkienice, wies powiatu brzeskiego; Rozwoj od 1900 do 1911," *Rozprawy Akademii Umiejetnosci,* Wydzial Historyczno-Filozoficzny (Krakow: 1914), t. LVIII, 111. This point is further confirmed by one of his students, Eliasz Wytanowicz, *op. cit.,* 283.

87. According to the findings of Herman Diamand, the mortgage indebtedness of manorial estates *(wlasnosc tabularna)* increased from 315 million crowns in 1880 to 343.5 million in 1890, to 516 million in 1900, to 751 million in 1910. See his, *Polozenie gospodarcze Galicyi przed wojna* (Lipsk: 1915), 34.

88. See, for example, Tadeusz Pilat, "Wlasnosc tabularna w Galicyi," *Wiadomosci statystyczne o stosunkach krajowych* (Lwow: 1889), t. XII; Jozef Buzek, "Wlasnosc tabularna w Galicyi wedlug stanu z koncem r. 1902," *ibid.* (1902), t. XX, zesz. III; Tadeusz Brzeski, "Parcelacya wlasnosci tabularnej w Galicyi," *ibid.* (1912), t. XXIII, zesz. II. Helena Landau-Bauer took rather sharp issue with such writers in general and with Brzeski specifically. Using the latter's statistics, she equated the negligible amount of land transferred from the tabular rolls during the period 1868–1888 with the negligible volume of emigration during that period; the increased transfers during the period 1888–1902 with the corresponding increases in emigration volume and, finally, the very substantial transfers during the flood-tide of emigration in the decade before the war. See her, "Kurja wiekszej wlasnosci," *Krytyka* (Krakow: pazdz. 1912), R. XIV, t. XXXV, 118–123. See also, Edward Maurizio, "Przeobrazenie wsi galicyjskiej," *ibid.,* R. XIV, t. XXXIII, 227–232; Witold Kula, *Historia gospodarcza Polski, 1864–1914* (Warszawa: 1947), 64. For those who

continued to explain that the large volume of parcelation was the direct result of declining grain prices on the European market, she noted that the process accelerated rather than diminished after 1907 when the agricultural crisis had passed and continued to increase after 1909 ". . . when the price of grain exceeded the highest expectations of Galician agricultural interests." See her, "Emigracya a ruch parcelacyjny w Galicyi" in *Srodkowo-europejski zwiazek gospodarczy a Polska. Studya ekonomiczne* (Krakow: 1916), 115 ff., and her, "Z zagadnien emigracyjnych," *Krytyka* (Krakow), R. XVI, t. XLI, luty 1914, 164-168. Similar judgments were being advanced in Russian Poland by the turn of the century. See, for example, Jan Rozwadowski, "Znaczenie parcelacyi wiekszej wlasnosci," *Ekonomista* (Warszawa: 1901), R. I, t. I, 283-304 and Kor., "Na widnokregach," *Glos* (Warszawa), R. XVII, nr. 21, 11 (22) maja 1902, 336.

89. For a summary of subjects discussed and papers read at this meeting as well as some commentary upon them, see, Jozef Milewski, "Pierwszy zjazd prawnikow i ekonomistow polskich w Krakowie," *Biblioteka Warszawska* (1887), t. 188, 116-126.

90. Tadeusz Smarzewski, "Wiedza prawno-ekonomiczna na zjezdzie naukowym," *Biblioteka Warszawska* (1893), t. 212, 331. See also, Jozef Kleczynski, "Trzeci zjazd prawnikow i ekonomistow polskich," *Przeglad Polski* (Krakow: listopad 1893), 396-411, and U., "Kronika galicyjska," *Biblioteka Warszawska* (1893), t. 211, 88.

91. The largest postal receipts were noted in the counties of: Jaslo (659,094 kr.), Gorlice (577,746 kr.), Sanok (442,670 kr.), Mielec (281, 062 kr.), Nowy Targ (273,650 kr.), Pilzno (259,498 kr.), Krosno (226,594 kr.) — all in the central part of Galicia — and Rohatyn (357,460 kr.) in eastern Galicia. U., "Kronika galicyjska," *Biblioteka Warszawska* (1896), t. 221, 105-106. To facilitate comparison and to maintain uniformity all monetary units have been reduced to their equivalents in crowns. Between 1892 and the outbreak of the war, there were no substantial changes in the value of Austrian currency with the crown established at .2026 of the United States dollar and the florin (gulden, zl. r.) at .4052, or double the value of the crown. See, United States Bureau of the Mint, *The Monetary Systems of the Principal Countries of the World. 1913* (Washington, D.C.: 1913), 4-5.

92. Quoted in Waclaw Kruszka, *Historja Polska w Ameryce* (Milwaukee: 1905), I, 46.

93. *Stenog. Sprawozd.*, I ses., VIII per., 21 pos. (15 wrzesien 1903), 1314, 1317.

94. *Ibid.*, II ses., VIII per., 48 pos. (9 listopad 1905), 2541-2542. The more careful contemporary observer, Franciszek Bujak, estimated that the average "temporary" emigrant in the United States at approximately that time realized a net saving of about 1200 crowns per year, though he had heard of some who managed to save from 1600 to 2000 crowns. See his, "Rozwoj wsi zachodnio-galicyjskiej w drugiej polowie XIX w.," *op. cit.*, 121-122. By 1911, however, he estimated that the annual net savings of the Polish emigrant in the United States averaged about 1000 crowns. *Maszkienice . . . ,* II, III. At the current exchange of approximately 5:1 this represented about 200 dollars per year.

95. Ignacy Daszynski, *Pamietniki* (Krakow: 1925), I, 16.

96. Skolyszewski estimated that about 60 million crowns came to Galicia annually from the United States alone. That money was utilized not only for

the purchase of land but, via taxes, was drawn into the fiscal mechanism of the government. *Stenog. Sprawozd.,* I ses., IX per., 20 pos. (17 pazdz. 1908), 924, 927. The validity of this contention was confirmed in 1910 when, as a result of agitation for the reform of the curia system it was found that the largest quota of taxes was paid by the cities (44.4 percent of the total); next came the peasant villages *(gminy wiejskie)* with 42.6 percent of the total taxes and, lastly the landed curia *(wielka wlasnosc)* with only 13.0 percent of the total taxes paid in Galicia. Marcin Nadobnik, "Podatki bezposrednie w Galicyi," *Wiadomosci statystyczne . . . ,* t. XXIII, zesz. III, 15–16 and Table V.

97. *Stenog. Sprawozd.,* III ses., VIII per., 28 pos. (27 wrzesien 1907), 1833; *ibid.,* 29 pos. (28 wrzesien 1907), 1875. See also, *ibid.,* I ses., IX per., 20 pos. (17 pazdz. 1908), 924–925.

98. *Ibid.,* 68 pos. (27 styczen 1910), 4060. The extent of the dependence of the Galician economy upon the emigrant earnings in the United States was graphically illustrated by the failure of the privately operated Parcelation Bank *(Bank Parcelacyjny)* of Galicia. This institution, like other speculative undertakings of its kind, operated on a small margin of original capitalization and a large volume of land acquisitions for which they made only a deposit payment to the former owner. With the advent of an economic recession in the United States after the turn of the century, emigrant earnings and transmittals declined, and peasant buyers in Galicia were obliged either to default on their payments or, more often, to restrain their desire to buy land from that bank. As a result of this, the bank found itself with much purchased land on its hands which it was unable to liquidate, while its financial obligations to the Provincial Bank *(Bank Krajowy)* and operating expenses were exhausting its original capitalization fund. In the case of the Parcelation Bank, it was forced into bankruptcy. Brzeski, *op. cit.,* 39; Skolyszewski in *Stenog. Sprawozd.,* I ses., IX per., 68 pos. (27 styczen 1910), 4057–4059; Kozlowski in *ibid.,* 69 pos. (28 styczen 1910), 4093. Leopold Caro, considering specifically the seasonal emigration from both the Kingdom and Galicia, concluded that it was the chief item of national export. Caro, "Nasi robotnicy sezonowi," *Przeglad Powszechny* (Krakow) luty 1908, t. XCVII, nr. 290, 183. Count Baworowski, the Galician deputy to the *Reichsrat,* addressing himself on behalf of the contemplated emigration law of 1912 in that body, came to the same conclusion. ____, "Mowa posla hr. Baworowskiego," *Polski Przeglad Emigracyjny* (Krakow), R. VI, maj-czerwiec 1912, 189. Wojciech Szukiewicz, concluding that the capital increment from emigration into all sectors of pre-war Poland was important in the fiscal balance of the nation, could still marvel that the most notable and serious economists were not recognizing that fact. See his, "Z zagadnien emigracyjnych," *Ekonomista* (Warszawa: 1910), R. X, t. II, 80–81.

99. Franciszek Bujak, "Podstawy rozwoju przemyslu w Galicji," *Z odleglej i blizkiej przeszlosci . . .* (Lwow: 1924), 216. The Galician deputy to the *Reichsrat,* Count Lasocki, speaking on behalf of the projected emigration law of 1912 in that body, estimated that the annual increment into the empire from both continental and overseas emigration amounted to about 250 million crowns — a very consequential factor in that nation's fiscal balance. ____, "Mowa posla hr. Lasockiego," *Polski Przeglad Emigracyjny* (Krakow), R. VI, maj-czerwiec 1912, 191–193.

100. Wilhelm Feldman, "Unarodowienie ziemi," *Krytyka* (Krakow: 15 kwiecien 1914), R. XVI, nr. VIII, 65.

101. Wladyslaw Gumplowicz, "Socjalism a kwestja Polska," *Krytyka* (Krakow: pazdz. 1906), R. VIII, zesz. 10, 272.

CHAPTER SIX

1. There is some evidence suggesting that the subject of emigration may have been studiously ignored in the *sejm*. On the several occasions that emigration, as such, was mentioned, it was only to be vigorously denied. In 1868, the deputies Skrzynski and Krainski affirmed that the Polish peasant did not and would not emigrate because of his attachment to the land. *Stenog. Sprawozd.*, II ses., II per., 15 pos. (16 wrzes. 1868), 266; *ibid.*, 16 pos. (17 wrzes. 1868), 296-297, 302-303, 306. In 1874 the deputy Skrzynski again denied the existence of emigration. *Ibid.*, V ses., III per., 20 pos. (15 pazdz. 1874), 508. The only explicit affirmation of its existence occurred in 1880 when Deputy Rapaport raised a motion ". . . to inquire into the ways and means of restraining emigration." Without any discussion on its merits, it was passed onto a committee which never reported on it. *Ibid.*, III ses., IV per., 3 pos. (12 czerw. 1880), 20; *ibid.*, 6 pos. (18 czerw. 1880), 111-114. In 1883 a denial of the existence of any emigration was made by Hausner. *Ibid.*, I ses., V per., 21 pos. (17 pazdz. 1883), 540, 542. Though a motion ". . . to collect all pertinent data and information on the causes, extent, direction and organization of emigration," was made by Teofil Merunowicz in 1895, and reported out by the Executive Department sitting as a committee, its findings were not published. U., "Kronika galicyjska," *Biblioteka Warszawska* (1896), t. 221, 103-104; J. Siemiradzki, "W sprawie emigracyi wloscianskiej w Brazylii," *ibid.* (1900), t. 236, 131-133. In 1904, Bujak expressed astonishment that, in view of the dependence of economic life in Galicia upon emigrant earnings, the Galician *sejm* had still failed to take the phenomenon under advisement. Franciszek Bujak, "Rozwoj wsi zachodnio-galicyjskiej w drugiej polowie XIX w.," *Z odleglej i blizkiej przeszlosci. Studja historyczno-gospodarcze* (Lwow: 1924), 114. In the *sejm* of that year, Baworowski, a deputy from the landed curia in eastern Galicia, publicly asserted that there was a time when the subject of emigration was deliberately ignored in the public discussions of that body for fear that such discussions would "waken the sleeping dog." *Stenog. Sprawozd.*, II ses., VIII per., 12 pos. (20 pazdz. 1904), 520.

In 1908, Deputy Skolyszewski, raising a motion to discuss emigration to Brazil, remarked that he had been privately reprimanded by someone whom he identified only as "a high official in the government" who asked him to ". . . please draw me a line of demarcation between that which can be considered discussion and that which is encouragement to emigration." *Ibid.*, I ses., IX per., 20 pos. (17 pazdz. 1908), 924.

The academic establishment showed a similar reluctance to legitimize the subject. An effort was made to establish a "free university" in Krakow in 1911 which offered a three-hour course by Leopold Caro entitled "Emigration and Colonization," a two-hour course by B. Limanowski entitled "A History of Polish Emigration in the 19th Century" and others by Wilhelm Feldman, Wl. Gumplowicz, Ludwik Krzywicki, Zofia Daszynska-Golinska and Franciszek Bujak. Confronted with this challenge, the faculty of the University of Jagiello

established a parallel program called the Polish School of Political Science
(Polska Szkola Nauk Politycznych) which, supported by the governments in
Lwow and Vienna, apparently drained off a sufficient number of students to
force the original institution *(Szkola Nauk Spoleczno-Politycznych w Krakowie)* to severely curtail its offerings and subsequently fold. In any case, the
subject of emigration — dealt with directly as such — was not included among
those projected for the following year. _____, "Szkola nauk spoleczno-politycznych w Krakowie," *Krytyka* (Krakow), R. XIII, t. XXIX, 1911, 333–335
and *ibid.*, R. XIV, t. XXXV, 1912, 147–149. Zofia Daszynska-Golinska, in
making the case for Demography as a legitimate *Wissenschaft,* stressed its
radical and existential relevance inasmuch as, like emerging Sociology but
unlike traditional History, its concern was with the condition of the total
population. The latter she saw as seriously constrained by its tradition of "by
mandarins, for mandarins and about mandarins." Quite apparently she saw
Demography as an academic vehicle and instrument for the advancement of
social democracy. See her: "Demografia jako nauka," *Ekonomista* (Warszawa: 1911), R. XI, t. III, 1–22.

2. *Supra,* 79 ff.
3. *Supra,* 86 ff.
4. *Stenog. Sprawozd.,* II ses., III per., 5 pos. (19 wrzes. 1871), 5; *ibid.,* V
ses., III per., 8 pos. (28 wrzes. 1874), 96.
5. *Ibid.,* V ses., IV per., 31 pos. (21 pazdz. 1882), 816. As a concomitant of
this movement to "control" the provincial labor supply a motion was raised by
Jozef Mecinski, a large landowner, to limit or otherwise reduce the number of
market and fair days *(targi i jarmarki)* by law. He argued that their proliferation and the disposition of the peasants to attend as many as possible tended to
increase laziness among the peasantry, fostered careless attention to their land
and, in general, gravitated against their material and moral well-being. He
reiterated that "landowners complain for lack of field workers. How often do
we see during harvest time [when need for field workers was most imperative]
hundreds of people trudging to distant fairs needlessly?" *Ibid.,* I ses., V per., 12
pos. (6 pazdz. 1883), 274. It may be pertinent to note that these "fairs" and
Jahrmarkts were not only the chief source of information for the peasant on
the conditions of the market for his produce but also for information on the
"outside" conditions of the labor market.
6. "Sprawozdanie Wydzialu Krajowego z projektem ustawy zawierajacej
przepisy o stosunkach slug i o najmie robotnikow do wiejskiego gospodarstwa," *Alegata do sprawozdan stenograficznych sejmu krajowego . . . z r.
1883,* Alegat I. See also, *supra,* 82.
7. *Stenog. Sprawozd.,* II ses., V per., 11 pos. (6 pazdz. 1884), 277–278;
ibid., 21 pos. (18 pazdz. 1884), 635–636; *ibid.* (1886/1887), 143, 751; *ibid.*
(1887/1888), 794–797, 799–811.
8. *Ibid.,* VI ses., V per., 30 pos. (12 styczen 1889), 65–83; *ibid.,* 31 pos. (14
styczen 1889), 89–101; *ibid.,* 37 pos. (24 styczen 1889), 296–299, 322–338. See
also, *Alegata do sprawozdan stenograficznych sejmu krajowego . . . z r.
1888/1889,* Alegat 139 and Alegat 185.
9. Nevertheless, as late as 1907 a motion was made by Zdislaw Tarnowski
". . . to regularize, by legislative sanction," the contractual relationship between agricultural employer and employee [see *Stenog. Sprawozd.,* III ses.,
VIII per., 18 pos. (13 marzec 1907), 1029–1030] and as late as 1909 complaints

were made by Ukrainian deputies against the forcible impressment of Ukrainian peasants by provincial executive authorities. *Ibid.,* I ses., IX per., 41 pos. (25 wrzes, 1909), 2586–2587, 2591.

10. Wilhelm Feldman maintains that the last decade of the nineteenth century saw the bankruptcy of the conservative loyalist orientation and the emergence of the patriotic-irredentist ideology. See his, *Dzieje polskiej mysli politycznej; 1864–1914* (Warszawa: 1933), II, 211 ff. This new orientation was signalized by the nationalistic program adopted by the Polish socialists *(Zwiazek zagraniczny socjalistow polskich)* at the Paris convention in 1892. *Ibid.,* 218–219, 266. This program was substantially adopted by the social democratic party in Galicia. *Ibid.,* 268. The national democratic group were nationalistic from their beginnings. *Ibid.,* 275–296. For the emergence of the peasant party, see *ibid.,* 256–257. For conservative-clerical response to the proliferation of Populist-peasant press in the last decades of the nineteenth century, see, for example, Ks. Jan Badeni, "Ruch ludowy w Galicyi," *Przeglad Powszechny* (Krakow), styczen 1895, t. XLV, nr. 133, 1–36. For a socialist appraisal of the "democratic opposition" which developed in Galicia, see I. D. [Ignacy Daszynski], "Bankructwo demokracyi Galicyjskiej," *Przedswit* (Londyn), Ser. III, nr. 1–3, marzec 1895, 3–6; *ibid.,* nr. 4, kwiecien 1895, 1–4; *ibid.,* nr. 5, maj 1895, 2–5.

St. Poraj, in the social-democratic *Krytyka,* ventures an interesting distinction between the Populist-peasant movement in the Kingdom and Galicia. In the former area, because of the political restraints of the Russian authorities and the equally repressive influences of the clerical-gentry elements, the peasant party movement evolved later and with greater difficulty than in Galicia. Where in Galicia it began without preliminary peasant social, economic or educational organizational structures and hence had a tendency to be heavily idealistic and "Christian" in its orientation, in the Kingdom it was preceded by a fairly extensive organizational experience in peasant credit unions, producer co-ops, agricultural associations and self-help structures. Where the directive leadership of peasant parties in Galicia was oftentimes taken over by clerical elements, as late as 1912, the peasant party movement in the Kingdom was still subject to episcopal anathema and the excommunication of its leadership — hence, had a tendency to be distinguishably anti-clerical. St. Poraj, "O ruchu ludowy w Krolestwie," *op. cit.,* R. XIV, t. XXXIII, 1912, 265–273.

11. *Stenog. Sprawozd.,* I ses., VIII per. (5 lipiec 1902), 513. See also, Jozef Buzek, *Poglad na wzrost ludnosci ziem polskich w wieku XIX-tym* (Krakow: 1915), 42 and Zofia Daszynska-Golinska, "Kapitalizm bierny i czynny," *Krytyka* (Krakow: luty 1903), R. V, zesz. 2, fn. 1, p. 131. For the "Brazilian Fever" in the Kingdom, see *supra,* 61 ff.

12. For details of this trial see, Leopold Caro, "Uber das Auswanderungsproblem," *Volkswirtschaftliche Wochenschrift* (Wien: 1907), a summary of a paper read by that author before the Society of Austrian Economists in that year. See also, Caro and Englisch, *Emigracya i polityka emigracyjna* (Poznan: 1914), 82–85; Tadeusz F. Grodynski, *Ustawodawstwo emigracyjne na tle porownawczem ze szczegolnem uwzglednieniem projektu ustawy austriackiej z r. 1904* (Krakow: 1912), 32 ff.; Leon Papieski, *Emigracya i kolonizacya oraz zadanie polskiej polityki emigracyjnej* (Warszawa: 1918), 63–64. Caro, in his "Nasi wychodzcy zamorscy," *Przeglad Powszechny* (Krakow), sierp. 1908, t.

IC, nr. 296, 161–165, dates this trial in 1889–1890. Grodynski, in his "Ustawodawstwo emigracyjne . . . ," *Czasopismo prawnicze i ekonomiczne* (Krakow: 1911), R. XII, 116, dates it in 1896.

13. Jozef Siemiradzki, "Stosunki osadnicze w Brazylii," *Biblioteka Warszawska* (1892), t. 205, 104–126. Although some have recorded the origins of the Polish Commercial-Geographical Association as of the above date (i.e., April 15, 1894), the editors of the *Przeglad Wszechpolski,* in the prologue to their inaugural issue, (Lwow), R. I, nr. 1, 1 stycznia 1895, p. 1, claimed that the Polish Commercial-Geographical Association was the founder of the *Przeglad Emigracyjny* which began publication in 1892.

14. Tadeusz Smarzewski, "Wiedza prawno-ekonomiczna na zjezdzie naukowym," *Biblioteka Warszawska* (1893), t. 212, 331; J. Okolowicz, "Od redakcyi," *Polski Przeglad Emigracyjny* (Lwow), R. I, nr. 1, 10 pazdz. 1907, 1.

15. As president, they elected Count Tadeusz Dzieduszycki and its governing board included, among others: Emil Dunikowski, Stanislaw Glabinski, Stanislaw Klobukowski, Aleksander Lisiewicz, Jozef Siemiradzki, the banker Terenkoczy and the lawyer Wiktor Ungar. Jozef Okolowicz, *Wychodztwo i osadnictwo polskie przed wojna swiatowa* (Warszawa: 1920), 394; Mieczyslaw Szawleski, *Kwestja emigracji w Polsce* (Warszawa: 1927), 116; Manoel F. Ferreira-Correia and Serro Azul, *Opis stanu Parana w Brazylii wraz z informacyami dla wychodzcow* [translated by Jozef Siemiradzki] (Lwow: 1896), in advertisements preceding text.

16. Ferreira-Correia and Azul, *loc. cit.;* Okolowicz, *loc. cit.;* _____, "Komisya emigracyjna w Warszawie," *Polski Przeglad Emigracyjny* (Lwow), R. I, nr. 1, 10 pazdz. 1907, 5. The editorial board of the original *Przeglad Emigracyjny* was made up of Stanislaw Klobukowski, Aleksander Lisiewicz, Jozef Siemiradzki and Wiktor Ungar. Its masthead defined it as an "economic-social bi-monthly — organ of The Polish Commercial-Geographical Association." The *Polskie Towarzystwo Handlowo-Geograficzne* was an entrepreneurial organization apparently modeled on the German *Kolonialvereins* — commercially and nationalistically oriented along N.D. political lines. It also had overtones of the German *Alldeutscher Verband*—"idea *Wszechpolski*"— to keep in touch with emigrant Poles throughout the world and specifically committed to redirecting Polish peasant emigration to Brazil (Parana). Frequently the *Przeglad Emigracyjny* included correspondence disparaging seasonal emigration to Germany. For a judicious appraisal of ideological-political stance of the *Przeglad Wszechpolski,* from the Social Democratic point of view, see Jozef Feldman, "Ewolucja w Galicyi," *Krytyka* (Krakow), R. XII, t. I, 1910, 269–276. Jeske-Choinski briefly deals with the original anti-clerical, anti-gentry, pro-populist position of Dmowski's party and its subsequent accommodation with the Church. See his, "Listy z Warszawy," *Przeglad Powszechny* (Krakow), listopad 1908, t. C, nr. 209, 280–284.

17. Among its peripheral projects was one which singled out the state of Washington as an ideal place for the concentration of the dispersed Polish immigrants in the United States. Okolowicz, *op. cit.,* 395. As late as September 28, 1907, this idea of concentrating immigrant Poles on agricultural settlements in the United States was reiterated in the Galician *sejm.* Skolyszewski, raising a motion for the *sejm* to instruct the *Wydzial Krajowy* to provide funds for the study of the emigration problem, sought to bolster his case by stating the need for "directing and controlling" that emigration which is going over-

seas in such a way as to concentrate it in masses which would resist assimilation. To this end, he informed that body that "there were large expanses of fertile land in the United States which would serve well for such a purpose." *Stenog. Sprawozd.,* III ses., VIII per., 29 pos. (1907), 1875. See also: Wiktor Ungar, "Dwa glosy w sprawie emigracyjno-kolonialnej," *Przeglad Emigracyjny* (Lwow), R. III, nr. 15, 1 sierp. 1894, 141–147; R. Kudrzanski, "W kwestyi emigracyjnej," in *ibid.,* R. III, nr. 17, 1 wrzesien 1894, 165; _____, "Polska kolonizacya nad Oceanem Spokojnem," in *ibid.,* R. III, nr. 19, 1 pazdz. 1894, 180–181.

18. According to Dunikowski, the revelations brought out by the "Wadowice Trial," the mass emigration from Russian Poland in the early 1890's, the resolutions of the Second Congress of Polish Jurists and Economists in 1889, and his journeys to the United States were responsible for the awakened interest in the "emigration problem" in the last decade of the nineteenth century. Emil H. Dunikowski, *Wsrod Polonii Amerykanskiej* (Lwow: 1903), 1. Another factor which caused this awakened interest, according to the author, was the fact that ". . . almost every session of the *sejm* has been the recipient of a multitude of petitions from Poles in the United States requesting help and advice on such matters as education, the Church, etc." *Ibid.,* 11. Though the *Stenographic Reports* of the Galician *sejm* have all petitions addressed to that body scrupulously recorded, this searcher has been unable to find any such petitions from the United States in any of the volumes between 1868 and 1913. Dunikowski seems to have been equally in error as far as the resolutions passed by the Second Congress of Polish Jurists and Economists. Klobukowski had, in fact, delivered a paper at this meeting in which he broke with the traditional policy of restriction and discouragement of emigration — a policy which he found both indefensible and impossible. His motion that overseas emigration be restricted, in the national interest, into concentrated agricultural enclaves apparently disturbed many of his auditors and his motion was voted down. The subject was remanded for further consideration at some future meeting of that body. Oswald Balzer, "Drugi zjazd prawnikow i ekonomistow polskich," *Przeglad sadowy i administracyjny* (Lwow), R. XIV, zesz. X, pazdz. 1889, 725; Adolf Suligowski, "Drugi zjazd prawnikow i ekonomistow polskich," *Ateneum* (Warszawa: 1889), t. LVI, 517–519. See also Dunikowski's: "Z podrozy do Ameryki," *Kosmos* (Lwow), 1892, zesz. I–III, 1–57; *ibid.,* zesz. IV–V, 142–217; *ibid.,* zesz. VI, 264–298; *ibid.,* zesz. VII–VIII, 307–373; *ibid.,* zesz. IX–X, 420–442; *ibid.,* zesz. XI–XII, 534–560; his "O szkolnictwie w Stanach Zjednoczonych," *Muzeum* (Lwow: kwiecien 1893), 271–283 and *ibid.,* maj 1893, 373–383; his "O Polskich koloniach w Polnocnej Ameryce," *Przeglad Emigracyjny* (Lwow: 1893), R. II, nr. 18; his *Program wycieczki polskich turystow pod przewodnictwem . . . do Chicago i w glab Ameryki* (Lwow: 1893); and his *Od Atlantyku poza gory skaliste, szkice przyrodnicze z dwukrotnej podrozy do Ameryki Polnocnej* (Lwow: 1893).

19. Stanislaw Klobukowski, "Roczna emigracya polska i srodki zapobiegajace zlemu z niej wyplywajacemu," *Zjazd II prawnikow i ekonomistow polskich* (Lwow: 1889); the same essay simultaneously published in the periodical: *Ateneum* (Warszawa), t. LVI, listopad 1889, 283–308; *ibid.,* t. LVI, grudzien 1889, 475–495; *ibid.,* 1890, t. LX, 138–147, and, *Ekonomista Polski* (Lwow), t. I, 15 styczen 1890, nr. 1, 104–112; *ibid.,* 15 luty 1890, nr. 2, 210–243. See also, his "Wycieczka do Parany. Dziennik podrozy," *Przewodnik nau-*

kowy i literacki (Lwow), R. XXXVI, zesz. I, styczen 1908, 22–41, and each succeeding month throughout that year; his, *Wyspomnienia z podrozy po Brazylii, Argentynie, Paragwaji, Patagonii i Ziemi Ognistej* (Lwow: 1899); and his *Wycieczka do Parany* (Lwow: 1907).

20. U., "Kronika galicyjska," *Biblioteka Warszawska* (1895), t. 218, 118; *ibid.*, t. 219, 111–112; *ibid.* (1896), t. 221, 107. See also, Szawleski, *op. cit.*, 16 ff.

21. Okolowicz, *op. cit.*, 182–183.

22. Jozef Siemiradzki, "Wychodztwo Polskie w Brazylii," *Przeglad Powszechny* (Krakow), czerwiec 1897, 360–369; *ibid.*, sierpien 1897, 193–218; *ibid.*, kwiecien 1898, 34–47.

23. Jozef Siemiradzki, "W sprawie emigracyi wloscianskiej w Brazylii," *Biblioteka Warszawska* (1900), t. 236, 130.

24. U., "Kronika galicyjska," *Biblioteka Warszawska* (1896), t. 221, 107.

25. *Ibid.* (1895), t. 218, 118–119.

26. *Ibid.* (1896), t. 221, 108–109. As a matter of fact, though Siemiradzki, acting on behalf of the Polish organization, was instrumental in gaining the German organization its "concession," he later vigorously deplored its activity — that by accepting the disbursal of tickets it had inadvertently become forwarding agent of the Galician emigrants; that its presence gave authority and authenticity to those agents who were promoting emigration and thereby caused a rush upon their offices in Lwow. J. Siemiradzki, "W sprawie emigracyi . . . ," *Biblioteka Warszawska* (1900), t. 236, 129–131. Despite this criticism, in its official handbook the Polish Commercial-Geographical Association claimed to have cooperated with the St. Raphael Society in sending five contingents of emigrants to Brazil under the leadership of the Reverend Aleksy Iwanow, Feliks Krzyzanowski, Stanislaw Klobukowski, the Reverend Stanislaw Ossowski and Aleksander Enzinger, in 1895 and 1896. Ferreira-Correia and Azul, *op. cit.*, 77. See also: Stanislaw Klobukowski, "Wycieczka do Parany," *Przewodnik naukowy i literacki* (Lwow: 1908), R. XXXVI, 24.

27. Ferreira-Correia and Azul, *op. cit.*, 56.

28. *Ibid.*, 58.

29. *Ibid.*, 13.

30. *Ibid.*, 61.

31. *Ibid.*, 80.

32. U., "Kronika galicyjska," *Biblioteka Warszawska* (1896), t. 221, 108–109; Caro and Englisch, *op. cit.*, 369. For a brief historical sketch of the St. Raphael Society see, *ibid.*, 366 ff.

33. Siemiradzki, "W sprawie emigracyi . . . ," *Biblioteka Warszawska* (1900), t. 236, 136.

34. U., "Kronika galicyjska," *Biblioteka Warszawska* (1895), t. 218, 118–119.

35. *Ibid.* (1896), t. 221, 107–108.

36. Siemiradzki, "W sprawie emigracyi . . . ," *Biblioteka Warszawska* (1900), t. 236, 136, 138.

37. *Ibid.*, 131; Szawleski, *op. cit.*, 49; Buzek, *op. cit.*, 41; Caro and Englisch, *op. cit.*, 217; U., "Kronika galicyjska," *Biblioteka Warszawska* (1896), t. 221, 107; Erasmus Piltz, *et al.*, *Poland* (London: 1918), 261–262. According to Brazilian statistics quoted by Okolowicz, a total of 27,127

immigrants of *all* nationalities arrived in Parana in the years 1895 and 1896. Okolowicz, *op. cit.*, 183–184.
    38. Okolowicz, *op. cit.*, 183.
    39. See footnote 19, *supra.*
    40. See his, "Wychodztwo do Brazylii," *Ateneum* (Warszawa), kwiecien 1891, 27–45; "Z historyi ostatniego bezrobocia," *ibid.*, styczen 1893; and *Do Parany* (Warszawa: 1903).
    41. See his, "Nowy exodus, czyli wyjscie ludu," *Ateneum* (Warszawa), styczen 1891, tom LXI, 1–7. This may, in fact, be a pseudonym of Klobukowski who was one of the earliest writers on the subject of emigration to view it as essentially a response to a demographic imbalance rather than a mischievous consequence of "agents-promoters."
    42. Kazimierz Gluchowski, "Polacy w Brazylii," *Kwartalnik instytutu Naukowego do badan emigracyi i kolonizacyi* (Warszawa) kw.–czerw. 1927, R. II, nr. 2, 107–114.
    43. Okolowicz, *op. cit.*, 395; ____, "Od redakcyi," *Polski Przeglad Emigracyjny* (Lwow), R. I, nr. 1, 10 pazdz. 1907, 1–2.
    44. For some details concerning this emigration movement see: Caro and Englisch, *op. cit.*, 184–208; Jozef Wlodek, *Argentyna i emigracja* (Warszawa: 1923), 361 ff.; Estanislao Pyzik, *Los polacos en la Republica Argentina, 1812–1910* (Buenos Aires: 1944), 281 ff. See also, Roman Jordan, *Argentyna jako teren dla polskiego wychodztwa. Sprawozdanie z podrozy informacyjnej* (Krakow: 1912). Wlodek, *op. cit.*, 363, and Buzek, *op. cit.*, 50, find that 1,004 Galician emigrants settled in Argentina in 1897. These, according to Pyzik, were mostly from the eastern Galician districts of Obertyn, Horodenko, Tlumacz, Buczacz, Zaleszczyki, Tarnopol and Husiatyn. *Op. cit.*, 281.
    45. At its head, as president, was the Prince Kazimierz Lubomirski; Dr. Jan Kanty Steczkowski was appointed vice-president, and Siemiradzki, Terenkoczy and Ungar comprised its board of directors. Okolowicz, *loc. cit.;* Szawleski, *op. cit.*, 66; J. Siemiradzki, "W sprawie emigracyi . . . ," *Biblioteka Warszawska* (1900), t. 236, 149–150, 153–154; ____, "Od redakcyi," *Polski Przeglad Emigracyjny* (Lwow), R. I, nr. 1, 10 pazdz. 1907, 2.
    46. Zenon Lewandowski, "Wychodztwo polskie i stan Parana w Brazylii," *Roczniki Towarzystwa Przyjaciol Nauk Poznanskiego* (Poznan: 1902), t. XXIX.
    47. Okolowicz, *loc. cit.;* Siemiradzki, *loc. cit.* Adam Krzyzanowski in his "Osadnictwo polskie," *Przeglad Powszechny* (Krakow), pazdz. 1900, t. XVIII, nr. 202, 143–144, mentioned the purchase of 50,000 hectares of land in Parana by Lewandowski on behalf of the Polish Colonization and Commercial Association. See also informational handbook entitled, *Kolonizacya polska zamorska, kilka slow o potrzebie organizacyi wychodztwa i skupienia polskiej ludnosci wychodzczej w brazylijskiem stanie Parana, Nowa Polska, wraz z mapa sytuacyjna kolonij rolniczych w poludniowych brazylijskich stanach, rzecz wydana staraniem Towarzystwa Kolonizacyjno-Handlowego we Lwowie* (Lwow: 1899), 41 pp.
    48. Okolowicz, *op. cit.*, 395–396; Szawleski, *loc. cit.*
    49. Charles Hurlbert Young, *The Ukrainian Canadians; A Study in Assimilation* (Toronto: 1931), 40. For a pamphlet said to have been very instrumental in diverting Ukrainian emigration to Canada, see Jozef Oleskow, *Rolnictwo za oceanem a przesiedlna emigracya* (Zolkiew: 1896).

50. *Stenog. Sprawozd.,* I ses., VIII per. (5 lipiec 1902), 515.

51. Franciszek Bujak, *Galicya* (Lwow: 1908/1910), I, 213. See also *supra,* 30.

52. Semen Wityk, *Precz z Rusinami! Za San z Polakami* (Lwow: 1903), 1-2, 6-9, reprinted in part in, *Galicja w dobie autonomicznej, 1850-1914. Wybor tekstow,* ed. by Stefan Kieniewicz (Wroclaw: 1952), 332-336. See also, Ignacy Daszynski, *Strejki rolne w Galicyi przed forum parlamentu* [Dwie mowy posla Daszynskiego, dnia 28 i 30 pazdziernika 1902 r., doslowny przeklad z protokolu stenograficznego] (Krakow: 1902), passim, and Wilhelm Feldman, *Stronnictwa i programy polityczne w Galicyi, 1846-1906* (Krakow: 1907), I, 236 ff.

53. Jan Rutkowski, *Historia Gospodarcza Polski; Czasy porozbiorowe* (Poznan: 1950), II, 376; and Feldman, *op. cit.,* 241-242.

54. *Stenog. Sprawozd.,* I ses., VIII per. (21 czerwiec 1902), 171.

55. Zygmunt Gargas reported that the strike was easily broken when alternative sources of labor were found. For this reason, the Ukrainian deputies in the *sejm* were opposed to the law because the position of their constituents would be stronger if eastern Galician agriculture — largely dominated by Polish gentry — was exclusively dependent on the local labor supply. See his, "Publiczne posrednictwo pracy w Galicyi," *Ekonomista* (Warszawa: 1910), R. X, t. IV, 73-75. Both Rutkowski, *loc. cit.* and Feldman, *loc. cit.,* maintain that the support of the eastern Galician gentry was won when they were convinced that agencies which would import farm workers from western Galicia to eastern Galicia could be used to provide the necessary manpower to break any threatened strikes in the future and, at the same time, contribute to the reduction of wages. Okolowicz, *op. cit.,* 264, may have confused the chronology of the events when he contends that its passage caused great alarm among German landholders and resulted in the establishment of the *Centralstelle zur Beschaffung der deutschen Ansiedler und Feldarbeiter.* It is entirely possible, and even very likely, that its passage caused some alarm among Prussian landholders, but the fact remains that the German organization antedated the Galician ones since it was established in the summer of 1903 and the Galician law providing for establishment of public employment bureaus was passed in the spring of 1904. See Richard W. Tims, *Germanizing Prussian Poland* (New York: 1941), 121.

56. Not a few seem to have utilized that and later occasions to express publicly their solicitude for the Polish peasants and to enumerate, in thrilling detail, the malpractices and even brutalities practiced by German agents, officials, police and employers. Since many of these are strikingly similar in context and some even repetitive, it may, with some justice, be presumed that a number of the deputies were speaking for the record rather than for the information of their colleagues. See, for example, *Stenog. Sprawozd.,* II ses., VIII per., 7 pos. (11 pazdz. 1904), 268-270; *ibid.,* 8 pos. (13 pazdz. 1904), 326 ff.; *ibid.,* 30 pos. (11 listop. 1904), 1680; *ibid.,* 50 pos. (15 listop. 1905), 2911-2926. See also, *Alegata do sprawozdan stenograficznych sejmu krajowego . . . z r. 1904,* Alegat 323. On one such occasion, the Ukrainian deputy, Jozef Huryk, took the opportunity to question these sentiments. He expressed the opinion that their harrowing details were calculated to frighten all peasants from venturing abroad and asked them ". . . where were you about fifteen years ago when agricultural laborers in this country were paid five to ten

cents and treated like dirt, while abroad, for comparable labor, a worker was paid three marks and even two dollars . . . and how much does he, even today, earn here?" *Stenog. Sprawozd.,* II ses., VIII per., 53 pos. (15 listop. 1905), 2921-2922.
    57. *Ibid.,* III ses., VIII per., 18 pos. (13 marzec 1907), 1029-1030.
    58. *Ibid.,* 1055.
    59. *Ibid.,* 1051-1052.
    60. *Ibid.*
    61. *Ibid.,* 1056.
    62. *Ibid.,* 1048.
    63. *Alegaty do sprawozdan stenograficznych sejmu krajowego . . . z r. 1908,* Alegat 74 [LW 65061/1908, 25 czerw. 1908].
    64. *Stenog. Sprawozd.,* I ses., VIII per., 26 pos. (3 pazdz. 1903), 1596-1597.
    65. *Ibid.,* II ses., VII per., 20 pos. (29 pazdz. 1904), 852.
    66. See, for example, Staruch in *ibid.,* I ses., IX per., 16 pos. (9 pazdz. 1908), 725; Sandulak in *ibid.,* 29 pos. (28 pazdz. 1908), 1518; Kurowiec in *ibid.,* 41 pos. (25 wrzes. 1909), 2591; Makuch in *ibid.,* 2586-2587, 2594; Lewicki in *ibid.,* 83 pos. (18 luty 1910), 4852. The socialist deputy, Ignacy Daszynski, confirmed the existence of these practices already in the 1880's. See his, *Pamietniki* (Krakow: 1925), I, 14-15. See also, Emily Greene Balch, *Our Slavic Fellow Citizens* (New York: 1910), 136-137; Wasyl Halich, *Ukrainians in the United States* (Chicago: 1937), 18-19; Nicholas Andrusiak, "The Ukrainian Movement in Galicia," *The Slavonic and East European Review* (July, 1935), Vol. XIV, No. 40.
    67. Okolowicz, *op. cit.,* 396. The Galician employment bureaus continued to exist up to the outbreak of the war, though they never succeeded in extending their operations on any notable scale. The domestic job offers registered at its offices continued to exceed the job applications. Its greatest success was in contracting jobs for seasonal emigrants outside of Galicia — a function it was created to arrest. Leon Papieski, *Emigracya i kolonizacya oraz zadanie polskiej polityki emigracyjnej* (Warszawa: 1918), 73-74; Zbigniew Pazdro, "Projekt ustawy emigracyjnej z roku 1913," *Ekonomista* (Warszawa: 1913), R. XIII, t. I, 24, and his, "Sprawy krajowe. Trzy lata dzialalnosci publicznych biur pracy w Galicyi (1905-1907)," *Przeglad Polski* (Krakow: 1908), R. XLIII, t. 169, 502-526. For a more extended discussion of what may be called "the politics of emigration," see *infra,* 165ff.
    68. Among its members were: Jan Hupka, as president (member of the *sejm);* Professor Dr. Alfred Halban, as vice president (member of the *sejm* and *Reichsrat);* Dr. Ernest Adam (member of the *sejm);* Professor Dr. Antoni Gorski (member of the *sejm);* Cezar Haller (member of the *Reichsrat);* The Reverend Dr. Adam Kopycinski (member of the *Reichsrat);* Professor Dr. Adam Krzyzanowski; the editor, Bronislaw Laskownicki; the banker, Dr. Witold Lewicki; Dr. Aleksander Lisiewicz (member of the *Reichsrat);* the lawyer, Dr. Stanislaw Rowinski; the banker, Jan Rozwadowski; the editor, Stanislaw Rymar; Tadeusz Starzewski; Dr. Jan Kanty Steczkowski; Dr. Wladyslaw Steslowicz (member of the *Reichsrat);* Jan Wasung (member of the *sejm);* Franciszek Wojcik (member of the *sejm);* and Dr. Ignacy Wrobel (member of the *sejm).* Its board of directors was composed of Jozef Okolowicz (Chairman), Dr. Franciszek Bardel, Antoni Doerman, Dr. Jozef Raczynski

and Tadeusz Tabaczynski. Wojciech Szukiewicz, "Sprawa wychodztwa," *Biblioteka Warszawska* (1910), t. 278, 102; Okolowicz, *op. cit.,* 396–397; Szawleski, *op. cit.,* 66.
69. Szukiewicz, *op. cit.,* 108. See also, articles by Zenon Pazdro, Leopold Caro, K. W. Kumaniecki, J. Okolowicz and others in the *Polski Przeglad Emigracyjny,* No. 6 (1907) and Nos. 1, 5, 6, 7, 8 (1908). President Hupka, in his address to the annual meeting of the P.T.E. in 1912 openly admitted that he understood the primary function of that organization to be the redirection of seasonal emigrants to other outlets than Germany. ____, "P.T.E., Walne zwyczajne zgromadzenie czlonkow," *Polski Przeglad Emigracyjny* (Krakow), R. IV, nr. 3–4, marzec–kw. 1912, 80.
70. This represented a continuation of the policy initiated by the Polish Commercial-Geographical Association and the *Przeglad Emigracyjny.* Jozef Warchalowski, "Nowa kolonizacya Brazylii," *Polski Przeglad Emigracyjny* (Lwow), R. I, nr. 1, 10 pazdz. 1907, 2–3; Szukiewicz, *op. cit.,* 104–105. This concept of "controlling" emigration and "concentrating" it abroad "in the national interest" was reiterated by Wiktor Skolyszewski in the Galician *sejm* on October 17, 1908. *Stenog. Sprawozd.* (1908), I ses., IX per., 20 pos., 926. Skolyszewski was subsequently accused in the conservative-clerical *Przeglad Powszechny* of operating a private agency to redirect seasonal emigration to France and Switzerland. K. Krotoski, "Emigracya Polska do Francyi w najnowszej dobie," *op. cit.,* kw.–czerwiec 1911, t. CX, 28–29. The same author charged the P.T.E. for being largely responsible for redirecting seasonal emigration to France and with entering into agreement with an unscrupulous French employment syndicate toward that end. *Ibid.,* 26. The editors of the P.T.E.'s *Polski Przeglad Emigracyjny* reported the redirection of seasonal emigrants to France was supported by some of the Populist-peasant press. ____, "Przeglad prasy," *op. cit.,* R. I, nr. 1, 10 pazdz. 1907, 14.
71. Desirous of obtaining information on the changing state of the labor market in various industries throughout the United States, the P.T.E. concluded an agreement with the Executive Committee of the Polish-American Z.N.P. to have the latter's component groups periodically forward to the Executive Committee a completed questionnaire on the conditions of the labor market in their locality. A summary of these findings was to be forwarded by the Z.N.P. to the P.T.E. in Krakow to be published in its official organs. Though accepted by the Executive Committee of the Z.N.P., this project was never put into operation because the authorities of the Z.N.P. subsequently became convinced that it would meet with the opposition of the United States immigration authorities and others. Okolowicz, *op. cit.,* fn. 1, 102.
72. Okolowicz, *op. cit.,* 16.
73. Szawleski, *op. cit.,* 66. Szukiewicz, *op. cit.,* 101. Okolowicz, *op. cit.,* 397ff. For other calendars, brochures, handbooks and dictionaries issued by the P.T.E., see: *Polski Przeglad Emigracyjny* (Krakow), R. IV, nr. 2, styczen 1910, 13, 15–16 and ____, "O tem, jak mozna dawanie 'Napiwkow' na wsi zastapic lub uzupelniac szerzeniem oswiaty," *op. cit.,* R. VI, lipiec 1912, 296–298.
74. See, for example, investigative operations undertaken into the economic feasibility of seasonal agricultural migration to Argentina in 1911. Okolowicz, *Wychodztwo i osadnictwo* . . . , 244–249; Caro and Englisch, *op.*

cit., 203-204. See also, findings of investigative journey to that country by its representative Roman Jordan, published serially in the *Polski Przeglad Emigracyjny* throughout 1912 as well as under one cover in *Argentyna jako teren dla polskiego wychodztwa. Sprawozdanie podrozy informacyjnej* (Krakow: 1912). The editor of the *Polski Przeglad Emigracyjny* reported that several Hakatist-oriented newspapers were attributing conspiratorial, anti-German designs to the P.T.E.; that the P.T.E. was receiving commissions from French employers with which it was building a war chest in the projected war with Germany and Germanism. This expression of Hakatist paranoia was received with a sense of self-esteem by the editor, Okolowicz. His, "Prasa Hakatystyczna o P.T.E.," *op. cit.*, R. VI, luty 1912, 72-74.

75. Charles F. Caillard, *Les migrations temporaires dans les campagnes francaises* (Paris: 1912), 81-82; 86-87, 91-92; Jan Rozwadowski, *Emigracja polska we Francji* (La Madelaine-les-Lille: 1927), 94-95; Zdzislaw Ludkiewicz, *Kwestja rolna w Galicyi* (Lwow-Krakow: 1910), 93, 114-115; Emile Blanchard, *Le maine d'oeuvre etrangere dans l'agriculture francaise* (Paris: 1913), 162, 167-168, 217, 221-222, fn. 1, p. 213; Szawleski, *op. cit.*, 56; Okolowicz, "Wychodztwo," in Janicki, *op. cit.*, 115. Okolowicz maintained that, on the basis of French statistics which were available to him, the annual immigration of Polish agricultural workers into France in the years immediately preceding the war was about 10,000. The Austro-Hungarian consular service placed it at about 8,000 while government spokesmen, during the deliberations on the projected Austrian emigration law of 1913, estimated the total between two and three thousand annually. Okolowicz, *Wychodztwo i osadnictwo . . .* , 325.

76. Okolowicz, *Wychodztwo i osadnictwo . . .* , 328; Szawleski, *loc. cit.;* Rozwadowski, *op. cit.*, 94-96. See also letter of a Polish miner in Barlin published in *Polski Przeglad Emigracyjny* (Krakow), R. VI, sierp. 1912, 358 and *Praca* (Krakow: 1912), 421. There were, according to Okolowicz, 400 Polish immigrants employed in the steel foundries of Mont St. Martin in 1913. Okolowicz, *op. cit.*, 333. Independent of both these movements, though contemporaneous with them, was a migration of artisans and craftsmen from Russian Poland. M. Huber, "Les etrangers a Paris d'apres le recensement de 1911," *Bulletin de la Statistique Generale de la France* (Paris: juillet 1915), cited by S. Wlocevski [Stefan Wloszczewski], *L'establissement des polonais en France* (Paris: 1936), 63. For attempt to locate Polish emigrants in Ressaix, Mariemont, Peronne and Morlanwetz in Belgium, see, Okolowicz, *op. cit.*, 303, 335-336.

77. Okolowicz, *Wychodztwo i osadnictwo . . .* , 344-349; Okolowicz, "Wychodztwo," in Janicki, *op. cit.*, 115; Szawleski, *op. cit.*, 57; Caro and Englisch, *op. cit.*, 307.

78. Okolowicz, *Wychodztwo i osadnictwo . . .* , 337-343; Caro and Englisch, *op. cit.*, 312. See also essays by Mieczyslaw Dukszta in *Wychodzca Polski* (Warszawa: 1912), No. 12 and *Praca* (Krakow: 1912), 366 ff.; *Czwarty rok dzialalnosci Polskiego Towarzystwa Emigracyjnego* (Krakow: 1913), 16, 25; Adam Woroniecki, "Polscy obiezysasi w Szwajcarji," *Ruch chrzescijansko-spoleczny* (Poznan: pazdz. 1905), R. IV; [Anon.], "Polacy na tulaczce. Robotnicy polscy w Szwajcaryi," *Straz polska* (styczen 1911), R. IV, nr. 33; K. Op., "Emigracya polskich robotnikow rolnych w Szwajcaryi," *Przedswit* (styczen-luty 1911), R. XXX, nr. 1-2.

79. Okolowicz, *Wychodztwo i osadnictwo* . . . , 285–298; Okolowicz, "Wychodztwo," in Janicki, *op. cit.,* 113–115; Caro and Englisch, *op. cit.,* 61, 307–309; Szawleski, *op. cit.,* 56; Rozwadowski, *op. cit.,* 53; Rutkowski, *op. cit.,* II, 239; Papieski, *op. cit.,* 66, 70, 75; Bujak, *Maszkienice* . . . , II, 99–100; Wojciech Szukiewicz, "Sprawa wychodztwa," *Biblioteka Warszawska* (1910), t. 278, 110 ff. See also, Andrzej Mytkowicz, *Powstanie i rozwoj emigracji sezonowej* (Krakow: 1917), 153–155, and anonymous pamphlet entitled, *Odezwa o sprawie wychodztwa polskiego do Danii* (Poznan: 1913).

80. Okolowicz, *Wychodztwo i osadnictwo* . . . , 299–301; Okolowicz, "Wychodztwo," in Janicki, *op. cit.,* 115; Caro and Englisch, *op. cit.,* 312; Szawleski, *loc. cit.* See also report of Austro-Hungarian consul in Malmo in, *Praca* (Krakow: 1912), 42.

81. For a summary report of its three years of operation, 1909–1911, see, _____, "Rozmaitosc," *Polski Przeglad Emigracyjny* (Krakow), R. VI, nr. 1, styczen 1912, 23–24 and *ibid.,* nr. 3–4, marzec–kw. 1912, 77 ff. and 124 ff.

82. Okolowicz, *Wychodztwo i osadnictwo* . . . , 159, 190, 224 ff.; Gustaw L. Zalecki, *Studja kolonjalne* (Warszawa: 1925/1928), II, 94–95; Jozef Siemiradzki, "W sprawie emigracji . . . , " *Biblioteka Warszawska* (1900), t. 236, 140 ff.; Caro and Englisch, *op. cit.,* 220–221, 239–242, 248–249, 371. See also, *supra,* fn. 19, 37, 38, 40, 41. For information on earlier Polish immigrant settlements in Parana, see: Okolowicz, *op. cit.,* 178–182; Jozef Siemiradzki, "Stosunki osadnicze w Brazylii," *Biblioteka Warszawska* (1892), t. 205, 105–107; Siemiradzki, *op. cit.* (1900), t. 236, 143–144; Ferreira-Correia and Azul, *op. cit.,* 66–71; E. Lloyd Rolfe, *The State of Parana, Brazil* (Curitiba: c. 1920), Ch. X, 4–44; Alfredo Romario Martins, *Historia do Parana* (Sao Paulo: 1939), Ch. XIV, 405–433; Kazimierz Gluchowski, "Polacy w Brazylii," *Kwartalnik Instytutu Naukowego do badan emigracji i kolonizacji* (Warszawa: kw.–czerw. 1927), R. II, nr. 2, 107 ff.; Kazimierz Gluchowski, *Materialy do problemu osadnictwa polskiego w Brazylii* (Warszawa: 1927), passim. For attempt and failure to establish Polish secular schools see: Okolowicz, *op. cit.,* 214, 216–217; Caro and Englisch, *op. cit.,* 237; Memoir No. 16, "Farmer in Santa Catarina, son of tenant near Gopla, born 1879," *Pamietniki Emigrantow: Ameryka poludniowa* (Warszawa: 1939), 277 and Memoir No. 24, "Laborer in Rio Grande do Sul, son of laborer in Lodz, born 1897," *ibid.,* 400–402.

83. Okolowicz, *op. cit.,* 311–314; fn. 1, 325. For a perceptive analysis of the ideological distinction between Populist-peasant press in Galicia and the Kingdom, see fn. 10, *supra.* Not the least of its problems were the criticisms levelled against it by operators of private emigration agencies. The socialist *Przedswit* reported a suit brought by the Rev. Szponder — a member of the Polish caucus in the *Reichsrat* — against Okolowicz, the editor of the *Polski Przeglad Emigracyjny.* The court subsequently ruled in Okolowicz's favor when evidence, brought out in the trial, established that Szponder himself was illegally engaged in the operations of an emigration agency, though as a silent partner, and, in fact, engaging in sundry and varied unsavory practices with which he, apparently, had charged Okolowicz initially. St. Os . . . arz, "Z calego kraju," *op. cit.,* R. XXX, nr. 4, 1911, 185–186.

84. Okolowicz, *op. cit.,* 159–160. For criticisms of overseas operations of the P.T.E. by Leopold Caro, see his, *Odprawa P. Hupce i prawda o P.T.E.* (Krakow: 1914) and his, *Prawdziwa dzialalnosc P.T.E. Ignorancya czy zla*

wola? (Krakow: 1914). For their rejoinder see, "Dr. Leopold Caro a P.T.E.," *Polski Przeglad Emigracyjny* (Krakow: 1914). Quite apparently the P.T.E., by 1912, was abandoning its traditional policy of supporting overseas emigration to Brazil. Taking note of the renewed policy of the Brazilian government to provide free transportation to that country, the editor of the *Polski Przeglad Emigracyjny* affirmed that the P.T.E., in cooperation with the Warsaw Emigrant Aid Society, were making vigorous efforts to neutralize the activities of Hamburg agents promoting this emigration in the Kingdom. _____, "Rozmaitosc," *op. cit.,* R. VI, luty 1912, 75. See also, fn. 67, Ch. 4, *supra.* Also in that year (1912), Jan Hupka, the president of the P.T.E., moved for the liquidation of that organization and the transfer of its assets, etc., to the newly authorized Galician Emigration Association *(Krajowe Towarzystwo Emigracyjne).* As an official government agency, the latter would have the authority and influence to carry on the functions of the P.T.E. — and to expand upon them. He suggested the transformation of the P.T.E. into an exclusively educational-humanitarian organization. This reorganizational move was apparently approved by the membership and a committee was appointed to revise its statutes to that end. _____, "P.T.E. Walne zwyczajne zgromadzenie czlonkow," *Polski Przeglad Emigracyjny* (Krakow), R. VI, nr. 3–4, marzec-kw. 1912, 81 ff. and 166 ff.

85. See, for example, Szawleski, *op. cit.,* 53; Okolowicz, *Wychodztwo i osadnictwo* . . . , 263 and "Zmniejszenie emigracyi polskiej do Niemiec i dzialalnosc Polskiego Towarzystwa Emigracyjnego," *Bojkot* (sierpien 1912), R. II, nr. 8.

86. For statistical compilations of seasonal emigration from Galicia to Germany see: Szawleski, *op. cit.,* 52–53; Caro and Englisch, *op. cit.,* 285; Okolowicz, *Wychodztwo i osadnictwo* . . . , fn. 1, 258, 260–262; Marya Balsiger, "Polskie wychodztwo sezonowe do Niemiec," *Srodkowo-europejski zwiazek gospodarczy a Polska. Studya ekonomiczne* (Krakow: 1916), 92–93; Karl Englisch, "Die oesterreichische Auswanderungsstatistik," *Statistische Monatsschrift* (Wien: Feb.–Marz 1913), 144; Stanislaw A. Kempner, *Rozwoj gospodarczy Polski, od rozbiorow do niepodleglosci* (Warszawa: 1924), 178; Zdzislaw Ludkiewicz, *Zagadnienie programu agrarnego a emigracja* (Warszawa: 1929), 7; Buzek, *op. cit.,* 47; Jacob Lestschinsky, "National Groups in Polish Emigration," *Jewish Social Studies* (New York: April, 1943), Vol. V, No. 2, 102; *Rocznik Statystyki, 1926–1927* (Warszawa: 1927), 103.

87. Szawleski, *loc. cit.;* Kempner, *loc. cit.;* Ludkiewicz, *loc. cit.;* Buzek, *loc. cit.;* Lestschinsky, *loc. cit.; Rocznik Statystyki, 1926–1927, loc. cit.*

88. Some of these considerations are candidly stated by Balsigerowa, *op. cit.,* 91–93, while others must be inferred from the evaluation of the available data in Szawleski, *op. cit.,* 53; Okolowicz, *op. cit.,* 257–259; Buzek, *op. cit.,* 42.

89. Balsiger, *op. cit.,* 100.

90. Franciszek Bujak, "Rozwoj wsi zachodnio-galicyjskiej w drugiej polowie XIX w," *Z odleglej i blizkiej przeszlosci* (Lwow: 1924), 121; Bujak, *Maszkienice* . . . , II, 90–91, 93–94. See also, Balsiger, *op. cit.,* 91; Rutkowski, *op. cit.,* II, 238.

91. Okolowicz, *Wychodztwo i osadnictwo* . . . , 383–384. For detailed analysis of wage scales for agricultural laborers in all three sectors of Poland see, Rutkowski, *op. cit.,* II, 288–296.

CHAPTER SEVEN

1. Leopold Caro and Karl Englisch, *Emigracya i polityka emigracyjna* (Poznan: 1914), 316; Tadeusz F. Grodynski, *Ustawodawstwo emigracyjne na tle porownawczem ze szczegolnem uwzglednieniem projektu ustawy austryackiej z r. 1904* (Krakow: 1912), 14; Felix Klezl, "Austria," in *International Migrations,* ed. by Walter F. Willcox (New York: 1931), II, 392. Grodynski's pamphlet is essentially a reprint of an article under the same title in the periodical *Czasopismo prawnicze i ekonomiczne* (Krakow: 1911), R. XII, 87–146.

2. *Dz. p. p.,* nr. 80, IV oddz., sect. 15, cited by Caro and Englisch, *op. cit.,* fn. 1, 331.

3. Wehrgesetz von 11/IV/1889, *Dz. p. p.,* nr. 41; Disposition of Minister of Defense, 7/XI/1889, L. 12686, 2040/11a; and Disposition of Minister of Defense, Sect. 8, *Dz. p. p.,* 1890, nr. 207, cited in *ibid.* While the law stipulated that emigration to avoid military obligations was legally punishable, apparently some courts liberally interpreted this to mean that if a person emigrated for economic reasons — rather than to avoid the draft — he was not legally punishable. See, K. Splawski, "O emigracyi naszego ludu do Ameryki polnocnej i o wystepku z ustepu 45 ustawy wojskowej z r. 1889," *Przeglad sadowy i administracyjny* (Lwow: grudzien 1891), R. XVI, 562–567.

4. Grodynski, *op. cit.,* 23.

5. Disposition of Minister of Internal Affairs, October 23, 1852, L. 25.748, cited in Caro and Englisch, *op. cit.,* 316–319.

6. Disposition of Minister of Internal Affairs, September 30, 1852, L. 624, cited in, *ibid.*

7. Police Law of October 23, 1852, L. 6251, cited in, *ibid.*

8. Caro and Englisch, *op. cit.,* 61 ff.; Grodynski, *op. cit.,* 8–10, 13. See also, Leopold Caro, "Nasi wychodzcy zamorscy," *Przeglad Powszechny* (Krakow), t. IC, nr. 296, sierp. 1908, 149–165; *ibid.,* t. IC, nr. 297, wrzesien 1908, 352–372.

9. Grodynski, *op. cit.,* 8–10; Caro and Englisch, *op. cit.,* 316–319.

10. Grodynski, *loc. cit.;* Caro and Englisch, *op. cit.,* 328, 339–341. The enforcement of these laws and directives was further complicated, and frequently nullified, by the fact that "emigration" was not clearly defined in Austrian law. See Grodynski, *op. cit.,* 7 ff., and Caro and Englisch, *op. cit.,* 315 ff.

11. *Stenog. Sprawozd.,* III ses., IV per., 6 pos. (18 czerwiec 1880), 112.

12. Tadeusz Smarzewski, "Wiedza prawno-ekonomiczna na zjezdzie naukowyn," *Biblioteka Warszawska* (1893), t. 212, 331.

13. *Stenog. Sprawozd.,* I ses., VIII per. (1 lipiec 1902), 453.

14. *Ibid.*

15. *Ibid.* (5 lipiec 1902), 514.

16. *Ibid.*

17. *Ibid.,* 515.

18. *Ibid.*

19. It is probably significant that, almost without exception, the cosigners of Merunowicz's motion were deputies representing urban constituencies. *Ibid.* (1 lipiec 1902), 453–454.

20. *Ibid.*, II ses., VIII per., 7 pos. (11 pazdz. 1904), 268–270.
21. *Ibid.*
22. *Ibid.*, 12 pos. (20 pazdz. 1904), 524.
23. "Sprawozdanie komisyi dla reform rolnych o wniosku posla Baworowskiego w przedmiocie akcyi ochronnej dla emigracyi z naszego kraju," *Alegaty do Sprawozdan Stenograficznych sejmu krajowego . . . z r. 1904,* Alegat 323 [Ls. 2.023/or].
24. *Stenog. Sprawozd.,* II ses., VIII per., 30 pos. (11 listopad 1904), 1680.
25. *Ibid.*, 1670–1674.
26. See *supra,* 98 ff.
27. *Stenog. Sprawozd.,* I ses., VIII per. (29 grudzien 1902), 1009.
28. *Ibid.* (15 wrzesien 1903), 1312.
29. These included the depositions of: Michal Kochanek, Wies Podlipa, Pow. Dabrowa; Franciszek Rybicki, Wies Ustrobiny, Pow. Krosno; Andrzej Dzialowski, Wies Lysakow, Pow. Mielec; Wojciech Wicinski, Wies Wrzaw, Pow. Tarnobrzeg; Franciszek Morawiec, Wies Szwarow, Pow. Dabrowa; Piotr Decowski, Wies Zolyn, Pow. Lancut; Wladyslaw Grzenia, Wies Uniszowa, Pow. Tarnow; and Stanislaw Konisar, Wies Niepla, Pow. Jaslo. *Ibid.*, 1316–1317.
30. *Ibid.*, 21 pos. (15 wrzesien 1903), 1318. The case of one Franciszek Gajewski he regarded as typical. Upon his return to Galicia he was incarcerated for a time, inducted into the army where he served his regular enlistment and, as a punishment for desertion, had an extra year of service imposed upon him. Stapinski addressed an interpellation to the *komisarz rzadowy* on his behalf but that official declined an answer. When a petition on Gajewski's behalf was addressed to the *sejm,* it was remanded to the Commission on Petitions which never reported any action upon it. *Ibid.*, 39 pos. (22 pazdz. 1903), 2154–2155 and *ibid.*, 47 pos., 2761.
31. A similar observation, but in another context, was made previously by Merunowicz before that body. According to his information the directive of the Minister of Defense of 1882, which was calculated to prohibit the emigration of those liable for military conscription without authorization of the district *starosta,* was variously interpreted by those officials. In some districts his permission was readily granted while in others it was extremely difficult, if not impossible, to obtain. *Ibid.* (5 lipiec 1902), 514.
32. *Ibid.*, 21 pos. (15 wrzesien 1903), 1316.
33. *Ibid.*, 1315.
34. *Alegata do Sprawozdan Stenograficznych sejmu krajowego . . . z r. 1902/1903,* Alegat 510 [Ls. 3.260/1903].
35. *Stenog. Sprawozd.,* I ses., VIII per., 49 pos. (3 listopad 1903), 3066.
36. *Ibid.*, II ses., VIII per., 7 pos. (11 pazdz. 1904), 269. Elsewhere he estimated that about three-fourths of the emigration abroad was without passports or with passports to Germany only. *Ibid.*, 12 pos. (20 pazdz. 1904), 525. Klezl maintains that ". . . the most numerous class of emigrants [from Austria] were those who left without knowledge of the authorities." Felix Klezl, "Austria," in Willcox, *op. cit.,* II, 392, 397. See also, Jozef Okolowicz, *Wychodztwo i osadnictwo polskie przed wojna swiatowa* (Warszawa: 1920), 386.
37. *Stenog. Sprawozd.,* III ses., VIII per., 27 pos. (23 wrzes. 1907), 1775–1776; *ibid.*, 28 pos. (26 wrzes. 1907), 1833–1835. See also, *Alegata do*

Sprawozdan Stenograficznych sejmu krajowego . . . z r. 1907, Alegat 327.
Though Caro was apparently distressed by the ease with which the Army Law
of 1889 could be legally by-passed, he felt the law in question should be
sufficiently modified to permit postponement of military service until the
emigrant returned from abroad. Caro and Englisch, *op. cit.,* fn. 1, 331,
376–377. Grodynski repeated this point of view. *Op. cit.,* 8, 14, 61, and his,
"Ustawodawstwo emigracyjne . . . ," *Czasopismo prawnicze i ekonomiczne*
(Krakow: 1911), R. XII, 98–99, 145. That the prospect of eventual military
service would have been as much a deterrent to remigration as prosecution for
"desertion" apparently did not occur to either of them. Caro even seemed to
think that the Austro-American repatriation convention of September 20,
1870, which stipulated that acceptance of foreign citizenship did not free the
emigrant from obligations incurred while the subject of his former country,
also included the matter of military obligations. *Op. cit.,* 374–375. See also,
W. K. Kumaniecki's remarks at the Fourth Congress of Polish Jurists and
Economists in "Obrady sekcyi ekonomicznej. II. Emigracya," *Czasopismo
prawnicze i ekonomiczne* (Krakow: 1907), R. VIII, 165 and his, "W naszych
sprawach spolecznych. Oswiata i emigracya," *Przeglad Powszechny* (Krakow), pazdz. 1906, t. XCI, 152–153.

38. Quoting the testimony of an "expert," Frey, during the enquiry held on
the proposed emigration law of 1904. Grodynski, *op. cit.,* 48; Caro and
Englisch, *op. cit.,* 189, 331–332.

39. *Op. cit.,* 20. See also, Karl Englisch, "Die Methoden der statistischen
Erfassung der Auswanderung," *Statistische Monatsschrift* (Bern), Marzheft
1908; Kazimierz W. Kumaniecki, "Studya z zakresu statystyki wedrowek,"
Czasopismo prawnicze i ekonomiczne (Krakow: 1909), R. X, zesz. 1–3, 97–
145; L. Caro, "Nasi wychodzcy zamorscy," *Przeglad Powszechny* (Krakow),
sierpien 1908, t. IC, nr. 296, 150–151, 154–155; Helena Landau, "Ostatni
spis ludnosci w Galicyi," *Krytyka* (Krakow: 1912), R. XIV, t. XXXIII, 139 ff.
Despite Caro's frequently reiterated remarks on the lack of credibility of
Austrian statistics, in general, and emigration statistics, in particular, his
magnum opus, *Auswanderung und Auswanderungspolitik* and its Polish
translation indicate a singular preoccupation with impressive but, in the final
analysis, inconsequential statistics. See, for example, Dr. A. Tomaszewski,
"Ksiazka o emigracyi [L. Caro]," *Przeglad Powszechny* (Krakow), lipiec–
wrzesien 1911, t. CXI, 43–57, 229–245.

40. Karl Englisch, "Zur unserer Auswanderungsfrage," *Statistische
Monatsschrift,* Febr.–Marzheft 1911.

41. Franciszek Bujak, *Galicya* (Lwow: 1908/1910), I, fn. 1, 411. As early
as 1894 a formal petition was addressed to the Galician deputies in Vienna, to
provide consular protection for its nationals in Brazil because of the outrages
visited upon them during the course of the current civil war there. The petition
was apparently unacknowledged. ____, "W sprawie opieki nad Polakami w
Brazylii," *Przeglad Emigracyjny* (Lwow), R. III, nr. 18, 1 wrzesien 1894,
174–175.

42. Caro and Englisch, *op. cit.,* fn. 1, 373.

43. Grodynski, *op. cit.,* 56; Caro and Englisch, *op. cit.,* 372–374.

44. Caro and Englisch, *op. cit.,* 7, 233–235, 372, 374. For a thoroughgoing
indictment of Austro-Hungarian consular establishment, see: Zygmunt Gargas, "Reforma konsularna," *Przeglad sadowy i administracyjny* (Lwow),
grudzien 1912, R. XXXVII, zesz. 12, 1133–1151; *ibid.,* styczen 1913, R.

XXXVIII, zesz. 1, 55–74; *ibid.,* luty 1913, R. XXXVIII,zesz. 2, 146–155; *ibid.,* marzec 1913, R. XXXVIII, zesz. 3, 181–203.
    45. Caro and Englisch, *op. cit.,* 322. As early as April 1894, Dr. Wielowiejski, a Galician deputy to the *Reichsrat,* was reported to have taken the initiative in establishing some control over the growing tide of emigration by conjoining it with a rational policy of colonization. Wiktor Ungar, "Dwa glosy w sprawie emigracyjno-kolonialnej," *Przeglad Emigracyjny* (Lwow), R. III, nr. 15, 1 sierpien 1894, 147. A similar policy was suggested at that time, from the Polish point of interest, by Modest Maryanski in his, *O emigracyi polskiej do Stanow Zjednoczonych Polnocnej Ameryki i o koniecznej potrzebie jej zorganizowania* (Chicago: 1893) and, from the Austrian point of interest by Richard Schroft, *Die Osterr.-Ungar. uberseeische Kulturarbeit und Auswanderung. Ein patriotisches Mahnwort* (Wien: 1894). Ungar, *op. cit.,* 141–147.
    46. Grodynski, *op. cit.,* 10–11; Caro and Englisch, *op. cit.,* 322–323.
    47. Grodynski, *op. cit.,* 57–58; Grodynski, "Ustawodawstwo emigracyjne . . . ," *Czasopismo prawnicze i ekonomiczne* (Krakow: 1911), R. XII, 93, 141. For testimony of other experts see, Caro and Englisch, *op. cit.,* 82, 92, 94, 95, 322–324 and Leopold Caro, "Unsere überseeischen Auswanderer und die Enquete vom 1905," *Zeitschrift fur Volkswirtschaft, Socialpolitik und Verwaltung* (Wien: November, 1907), XVI, 529 ff. For complete text of projected law of 1904 see, Franz von Srbik, *Die Auswanderungsgesetzgebung* (Wien: 1911), II, 1–13. The P.T.E., reporting the receipt of a subsidy from the Austrian Ministry of Interior to establish an emigrant shelter in Krakow and an agency authorized to sell steamship tickets, admitted its special commitment to Austro-Americana and the port of Trieste. ____, "Rozmaitosc," *Polski Przeglad Emigracyjny* (Krakow), R. IV, nr. 2, 30 styczen 1910, 10.
    48. Grodynski, *op. cit.,* 10–11.
    49. Significantly enough, the initiative for this law in the Austrian parliament was provided by the motion of Deputy Friedmann on December 14, 1912. The author of this motion was also the secretary of the Austrian Central Bureau of Manufactures who had just recently issued a book emphasizing the losses suffered by native industrial interests because of emigration. Caro and Englisch, *op. cit.,* 8, fn. 4, p. 8, and 324. See also Friedmann, *Arbeitermangel und Auswanderung* (Wien: 1907).
    50. For complete text of proposed law of 1908 see Srbik, *op. cit.,* II, 15–27. For details of hearings on proposed law of 1912 see, *Protokoll der im K. K. Handelsministerium durchgefuhrten Vernehmung von Auskunftspersonen uber die Auswanderung aus Oesterreich* (Wien: 1912), and Karl Englisch, "Die osterreichische Auswanderungsenquete," *Arbeitsnachweis* (Wien: mai 1912). See also, Zdzislaw Ludkiewicz, *Kwestya rolna w Galicyi* (Lwow: 1910), 140–142; Marya Balsiger, "Polskie wychodztwo sezonowe do Niemiec," *Srodkowo-europejski zwiazek gospodarczy a Polska* (Krakow: 1916), 106.
    51. Caro and Englisch, *op. cit.,* 336–337; Grodynski, *op. cit.,* 22. The logic of Grodynski is quite illuminating. He argued vigorously for a comprehensive emigration law which would restrict the activities of "agents," who, in his view, stimulate unnecessary emigration and expose the emigrants to a life of poverty and hardship abroad — ". . . conditions, though not worse, at least equal to those of their native land. . . ." *Ibid.,* 4.
    52. Caro and Englisch, *op. cit.,* 332–333, 357–358.

53. Okolowicz, *op. cit.*, fn. 1, 125.
54. Testimony of Merwin at enquiry of 1912, cited by Caro and Englisch, *op. cit.*, 362.
55. *Ibid.*, 41, 364.
56. Okolowicz, *loc. cit.* As early as 1906, Artur Benis maintained that "pool" arrangements existed between Hapag, North-German Lloyd, Red Star and Holland-America — a periodically renewed cartel dividing among themselves the bulk of Galician overseas emigration. See his, "Emigracya," [IV Zjazd Prawnikow i Ekonomistow Polskich], *Czasopismo prawnicze i ekonomiczne* (Krakow: 1906), R. VII, 31. Grodynski, however, as late as 1911 held that no such pooling agreement existed among the several shipping companies transporting emigrants. See his, "Ustawodawstwo emigracyjne ...," *op. cit.*, R. XII, 118.
57. Artur Benis, *op. cit.*, R. VII, 42–43.
58. Battaglia maintained that the regulation and control of all emigration — both seasonal-continental and overseas — was within the purview of the Galician *sejm*. IV Zjazd Prawnikow i Ekonomistow Polskich, "Obrady sekcyi ekonomicznej. II. Emigracya," *Czasopismo prawnicze i ekonomiczne* (Krakow: 1907), R. VIII, 181–182.
59. *Ibid.*, 174–176.
60. See, for example, Grodynski's "Ustawodawstwo emigracyjne ...," *Czasopismo prawnicze i ekonomiczne* (Krakow: 1911), R. XII, 87–146. He affirmed that the redirection of overseas emigration via Trieste was not exclusively propounded by spokesmen for Austro-Americana but also by disinterested individuals who felt that Austrian authorities would be able to effectively obviate the exploitative practices in their own territorial domains. Nevertheless, he held that such a legal monopoly to Austro-Americana would be potentially mischievous and disadvantageous for the emigrants. *Op. cit.*, 141–143, 145.
61. L. Caro, "Nasi wychodzcy zamorscy," *Przeglad Powszechny* (Krakow), sierpien 1908, t. IC, 149–150 and his, "Sprawa naszych wychodzcow i robotnikow sezonowych na konferencyi Budapesztanskiej" in *ibid.*, pazdz.-grudzien 1910, t. CVIII, 325–347. He claimed that, if nothing else, the various hearings and public discussions had the effect of exposing to public attention the magnitude of practices and conditions that oppressed the emigrants, thereby publicly indicting Germany.
62. Okolowicz, "W sprawie noweli emigracyjney," *Polski Przeglad Emigracyjny* (Krakow), R. VI, luty 1912, 33–36. At a time when the Poles were attempting to redirect seasonal emigration to other than German areas and when a broader economic boycott of Germany and German goods was being considered, the editor of the *Polski Przeglad Emigracyjny* reported on a new directive of the K.K. directory of national railways which provided for scheduled working-class, through trains from eastern Galicia via Debica and Rzeszow to Krakow and from there to the frontier towns of Oswiecim and Myslowic — all this, obviously, to facilitate seasonal emigration to Germany. This policy, in the view of the editor, quite simply reflected the Austrian government's cooperation with Germany in providing "Galician grist for the Prussian mill." ____, "Rozmaitosc," *ibid.*, 76.
The Galician deputy to the *Reichsrat,* Count Lasocki, citing the periodicals *Das Auswanderer* and the *Neue freie Press* (8 Feb. 1908) as his sources, main-

tained that German capital — and, specifically, North German shipping interests — had assured themselves a substantial influence over the operations of Austro-Americana by acquiring substantial blocks of the latter's stock issue — in fact, about half of it amounting to about 18 million crowns with options to buy more. For these reasons, he seriously questioned the advisability of the 1,475,000 crown subsidy provided by the government to Austro-Americana — especially since certain specifically named directors of North German shipping interests were also on the board of directors of Austro-Americana. This, in his view, went a long way toward explaining the latter's opposition to a rational and consequential emigration law over the years.
_____, "Mowa posla hr. Lasockiego," *Polski Przeglad Emigracyjny* (Krakow), R. VI, maj–czerwiec 1912, 195 ff.
63. *Stenog. Sprawozd.,* II ses., VIII per., 53 pos. (15 listopad 1905), 2920.

CHAPTER EIGHT

1. See, for example, editorial entitled, "Emigracya naszych wloscian," *Przeglad Powszechny* (Krakow), wrzesien 1885, t. VII, nr. 21, 344 ff. For earlier expressions of this "conspiracy theory" of emigration, see *supra,* 55, 60 ff.
2. Tadeusz Smarzewski, "Wiedza prawno-ekonomiczna na zjezdzie naukowym," *Biblioteka Warszawska,* t. 212 (1893), 332.
3. *Ibid.,* 330. See also: Jozef Kleczynski, "Trzeci zjazd prawnikow i ekonomistow polskich," *Przeglad Polski* (Krakow), R. XXVIII, t. 110, listopad 1893, 396–411; Stanislaw Klobukowski, "Roczna emigracya polska i srodki przeciw niej zaradcze," *Ateneum* (Warszawa), listopad 1889, 283–308; *ibid.,* grudzien 1889, 475–495; *ibid.,* pazdziernik 1890; Stanislaw Klobukowski, "Roczna emigracja polska," *Ekonomista Polski* (Lwow), t. I, nr. 1, 15 styczen 1890, 104–112; *ibid.,* t. I, nr. 2, 15 luty 1890, 210–243. See also: Oswald Balzer, "Drugi zjazd prawnikow i ekonomistow polskich," *Przeglad sadowy i administracyjny* (Lwow), R. XIV, zesz. X, pazdz. 1889, 725 and Adolf Suligowski, "Drugi zjazd prawnikow i ekonomistow polskich," *Ateneum* (Warszawa: 1889), t. LVI, 517–519.
4. Jozef Siemiradzki, "Stosunki osadnicze w Brazylii," *Biblioteka Warszawska,* t. 205 (1892), 105–108. This estimate of the volume of that emigration was subsequently revised by Siemiradzki to approximately 30,000 in his, "W sprawie emigracji . . . ," *Biblioteka Warszawska* (1900), t. 236, 144. See also, Jozef Okolowicz, *Wychodztwo i osadnictwo polskie przed wojna swiatowa* (Warszawa: 1920), 198 and his, "Wychodztwo" in Stanislaw Janicki (ed.), *Stosunki rolnicze Krolestwa Kongresowego* (Warszawa: 1918), 107.
5. Inevitably perhaps, a stereotyped terminology developed in most general references made to that emigration. Szawleski's may be regarded as more or less characteristic when he speaks of ". . . the tragic experience of the Brazilian fever" which "infected several tens of thousands," etc. See his: *Wychodztwo polskie w Stanach Zjednoczonych Ameryki* (Lwow: 1924), 15 and his *Kwestja emigracji w Polsce* (Warszawa: 1927), 34.
6. Zofia Daszynska-Golinska, *Zarys ekonomii spolecznej* (Lwow: 1898), 66.
7. See, for example, his: "Das Problem der Auswanderungsfrage,"

Volkswirtschaftliche Wochenschrift (Wien: 1907), Nos. 1215, 1217, 1218; "Unserer uberseeischen Auswanderer und die Enquete vom Jahre 1905," *Zeitschrift fur Volkswirtschaft, Sozialpolitik und Verwaltung* (Berlin: Nov., 1907); "Wychodztwo Polskie," *Ekonomista* (Warszawa: 1907), R. VII, t. II, 1–14; "Unsere Auswanderer in Brasilien," *Oesterreichische Rundschau* (Wien: 1 Feb. 1908); "Nasi wychodzcy sezonowi," *Przeglad Powszechny* (Krakow), luty 1908, t. XCVII, nr. 290, 181–199; "Nasi wychodzcy zamorscy," *ibid.,* sierp. 1908, t. IC, nr. 296, 149–166; *ibid.,* wrzes. 1908, t. IC, nr. 297, 352–373; "Arbeitsvermittlung," *Sitzungsberichte des VIII internationalen landwirtschaftlichen Kongresse* (Wien: 1907), Band 1; "Das internationale Problem der Auswanderungsfrage," *Verhandlungen der Mitteleuropaischen Wirtschaftskonferenz* (Berlin: 17 u. 18 Mai 1909); "Miedzynarodowy problem emigracyi," *Przeglad Powszechny* (Krakow), kwiecien–czerwiec 1909, t. CII, 321–335; "Sprawa naszych wychodzcow i robotnikow sezonowych na konferencyi budapesztanskiej," *ibid.,* grudzien 1910, t. CVIII, 325–348; *Auswanderung und Auswanderungspolitik in Oesterreich* [Schriften des Vereines fur Socialpolitik, Bd. 131], (Leipzig: 1909); "Wspolna akcya w sprawie wychodztwa," *Przeglad Powszechny* (Krakow), listopad 1912, t. CXVI, nr. 347, 143–165; "Obrona narodowej pracy," *ibid.,* marzec 1913, t. CXVII, 337–352; *Emigracya i polityka emigracyjna ze szczegolnem uwzglednieniem stosunkow polskich* [translated and supplemented by Karl Englisch] (Poznan: 1914).

8. Leopold Caro and Karl Englisch, *Emigracya i polityka emigracyjna* (Poznan: 1914), fn. 1, p. 133, 176, 248.

9. *Ibid.,* 82–95, fn. 1, 133, 177, 387.

10. *Ibid.,* fn. 1, 323.

11. See especially his discussion on the projected Austrian emigration laws of 1904, 1908 and 1912 in *ibid.*

12. *Ibid.,* 270. This was in response to remarks made by Benis in his inaugural statement on the subject of emigration at the Fourth Congress of Polish Jurists and Economists held in Krakow in 1906. See his, "Emigracya. [IV Zjazd prawnikow i ekonomistow polskich]," *Czasopismo prawnicze i ekonomiczne* (Krakow: 1906), t. VII, 1–57. For other points of contention between Benis and Caro at this meeting, see, *supra,* 128–129. Caro also carried on an exchange with the P.T.E. See his: *Odprawa P. Hupce i prawda o P.T.E.* (Krakow: 1914) and *Prawdziwa dzialalnosc P.T.E. Ignorancya czy zla wola?* (Krakow: 1914). See also, "Dr. Leopold Caro a P.T.E.," *Polski Przeglad Emigracyjny* (Krakow: 1914), R. VIII.

13. Helena Landau, "Z zagadnien emigracyjnych," *Krytyka* (Krakow), 1 luty 1914, R. XVI, t. XLI, 164, 165, 167. See also, Gustaw L. Zalecki, *Polska polityka kolonjalna i kolonizacyjna; Studja kolonjalne* (Warszawa: 1925–1928), II, 49. Even in the postwar period the "agent" continued to be regarded as a malignant influence on all concerned. Though the more reputable writers conceded that the influence of the "agents" had frequently been exaggerated— that their influence was of a secondary nature and effective only where the primary economic internal and external factors existed — they continued to rage against them frequently using Caro's terminology. See, e.g., Okolowicz, *Wychodztwo i osadnictwo . . . ,* 18, 19–20, 22–23, 116 and fn. 1, 117–119; Szawleski, *Wychodztwo polskie . . . ,* 11, 12, 356, and Marja Niemyska, *Wychodzcy po powrocie do kraju* (Warszawa: 1936), 14.

American authorities frequently ascribed primary influence to such agents, also. See Henry Pratt Fairchild, *Immigration, A World Movement and its American Significance* (New York: 1913), 150–151, 163; the uncritical acceptance of the testimony of an authority before the United States Immigration Commission in Philip Davis (ed.), *Immigration and Americanization* (Boston: 1920), 76 and W. I. Thomas and Floryan Znaniecki, *The Polish Peasant in Europe and America* (Chicago: 1918–1920), II, 1490–1492. The more astute Emily Balch considered the promotional activities of "agents" as a factor in emigration grossly exaggerated. As a matter of fact, it was the author's impression that ". . . the less direct and concrete knowledge a man has, the more weight he lays on this factor." She regarded it as something of a "rhetorical commonplace" which a public speaker was likely to make. Agents facilitated rather than caused emigration. "Where the circumstances are such as to produce emigration, men will learn the facts and act on them in the course of time, even if advertising is absolutely excluded." *Our Slavic Fellow Citizens* (New York: 1910), 52–53.

14. See, e.g., Okolowicz, *op. cit.*, 18 and Karol Wachtl, *Polonja w Ameryce, dzieje i dorobek* (Philadelphia: 1944), 67–68.

15. Leopold Caro, "Nasi wychodzcy zamorscy," *Przeglad Powszechny* (Krakow), sierpien 1908, t. IC, nr. 296, 157–158; Caro and Englisch, *op. cit.*, 74. Caro's correlation of illiteracy with emigration seems to have been intended as a rejoinder to an early essay in the *Przeglad Powszechny* by Dr. K. W. Kumaniecki who saw increases in literacy among Galicians to be vaguely related to increased evidence of emigration. Kumaniecki, "Z naszych sprawach spolecznych," *op. cit.*, pazdz. 1906, t. XCI, 144–149.

16. Caro and Englisch, *op. cit.*, 95. The authors appear to be unaware of the contradiction in their contention when elsewhere in the text, citing the general census of December 31, 1900, they note that at that time the illiteracy ratio for males in Galicia was 52 percent and 59.99 percent among females. *Ibid.*, 75.

17. *Ibid.*, 96–97.

18. *Ibid.*, 75; L. Caro, "Nasi wychodzcy zamorscy," *Przeglad Powszechny* (Krakow), sierpien 1908, t. IC, nr. 296, 158.

19. Caro and Englisch, *loc. cit.*

20. Jan Rutkowski, *Historia Gospodarcza Polski; Czasy porozbiorowe* (Poznan: 1950), II, 240. See also, Szawleski, *op. cit.*, 12.

21. Daszynska-Golinska, *op. cit.*, 66. Florian Znaniecki, in his "Wychodztwo i polozenie ludnosci wiejskiej, zarobkujacej w Krolestwie Polskiem," *Wychodzca Polski* (Warszawa), zesz. 3, grudzien 1911, 9–16, essentially reaffirmed this point of view and went on to say that those frustrated and disaffected elements of the population had two alternatives: (1) to venture abroad in an effort to realize their expectations in more promising circumstances, or (2) remain at home and work toward changing the existing and unsatisfactory conditions which were frustrating the realization of their expectations. That being the case, it would behoove the "conservatives" not to impede but rather even encourage the emigration of those potentially "troublesome" elements. The progressive and reformist elements, on their part and for the same reasons, should have discouraged and otherwise opposed emigration — a posture which was at variance to those political groupings in pre-war Poland.

22. Landau, *op. cit.*, 164-168. In this same review article of Caro's revised and translated work — from the German monograph of 1909 — Landau disputed its claim to comprehensiveness inasmuch as it was primarily concerned with emigration from Galicia. In fact, it was primarily concerned with peasant emigration from Galicia.

23. Jozef Buzek, *Poglad na wzrost ludnosci ziem polskich w wieku 19-tym* (Krakow: 1915), 16, 39. See also his *Studya z zakresu administracyi wychowania publicznego* (Lwow: 1904).

24. Franciszek Bujak, in his studies of Maszkienice, was apparently the first to perceive this phenomenon. "Wychodztwo zarobkowe w Galicyi," *Z odleglej i blizkiej przeszlosci. Studja historyczno-gospodarcze* (Lwow: 1924), 229-230. This point was subsequently reiterated by: Marya Balsiger, "Polskie wychodztwo sezonowe do Niemiec," *Srodkowo-europejski zwiazek gospodarczy a Polska. Studja ekonomiczne* (Krakow: 1916), 94; Leon Papieski, *Emigracya i kolonizacya, oraz zadanie polskiej polityki emigracyjnej* (Warszawa: 1918), 32, 50-51; Szawleski, *Wychodztwo polskie . . .*, 11-12; Szawleski, *Kwestja emigracji . . .*, 22; Okolowicz, *op. cit.*, 21-22. See also, Balch, *op. cit.*, 50 and Thomas and Znaniecki, *op. cit.*, II, 1487-1489.

25. Szawleski, *Wychodztwo polskie . . .*, 81. See also, Thomas and Znaniecki, *op. cit.*, II, 1472, 1485 and Florian Znaniecki, "The Poles," in H. P. Fairchild, *Immigrant Backgrounds* (New York: 1927), 202.

26. From a letter dated "1879" quoted by Szawleski, *op. cit.*, 99.

27. *Ibid.*, 98.

28. *Ibid.*, 11. See also, Okolowicz, *op. cit.*, 22-23.

29. Wojciech Szukiewicz, "Sprawa wychodztwa," *Biblioteka Warszawska* (1910), t. 278, 117. Even "Pogroms" as factors of emigration tended to lose currency later on. Salo Baron, among others, was able to point out statistically that in Austrian Poland, where there were no spectacular pogroms like in the Russian empire, emigration of Jewish population to the United States accelerated rapidly in the same periods. See his, *A Social and Religious History of the Jews* (New York: 1937), II, 265. Handlin makes the cogent observation that religious persecution drove no one away. To emphasize his point he notes that ". . . the bitter policy of the Hapsburgs in Galicia in the first half of the nineteenth century created no exiles. . . ." When the volume of Jewish emigration increased after 1870 it was as high in Austria Hungary ". . . where there were no pogroms and where the government's policy was by then relatively liberal, as in Russia where the reverse was true." Oscar Handlin, *Adventures in Freedom* (New York: 1954), 81-82.

30. Jozef Siemiradzki, "Stosunki osadnicze w Brazylii," *Biblioteka Warszawska* (1892), t. 205, 105.

31. Szukiewicz, *op. cit.*, 116-118. See also: Fairchild, *op. cit.*, 157-162; Wasyl Halicz, *Ukrainians in the United States* (Chicago: 1937), 15-17 and Charles H. Young, *The Ukrainian Canadians* (Toronto: 1931), 38.

32. Okolowicz, *op. cit.*, 19.

33. Stanislaw Szczepanowski, *Nedza Galicyi w cyfrach i program energicznego rozwoju gospodarstwa krajowego* (Lwow: 1888).

34. Tadeusz Pilat, "Przeglad pracy Szczepanowskiego," *Biblioteka Warszawska* (maj 1888), t. 190; Jozef Kleczynski, "Stan ekonomiczny Galicyi," *Przeglad Polski* (Krakow), R. XXII, t. 88, kw.-czerwiec 1888, 209-240. See also the review by Witold Zalecki in *Niwa* (Warszawa), R. XVII, 1 maj 1888,

660–675. A rather revealing criticism of Szczepanowski's publication was made by one Antoni Molicki in his *Odpowiedz p. Szczepanowskiemu na jego Nedza Galicji* published in Krakow in 1890. In it the author stated that industrialization would bring about the "demoralization of the classes." To Szczepanowski's contention that the peasant was improperly fed, he remarked that it was far better for the people to eat potatoes rather than meat since the former had a tendency toward "placating the character."

35. Szczepanowski, *op. cit.*, 22. For pertinent commentary see: Szawleski, *Kwestja emigracji* . . . , 45; Jozef Poniatowski, *Przeludnienie wsi i rolnictwa* (Warszawa: 1936), 61 and Wojciech Saryusz-Zaleski, *Dzieje przemyslu w bylej Galicji, 1804–1829* (Krakow: 1930), 141–142.

36. Tadeusz Smarzewski, "Wiedza prawno-ekonomiczna na zjezdzie naukowym," *Biblioteka Warszawska* (1893), t. 212, 319–333.

37. Franciszek Bujak, *Zmiaca, wies powiatu limanowskiego* (Krakow: 1903).

38. Franciszek Bujak, *Limanowa. Miasteczko powiatowe w zachodniej Galicyi. Stan spoleczny i gospodarczy* (Krakow: 1902).

39. Franciszek Bujak, "Maszkienice, Wies powiatu brzeskiego; Stosunki gospodarcze i spoleczne," *Rozprawy Akademji Umiejetnosci*, Wydzial Historyczno-Filozoficzny (Krakow: 1902), t. XXXI, 76–182 and "Maszkienice, Wies Powiatu brzeskiego; Rozwoj od r. 1900 do 1911," *Rozprawy Akademji Umietjetnosci*, Wydzial Historyczno-Filozoficzny (Krakow: 1914), t. LVIII, 1–164, hereinafter cited as *Maszkienice . . .* , I and *Maszkienice . . .* , II respectively.

40. Bujak, *Maszkienice . . .* , I, 95, 117. On the basis of statistical analysis of this west Galician village for the period 1900–1911, the author found that while marriage generally ended the career of women as seasonal migrants, the men, on the contrary, found themselves impelled to continue — or even to undertake the practice if they had not previously engaged in it. A considerable proportion of them continued to do so throughout their physically productive lives. Thus, seasonal emigration was accepted by them as a permanent element of their economic existence rather than a temporary expedient. Franciszek Bujak, "Wychodztwo zarobkowe w Galicji," *Z odleglej i blizkiej przeszlosci . . .* , 230.

Wilhelm Feldman, taking stock of the economic condition of Galicia at about the same time (1899), pointed out that, in spite of the qualified optimism expressed by the spokesmen of the ruling classes ("conditions poor but improving, slowly but surely"), there was statistical evidence indicating an absolute as well as a relative degree of economic decline in almost all strata of population during the period 1878–1897. Though there was some concentration of wealth in industry (especially petroleum which was largely foreign-owned) and in agriculture of magnatorial proportion, not only was the peasant the victim of progressive proletarization but that the small artisan, craftsman and merchant were being removed from the economic scene even more dramatically. See his, "Proletaryzacya Galicyi," *Krytyka* (Krakow), R. I, zesz. 1, kwiecien 1899, 76–85, 129–141.

41. Bujak, *Maszkienice . . .* , I, 120.

42. *Ibid.*, 97–98. Waclaw Budzynowski in his, "Chlopska posiadlosc w Galicyi," *Krytyka* (Krakow), R. III, t. 1, 1901, 358–359, pointed out that, in the decades since their emancipation, peasant landholds in the 0–1.94 morg

category increased by 250 percent and in the 1.94–3.90 category they increased by 154 percent. This prompted him to refer to it not just as "fragmentation" but "pulverization" — the creation of an "agronomical absurdity."
43. Bujak, *Maszkienice* . . . , I, 102.
44. Bujak, *Z odleglej i blizkiej przeszlosci* . . . , 120. See also, Saryusz-Zaleski, *op. cit.*, 99.
45. Bujak, *Maszkienice* . . . , I, 88.
46. Bujak, *Maszkienice* . . . , II, 85, 94–95.
47. Stanislaw Koszutski, *Rozwoj ekonomiczny Krolestwa Polskiego w ostatnien trzydziestoleciu, 1870–1900* (Warszawa: 1905), 203 ff.
48. *Ibid.*, 207–208.
49. *Ibid.*, 217. For an abstraction and interpretation of Filipowicz's findings see, *ibid.*, 209–214.
50. *Ibid.*, 203.
51. See, for example, Stefan L. Zaleski, "General Demography of Poland," *Polish Encyclopaedia* (Geneva: 1921), Vol. II, No. 2, 127; Buzek, *op. cit.*, 3–4, 10–11, 35–37; Rutkowski, *op. cit.*, II, 1–2, 229–231; Witold Zaleski, *Statystyka porownawcza Krolestwa Polskiego; Ludnosc i stosunki ekonomiczne* (Warszawa: 1876), 119; Julian B. Marchlewski, *Stosunki spoleczno-ekonomiczne pod panowaniem pruskiem* (Warszawa: 1903), 3–4; Stanislaw A. Kempner, *Rozwoj gospodarczy Polski, od rozbiorow do niepodleglosci* (Warszawa: 1924), 143 and Leon Papieski, *op. cit.*, 54.
52. Zdzislaw Ludkiewicz, *Kwestya rolna w Galicyi* (Lwow: 1910), 46. See also, his "Ziemia i ludnosc rolnicza," in Stanislaw A. Kempner (ed.), *Dzieje gospodarcze Polski porozbiorowej* (Warszawa: 1920), Vol. II, Sect. II, 63–108.
53. Wladyslaw Grabski, *Spoleczne gospodarstwo agrarne w Polsce* (Warszawa: 1923), 48.
54. Okolowicz, *op. cit.*, 15.
55. *Ibid.* See also, Rutkowski, *op. cit.*, II, 233.
56. Ludkiewicz, *op. cit.*, 46.
57. Grabski, *loc. cit.*
58. Ludkiewicz, *op. cit.*, 85.
59. Cited by Herman Diamand, *Polozenie gospodarcze Galicyi przed wojna* (Lipsk: 1915), 102. To Bujak, the relationship between a glutted agricultural labor market and peasant emigration was abundantly clear: "Today, the cultivation of the soil does not sufficiently utilize the labor manpower potential of the rural population. A considerable part of this [productive] potential is without employment throughout the year — another part, while necessary to the cultivation of the soil, thus far cannot be permanently employed with the result that its remuneration, in proportion to its year-around needs, is insufficient. The result is a pressure for emigration. On the one hand, there is the pressure resulting from lack of sufficient employment of manpower resources and, on the other, the inability of a large segment of the population to find means, at home, to satisfy their most basic needs. For these reasons the Galician peasant needs must be the exporter of his manpower potential — which can be more effectively utilized abroad." *Galicya* (Lwow: 1908/1910), I, 218–219.
60. Szawleski, *Kwestja emigracji* . . . , 49.
61. *Ibid.*, 33.

62. Gustaw L. Zalecki, *Studja kolonjalne* (Warszawa: 1925/1928), II, 61.
63. *Prace Warszawskiego Komitetu Statystycznego,* t. XXXIX, table 1, 13 ff. reproduced in Wladyslaw Grabski, *Rocznik statystyczny Krolestwa Polskiego, rok 1914* (Warszawa: 1915), 52–53, 60. See also, Okolowicz, *op. cit.,* 14.
64. *Ibid.,* 16 and Okolowicz, "Wychodztwo" in Janicki, *op. cit.,* 98. As late as 1918 the phenomenon of increasing emigration was incomprehensible to Papieski since "... the wage scale in the country equalled that paid abroad, as, for example, in Russian Poland after the agricultural strike in 1904." Leon Papieski, *op. cit.,* 65. See also Caro and Englisch, *op. cit.,* 78.
65. See, for example, Ludkiewicz, *op. cit.,* 92; Caro and Englisch, *loc. cit.;* Balsiger, *op. cit.,* 94–95, and Bujak, *Galicya,* I, 218–219.
66. Erasmus Piltz, *et al., Poland* (London: 1918), fn. 1, p. 259. For other comparative agricultural wage scales in Russian Poland and abroad see: Okolowicz, *Wychodztwo i osadnictwo...,* 14; Okolowicz, "Wychodztwo," in Janicki, *loc. cit.,* and Grabski, *op. cit.,* 60.
67. Jordan Kanski, "Robotnicy rolni w Krolestwie Polskiem," *Biblioteka Warszawska* (1906), t. 261, dodatek *Praca,* No. 2, 12.
68. Bujak, *Galicya,* I, fn. 2, p. 403. The author estimated that wages for field workers in Germany and the provinces of western Austria were two and sometimes three times higher than in Galicia. *Ibid.,* 405. In a paper read at the meeting of Polish Jurists and Economists in 1893, Jozef Kleczynski estimated that a peasant emigrant in the United States sometimes earned twenty times more in day wages than he could in Galicia. T. Smarzewski, "Wiedza prawno-ekonomiczna ... ," *Biblioteka Warszawska* (1893), t. 212, 331. Znaniecki estimated that the wages of emigrant agricultural workers in Germany were about 50 percent higher than in either Russian Poland or Galicia. Thomas and Znaniecki, *op. cit.,* I, 199.
69. Saryusz-Zaleski, *op. cit.,* 97–99. For more detailed compilations of prevailing wage scale for industrial workers in Russian Poland during the last half of the nineteenth century and the early twentieth century see: Rutkowski, *op. cit.,* II, 385–386; Grabski, *op. cit.,* 125, 129–131; Koszutski, *op. cit.,* 232–236; Klimecki, *op. cit.,* 539–540 and Aleksander Woycicki, "Historja rozwoju warstwy robotniczej w nowszych czasach" in Kempner, *op. cit.,* II, 151. Comparative compilations for Galicia can be found in: Piltz, *op. cit.,* fn. 4, p. 254 and Herman Diamand, *Tablice statystyczne gospodarstwa spolecznego w Austryi ze szczegolnem uwzglednieniem Galicyi* (Krakow: 1913), 17. At a conference of mine operators in the Zaglebie Basin *(Zaglebie Dabrowieckie)* held at the turn of the century, the participants apparently concluded that the shortage of mine workers in that area was due to the psychological indisposition of the peasants to work underground — this, in spite of the otherwise "splendid" working conditions existing there. A writer in the populist-peasant oriented *Glos* took strong exception to these conclusions. Using the Hakatist Alldeutschen Verbandes' publication, *Die Polen in Rheinisch-Westfalischen Steinkohlen Bezirke* (München: 1901) as his source, he pointed out the very considerable number of Polish peasant migrants from the Eastern Marches who were employed in the mining industry of the Reich. W., "Emigracya do kopaln Westfalskich," *op. cit.,* R. XVI, nr. 4, 13 (26) styczen 1901, 49–50.
70. Helena Landau, "Ostatni spis ludnosci w Galicyi," *Krytyka* (Krakow:

marzec 1912), t. XIV, 140–141. For detailed compilations of prevailing wage scales for agricultural workers in Russian Poland in the decade before the war see: Kempner, *op. cit.,* 121–129; Venceslas Ponikowski and Stefan L. Zaleski, "Kingdom of Poland," *Polish Encyclopaedia* (Geneva: 1921), Vol. III, Part III, 414; Leo Klimecki, "Kingdom of Poland," in *ibid.,* 534–538 and Grabski, *op. cit.,* 71–72. For an analysis of the comparative wage scales of agricultural workers in all three sectors of pre-war Poland, see Rutkowski, *op. cit.,* II, 288–296.

71. Buzek, *op. cit.,* 39–40. See also, Okolowicz, *Wychodztwo i osadnictwo* . . . , 22.

72. Piltz, *et al., op. cit.,* 259. For statistics on the earnings of Polish immigrants in various industries in the United States see: Szawleski, *Wychodztwo* . . . , 57–64.

73. See, for example, Okolowicz, *op. cit.,* 16–17 and Balch, *op. cit.,* 54–56.

74. See, for example, Eugene M. Kulischer, *Europe on the Move; War and Population Changes, 1917–1947* (New York: 1948), 11 ff.

75. At least one writer on the subject questioned this generally accepted and frequently reiterated solution for over-population and rural poverty. This fallacy, in his view, stemmed from the generally accepted belief that Russian Poland was a grain importing country by the turn of the century. Statistics showing an excess of grain imports over exports dealt only with imports and exports by rail and failed to take into account the large volume of grain exports, especially from the provinces of Suwalki, Plock and Kalisz to Germany, via river traffic and wagons. Except for the districts around Warszawa, Lodz, Czestochowa and Bedzin, all Russian Poland normally had a surplus of grain production. In view of these facts, the author unequivocally reiterates that there can be no doubt that Russian Poland was — in 1901 — a grain *exporting* country. This being the case, the intensification of grain production, with its increased per volume costs (fertilizer, labor, etc.), for export trade was not economically feasible — and as a solution to the ills of agriculture, an illusion — in view of the world market conditions (*e.g.,* protective tariffs for domestic grain producers; competition from exporters like the United States, which because of large, virginal expanses of cheap land could produce at minimum costs, etc.). S. Krzeczkowski, "Wychodztwo wloscian z Krolestwa na zarobki," *Biblioteka Warszawska* (1901), t. 243, 51–52.

76. Rutkowski, *op. cit.,* II, 239.

77. The author apparently had in mind the freedom of movement and "expatriation" only within the borders of "historical Poland" — the ancient Polish Commonwealth. Stefan L. Zaleski, "General Demography of Poland," *Polish Encyclopaedia* (Geneva: 1921), Vol. II, No. 2, 202–203.

78. Papieski, *op. cit.,* 64.

79. Szawleski, *Wychodztwo* . . . , 12.

80. Szawleski, *Kwestja emigracji* . . . , 33.

81. Okolowicz, *op. cit.,* 13.

82. *Ibid.,* 12–13. See also, Zalecki, *op. cit.,* II, 56.

83. Okolowicz, *op. cit.,* II, 14. Okolowicz perceived a correlation between the years of presidential elections in the United States and the volume of Polish emigration to that country. He explained this phenomenon by stating that years of presidential elections are usually marked by a decline in the

nation's economic activity which in turn makes for a reduced volume of emigration. Okolowicz, "Wychodztwo" in Janicki, *op. cit.,* 99. Artificial restraints imposed by authorities of the country of emigration were subsequently acknowledged as useless. Diamand, for instance, concluded that, given a favorable labor market abroad, money could be found to pay higher steamship and other transportation costs as well as intercessors in obtaining restricted passports. Failing that, village or border officials could be "bought" and failing this, competent "guides" to smuggle them across the border could be hired. Diamand, *Polozenie gospodarcze Galicyi . . . ,* 103. As early as the turn of the century, two as ideologically diverse commentators as Roger Battaglia and the editor of the periodical *Glos,* had come to the same conclusion. See, Battaglia's "Zarys systemu nowoczesnego prawa emigracyjnego," *Przeglad sadowy i administracyjny* (Lwow), R. XXII, 1897, 599, and W., "Wychodztwo wiejskie," *Glos* (Warszawa), R. VI, nr. 12, 10 (23) marzec 1901, 165–166.

84. Jan Bloch, "Ziemia i jej obdluzenie," *Biblioteka Warszawska* (1891), t. 204, 68. The editor of the social-democratic *Krytyka* essentially concurred with this view. Given the tolerance of the peasants for a depressed standard of existence, their emigration must be regarded as a radical response to an intolerable, even for them, situation. Hence, a revolutionary act. _____, "Emigracya Polska," *op. cit.,* R. I, zesz. 1, kwiecien 1899, 105.

85. Wojciech Szukiewicz, "Sprawa wychodztwa," *Biblioteka Warszawska* (1910), t. 278, 104. See also the excerpts of letters addressed to the Emigrants Protective Association of Warsaw in Thomas and Znaniecki, *op. cit.,* I, 1504–1510. Apparently all — with possibly one qualified exception — had decided on emigration and asked only to be advised *where* to go.

86. Franciszek Bujak, "Wychodztwo zarobkowe w Galicyi," *Z odleglej i blizkiej przeszlosci . . . ,* 226.

CHAPTER NINE

1. Jozef Kazmierczak, "Wychodztwo do Niemiec," *Praca* (Krakow: 1912), 39–41. The same argument had been made by a speaker at the Fourth Congress of Polish Jurists and Economists (1906). He spoke not only of the large proportion of physical and moral debilitation but also an equally high incidence of illegitimacy and indigence. Still others disappeared "in the sea of Germanism." Kaz. Rakowski, "Wychodzcy polscy w Niemczech," [IV Zjazd prawnikow i ekonomistow polskich], *Czasopismo prawnicze i ekonomiczne* (Krakow: 1906), t. VII, 6–7. See also, *supra,* 55.

2. Stanislaw Ciechanowski, *Wychodztwo pod wzgledem hygieniczno-spolecznem* (Warszawa: 1914), cited by Jozef Okolowicz, *Wychodztwo i osadnictwo Polskie przed wojna swiatowa* (Warszawa: 1920), 390–391. See also, *supra,* fn. 71, Ch. 4. Bujak seems to have occupied an ambivalent position on this point. On several occasions he reiterated that seasonal emigration tended to affect population increases adversely: it postponed entry upon marriage for both men and women; it tended to reduce birthrate because of reduced period of cohabitation of married couples and it tended to reduce the fertility of the women. Elsewhere he noted the loss of the major part of the natural increase of the population of Maszkienice due to permanent establish-

ment in the United States and elsewhere in Galicia. Simultaneously, however, he added that because of the increased fecundity of the remaining families, the birth rate during the 1900–1910 period nevertheless showed an increase over previous decades. Franciszek Bujak, "Wychodztwo zarobkowe w Galicji," *Z odleglej i blizkiej przeszlosci; Studja historyczno-gospodarcze* (Lwow: 1924), 233 and Franciszek Bujak, *Maszkienice* . . . , II, 107, 4–5 and 8. Roman Dmowski was one of the few observers who, as early as 1900, was aware of the fact that emigration did not decrease the rate of the natural increase of the population. Roman Dmowski, *Wychodztwo i osadnictwo* (Lwow: 1900), cited by Mieczyslaw Szawleski, *Kwestja emigracji w Polsce* (Warszawa: 1927), 173–174.

3. Leopold Caro and Karl Englisch, *Emigracya i polityka emigracyjna; Ze szczegolnem uwzglednieniem stosunkow polskich* (Poznan: 1914), 8.

4. Mieczyslaw Szawleski, *Wychodztwo polskie w stanach zjednoczonych Ameryki* (Lwow: 1924), 76–77. An earlier commentator on emigration to the U.S. saw it as less deplorable than emigration to Saxony, Westphalia and the Rhineland provinces since the former settled in cohesive enclaves and retained their religious and national integrity while the latter returned contaminated with cynicism, socialism and infectious agnosticism to their native villages. ____, "Emigracya naszych wloscian," *Przeglad Powszechny* (Krakow), wrzesien 1885, t. VII, nr. 21, 346–347.

5. Caro and Englisch, *op. cit.,* 8–9.

6. Daszynska-Golinska, a former socialist, became one of the most eloquent proponents of the "regulation and control" of emigration. In her opinion, insofar as emigration is not regulated or otherwise controlled, *i.e.,* left to its own devices, ". . . not the least but the most desirable and valuable elements in the country will emigrate . . ." — a kind of Gresham's Law of emigration. Zofia [Daszynska-] Golinska, *Zarys ekonomii spolecznej* (Lwow: 1898), 66 ff. See also, Kazimierz Rakowski, "Gospodarcze niedobory naszego kraju," *Biblioteka Warszawska* (1906), t. 263, 135–136. Caro, in his: "Nasi wychodzcy zamorscy," *Przeglad Powszechny* (Krakow), sierpien 1908, t. IC, nr. 296, 153, continued to deplore, in the national interest, the unwarrantable loss of the most energetic and vigorous elements. Jozef Milewski concurred with this view but in the interest of the industrial development of Poland. ____, "V Zjazd prawnikow i ekonomistow we Lwowie," *Ekonomista* (Warszawa: 1913), R. III, t. 1, 136. Wojciech Szukiewicz, while acknowledging the probable validity of this argument when emigration was just developing, maintained that it no longer was the case in the years immediately preceding the war when the patterns and routes of emigration were well established. With the advent of remittances and "prepaids" from friends and relatives abroad, emigration rarely entailed any drain of money from the country. American money was paying the cost of emigration. Hence, more frequently than not, weaker and less vital elements of the population — as well as the most indigent — could, and in fact did, emigrate, thereby relieving the economic pressure at home. See his, "Z zagadnien emigracyjnych," *Ekonomista* (Warszawa: 1910), R. X, t. II, 81–82, 84, 86.

7. As early as 1889 he argued that the unemployed — and unemployable — elements of the population represented an economic burden on the total society. Consequently, he argued, any policy to stem the tide of emigration either by police action or prohibitive legislation would be not only

morally indefensible but cataclysmic in its consequences. St. Klobukowski, "Roczna emigracya polska i srodki przeciw niej zaradcze," *Ateneum* (Warszawa: 1889), t. LVI, 476 ff., and his, "Roczna emigracya polska," *Ekonomista Polski* (Lwow: 1890), t. I, 222–225. He accused the historian Michal Bobrzynski in his standard text, *Dzieje Polskie w Zarysie* (3rd edition), Vol. II, p. 338, as one of the most notable propagators of this mercantilistic concept of population. He charged Bobrzynski with bemoaning the historical expansion — and, therefore, dispersal — of Poland into Lithuania and the Ukraine. Had the Poles remained in their historical-ethnographic boundaries, that concentration of population, wealth and culture would have forced the economic evolution of Poland into modern commercial-industrial times and created a formidable and vigorous middle class. See the above essay in *Ekonomista Polski* (Lwow: 1890), t. I, fn. 1 on p. 212–213, and his, "Wedrowka ludu polskiego do Niemiec," *ibid.*, t. IV, 65–66.

8. P. Pawlowski and Dr. Milewski, among others, reaffirmed this view at the Fifth Congress of Polish Jurists and Economists in 1913. The former, commenting on the papers read at the congress, remarked upon the adverse effect emigration had upon the industrialization of Poland. The landless-proletarized peasant not only frequently remained permanently abroad but, even if he returned, he located his earnings in land — via parcelation — and thereby lost his proletarized status. To the degree that he remained attached to — and sustained by — the land, he would not add to the reservoir of cheap labor necessary to facilitate industrialization. Furthermore, he maintained, to the degree that the public employment bureaus (in Galicia) aided and abetted emigration, they were working counter to those forces seeking the industrial development of that area. ____, "V Zjazd prawnikow i ekonomistow we Lwowie," *Ekonomista* (Warszawa: 1913), R. XIII, t. I, 133. Dr. Milewski, in his closing remarks at the conference, remarked that the industrial development of Galicia and the Kingdom found itself in a vicious circle. The insufficient industrial development of those areas created conditions auspicious for emigration. This export of Polish labor — to Germany especially — facilitated the development of German industries and thereby helped create in that country the most competitive impediment to the industrial development of the two Polish sectors. *Ibid.*, 151–152.

9. When Tadeusz Kudelka, writing in the publication *Przeglad Powszechny* at the turn of the century, ventured to suggest that the effects of seasonal emigration to Germany were generally beneficent (that the emigrants developed self-reliance and self-assurance as a result of exposure to higher culture; that they acquired habits of orderliness and cleanliness; that their savings represented a formidable economic increment into the country; that temporary-seasonal emigration diminished permanent-overseas emigration and, finally, that exposure to alien culture frequently awakened the dormant sense of nationality in the peasant) he was subjected to an almost immediate, point by point, rebuttal by two clergymen in subsequent issues of that publication. Tadeusz Kudelka, "Obiezysasi," *Przeglad Powszechny* (Krakow), luty 1900, t. LXV, nr. 194, 226–229; Ks. A. Boc., "Emigracya polska na zachodniem pomorzu," in *ibid.*, marzec 1900, t. LXV, nr. 195, 495–502; Ks. Wiktor Wiecki, "'Charitas' o emigracyi polskiej," in *ibid.*, sierpien 1900, t. LXVII, nr. 200, 299–301.

That "demoralization," in the sociological sense, was a natural consequence of the incursion of the ethical concepts, values and attitudes of capitalism on the "moral" concepts of an essentially agrarian society has been established by William I. Thomas and Florian Znaniecki in their monumental *The Polish Peasants in Europe and America* (Chicago: 1918-1920), especially in the first two volumes. It was, however, in the vernacular sense that Bystron reaffirmed the demoralizing influences of the remigrants. Jan Stanislaw Bystron, *Kultura ludowa* (Warszawa: 1936), 342. Emily Balch also found that a sojourn in the United States had a socially vulgarizing effect on the remigrant in Poland, especially as regards his speech. This, she concluded, ". . . was a result of being brought into contact in America with the roughest elements of an industrial civilization. . . . Swearing is an integral part of their English as they learn it. . . ." Emily Greene Balch, *Our Slavic Fellow Citizens* (New York: 1910), 143.

10. For a more detailed discussion on this point see, Szawleski, *Wychodztwo* . . . , 47, 91, 251. When the clergyman Waclaw Kruszka gave a rather sympathetic treatment of Americanisms that had been adopted and "Polonized" by Polish Americans, recognizing the inevitability of the process and even its functional practicability, he reported that he was widely criticized as "an advocate of assimilation." Waclaw Kruszka, *Historja Polska w Ameryce* (Milwaukee: 1905), Vol. V, Section XIII, 111-120. Dr. Janik related an incident which gave him a chuckle when he visited America: upon overhearing the "curious jargon" of children in a Polish American community and inquiring of them where they learned this "Anglicism," he was told that "it fell upon them like the rain from heaven." Michal Janik, "Ludnosc polska w Stanach Zjednoczonych Ameryki polnocnej," *Lud* (Lwow: 1905), t. XI, zesz. III, 260.

11. See, for example, Caro and Englisch, *op. cit.,* 261. Leopold Caro, one of the foremost advocates of "regulation and control" of emigration, persistently argued that the total gain for the country of immigration far outweighed the gains of the country supplying the emigrants. See his, "Sprawa naszych wychodzcow i robotnikow sezonowych na konferencyi Budapesztanskiej," *Przeglad Powszechny* (Krakow), pazdz.-grudzien 1910, t. CVIII, 325-347. Henry Pratt Fairchild, one of the many American writers on immigration after the first World War, expressed similarly pessimistic views of the effects of emigration on both the emigrant and the country of emigration. Citing authorities like John Stuart Mill, Roscher, Jannasch, Malthus and others, he generalized that emigration was not likely to reduce over-population. Basing his contentions on his own researches into Greek emigration and those of Antonio Mangano into Italian emigration, he hinted darkly of "certain undesirable consequences, insidious and persistent in their nature, and likely to make themselves more manifest with the passage of years" insofar as the emigrant himself is concerned. Although disposed to concede that there was evidence of material gain for the country of emigration, he questioned "whether it is a healthy state of affairs for any nation to be largely supported by money earned in another land and sent back in a form which gives it the nature of a gift in the eyes of the common people." Henry Pratt Fairchild, *Immigration, a World Movement and its Significance* (New York: 1913), 478-479, 485-491.

12. As evidence of this, he pointed to the province of Plock in which the parcellation activity of the "Peasant Bank" developed slowly and, up to 1901, had not reached any relatively notable volume of operations in spite of the fact that that province had contributed a large volume of participants in emigra-

tion. This, in the editor's view, illustrated graphically the fact that emigration as a means of accumulating the requisite capital for buying more land was a failure. He failed, however, to consider other factors, peculiar to Plock province, which may have accounted for the small progress of parcellation activity there; for example, the amount of land available for parcellation in that province, the relatively large proportion of petit-gentry there who were ineligible for loans from the "Peasant Bank" and, possibly, the large percentage of permanent emigrants from there. Adam Krasinski, "Kronika miesieczna," *Biblioteka Warszawska* (1902), t. 247, 188.

13. *Prace Warszawskiego Komitetu Statystycznego* (Warszawa: 1902/ 1903), t. XIX, 57. See also, Stanislaw Koszutski, *Rozwoj ekonomiczny Krolestwa Polskiego w ostatniem trzydziestoleciu, 1870–1900* (Warszawa: 1905), 222 and Okolowicz, *op. cit.,* 280.

14. Wladyslaw Grabski, *Materjaly w sprawie wloscianskiej* (Warszawa: 1907/1919), II, 136. See also, Stanislava von Kuzelewska, *Die Landarbeitern-verhaltnisse im Koenigreich Polen* (Breslau: 1909), 74, citing Vol. XXII of the *Prace Warszawskiego Komitetu Statystycznego,* and Stanislaw A. Kempner, *Rozwoj gospodarczy Polski, od rozbiorow do niepodleglosci* (Warszawa: 1924), 145.

15. Aleksander Klobukowski, "Wlasnosc ziemska w Krolestwie Polskiem," *Biblioteka Warszawska* (1903), t. 249, 521; Koszutski, *op. cit.,* fn., p. 215. The growing dependence of Russian Poland on remittances from its emigrants was demonstrated by Henryk Sienkiewicz's open letter to "Rodacy" in the United States, published in the Warszawa newspapers to be picked up by the Polish-American press, imploring them for their "continued aid" to the unemployed of Russian Poland and for the establishment of an educational fund for the future. Adam Krasinski, "Kronika miesieczna," *Biblioteka Warszawska* (1906), t. 262, 190–191. Sienkiewicz himself was one of the foremost literary exponents of the strategy to discourage emigration by presenting the plight of the peasant-emigrant abroad in the most harrowing light. His *Za chlebem* — variously translated as *Peasants in Exile* (Notre Dame [Indiana]: 1898) and *Her Tragic Fate* (New York: 1899) — is an example. In the words of Emily Balch, the presentation of the travails of the Polish immigrant "is reminiscent of *Martin Chuzzlewit.*" She goes on to say that "the story is said to have been written in the interests of the Polish landlords with the intention of deterring from emigration." Balch, *op. cit.,* 333 and fn. For a bitterly critical analysis of Sienkiewicz's role in the social and intellectual history of nineteenth and even twentieth century Poland, see Jozef Chalasin-ski, *Przeszlosc i przyszlosc inteligencji polskiej* (Rome: 1947), 73 ff.

16. Poznanczyk, "Stosunki ekonomiczne w Poznanskiem," *Biblioteka Warszawska* (1901), t. 241, 440.

17. Bujak, *Maszkienice . . . ,* I, 125–126, 133. These findings were substantially reaffirmed by the author when he conducted an even more intensive examination of that village about a decade later. At that time he found the net income to the village of Maszkienice from earnings abroad amounting to approximately 100,000 crowns. Estimating the average income from each *morg* of land at that time to be about 95 crowns, he found the total net income from the agricultural production of the village to be about 100,000 crowns. Bujak, *Maszkienice . . . ,* II, 105–106. Wladyslaw Skowron, writing somewhat later, maintained that the economic life of the rural population in the border

counties of Russian Poland, as, for example, Wielun and Czestochowa, was wholly dependent upon earnings of seasonal emigrants. See his: *Kryzys i skutki emigracji sezonowej* (Warszawa: 1932), 11 and ff. To the contention of the conservative elements that the emigrant worker was deceived of his money, philandered it on useless finery or otherwise wasted it, Bujak pointed out that of the 116 migrant workers in this village, only seven did not save any money from their earnings. More than a third of them saved between a half and two-thirds of their total wages; a third saved between 66 and 70 percent of their total wages; and more than a fifth of them returned home with between 71 and 85 percent of their gross wages earned abroad. Bujak, *Maszkienice . . .*, I, 133.

18. Stanislaw Hupka, *Uber die Entwicklung der westgalizischen Dorf-zustande in der zweite Halfte des 19. Jahrhunderts* (Teschen: 1910), cited by Caro and Englisch, *op. cit.*, 77. See also Hupka's *Stan wspolczesny i metoda badan wsi polskiej w Galicyi* (Krakow: 1912), 34.

19. Erasmus Piltz, *et al., Poland* (London: 1918), 261. See also, *supra,* 98 ff.

20. *Ibid.* See also Caro and Englisch, *op. cit.,* 261.

21. Francis Bujak, "Galicia and Silesia of Cieszyn," *Polish Encyclopaedia* (Fribourg: 1922), Vol. III, Pt. II, 241.

22. Szawleski, *Kwestja emigracji . . .*, 182-183. Of total "Polish" immigration to the United States in the year 1912/13, 119,633 came at their own expense and 54,732 had "prepaid" passage tickets. These were usually purchased by either a member of the immigrant's family or some relative of his living in the United States. From whatever source, these prepaids may also be regarded as a type of capital transmitted from abroad. See Okolowicz, *op. cit.,* 112-113.

23. *Ibid.,* 389. Krzyzanowski concurred with this point of view. Writing in 1926, he remarked: "Now emigration has declined and unemployment has increased. . . . It could not be otherwise." Adam Krzyzanowski, *Pauperyzacja Polski wspolczesnej* (Krakow: 1926), 57.

24. Franciszek Bujak, "Rozwoj wsi zachodnio-galicyjskiej w drugiej po-lowie XIX w.," *Z odleglej i blizkiej przeszlosci . . .*, 122; *Maszkienice . . .*, I, 156; and *Maszkienice . . .*, II, 112. The persistence of the fiction of the peasant as a guileless and naive creditor was to a degree perpetuated by Thomas and Znaniecki. In their view, the concept of money held by the peasant was essentially non-capitalistic. "Money is a relatively new kind of property . . . whose importance grows as the modern economic life penetrates the peasant community. . . . For the peasant, money property has originally not the character of capital. . . . He does not at first even think of making money produce; he simply keeps it at home. And if he lends it privately, the medieval principle of no interest prevails, or at most . . . a reward in money or products is taken for the service. *Even now interest on private loans from peasant to peasant is very low.* "(The italics mine.) Thomas and Znaniecki, *op. cit.*, I, 164. Handlin expresses the same point of view: "Peasant solidarity thus demanded that loans be without interest and hospitality without cost. 'Am I a Jewess or a trader, to take money for a little fire and water?' asked the goodwife." Oscar Handlin, *The Uprooted; The Epic Story of the Great Migrations that Made the American People* (Boston: 1951), 16. That this view is without basis is demonstrated by Bujak who found that as late as 1900 private loans — loans in which peasants increasingly participated as *creditors* — still cost as much as 40

percent in interest. Bujak, *Maszkienice* . . . , I, 151. Earlier, deputy Krukowiecki, at that time probably the most outspoken champion of the interests
of the peasants in the *sejm,* readily admitted that the peasant himself was the
most outrageous in his demands when he was a *creditor.* While the speaker
castigated the notorious Peasant Bank and declared the incompetence of the
community banks *(Gminne kasy porzyczkowe)* existing in the peasant villages, he remarked that at that time the only recourse available to a peasant
seeking a loan was another peasant. In his opinion, however, the peasant as a
creditor was probably the most demanding creditor. "The Peasant Bank
cannot hold a candle to the peasant as a lender." In the Przemysl district (his
constituency) a peasant creditor, in repayment of a loan, received cash and
other emoluments to the end that the debtor paid as much as 180 percent per
year interest on a personal loan. *Stenog. Sprawozd.,* II ses., IV per., 14 pos. (8
pazdz. 1878), 374–375 and *ibid.,* IV ses., IV per., 22 pos. (18 pazdz. 1881), 498.
According to interviews made among emigrants to Brazil in 1895 by the St.
Raphael Society in Galicia, the chief causes of their emigration were: (1) lack
of sufficient land and (2) the extremely difficult credit facilities, especially the
usurious credit practices of the more affluent peasants. U., "Kronika galicyjska," *Biblioteka Warszawska* (1895), t. 219, 113. See also, N., "Lichwa, jej
przyczyny i skutki," *Przedswit* (Londyn), Ser. III, nr. 9, wrzesien 1896, 2–6.

25. Bujak, *Maszkienice* . . . , II, 118.
26. Bujak, *Maszkienice* . . . , I, 151.
27. *Ibid.,* 148–149.
28. Bujak, *Maszkienice* . . . , II, 118–119. See also, Witold Kula, *Historia
gospodarcza Polski, 1864–1918* (Warszawa: 1947), 24. For effects of the
decline of emigration in the post-war period on the cost of credit see,
Krzyzanowski, *op. cit.,* Sect. IV, 34 ff.
29. Okolowicz, *op. cit.,* fn. 1, p. 17.
30. Jan Rutkowski, *Historia gospodarcza Polski; Czasy porozbiorowe*
(Poznan: 1950), II, 297.
31. Kempner, *op. cit.,* 225. Bujak, though he readily recognizes the far-
reaching importance of emigrant earnings, does not go to the extreme position
indicated in the above statement. He found that of the 82 villagers of Maszkienice who acquired land in the parcellation of a local estate in 1899–1900, 39
were full-time farmers and 43 were workers who earned their chief, if not sole,
livelihood from migrant labor. Though the farmers bought up the larger share
of the parcelled land, the latter had larger capital resources at their disposal
since they paid for their total acquisitions as follows: 76 percent in cash and 24
percent by loans as compared to 40 percent and 60 percent respectively by the
farmers. Bujak, *Maszkienice* . . . , I, 154–155.
32. Stanislaw Klobukowski in his "Wedrowka ludu polskiego w glab
Niemiec," *Ateneum* (Warszawa: 1890), t. LX, 146–147, appears to have been
one of the earliest to see the determining influence of Polish emigrant
earnings — especially from the Rheinland-Westfalen industrial areas — in
countervailing the efforts of the German colonization commission in the
Eastern Marches. While both German and Polish speaking elements in
Prussian Poland migrated to the higher paying areas in the west and southwest
of Germany, the Poles tended to return to their places of origin and locate their
savings in land. Dr. Witold Skarzynski, in one speech delivered at the Second
Congress of Polish Jurists and Economists in 1889, maintained that, in

general, both large and small Polish landholds were gaining rather than losing ground in that area, despite the hostile and discriminatory policies of the government. For these reasons, he concluded that the Prussian policy was failing. D., "Drugi zjazd prawnikow i ekonomistow polskich," *Przewodnik naukowy i literacki* (Lwow: 1889), R. XVII, 943–944. In apparently another address at the same congress, he (Skarzynski) observed that while the Polish landed gentry was losing ground at approximately 30,000 *morgs* per annum during the decade 1878–1888, the Polish peasant landholders were demonstrating a remarkable resilience to the Prussian program of Germanizing the Eastern Marches. This latter manifestation, however, he credited to the selfless moral and material efforts of the Polish gentry in discharging their historically defined aristocratic duties and responsibilities. No mention was made of any increment of emigrant earnings. See, Adolf Suligowski, "Drugi zjazd prawnikow i ekonomistow polskich," *Ateneum* (Warszawa: 1889), t. LVI, 351. By the turn of the century, a writer in the clerical-gentry oriented *Przeglad Powszechny,* while acknowledging the extensive migration of Poles into the mines and factories of Rheinland-Westfalen, apparently sought to reassure his readers that those elements were sustaining their cultural and national integrity — a view which seems to reflect a reconciliation with the fact of that emigration. M., "Polacy na obczyznie," *Przeglad Powszechny* (Krakow), sierpien 1899, t. LXIII, nr. 188, 316–324.

Shortly after the turn of the century, one observer reported the pessimistic valedictory speech of Burgomeister Witting of Poznan in which he conceded that, in spite of Hakatist efforts, Germanism was losing ground — even in the cities of Prussian Poland. ("Niemczyzna sie cofa.") Still no acknowledgement was made of the factor of emigrant earnings in that process. R. Zm., "Wyznanie wlasnej bezsilnosci," *Niwa Polska* (Warszawa), 7 (20) grudnia 1902, R. XXX, nr. 51, 801–802. Thereafter, however, the integral correlation between emigrant earnings and the apparently successful counter-offensive against Germanism, especially in the countryside, came to be increasingly, albeit still grudgingly, recognized. C. Rydlewski, for example, quite unequivocally reported that by that year (1904) the corner had been turned in the Polish-German confrontation in the Eastern Marches. A singular factor in this turn of the German tide was the inflow of emigrant earnings from abroad and from the industrial areas of the Reich. See his, "Walka ekonomiczna zywiolu poskiego pod rzadem pruskim," *Ekonomista* (Warszawa: 1904), R. IV, t. I, 3–8, 238–250. An equally unequivocal observation was made by Ludwik Krzywicki in his, "Nasi wychodzcy," *Ateneum* (Warszawa: 1901), t. CI, 440–441. Nevertheless, as late as 1908, Jozef Adamczewski could still hedge on the issue in one of his essays. He conceded that emigrant earnings in Westphalia and Saxony played "a not insignificant" role in turning the balance in the "conflict for the land" in favor of the Poles, though he continued to give priority status in this reversal to such factors as growth of banking and credit facilities, the development of railroads, etc. See his, "Walka ekonomiczno-polityczna o ziemie w Krolestwie Poznanskiem," *Ekonomista* (Warszawa: 1908), R. VIII, t. I, 332–333, 339, 344, 352–353, 355. In a subsequent essay in the same publication, however, he appeared to be less ambivalent on the impact of emigrant earnings from the western industrial provinces. For that reason, enjoined against any restrictions upon or discouragement of that vital source of capital, though he foresaw that the increment of that capital seemed to be reversing the traditional socio-economic patterns in that area. Where formerly the gentry had been absorbing the peasant landholds, the reverse was the case in 1908. Such a pattern of change, he seemed to warn, would be followed by equally basic political changes — conceivably in the direction of populism or social democracy. See, *ibid.*, R. VIII, t. II, 76, 95–96, 100. For subsequent political impact on Prussian Poland of emigrant concentrations in Rheinland-Westfalen area, see, Czeslaw Demel, "Wplyw polskiej emigracyi robotniczej z Westfalii-Nadrenii na zycie polityczne Wielkopolski w latach 1916–1918," *Przeglad Zachodni* (Poznan: 1973), t. 29, nr. 1, 72–109. A writer in the social democratic *Krytyka* had no such qualms or reservations. He unequivocally affirmed that the transfer of land from Polish ownership to German — transfers greatly facilitated by the operations of the German colonization commission — had been reversed by the turn of the century. This reversal, in his view, was almost exclusively due to the money earned by Polish emigrants to the industrial centers of the Reich — savings that were frequently located in land. J.K.M., "Zabor pruski wobec ustawy ekspropryacyjnej," *op. cit.*, 1908, R. X, t. I, 55–65. This point was essentially reaffirmed by Jozef Frejlich in the more conservative *Czasopismo prawnicze i ekonomiczne* a few years later. See his, "Polskie wychodztwo zarobkowe w obwodzie przemyslowem westfalsko-nadrenskiem," *op. cit.* (Krakow: 1911), R. XII, 42, 84. William W. Hagen comprehensively examined the elaborate Polish organizational structures that developed in Prussian Poland as counters to German policies in that area in his, "National Solidarity and Organic Work in Prussian Poland, 1814–1914," *The Journal of Modern History* (Chicago), Vol. 44, No. 1, March 1972, 38–64. Unaccountably, however, he failed to even mention the emigrant capital — especially from the industrial areas of the Reich — which made those structures functionally successful.

    33. Kula, *op. cit.,* 25; Balch, *op. cit.,* 144.

    34. Kula, *loc. cit.*

    35. Juliusz Makarewicz, "Walka z spekulacja parcelacyjna," *Przeglad Powszechny* (Krakow), wrzesien 1904, t. LXXXIII, nr. 249, 321–322. Dr. Gross, a participant at the Fourth Congress of Jurists and Economists in 1906, took strong exception to the oft-repeated argument that inflated prices of parcels of land were a consequence of profit-oriented agents and alien speculators — presumably Jews. In his view, that state of affairs had, in fact, been created by government sponsored and officially licensed agencies like the Galician Peasant Bank, the Galician Parcelation Bank and others. In spite of their pious professions of concern for the interests of the peasantry, they were basically profit oriented in the interest of the landowners who put their land up for sale. IV Zjazd prawnikow i ekonomistow polskich, "Obrady sekcyi ekonomicznej," *Czasopismo prawnicze i ekonomiczne* (Krakow: 1907), R. VIII, 147ff.

    36. Bujak, *Maszkienice . . . ,* I, 100.

    37. Bujak, *Maszkienice . . . ,* II, 26.

    38. Bujak, *Maszkienice . . . ,* I, 99–100.

    39. Roman Buczynski, "Nasza wlasnosc ziemska," *Biblioteka Warszawska* (1882), t. 168, 155–156. See also: Jozef Kleczynski, "Ceny ziemi wloscianskiej w Galicyi," *Niwa* (Warszawa: 15 kwiecien 1879), XV, 553ff. and his, "Stosunki ekonomiczne w Galicyi," *Wiadomosci statystyczne o stosunkach krajowych* (Lwow: 1881), R. VII.

40. C. H. Young, citing E. H. Oliver as his authority, stressing the poverty of newly arrived Ukrainian elements to Canada, states that even those who had land to sell before emigrating realized little from its sale because "... the land was not always marketable, and the day came not later than 1904 when, with the peasants emigrating and the land market flooded, it was difficult or impossible to sell." E. H. Oliver, *Land Settlement in Saskatchewan* (n.p.: n.d.), 78, cited by Charles Hurlbert Young, *The Ukrainian Canadians; A Study in Assimilation* (Toronto: 1931), 42–43, 45. This, in view of the statistical evidence cited immediately above and excluding isolated and exceptional circumstances, seems to be unlikely.

41. Leon Wasilewski, "Zapomniani," *Krytyka* (Krakow), lipiec–sierpien 1911, R. XIII, 46. See also, Edmund Kolodziejczyk, *Ludnosc polska na gornych Wegrach* (Krakow: 1910), 34.

42. Bujak, *Maszkienice* . . . , II, 96, 110–111.

43. See, for example, Okolowicz, *op. cit.*, 280–281, 389–390; Jozef Okolowicz, "Wychodztwo" in Stanislaw Janicki (ed.), *Stosunki rolnicze Krolestwa Kongresowego* (Warszawa: 1918), 116–117; Szawleski, *Kwestja emigracji . . .*, 66.

44. Bujak, *Maszkienice* . . . , I, 154–155. See also, *supra*, 152.

45. *Ibid.*, 128. See also, U., "Kronika galicyjska," *Biblioteka Warszawska* (1896), t. 221, 106.

46. See, for example, Okolowicz, *Wychodztwo i osadnictwo* . . . , 390; Caro and Englisch, *op. cit.*, 273; Marya Balsiger, "Polskie wychodztwo sezonowe do Niemiec," *Srodkowo Europejski Zwiazek Gospodarczy i Polska* (Krakow: 1916), 94–95.

47. Koszutski, *op. cit.*, 231, citing *Prace Warszawskiego Komitetu Statystycznego* (Warszawa: 1902/1903), t. XIX.

48. *Ibid.*, 226–230, 232.

49. Franciszek Bujak, *Galicya* (Lwow: 1908/1910), I, 398–399.

50. The author explained the varying rates of increase by the fact that a higher proportion of men migrated seasonally and therefore the manual labor which they would have performed (*e.g.*, mowing, threshing) paid premium wages. Harvest field work, a function usually fulfilled by girls and women, did not feel the pinch of scarcity, because relatively fewer girls and women emigrated seasonally. Teamsters always owned their own horses and, therefore, were invariably the more affluent farmers. Affluent farmers seldom migrated seasonally since they were sufficiently occupied on their own land. Bujak, *Maszkienice* . . . , II, 66.

51. *Ibid.*, 67.

52. *Ibid.*, 66–67.

53. Bujak, *Maszkienice* . . . , I, 119.

54. Bujak, *Maszkienice* . . . , II, 68.

55. *Ibid.*, 65, 109.

56. *Ibid.*, 67.

57. Stefan Schmidt, *Die Wanderarbeiter in der Landwirtschaft Sachsen und ihre Beschaftigung im Jahre 1910* (Berlin: 1911), 176.

58. Bujak, *Maszkienice* . . . , II, 65. Interestingly enough, while he found that rentals for land leases had increased during the 1900–1910 decade, these increases were not nearly as notable as the increases in the prices of land put up for sale. While the peasants were disposed to pay prices out of proportion to

their economic value in buying land for themselves, the leasing of land was regarded in terms of investment and profit with the value of his labor scrupulously considered. This, the author felt, was by then possible because there was a more remunerative market for his labor abroad. Formerly, when the value of his labor was not considered, rentals were correspondingly higher and, in many cases, made the leasing of land to the peasant more profitable than cultivating it by the landowner. *Maskienice* . . . , I, 108–109; and *Maszkienice* . . . , II, 27, 29–30, 46–48.

59. *Ibid.*, 67.

60. *Ibid.*, 64.

61. *Ibid.*, 67–68.

62. Some noteworthy changes were instituted in farm buildings: (1) old houses and buildings were replaced by new ones to a larger degree in the last decade than ever before; (2) the new houses were distinguished by higher walls, larger windows, a tendency to retain the natural coloration of the wood; (3) in 1911 a remigrant from the United States had built all his farm buildings from brick — "a construction material theretofore reserved almost exclusively for school buildings"; (4) the practice of using concrete for foundations, wells, and cellars had begun to gain acceptance — "a remigrant from the United States even built his barn and workshop from this material"; (5) there was a greater tendency to build stables separately from the peasants' living quarters; (6) the practice of using double windows (storm windows) in winter had gained acceptance; and (7) there was a more widespread use of wooden flooring in the living quarters — formerly the floor was always of clay. *Ibid.*, 34–38.

63. Bujak, "Rozwoj wsi zachodnio-galicyjskiego w drugiej polowie XIX. w.," *Z odleglej i blizkiej przeszlosci* . . . , III, 122 and *Maszkienice* . . . , II, 107, 109. Ludwik Krzywicki expressed similar sentiments on the stifling restraints of tradition. Impressed by the Bunyanesque accomplishments of the emigrants to Brazil — he compared them to the fabled strong-men *Wyrwideb* and *Waligor* — he found this question forcing itself upon his attention: "Why was this potential might discovered only abroad, among isolated surroundings and in the absence of any financial means or help of any kind?" To this the author answered: "Because the human being freed itself from the shackles of a tradition begun during the years of serfdom and intensified during the years of political imprisonment . . . oppressive conditions which increased from year to year as a result of the subdivision of the small landholds, lack of gainful employment . . . years during which circumstances contrived such a situation around this human being that any effort on his part was as fruitless as butting his head against a stone wall." Away from home, he was first able to tax his latent physical, moral, etc., resources. Ludwik Krzywicki in his introduction to *Pamietniki emigrantow: Ameryka Poludniowa* (Warszawa: 1931), v–vi, compiled and published by the Instytut Gospodarstwa Spolecznego.

64. Leon W. Biegeleisen, *Rozwoj gospodarczy nowoczesnej wsi polskiej* (Krakow: 1916), I, 16 and ff.

65. Stanislaw Hupka, *Über die Entwicklung der westgalizischen Dorfzustände in der zweite Hälfte des 19. Jahrhunderts* (Teschen: 1910), 105 and ff. Wladyslaw Rapacki, writing in 1874, i.e., before the development of any notable volume of emigration, was obliged to conclude that any improvement in peasant agriculture was impossible because of the lack of sufficient economic resources. See his, *Ludnosc Galicyi* (Lwow: 1874), 110–113, reprinted

in Stefan Kieniewicz (ed.), *Galicya w dobie autonomicznej, 1850–1914; Wybor tekstow* (Wroclaw: 1952), 191–193. As late as 1899, Bujak saw evidence of economic and cultural stagnation — and even regression — in certain areas of Galicia because of the ever-increasing disparity between the needs of the population and the means available to satisfy them. Bujak, *Maszkienice* . . . , I, 134.

66. IV Zjazd prawnikow i ekonomistow polskich, "Obrady sekcyi ekonomicznej. I. Parcelacya," *Czasopismo prawnicze i ekonomiczne* (Krakow: 1907), R. VIII, 96–164; *ibid.,* 165–209, 216–221.

67. See his, "Walka z spekulacja parcelacyjna," *op. cit.,* wrzesien 1904, t. LXXXIII, nr. 249, 321–322.

68. Helena Landau, "Parcelacya ziemi w Galicyi," *Krytyka* (Krakow), R. XIV, t. XXXIII, 1912, 195–199 and Edward Maurizio, "Przeobrazenie wsi galicyjskiej," *op. cit.,* 227–232. Although Landau remained unconvinced as to the economic feasibility of small landholds, in a subsequent essay she modified her views somewhat by advocating the creation of cooperative leaseholds as an alternative to the inefficient productive methods of small, peasant holdings. See her, "Kurya wiekszej wlasnosci," *op. cit.,* R. XIV, t. XXXV, 1912, 122.

This dilemma among social-democrats reflected a dilemma in socialist theory that went back at least to the turn of the century. In June 1899, Wladyslaw Gumplowicz challenged a position paper on the subject of the Socialist Party and ameliorative-reformist politics by the elder statesman of socialism, Friedrich Engels ("Kwestya wloscianska," *Przedswit* (Londyn), Ser. III, nr. 12, grudzien 1894, 1–7). Gumplowicz, in effect, asked: What should be the position of the Socialist Party toward ameliorative legislation, in general, and, specifically, such reform issues as parcelation, peasant credit facilities, leaseholds, etc. — measures which would have the effect of perpetuating individual ownership of land in the face of historical forces which foredoom them to economic extinction? He rejected the commonly held view of his socialist colleagues about "the proprietary fanaticism of the peasant" and argued that, in fact, they do manifest strong inclinations toward collectivism — inclinations not inconsistent with the aims of socialism. The old concept of *Markgenossenschaft* and *Mir* had contemporary counterparts in the renaissance of peasant agricultural associations and cooperatives *(spolki rolnicze)* which he saw as transitional stages in the direction of collective ownership — particularly if developed under the sponsorship and direction of socialists. This subject, in his view, was of more than theoretical interest because completely proletarized peasants were forced to emigrate — usually to industrial centers of Europe or America and constituted a debilitating influence on socialist unionism in those areas. W. Gumplowicz, "Kwestya agrarna," *Przedswit* (Londyn), czerwiec 1899, Ser. III, nr. 6, 3–5.

This view was, in principle, vigorously opposed by the Marxist theorist, Kazimierz Kelles-Krauz, who seemed to regard Gumplowicz as a well-intentioned "observer" rather than "a committed party activist." While recognizing the imperative need for bringing socialism to the peasants — a problem which occupied the deliberations of several party congresses in the early years of the 1890's — he contended that small peasant landholds, in contradistinction to middle-sized ones, survived precisely because they did not represent a competitive element to the latifundia. In fact, they provided an anchorage of a cheap and abundant labor supply for the latter. In essence, basing his argument on Kautsky's *Die Agrarfrage,* 1899, he maintained that socialists did not need a special agrarian program. In his view, ameliorative legislation — like, for example, parcelation — at best could only "neutralize" the potential opposition of small peasant landholders toward the socialist effort since the peasant, like the petit-bourgeois, was pulled in two directions: that of the proletarian and that of a private owner. Gumplowicz's position, in his judgment, seemed to be tainted with "Bernsteinism." Michal Lusnia [Kazimierz Kelles-Krauz], "O naszej taktyce na wsi," *op. cit.,* Ser. III, nr. 10, pazdz. 1899, 3–8.

This argument was renewed with the publication of David's *Sozialismus und Landwirtschaft. I. Die Betriebsfrage* (Berlin: 1903) in which the author challenged the "industrial socialism" of Kautsky and Kelles-Krauz. David argued that the process of amalgamation and absorption apparent in manufacture was not operative in agriculture. Small landholds, in his view, had a vitality and economic integrity, especially in intense areas of production. That being the case, it behooved the socialists to support reformist-ameliorative legislation aimed at helping the small peasant landholder. Like Gumplowicz, he saw peasant landholds increasingly forced in the direction of cooperatives which would be a transitional stage toward collective ownership. Michal Lusnia [K. Kelles-Krauz], "Nasza praca na wsi. Rewizja programu agrarnego," *op. cit.,* R. XXIV, nr. 9, wrzesien 1905, 360–367.

This position was essentially reaffirmed by Gumplowicz in 1905. While he saw little prospect for the socialist cause among large peasant landholders, ameliorative policies — such as support and encouragement of parcelation aimed at improving the condition of small and landless peasants — should be supported by the party. By acquiring land the peasant could bail himself out of feudalism — ". . . he deserves this long-overdue satisfaction." He could thus attain to a higher cultural-technical level, that is, gain broader intellectual horizons which, in fact, was the aim of the party. In the existential circumstances and until the party can take over parliamentary power and advance something better, it cannot do otherwise. Gumplowicz, "Nasze zadania na wsi," *op. cit.,* R. XXV, nr. 2, luty 1905, 82.

As late as 1914, Wilhelm Feldman, the editor of the social-democratic *Krytyka,* chided the doctrinnaire socialists for their continued opposition to parcelation. He pointed out that, ironically enough, their position very nearly corresponded to that of "neo-conservatives" like Grabski who would sanction parcelation only for the creation of middle-sized peasant landholds. He maintained that Grabski's policy simply would not solve the problem for the large majority of the peasants in Poland. Going somewhat beyond Landau, he advocated the remunerated expropriation and nationalization of the largest landholds — latifundia in excess of 10,000 hectares — and the creation of 5–10 hectare leaseholds extended over 50 to 70 years with the stipulation that they remain undivided. Like Gumplowicz and David, as well as Landau, he saw their ultimate organization along cooperative lines. (f.) [W. Feldman], "Unarodowienie ziemi jednem wyjsciem z nedzy galicyjskiej," *Krytyka* (Krakow), R. XVI, t. XLII, 15 kwiecien 1914, 67–70. For Grabski's prewar views on parcelation and feasible peasant landholds, see fn. 14, Ch. 4, *supra.* At a later date (1929) he pointedly affirmed that farmholds of 2–5 hectares (in western Galicia) showed economic vitality in the prewar period only when their income was augmented by money earned abroad. In the absence of such income, the minimum size of peasant landholds must perforce be revised upward. Wladyslaw Grabski, *Historya wsi w Polsce* (Warszawa: 1929), 403.

69. Bujak, *Maszkienice* . . . , I, 131. One peasant writer, in the face of the widespread claims of the demoralizing influences that the emigrants were subjected to abroad, cited the widespread demoralization among workers on Polish manorial estates. He was especially bitter in his indictment of the licentious conduct of the manorial "pushers," *i.e.,* overseers. He likened the majority of the estates to "Sodom and Gomorrah." Wojciech Wiacek, "Przyczyny emigracji sezonowej," in Stanislaw Pigon (ed.), *Wybor Pisarzy Ludowych* (Wroclaw: 1947–1948), I, 177–181. Another writer enumerated the deplorable economic conditions prevailing among the manorial employees in Galicia indicating a total disregard of the gentry for their most primitive needs. Zygmunt Zielinski, *Poglad krytyczny na nasze stosunki ekonomiczno-spoleczne w Galicyi* (Przemysl: 1899), 193–197, reproduced in Kieniewicz (ed.), *op. cit.,* 221–224.

70. Bujak, *Maszkienice* . . . , II, 108.

71. *Ibid.,* 12.

72. See, for example: Jozef Buzek, *Poglad na wzrost ludnosci ziem polskich w wieku 19-tym* (Krakow: 1915), 26, 33–34; Stefan L. Zaleski, "General Demography of Poland," *Polish Encyclopaedia* (Geneva: 1921), Vol. II, No. 2, 304, 333, 350–351; Wladyslaw Grabski, *Rocznik statystyczny Krolestwa Polskiego, rok 1914* (Warszawa: 1915), 45; T. Szturm de Szterm, "Ludnosc" in Janicki, *op. cit.,* fn. 1, p. 27; and Julian B. Marchlewski, *Stosunki spoleczno-ekonomiczne pod panowaniem pruskiem* (Warszawa: 1903), 6.

73. Bujak, *Maszkienice* . . . , I, 133–134.

74. *Ibid.,* 127. Helena Landau made essentially the same point in her, "Parcelacya ziemi w Galicyi," *Krytyka* (Krakow), R. XIV, t. XXXIII, 1912, 195–199.

75. Bujak, *Maszkienice* . . . , II, 106–107. Bystron, writing at a later date, saw much evidence among remigrants — from Germany and the United States especially — of certain refinements of manners and less traditional vulgarism in speech and social conduct. Bystron, *op. cit.,* 342ff.

76. Bujak, *Maszkienice* . . . , II, 135–136.

77. Janik, *op. cit.,* 266.

78. Szawleski, *Wychodztwo* . . . , 149. See also his, *Kwestja emigracji* . . . , 67 and Okolowicz, *Wychodztwo i osadnictwo* . . . , 390. Balch, with her usual perceptiveness, noted that, for good or evil, emigration had a modernizing influence upon the country of emigration and that the more striking cultural distinctions and traits between the countries concerned tended to be obliterated. Balch, *op. cit.,* 82. Taft concluded that the total advantages accruing to the country of emigration far outweigh the disadvantages. Donald R. Taft, *Human Migration; A Study of International Movements* (New York: 1936), 198–202. Such was his considered judgment as far as the emigrant as an individual was concerned. For these reasons he disagreed with Foerster's (R. H. Foerster, *Italian Emigration in Our Time* (Cambridge: 1919), Ch. 22) tendency to minimize the benefits of emigration to the Italians, as well as Louis Adamic's argument (in *The Promised Land*) that the Slav, "in quiet Carniola . . . works a little and starves a little and still lives to an old age." There he "belongs," here he is treated as "refuse." Though Taft was willing to acknowl-

edge that the debatable fields were the social, moral and, in some cases, the intellectual effects of emigration, he nevertheless pointed out the static character of Adamic's arguments by noting that the children of the immigrants often did "belong" here in America. *Op. cit.,* 197–198. See also, Taft's *Two Portuguese Communities in New England* (New York: 1935), 348.·

CHAPTER TEN

1. For the pervasive impact of the revolutionary developments of 1905–1906 in Russia on the currents of nationalism in all sectors of prewar Poland, see Stefan Kieniewicz, *Historia Polski, 1795–1918* (Warszawa: 1970), especially Ch. XXV, 433–460. For impact of pre-war currents of nationalism on socialist internationalism, see F. [Wilhelm Feldman], "Ewolucya w Galicyi," *Krytyka* (Krakow: 1910), R. XII, t. I, 269–276. The political-ideological changes during these years are treated in extensive detail by Jerzy Myslinski, *Studia nad polska prasa spoleczno-polityczna w zachodniej Galicyi, 1905–1914* (Warszawa: 1970), *passim* and Leszek Guzicki and Seweryn Zurawicki, *Historia polskiej mysli spoleczno-ekonomicznej* (Warszawa: 1969), Chapters VII and VIII.

2. Caro's publication of his *Auswanderung und Auswanderungspolitik in Oesterreich* in 1909, probably more than any other publication, went a long way toward revitalizing this older "devil" or "conspiracy" theory of the basic cause of emigration.

3. Bohdan Wasiutynski, for example, pointed out that while in 1899 the German agricultural bureaus *(Landwirtschaftkammern)* had provided only 14,500 seasonal workers for Prussian agriculture — approximately 1/15 of the total seasonal workers employed in that country in that year — by 1906, they had considerably expanded their function and efforts were being made to centralize their operations in an agency which would cover the whole of the Reich — a *Feldarbeiterzentrale.* Such an arrangement, in the author's view, was fraught with serious disadvantages, including a glutted labor market for the emigrants and a "politics of immigration" in the Reich to satisfy the paranoia of Hakatists resulting from an excessive dependence of German agriculture upon Polish workers — a politics which was manifest in the intensified recruitment of Germans from Transylvania, Italians, Slovaks and Ukrainians. See his, "Ruch wychodzczy z Krolestwa Polskiego," [IV Zjazd prawnikow i ekonomistow polskich], *Czasopismo prawnicze i ekonomiczne* (Krakow: 1906), t. VII, 21–22.

4. See, *supra,* 18, 22, 151 and fn. 32, Ch. IX.

5. See his: "Wychodztwo Polskie," *Ekonomista* (Warszawa: 1907), R. VII, t. II, 2ff.; his, "Nasi robotnicy sezonowi," *Przeglad Powszechny* (Krakow), luty 1908, t. XCII, nr. 290, 181–182; his, "Sprawa naszych wychodzcow i robotnikow sezonowych na konferencyi Budapesztanskiej," *ibid.,* pazdz.–grudzien 1910, t. CVIII, 325–347; his, "Katolicy niemieccy w Dreznie w sprawie naszych robotnikow," *ibid.,* pazdz.–grudzien 1911, t. CXII, *7–*8; and his, "Wspolna akcya w sprawie wychodztwa [referat wygloszony na zjezdzie jubileuszowym Piotra Skargi w Krakowie]," *ibid.,* listopad 1912, t. CXVI, nr. 347, 140–157. Artur Benis affirmed Germany's imperative need was especially apparent during the Russo-Japanese war when seasonal emigration

from Russian Poland severely declined. See his, "Emigracya" [IV Zjazd prawnikow i ekonomistow polskich], *Czasopismo prawnicze i ekonomiczne* (Krakow: 1906), t. VII, 7.

6. The issue of considerably expanded network of employment bureaus came under extended discussion during the Fourth Congress of Polish Jurists and Economists in Krakow in 1906. Caro, representing the majority opinion of that body, advocated the broader expansion of the existing government (*i.e.,* Galician) employment agencies. Artur Benis and Count Roger Battaglia, representing the minority opinion, favored private, licensed and bonded agricultural labor agencies to handle seasonal emigration. Both of the latter regarded public, provincial and county, bureaus as hamstrung by their bureaucratic methods and procedures. IV Zjazd prawnikow i ekonomistow polskich, "Obrady sekcyi ekonomicznej. II. Emigracya," *Czasopismo prawnicze i ekonomiczne* (Krakow: 1907), R. VIII, 96 ff.

7. See, *supra,* 112 ff.

8. The sanguine hopes for this enterprise were never realized. Kazimierz Bartoszewicz, chairman of the board of directors of the *Straz Polska,* pronounced it a "straw fire" by the end of that year. See his, "Dyskusya w kwestyi bojkotu," *Przeglad Powszechny* (Krakow), listopad 1908, t. C, nr. 299, *9– *24. Other commentators on the subject seemed to confirm his verdict. See, for example, Leopold Caro, "Kwestya obecnego u nas bojkotu," in *ibid., *1– *8; his, "Katolicy w Dreznie w sprawie naszych robotnikow," *ibid.,* pazdz.– grudzien 1911, t. CXII, *8 ff.; and his, "Wspolna akcya w sprawie wychodztwa" in *ibid.,* listopad 1912, t. CXVI, nr. 347, 140–157.

9. Mieczyslaw Szawleski, *Kwestja emigracji w Polsce* (Warszawa: 1927), 64–65; Szawleski, *Wychodztwo polskie w stanach zjednoczonych Ameryki* (Lwow: 1924), 17–18; and Jozef Okolowicz, *Wychodztwo i osadnictwo Polskie przed wojna* (Warszawa: 1920), 393. See also, *supra,* Ch. VII.

The editor of the social-democratic *Krytyka,* as early as 1899, accused both the provincial government in Lwow and the federal government in Vienna of total delinquency as far as protective legislation for emigrants was concerned in spite of the elaborate bureaucratic structure supported by peasant taxes. *Op. cit.,* R. I, zesz. 1, kwiecien 1899, 102–105.

10. Szawleski, *Wychodztwo . . . ,* 356. It is apparently impossible to determine with any degree of accuracy the amount of money transferred to pre-war Poland as inheritances after deceased emigrants in the United States and elsewhere. Quite possibly, the amounts may have been substantial and, viewed as a source of capital increment from abroad, played a significant part in the total economic effects of emigration.

11. One historian, commenting upon this policy of loyalism of the Galician *szlachta* in its relation to the crown, remarked that the Emperor needed only to summon the leader of the Polish Club in the Reichsrat and their support was forthcoming. This, he found, was in conformity with the *Stanczyk* interpretation of history which regarded the Emperor as their legitimate monarch. "They were more loyal to him than were their forefathers to their kings." It was this "Krakow school" of history which emphasized that it was precisely the lack of loyalty to their kings which caused the decline and fall of Poland. "Such were the paradoxical conclusions drawn from the study of history. All this actually was an ideological rationale for the social interests of

the Galician landed gentry which, not without reason, saw in the Austrian emperor a mainstay of its rule over the rest of the population." Henryk Wereszycki, *Historja polityczna Polski w dobie popowstaniowej, 1864–1918* (Warszawa: 1948), 162.

12. Szawleski, *Kwestja emigracji . . . ,* 65; Okolowicz, *op. cit.,* 197; Zdzislaw Ludkiewicz, *Kwestya rolna w Galicyi* (Lwow: 1910), 264.

13. Quoted in Wereszycki, *op. cit.,* 23–24.

14. Franciszek Bujak, *Maszkienice . . . ,* I, 133. Interestingly enough, the same writer, in advocating the more widespread organization and establishment of *Reiffeisenkassen,* urged the clergy to recommend them to the peasantry since the parish clergy ". . . possesses a sufficient confidence of the peasant in money matters. . . ." *Ibid.,* 101.

In a review essay of Reymont's *Peasants* published in the clerical-oriented *Przeglad Powszechny* in 1909, Antoni Mazanowski adjudged it to be only a fragmentary representation of village life since many determining and directive elements (*e.g.,* the gentry, the Jew, the teacher, the scribe, the priest, etc.) were imperfectly or not at all delineated. Furthermore, in that work's chief protagonist, the peasant Boryna — and especially in his dying words — the reviewer perceived an expression of deep-rooted class antagonism to the gentry, therefore at odds with the reviewer's ideal of class reconciliation in the national interest. Boryna and other characters in that novel were, in fact, articulating the historical hostility of their class to the self-appointed leadership of the gentry. "This is not our affair," *(Nie nasza to sprawa)* they answered to the gentry's call for national unity or enterprise. The aristocratic ideals of the latter were regarded as both alien and antithetical to peasant interests. Boryna, unsentimentally drawn, is not unlike Rolvaag's *Old Jules;* Jagusia, the chief female protagonist, was represented as a kind of earth-fertility nature-child. Both were regarded by the reviewer as lacking in the basic elements of Christian morality. *Op. cit.,* lipiec–wrzesien 1909, t. CIII, 321 ff.

15. Ignacy Daszynski, *Pamietniki* (Krakow: 1925), I, 14–15. See also his, *Szlachetczyzna a odrodzenie Galicyi* (Lwow: 1899). As early as 1885, the editor of the *Przeglad Powszechny,* remarking on the emigration tide that was developing in the southeastern counties of Poznan province, admitted that the effectiveness of the clergy in containing this movement was generally very limited. *Ibid.,* wrzesien 1885, t. VII, nr. 21, 351, 356–357.

16. William I. Thomas and Florian Znaniecki, *The Polish Peasant in Europe and America* (Chicago: 1918–1920), II, 1261. Znaniecki explains the nature of the influence of the Catholic church as follows: "[The] influence of the church consists in bringing to bear on each traditional definition [including emigration], whatever it may be, the entire weight of the religious system. The latter is so coherent, its many various elements are so closely associated with one another in the doctrine and practice of the church and in the consciousness of the believer, that the individual cannot reject any of them without rejecting all, unless he has developed a spirit of critical discrimination seldom found among the peasants who have not been influenced by educated classes; and even if he tries to discriminate, the church does not let him do it but forces him to make a choice between all religion or no religion, unless it sees the need of relaxing on certain points in view of certain tendencies generally prevalent in society. When thus the church attaches a negative or positive sanction to any definition of a social situation, this situation, even if it

has no intrinsic religious significance of itself, even if it has no bearing whatever on matters of religious worship, becomes nevertheless externally connected with the whole system, and this connection is imposed on every member of the church by all the means of control which the latter disposes." *Ibid.,* 1261-1262. Thus, emigration, since it was generally deplored by the clergy, may have been regarded as somewhat "irreligious" as well as "illegal" by the emigrant.

17. *Tygodnik Ilustrowany* (Warszawa: 1886), nr. 157, quoted by Jozef Chalasinski, *Przeszlosc i przyszlosc inteligencji polskiej* (Rome: 1947), 61. Already in the previous year, Prus had concluded that, "Those . . . who constitute the intelligentsia of the towns, that is, the doctors, the notary public, the apothecary, etc., live only with themselves, stimulating their minds with current news from the newspapers and not participating in the general affairs of the community. Of more interest to them are . . . Afghanistani, the Tonkin Chinese than the cobblers, tailors, masons and coopers — people who walk the same streets they do. Such is the result of our aristocratic tradition." *Kurjer Warszawski,* 1885, quoted in *ibid.*

18. Wladyslaw M. Kozlowski, *Z hasel umyslowosci wspolczesnej* (Krakow: 1902), 47-52. For his commentaries on the political, social and intellectual scene in the United States, see his, "Z Ameryki, Biblioteki i czytelnie w Stanach Zjednoczonych," *Biblioteka Warszawska* (1897), t. 228, 141-151 and "Stronnictwa polityczne w Stanach Zjednoczonych . . . ," *Ateneum* (Warszawa), maj-czerwiec 1897, 222-254, 470-495, also reproduced in his more popular, *Jak jest za oceanem, urzadzenie panstwowe i zycie spoleczne Stanow Zjednoczonych Ameryki Polnocnej* (Warszawa: 1902).

19. Hrabia Wojciech Dzieduszycki, *Listy ze wsi; serja I* (Lwow: 1889), 88. Italics mine.

20. For standard institutional histories of Polish-American organizations see: Stanislaw Osada, *Historya Zwiazku Narodowego Polskiego i rozwoj ruchu narodowego polskiego w Ameryce Polnocnej* (Chicago: 1905); Osada, *Sokolstwo polskie; jego dzieje ideologia i poslannictwo* (Pittsburgh: 1929); Osada, *Jak sie ksztaltowala polska dusza wychodztwa w Ameryce* (Pittsburgh: 1930); Karol Wachtl, *Z.P.R.K. Dzieje Zjednoczenia Polskiego Rzymskokatolickiego w Ameryce* (Chicago: 1913). For a critically incisive denunciation of Polish-American leadership in the U.S., see, John Dewey, "Autocracy in America," *The New Republic* (New York), Aug. 24, 1918, Vol. XVI, No. 199, 103ff. Okolowicz credited the Polish-American organizations with both resisting and facilitating assimilation — the latter by "striving to transform as many temporary immigrants into permanent citizens of the United States" to maintain their numerical strength and influence in that country. Okolowicz, *Wychodztwo i osadnictwo . . . ,* 36, 55.

21. In whole or in part, the following monographs have dealt with the Polish-American press: Stanislaw Osada, *Prasa i publicystyka polska w Ameryce* (Pittsburgh: 1930); Henryk Nagiel, *Dziennikarstwo polskie w Ameryce* (Chicago: 1894); Witold Doroszewski, *Jezyk Polski w Stanach Zjednoczonych A.P.* (Warszawa: 1938); Robert E. Park, *The Immigrant Press and Its Control* (New York: 1922); Oswald G. Villard, *Some Newspapers and Newspapermen* (New York: 1923), and the Magisterial essay by Edmund G. Olszyk entitled *The Polish Press in America* (Milwaukee: 1940). Though generally recognized as one of the foremost instrumentalities working against

cultural assimilation in the United States, the Polish-American press was increasingly criticized for its advocacy of "separatism" from the Fatherland, *i.e.,* permanent settlement, for fear of diminishing its subscribers. See, for example, Szawleski, *Wychodztwo . . . ,* 169; Okolowicz, *Wychodztwo i osadnictwo . . . ,* 58–61. The Polish press was frequently critical of the disposition of the Polish-American press to widely disregard the literary rights of Polish authors by reproducing their works in both the periodical press and in book form without either permission of or remuneration to the original authors. Wladyslaw Dyniewicz, the editor and publisher of the Chicago weekly, *Gazeta Polska,* was singled out as an outstanding offender in this respect and was simultaneously accused of fulfilling the function of "passenger agent" by "addressing letters to the country folk of Galicia advising them to sell their patrimony to foreigners and emigrate to America," and selling fraudulent land titles to his co-nationals in America. Wladyslaw Wislocki (ed.), *Przewodnik Bibliograficzny* (Krakow: 1882), V, 71; *ibid.,* 1883, VI, 76; *ibid.,* 1886, IX, 24; *ibid.,* czerwiec 1890, 115; *ibid.,* listopad 1895, 206–207; *ibid.,* grudzien 1895, 231–232.

22. Probably still the best extant sources on the historical development of Polish-American Catholic parishes are the first two volumes of Waclaw Kruszka, *Historja Polska w Ameryce* (Milwaukee: 1905) as well as his revised edition entitled: *Historja Polska w Ameryce; od czasow najdawniejszych az do najnowszych* (Milwaukee: 1937). See also: Stanislaw Targosz, *Polonia katolicka w Stanach Zjednoczonych w przekroju* (Detroit: 1943). Frequently the American-educated Polish Catholic clergy were criticized by the nationalistic elements at home for their apparent nationalistic indifferentism. Emil H. Dunikowski, *Wsrod Polonii Amerykanskiej* (Lwow: 1893), 140.

The "schismatic" movement in the Polish Catholic fold in the latter part of the 19th and early part of the 20th century attracted considerable criticism, especially in the clerically oriented journals in Poland. Kruszka, *op. cit.,* II, 47ff. gives a historical sketch of this development. Though less than sympathetic to the separatists, it is nonetheless a perceptive analysis of its causes, especially the assimilatory tendencies of the American Catholic hierarchy. A more sympathetic and a more representative nationalistic point of view was expressed by the distinguished expatriate Zygmunt Milkowski [T. T. Jez], *Opowiadania z wedrowki po koloniach polskich w Ameryce Polnocnej* (Paris: 1901), 52–60. See also, Joel B. Hayden, *Religious Work among Poles in America* (New York: 1916); Joseph E. Ciesluk, *National Parishes in the United States* (Washington, D.C.: 1944); Karol W. Strzelec, *The Burning Bush; Trial and Hope of the Polish People* (Chicago: 191-); Brand Blanshard, *The Church and the Polish Immigrant* (n.p.: 1920), and Theodore E. Abel, *Protestant Home Missions to Catholic Immigrants* (New York: 1933).

23. The Polish-American parochial schools, attached to churches and staffed primarily by Catholic nuns, were still frequently adjudged as inferior to public schools from the standpoint of building plant, curricula and the pedagogic arts. The teachers, representative of a generation born and educated in America, enjoyed little proficiency in the Polish language. As a result, they were frequently disposed to lecture in English and, in the case of need, to resort to a Polish-American jargon. Thus, unwittingly, they were serving as instruments of Americanization. Szawleski, *op. cit.,* 131–148; Emil H. Dunikowski, *Wsrod Polonii Amerykanskiej* (Lwow: 1893), 46, 66–67, 137; Dunikowski, "O

szkolnictwie w Stanach Zjednoczonych," *Muzeum* (Lwow: kw.-maj 1893), 271-283, 373-383. See also, Joel B. Hayden, *op. cit.,* 20-21 and Stanislaw Targosz, *op. cit.,* passim. More frequently, however, despite their apparent deficiencies, the parochial schools were adjudged superior to those in some parts of Poland and, by perpetuating the language among the children, even if imperfectly, were serving as potent instruments against assimilation. Michal Janik, "Ludnosc polska w Stanach Zjednoczonych Ameryki polnocnej," *Lud* (Lwow), listopad 1905, t. XI, zesz. III, 257 ff.

24. On the development of national identity abroad, see K. R. Zywicki [Ludwik Krzywicki], "Nasi wychozcy," *Ateneum* (Warszawa: 1901), t. CI, 440, 442. As early as 1879, Agaton Giller, while advocating a nationwide Polish-American organization in the United States, remarked that ". . . it is not seemly that we should forget about those who find themselves in foreign lands. Because the emigrants constitute a force which cannot be denied, it should be the task of a well-conceived patriotism to so direct them that the cause of the Fatherland would realize the greatest profit therefrom." Szawleski, *Wychodztwo . . . ,* 99. See also, Modest Maryanski, *O emigracyi a w szczegolnosci o emigracyi polskiej do Stanow Zjednoczonych Polnocnej Ameryki i o koniecznej potrzebie jej zorganizowania* (Chicago: 1893), *passim.*

25. The editor of the socialist *Przedswit* regarded this view as unrealistic. Stanislaw Mendelson, "Nasza emigracja. II. Emigracja ekonomiczna," *Przedswit* (Londyn), Ser. II, t. II, nr. 29, 16 stycznia 1892, 7. The Polish-American socialist, Wladyslaw Fishler, considered it not beyond the realm of possibility. See his, "Polska w Ameryce," in *ibid.,* Ser. III, nr. 8, sierpien 1894, 4-19. The editors of the *Przeglad Emigracyjny* of 1894 reported that it was the super-patriotic newspapers of the partitioning powers *(e.g., Posner Tageblatt* and Russian *Nowoje Wremie)* which first raised the alarm of a Polish Fennianist movement, capable of immediately mobilizing 40,000 troops, in the United States in the event of a war for Poland's independence. They generally dismissed it as a paranoic fantasy. ___, "Polonia Amerykanska wobec kwestyi polskiej," *ibid.,* R. III, nr. 20, 15 pazdz. 1894, 187-188. Mendelson subsequently accused the patriotic-democratic groupings in Poland with indisposition to carrying out their revolutionary activities at home and showing a singular disposition toward shifting their field of operation among the Polish-Americans whom they increasingly proclaimed "the fourth sector of Poland" *(czwarta dzielnica Polski).* These "democrats" were generally made up of petit-bourgeois elements who could not agree with the *Stanczyk* policy of accommodation in Poland. In America, "revolutionary rhetoric costs nothing *(i.e.,* meets no reprisals), and demagogic laurels are easy to come by." ___, "Terazniejszosc i przyszlosc polonii w Ameryce," *Przedswit* (Londyn), Ser. III, nr. 1, czerwiec 1895, 1-3.

26. Caro and Englisch, *op. cit.,* 369. Okolowicz, "Wychodztwo" in Janicki (ed.), *op. cit.,* 117. The tendency to limit the size of families in the United States was viewed as such an influence. It would have been reassuring for the champions of Parana to read the memoir of a peasant-emigrant who settled in the adjacent Santa Catarina. Large families, it appears, were very common among the immigrant settlers. He, himself, ". . . was blessed with six children and I hope for at least as many more. Older settlers than myself boast of fifteen, sixteen and even twenty-three children. When one moves out with such a battalion into the fields, the work just disappears. . . ." Memoir No. 16, "A

farmer in Santa Catarina, son of a tenant farmer from near Gopla, born in 1879," Instytut Gospodarstwa Spolecznego, *Pamietniki emigrantow: Ameryka Poludniowa* (Warszawa: 1939), 284.

27. Okolowicz, *op. cit.,* 108. Kazimierz Warchalowski, also identified with the Parana group, reaffirmed that, in Brazil, the Polish emigrants are the assimilators rather than the assimilated. See his remarks at the Fourth Congress of Polish Jurists and Economists in *Czasopismo prawnicze i ekonomiczne* (Krakow: 1907), t. VIII, 191. See also Ch. IV, fn. 58 and Ch. VI, 103 ff., *supra,* on the Polish Commercial-Geographical Association — the original promoter of the *Nowa Polonia* idea — and its successors.

28. Jozef Siemiradzki, "Stosunki osadnicze w Brazylii," *Biblioteka Warszawska* (1892), t. 205, 104–105. These critics included not only the proponents of *Nowa Polonia* in Parana but also such spokesmen of the National Democratic *(endek)* persuasion as Poplawski and Dmowski. The spokesmen for the ultra-conservative landed gentry, fearful of the ultimate effect of the urban-industrial milieu upon the peasant-emigrant even went so far as to increasingly favor temporary seasonal emigration to Germany over emigration to the United States. Zalecki, *op. cit.,* t. II, Cz. 1, 88. See also, Thomas and Znaniecki, *op. cit.,* II, 1484. Even Bujak added his influence behind this trend. Though he recognized that the earning potential of the emigrant in the United States was higher than elsewhere, he took care to emphasize that the conditions of labor there were much more exhausting. "Though many return from the United States with several hundreds of dollars, they also return with undermined health. . . . Only one with extraordinary health and strength can safely survive the rigors in the United States." Consistent with this attitude he reiterated the allegedly popular peasant aphorism: America for the oxen, Europe for the peasant. Bujak, *Maszkienice . . . ,* II, 108.

For some earlier initiatives in colonization, ranging from Prince Adam Czartoryski's "Adampol" on the Asiatic side of the Bosporus in 1835, to Korczak-Branicki's plans in Oceania (1875), to a plan to relocate political emigres in the Confederate South during the U.S. Civil War in return for military service, and other relocation projects in the U.S., see Leon Papieski, *Emigracya i kolonizacya oraz zadanie polskiej polityki emigracyjnej* (Warszawa: 1918), 42–47; Zalecki, *op. cit.,* I, 11–12; Kruszka, *op. cit.,* I, 80; Dunikowski, *op. cit.,* 149; Okolowicz, *op. cit.,* 44; Szawleski, *op. cit.,* 22 and fn.

Henry Sienkiewicz, in his *Listy z Ameryki,* published in 1876, mentioned a conflict between two colonizing interests in America: a secular organization advocating settlement in Arkansas and a clerical one advocating settlement in Nebraska. According to him, "both parties waged a bitter battle in which neither the one nor the other were too temperate in their means or their expressions." Quoted by Kruszka, *loc. cit.* See also prospectus drawn up by a Polish Emigration Land Company of Virginia entitled *By-Laws, Charter, Prospectus and "Odezwa"* (Washington, D.C.: 1870).

29. Dr. Artur Benis, "Emigracya," [IV Zjazd prawnikow i ekonomistow polskich], *Czasopismo prawnicze i ekonomiczne* (Krakow: 1906), t. VII, 15.

30. IV Zjazd prawnikow i ekonomistow polskich, "Obrady sekcyi ekonomicznej. II. Emigracya," *Czasopismo prawnicze i ekonomiczne* (Krakow: 1907), t. VIII, 174–179.

31. *Ibid.,* 188.

32. *Ibid.,* 190.

33. *Ibid.,* 164-165.
34. *Ibid.,* 168.
35. *Ibid.,* 195.
36. *Ibid.,* 204.
37. *Ibid.,* 205.
38. *Ibid.,* 206-207.
39. *Ibid.,* 172.
40. *Ibid.,* 180.
41. *Ibid.,* 169.
42. *Ibid.,* 203.
43. See *supra,* Ch. VI, fn. 84. By 1906 Kumaniecki was expressing qualms about the assimilatory capacities of government-sponsored German schools in Brazil and in 1907 Caro was expressing serious reservations about the Parana idea in general. K. W. Kumaniecki, "Z naszych sprawach spolecznych. Oswiata i emigracya," *Przeglad Powszechny* (Krakow), pazdz. 1906, t. XCI, 144-159 and Leopold Caro, "Wychodztwo Polskie," *Ekonomista* (Warszawa), 1907, R. VII, t. II, 8-9. These reservations about the durability of the cohesive agricultural enclaves in Parana were reiterated by Dr. A. Bielicki in his "Kwestja rolna w Galicyi. Zdzislaw Ludkiewicz," *Przeglad Powszechny* (Krakow), lipiec-wrzesien 1913, t. CXIX, 110-113.
44. See, for example, Caro and Englisch, *op. cit.,* 6, 337.
45. Okolowicz, *Wychodztwo i osadnictwo . . . ,* 197-198. Both Dmowski and Caro opposed Polish emigration to Canada because that country's policy of settlement favored dispersal of the settlers in the homestead areas specifically to preclude ethnic concentrations and was, therefore, premised on the idea of speedy assimilation of immigrants. IV Zjazd prawnikow i ekonomistow polskich, "Obrady sekcyi ekonomicznej. II. Emigracya," *Czasopismo prawnicze i ekonomiczne* (Krakow: 1907), t. VIII, 189, 219.
46. Szawleski, *op. cit.,* 337. Caro continued to regard the "prepaids" as a device of American industrialists and mine operators to by-pass United States legal prohibitions against contract labor. Caro and Englisch, *op. cit.,* 337.
47. Okolowicz, *op. cit.,* 10-11.
48. Czerkawski, for example, at the Fourth Congress of Polish Jurists and Economists, affirmed that considerations of "national strength" should be the basic assumption to any consideration of the problem of emigration. IV Zjazd prawnikow i ekonomistow polskich, "Obrady sekcyi ekonomicznej. II. Emigracya," *Czasopismo prawnicze i ekonomiczne* (Krakow: 1907), t. VIII, 169.
49. Handbill published by *Przedswit* (Londyn: 1881), 7-16, reproduced in Stefan Kieniewicz (ed.), *Galicya w dobie autonomicznej, 1850-1914; Wybor Tekstow* (Wroclaw: 1952), 182-190. In 1891, Stanislaw Mendelson, the editor of the socialist *Przedswit,* recognized its economically imperative character, simultaneously recognizing the understandable hostility it provoked among indigenous workers in the countries of immigration. As an advocate of international solidarity of working classes he advocated their speedy organization into workers' combinations which would make the Polish immigrants allies rather than competitors of their fellow workers. See his, "Emigracya robotnicza," *Przedswit* (Londyn), Ser. II, t. I, nr. 11, 12 wrzesien 1891, 2-3, and his "Nasza emigracya. II. Emigracya ekonomiczna," *ibid.,* Ser. II, t. II, nr. 29, 16 stycznia 1892, 6-8.
50. Wladyslaw Gumplowicz, "Socjalizm a kwestja Polska," *Krytyka*

(Krakow), pazdz. 1906, R. VIII, zesz. 10, 272. Gumplowicz, however, did concede that "in the existing circumstances the population has a right to unrestricted emigration in search of a better livelihood. . . ." and that, while the state should intercede in the material and cultural interests of its emigrants abroad, it should regard it as a temporary palliative to facilitate their cultural transition and to minimize the conflict resulting from the assimilative processes which are not only inevitable but desirable in the ultimate realization of a full life abroad. *Ibid.,* 270–272, 273, 277. Though favorably disposed to resistance to the forcible assimilation practiced in the Eastern Marches by the German government, a writer in the socialist *Przedswit,* in 1912, viewed with approbation the systematic assimilation of Polish immigrant workers in the Westphalia-Rhineland industrial area with their German counterparts in the interest of proletarian solidarity. B. P-in, "Asymilacya narodowa a socyalizm," *Przedswit* (Londyn), R. XXXI, nr. 7, styczen–czerwiec 1912, 64–74.

51. "Pierwszy Program Stronnictwa Ludowego," *Przyjaciel ludu* (1895), nr. 18, reprinted in Kieniewicz, *op. cit.,* 268–270.

52. Joseph Tenenbaum, *In Search of a Lost People; The Old and the New Poland* (New York: 1948), 168; Henryk Wereszycki, *Historia polityczna Polski w dobie popowstaniowej, 1864–1918* (Warszawa: 1948), 98–99. A writer in the clerical-conservative *Przeglad Powszechny* of 1894 saw the repressive May Laws of the Russian government, which forced the exodus of Jews from the western governments of the empire into the Kingdom and Lithuania, as basically motivated by the desire to dilute and diminish the growing currents of Polish nationalism — especially among the almost-assimilated Jewish Poles. In a word, a part and parcel of Russia's policy to deal with its chronic "Polish problem." He viewed it as a potentially workable (*i.e.,* successful) policy. That being the case, the author voiced sympathetic approbation of their emigration — especially to England where their numbers were relatively small, the government's policy (of immigration) was generally unrestrictive (*i.e.,* liberal) and their material prospects promising. Marek Lza, "Zydzi Polsko-Rosyjscy w Londynie," *op. cit.,* listopad 1894, t. XLIV, nr. 131, 201–221. That view was subsequently reiterated by Adam Skierko, "The Jews of Poland," *Polish Encyclopaedia* (Geneva: 1921), Vol. II, No. 5, 941. See also, *supra,* fn. 58, Ch. 3.

53. T. W-o, "Kwestya zydowska jako zagadnienie narodowe," *Przedswit* (Londyn), R. XXIV, nr. 5–6, maj–czerwiec 1904, 223.

54. See, for example, Lut., "Kronika miesieczna," *Ateneum* (Warszawa: 1892), t. LXVII, 179–183; P. W., "Zydzi w Stanach Zjednoczonych," *Niwa Polska* (Warszawa), 6 (19) lipca 1902, R. XXX, Nr. 29, 454–455; and D. n., "Syonizm-awangarda pangermanizmu," *Niwa Polska* (Warszawa), 31 sierp. (13 wrzesien) 1902, R. XXX, Nr. 37, 578–579.

55. Adam Krasinski, "Kronika miesieczna," *Biblioteka Warszawska* (1906), t. 264, 600–605.

56. J. Weyssenhoff, "Kronika miesieczna," *Biblioteka Warszawska* (1891), t. 203, 416; *ibid.* (1892), t. 206, 165–166. He bewailed the large volume of Jewish immigration to Galicia from Russia which Galician authorities "were powerless to restrain" and noted that the latter had undertaken measures to prevent Jewish immigrant settlement in Galicia — a policy which caused many of them to wander from town to town. *Ibid.* (1891), t. 203, 416.

57. Socjalista, "Z Galicyi," *Przedswit* (Londyn), Ser. II, t. I, nr. 14, 3 pazdz. 1891, 1.

58. *Stenog. Sprawozd.* (1901/1902), I ses., VIII per., 514. Stojalowski's ideological orientation and political fortunes inevitably invite comparison with and suggest some striking parallels to that of Father Coughlin in the United States in the 1930's. See, for example, Ks. Maryan Morawski, "List pasterski biskupow galicyjskich i pisma Ks. Stojalowskiego," *Przeglad Powszechny* (Krakow), maj 1895, t. XLVI, nr. 137, 314–320, and Ks. St. Ledochowski, "Zdjecia cenzur z ks. Stojalowskiego," in *ibid.*, pazdz. 1897, t. LVI, nr. 166, 144–146. For a detailed indictment of political perfidy and opportunism of Stojalowski, see, Wilhelm Feldman, "Ruch Chrzescijansko-spoleczny w Galicyi," *Krytyka* (Krakow), R. IX, t. I, 1907, 62–69, 230–239.

59. F. R., "Galicyjski apostol zydow," *Niwa Polska* (Warszawa), 23 listopad (6 grudnia) 1902, R. XXX, nr. 49, 770–771.

60. *Stenog. Sprawozd.*, III ses., VIII per., 20 pos. (15 marzec 1907), 1215–1223. Cogent particulars on the subject were also brought out by Kolischer and Abrahamowicz, *ibid.*, 19 marzec 1907, 1560–1564.

61. *Ibid.*, I ses., IX per., 25 pos. (23 pazdz. 1908), 1288.

62. *Ibid.*, 34 pos. (3 listopad 1908), 2075–2076.

63. ____, "Organizacya opieki nad emigrantami zydowskiemi," *Polski przeglad emigracyjny* (Krakow), R. VI, maj–czerwiec 1912, 234–239.

64. Caro and Englisch, *op. cit.*, 23, 28 ff. In the face of the growing temper of nationalism, the so-called *Podolian szlachta* of eastern Galicia found itself in a situation very much like that of its Junker counterpart in Prussian Poland. As the traditional keepers of the symbols of nationalism, it was incumbent that they assume leadership of and give support to the manifestations of nationalism at the turn of the century. In time, however, the extreme nationalistic elements began to look to the displacement of the Ukrainian elements as a simple solution to the nationalities problem in that area. Such a development would have deprived the gentry of its cheap labor supply and therefore, insofar as the gentry contributed to the rising tide of nationalism, it had created a situation wherein it was "hoist on its own petard."

65. This period saw a rather remarkable proliferation of statistical compilations with a decidedly "ethnographic" orientation. See, for example, Stefan Komornicki, *Polska na zachodzie w swietle cyfr i zdarzen, Cz. I: Zabory i kolonizacja niemiecka na ziemiach polskich* . . . (Lwow: 1894); J. L. Poplawski, *Galicya w liczbach* (Lwow: 1903); Zygmunt Gloger, *et al., Opis ziem zamieszkalych przez Polakow pod wzgledem geograficznem, etnograficznem, historycznem.* . . (Warszawa: 1904); Edward Czynski and T. Tillinger, *Etnograficzno-statystyczny zarys liczebnosci i rozsiedlenia ludnosci polskiej* (Warszawa: 1909); J. Grabiec [Jozef Dabrowski], *Wspolczesna Polska w cyfrach i faktach* (New York: 1911); Faustyn Rasinski, *Prace statystyczne, IV, Polska etnograficzna* (Warszawa: 1915); Eugeniusz Romer, *Geograficzno-statystyczny atlas* (Warszawa: 1916); Romer, *Ilu nas jest?* (Krakow: 1917); Romer, *Polacy na kresach pomorskich i pojeziernych* (Lwow: 1919); Stanislaw Thugutt, *Polska i Polacy. Ilosc i rozsiedlenie ludnosci polskiej* (Warszawa: 1915); and Wlodzimierz Wakar, *Ludnosc polska; ilosc i rospostrzenie* (Warszawa: 1915). See also, Witold Lewicki, "Emigracya Galicyi w swietle cyfr," *Polski przeglad emigracyjny* (Krakow), R. VI, luty 1912, 36–49.

66. Wladyslaw Studnicki, "Emigracya," *Krytyka* (Krakow: luty 1911), R.

XIII, 77–78. See also, Thomas and Znaniecki, *op. cit.,* II, 1484. By that year Roman Dmowski and his National Democratic *(Endek)* party's nationalism had degenerated into a virulent anti-Semitism in the Kingdom. In Galicia it was conjoined with an equally blatant "Ukraniophobia" moving in the direction of an alliance with the "Podolian gentry" in the eastern part of that sector. See, Bronislaw Potocki, "Kwestya ruska w Galicyi i project jej zalatwienia," *Krytyka* (Krakow), R. X, t. I, 1908, 129–139; Junius, "Wspolczesni politycy polacy. Roman Dmowski," in *ibid.,* R. XIV, t. XXXV, 1912, 135–138; and Socius, "Straszak Ukrainski," in *ibid.,* R. XV, t. XXXVII, 1913, 19–24. An earlier spokesman of the new orientation perceived a political-cultural coalition taking form between Ukrainian and Jewish nationalists in Galicia — the latter assuming a progressively intractable stance and, in eastern Galicia, cooperating with the Ukrainians. Alfred Kohl, "Prady i mysli w naszym kraju w kwestyi zydowskiej," *Ateneum Polskie* (Lwow), pazdz. 1908, t. IV, nr. 1, 76–83.

67. See Leopold Caro in ____, "V Zjazd prawnikow i ekonomistow we Lwowie," *Ekonomista* (Warszawa), 1913, R. XIII, t. I, 148 and Henryk Wielowieyski, "Emigracya ludu i program ochronny," *Przeglad Powszechny* (Krakow), styczen–marzec 1913, t. CXVII, 175–188.

68. Janusz Machnicki, "Piaty Zjazd Polskich Prawnikow i Ekonomistow," *Ekonomista* (Warszawa), 1912, R. XII, t. IV, 97–106; and ____, "Piaty Zjazd Prawnikow i Ekonomistow w Lwowie. Stenograficzne sprawozdanie," *ibid.,* 1913, R. VIII, t. I, 109–153. See also, Czerkawski and Milewski, *Polityka ekonomiczna* (Krakow: 1905), I, 109–110. The authors' historical basis for this revived neo-mercantilism was that the ancient eastward migrations of Polish elements into Russia resulted in a deterioration of the conditions of socage tenure in Poland proper thereby contributing to its economic decline and subsequent dismemberment by the European powers.

69. See, for example, Stefan L. Zaleski, "General Demography of Poland," *Polish Encyclopaedia* (Geneva: 1921), Vol. II, No. 2, 203–205.

70. See, for example, Zofia Daszynska-Golinska, "Utopia najblizszej przyszlosci," *Krytyka* (Krakow), styczen 1907, R. IX, zesz. 1, 14–22; *ibid.,* luty 1907, R. IX, zesz. II, 137–145 and her *Rozwoj i samodzielnosc gospodarcza ziem polskich* (Warszawa: 1914), *passim.*

71. As early as 1924 he was aware that the problem of emigration was still with them "because the economic conditions of today, as compared to those of pre-war Poland, have deteriorated rather than improved." Szawleski, *Wychodztwo . . . ,* 331.

72. Szawleski, *Kwestja emigracji . . . ,* 67. The author's pronouncements cannot be regarded simply as inconsequential utterances of a publicist or polemicist since the work is essentially a publication of a series of lectures which he delivered at the *Szkola Nauk Politycznych* of Warsaw in 1927.

73. Szawleski, *Wychodztwo . . . ,* 316.

74. *Ibid.,* 18, 356.

75. Szawleski, *Kwestja emigracji . . . ,* 190.

76. Szawleski, *Wychodztwo . . . ,* 18.

77. Szawleski, *Kwestja emigracji . . . ,* 192.

78. *Ibid.,* 25, 49–50, 59–60. The Polish attitudes toward the pre-war Jewish emigration attained the status of policy in the inter-war years. "[To] free Poland of Jews and turn over their jobs to the impoverished peasantry . . .

captured the imagination of not only the population but also the administration. . . ." Ariah Tartakower, *In Search of Home and Freedom* (London: 1950), 44–57 and *passim*, and Samuel L. Sharp, *Poland: White Eagle on a Red Field* (Cambridge: 1953), 98. The Polish representatives to the League of Nations demanded international measures for the annual removal of 100,000 Jews from Poland. Sharp, *op. cit.*, 91. The periodical, *Kwartalnik Naukowego Instytutu Emigracyjnego*, published in Warsaw, regularly published articles favoring these policies. See, for example, L. Kulczycki, "Emigracja i mniejszosci narodowe," *ibid.*, 1927, Vol. III, 17–21; Miecz. G., "Zagadnienia emigracji Zydowskiej z Polski," *ibid.*, 1929, Vol. I–II, R. IV, 320–326.

79. Okolowicz, *Wychodztwo i osadnictwo* . . . , 393.

80. Leopold Caro, *Ku nowej Polsce* (Lwow: 1923), 13.

81. Zofia Daszynska-Golinska, *Land Reform in Poland* (London: 1921), 16.

82. Daszynska-Golinska, *Zagadnienia polityki populacyjnej* (Warszawa: 1927), 37.

83. Instytut Gospodarstwa Spolecznego, *Pamietniki emigrantow. Francja* (Warszawa: 1939), nr. 1–37.

84. Instytut Gospodarstwa Spolecznego, *Pamietniki chlopow* (Warszawa: 1935), nr. 1–51. See also, Eugene M. Kulischer, "Population Changes behind the Iron Curtain," *Annals of the American Academy of Political and Social Science*, Vol. 271 (Sept. 1950), 101.

85. This deficit, according to one observer, was to some degree made up by the money sent from overseas, especially the United States, amounting to "several tens of millions of dollars" annually. J. Borenstein, "Zagadnienia pauperyzacji ludnosci zydowskiej w Polsce," *Zydzi w Polsce odrodzonej*, ed. by Ignacy Schiper, *et al.* (Warszawa: 1933), II, 407.

86. Wojciech Saryusz-Zaleski, *Dzieje przemyslu w B. Galicyi, 1804–1929* (Krakow: 1930), 195.

87. Antoni Zabko-Potopowicz, "Wies polska w swietle polskich prac naukowych i publicystycznych z okresu po uwlaszczeniu wloscian," *Roczniki Socjologii Wsi* (Warszawa: 1937), 67–151.

88. Jozef Poniatowski, *Przeludnienie wsi i rolnictwa* (Warszawa: 1936), 60.

89. *Ibid.*, 238.

90. *Ibid.*, 62, 107, 155, 161.

91. *Ibid.*, 107, 163.

92. Even such an astute scholar as Bujak could not sanction such an alternative to overpopulation. His rationale was as follows: "The concern for creating for their children a means of livelihood (land) without reducing the parents' level of existence could be affected either by the emigration of the total natural increase of the population . . . or by inducing the population to limit the natural increases to a minimum. Inasmuch as the thought of providing for their children as well as to advance themselves progressively is one of the motives for their economic efforts, any policy toward the limitation of progeny needs must be regarded as a restraint upon the cultural progress of the nation." Bujak, *Maszkienice* . . . , II, 33. Adam Krzyzanowski was apparently one of the few exponents of the Malthusian concepts in Poland. Though not wholly in agreement with Malthus' thesis, he favored a liberal policy of restraint upon the birth rate. He, also, first translated Malthus' works on

population into Polish in 1925. Poniatowski, *op. cit.,* 80–82.
    93. *Ibid.,* 107–108.
    94. *Ibid.,* 108–109, 114. See also, Eugene M. Kulischer, *Europe on the Move; War and Population Changes, 1917–1947* (New York: 1948), 28.
    95. Poniatowski, *op. cit.,* 163.
    96. *Ibid.,* 106. Nevertheless he felt impelled to justify his position by affirming that ". . . in the face of the present intensity of overpopulation which prevails in Polish agriculture, emigration is not only an economic necessity but also a supra-economic one . . . the national *raison d'etat* . . . which is the ultimate purpose of all policy. . . ." *Ibid.,* 5, 107, 119. This concept of the state appears to be strikingly like that advocated by Max Weber in his inaugural address wherein he stated: "It is not our task to pass on to our descendants for their journey through life peace and happiness, but rather the eternal struggle for the maintenance and enhancement of our national way. The power and interests of the nation are the last and decisive interests which economic policy has to serve. The *raison d'etat* of the nation-state is for us the ultimate yardstick for economic consideration." *Gesammelte politische Schriften* (Munich: 1921), 19 ff., quoted by Hans Kohn, *Prophets and People, Studies in Nineteenth Century Nationalism* (New York: 1946), 121. Kohn concludes that Weber ". . . shared Treitschke's fundamental position and Bismarck's faith in the power state." *Ibid.* The conclusion that inevitably suggests itself is that the Second Commonwealth, given its political-economic circumstances, was incapable of adequately sustaining its total population.

Bibliography

A. Books

Abel, Theodore F., *Protestant Home Missions to Catholic Immigrants*. New York: Institute of Social and Religious Research, 1933. 143 pp.

Balch, Emily Greene, *Our Slavic Fellow Citizens*. New York: Charities Publications Committee, 1910. 536 pp.

Bär, Max, *Westpreussen unter Friedrich dem Grossen*. 2 vols.; Leipzig: S. Hirzel, 1909.

Baron, Salo W., *A Social and Religious History of the Jews*. 3 vols.; New York: Columbia University Press, 1937.

Behrendt, Johannes, *Die polnische Frage und das oesterreichische-deutsche Bündnis 1885 bis 1887*. Berlin: K. Vowinckel g. m. b. h., 1927.

Bernhard, Ludwig, *Die Polenfrage*. Third edition; Munich and Leipzig: Duncker und Humblot, 1920. 572 pp.

Biegeleisen, Leon W., *Przewod spadkowo-opiekunczy a ustroj wlasnosci chlopskiej. Studyum z zakresu gospodarczo-prawnych stosunkow ludnosci wloscianskiej w Galicyi*. Lwow: H. Altenberg, G. Seyfarth, E. Wende i Sp., 1914. 405 pp.

―――, *Rozwoj gospodarczy nowoczesnej wsi polskiej*. 2 vols.; Krakow: Instytut Ekonomiczny N. K. N., 1916-1917.

Bismarck, Otto, Fürst von, *Die gesammelten Werke*. Berlin: O. Stollberg, 1924.

[Bitter, Rudolph von], *Handwörterbuch der preussischen Verwaltung*. 2 vols.; Leipzig: Rossberg, 1906.

Blanchard, Emile, *La main d'oeuvre étrangère dans l'agriculture française*. Paris: Marcel Riviere and Cie., 1913. 334 pp.

Blanshard, Brand, *The Church and the Polish Immigrant*. [n.p.]: [n. n.], 1920. 79 pp.

Bobrzynski, Jan, *Na przelomie polskiego przemyslu; Studyum ekonomiczne*. Warszawa: F. Hoesick, 1919. 176 pp.

Boleslawita, B. [pseud. for Jozef Ignacy Kraszewski], *Tulacze, opowiadania historyczne*. 3 vols.; Warszawa: Drukarnia artystyczna, 1897.

Browne, Lewis, *Stranger Than Fiction*. New York: The Macmillan Company, 1925. 377 pp.

Bujak, Franciszek, *Galicya*. 2 vols.; Lwow: H. Altenberg, 1908-1910.

―――, *Limanowa. Miasteczko powiatowe w zachodnej Galicyi. Stan spoleczny i gospodarczy*. Krakow: Gebethner i Sp., 1902, 221 pp.

―――, *O naprawie ustroju rolnego w Polsce*. Warszawa: Gebethner i Wolff, c. 1918. 160 pp.

_____, *Uwagi spoleczno-gospodarcze dla wloscian.* Lwow: Macierz Polska, 1916. 112 pp.

_____, *Zmiaca, wies powiatu limanowskiego.* Krakow: Gebethner i Sp., 1903. 152 pp.

_____, *Z odleglej i bliskiej przeszlosci. Studja historyczno gospodarcze.* Lwow: Zakl. Nar. im. Ossolinskich, 1924. 325 pp.

Bukowiecki, Stanislaw, *et al., W naszych sprawach, II: Szkice w kwestyach ekonomiczno-spolecznych.* Warszawa: Gebethner i Wolff, 1900. 581 pp.

Busch, Moritz, *Our Chancellor; Sketches for a Historical Picture.* 2 vols.; London: Macmillan and Company, 1884.

Buzek, Jozef, *Historya polityki narodowosciowej rzadu pruskiego wobec polakow; od traktatow wiedenskich do ustaw wyjatkowych z r. 1908.* Lwow: H. Altenberg, 1909. 569 pp.

_____, *Poglad na wzrost ludnosci ziem polskich w wieku 19-tym.* Krakow: Centralne Biuro Wydawnictw N. K. N., 1915. 74 pp.

_____, *Studya z zakresu administracyi wychowania publicznego.* Lwow, Krakow and Warszawa: E. Wende i Sp., 1904. 479 pp.

Bystron, Jan Stanislaw, *Kultura ludowa.* Warszawa: Zwiazek Nauczycielstwa Polskiego, 1936. 458 pp.

Caillard, Charles F., *Les Migrations Temporaires dans les Campagnes Françaises.* Paris: Edition du Temps Present, 1912.

Caro, Leopold, *Auswanderung und Auswanderungspolitik in Oesterreich.* Leipzig: Duncker und Humblot, 1909. 283 pp.

_____, *Ku nowej Polsce.* Lwow: Drukarnia naukowa, 1923. 152 pp.

_____, *Odprawa P. Hupce i prawda o P. T. E.* Krakow: druk. Glos Narodu, 1914. 63 pp.

_____, *Prawdziwa dzialalnosc P. T. E. Ignorancya czy zla wola?* Krakow: druk. Glos Narodu, 1914. 58 pp.

_____, and Karol Englisch, *Emigracya i polityka emigracyjna, ze szczegolnem uwzglednieniem stosunkow polskich.* Poznan: Ksiegarnia Sw. Wojciecha, 1914. 393 pp.

_____, *et al., Sitzungsberichte des VIII internationalen landwirtschaftlichen Kongresse.* Band I; Wien: 1907.

_____, *et al., Verhandlungen der Mitteleuropäischen Wirtschaftskonferenz.* Berlin: 17–18 Mai 1909.

Chalasinski, Jozef, *Przeszlosc i przyszlosc inteligencji polskiej.* Rome: Instytut literacki, 1947. 199 pp.

Ciechanowski, Stanislaw, *Wychodztwo pod wzgledem hygjeniczno-spolecznym.* Warszawa: nakl. autora, 1914.

Ciesluk, Joseph Edward, *National Parishes in the United States.* Washington, D.C.: The Catholic University of America Press, 1944. 178 pp.

Clausewitz, Karl von, *Politische Schriften und Briefe.* München: Drei Masken Verlag, 1922. 248 pp.

Czerkawski, Wlodzimierz, *Gestosc zaludnienia w Galicyi, 1890-1910.* Krakow: Drukarnia Uniwersytetu Jagiellonskiego, 1911. 27 pp.

_____, *Wielkie gospodarstwa, ich istota i znaczenie* [Odbitka z XXXIV tomu Rozpraw Wydzialu histor.-filoz. Akademii umiejetnosci]. Krakow: Drukarnia Uniwersytetu Jagiellonskiego, 1896. 163 pp.

_____, and Jozef Milewski, *Polityka ekonomiczna.* 2 vols.; Krakow: Spolka Wydawnicza Polska, 1905.

Czynski, Edward and T. Tillinger, *Etnograficzno-statystyczny zarys liczebnosci i rozsiedlenia ludnosci polskiej,* wydanie drugie. Warszawa: E. Wende i Sp., 1909. 115 pp. and maps.

Daszynski, Ignacy, *Strejki rolne w Galicyi przed forum parlamentu* [dodatek do numeru 13-go "Prawa ludu"]. B. m. w. i. dr., 1902. 66 pp.

———, *Szlachetczyzna a odrodzenie Galicyi.* Lwow: A. Goldman, 1899. 87 pp.

Davis, Philip, editor, *Immigration and Americanization; Selected Readings.* Boston: Ginn and Company, 1920. 770 pp.

Diamand, Herman, *Polozenie gospodarcze Galicyi przed wojna.* Lipsk:[n. n.], 1915. 106 pp.

———, *Tablice statystyczne gospodarstwa spolecznego w Austryi ze szczegolnem uwzglednieniem Galicyi. Ze zrodel urzedowych* . . . . Krakow: S. A. Krzyzanowski; Warszawa: E. Wende i Sp., 1913. 32 pp.

Dmowski, Roman, *Wychodztwo i osadnictwo.* Lwow: Tow. Wydawnicze; Warszawa: S. Sadowski; Poznan: A. Cybulski; Krakow: Anczyc i Sp., 1900. 109 pp.

Doroszewski, Witold, *Jezyk Polski w Stanach Zjednoczonych A. P.* Warszawa: Warsaw Society of Learning with the aid of the National Culture Fund, 1938. 353 pp.

Dworaczyk, Edward Joseph, *First Polish Colonies of America in Texas.* San Antonio, Texas: The Naylor Company, c. 1936. 201 pp.

Dygasinski, [Adolf], *Opowiadanie Kuby Cieluchowskiego o emigracyi do Brazylii.* Warszawa: J. Jesynski, 1892. 124 pp.

Fairchild, Henry Pratt, *Immigration, a World Movement and its American Significance.* New York: The Macmillan Company, 1913. 455 pp.

———, editor, *Immigrant Backgrounds.* New York: John Wiley and Sons, Inc., 1927.

Feldman, Jozef, *Bismarck a Polska.* Second revised edition; Krakow: Czytelnik, 1947. 430 pp.

———, *Mocarstwa wobec powstania styczniowego.* Krakow: [odbitka z "Przegladu Wspolczesnego," Nr. 81–82], 1929. 46 pp.

———, *Sprawa polska w roku 1848.* Krakow: Gebethner i Wolff, 1933. 350 pp.

Feldman, Wilhelm, *Dzieje polskiej mysli politycznej, 1864–1914,* wyd. drugie. Warszawa: Instytut Badania Najnowszej Historji Polskiej, 1933. 373 pp.

———, *Stronnictwa i programy polityczne w Galicyi, 1846–1906.* Krakow: Spolka "Ksiazka," 1907. 242 pp.

Filipowicz, Karol, *Parcelacja jako program spoleczny* [Odbitka z *Gazety rolniczej*]. Warszawa: Noskowski, 1883. 89 pp.

Friedmann, Karl, *Arbeitermangel und Auswanderung.* Wien: Verlag des Bundes oesterreichischer Industrieller, 1907.

Gloger, Zygmunt, *et al., Opis ziem zamieszkalych przez Polakow pod wzgledem geograficznym, etnograficznym, historycznem, artystycznem, przemyslowem, handlowem i statystycznem. Tom II, Krolestwo Polskie.* Warszawa: "Gazeta Polska," 1904. 347 pp.

Gluchowski, Kazimierz, *Materjaly do problemu osadnictwa polskiego w Brazylii.* Warszawa: Urzed Emigracyjny, 1927. 260 pp.

Golinska, Zofia (Daszynska), *Alkoholizm jako objaw choroby spolecznej. Krakow: W. L. Anczyc i Sp., 1905. 16 pp.*

———, *Land Reform in Poland.* London and Edinburgh: S. Low, Morston and Company, Ltd., 1921. 57 pp.

_____, *Rozwoj i samodzielnosc gospodarcza ziem polskich.* Warszawa: J. Mortkowicz, 1914. 216 pp.

_____, *Wlasnosc rolna w Galicyi, studyum statystyczno-spoleczne.* Warszawa: J. Cotta, 1900. 65 pp.

_____, *Zagadnienia polityki populacyjnej.* Warszawa: Ferdinand Hoesick, 1927. 357 pp.

_____, *Zarys ekonomii spolecznej.* Lwow: Ksiegarnia Polska, 1898. 368 pp.

Gorski, Ludwik, *Znaczenie wiekszej wlasnosci i obowiazki wiekszych wlascicieli ziemskich.* Warszawa: druk J. Berger, 1886. 195 pp.

Grabiec, J. [pseud. for Jozef Dabrowski], *Wspolczesna Polska w cyfrach i faktach.* New York: The Polish Book Importing Company, 1911. 272 pp.

Grabski, Wladyslaw, *Historja wsi w Polsce.* Warszawa: Gebethner i Wolff, 1929. 440 pp.

_____, *Materjaly w sprawie wloscianskiej.* 3 vols.; Warszawa: Gebethner i Wolff, 1907–1919.

_____, *Rocznik statystyczny Krolestwa polskiego, rok 1914.* Warszawa: Gebethner i Wolff, 1915. 283 pp.

_____, *Spoleczne gospodarstwo agrarne w Polsce.* Warszawa: J. Mianowski, 1923. 458 pp.

Grodynski, Tadeusz F., *Ustawodawstwo emigracyjne na tle porownawczem ze szczegolnem uwzglednieniem projektu ustawy austryackiej z r. 1904* [Odbitka z "Czasopisma prawniczego i ekonomicznego," rok XII]. Krakow: G. Gebethner i Sp., 1912. 62 pp.

Gross, Feliks, *The Polish Worker; A Study of a Social Stratum.* New York: Roy Publishers, 1946. 274 pp.

Guzicki, Leszek and Seweryn Zurawicki, *Historia polskiej mysli spolecznoekonomicznej do roku 1914.* Warszawa: Panstwowe Wydawnictwo Ekonomiczne, 1969. 358 pp.

Halich, Wasyl, *Ukrainians in the United States.* Chicago: University of Chicago Press, 1937. 149 pp.

Handlin, Oscar, *Adventure in Freedom; Three Hundred Years of Jewish Life in America.* New York: McGraw-Hill Book Company, Inc., 1954. 269 pp.

_____, *The Up-Rooted; The Epic Story of the Great Migrations that Made the American People.* Boston: Little, Brown and Company, 1951. 307 pp.

Hayden, Joel B., *Religious Work Among Poles in America.* New York: Missionary Education Movement, 1916. 48 pp.

Hirsch, Heinrich, *Überseeische Kolonisation durch Österreich-Ungarn.* Wien: Konegen, 1894. 341 pp.

Hupka, Stanislaw, *Stan wspolczesny i metoda badan wsi polskiej w Galicji Zachodnej.* Krakow: [n. n.], 1912. 34 pp.

_____, *Über die Entwicklung der westgalizischen Dorfzustände in der 2. Hälfte des 19. Jahrhunderts.* Teschen: P. Mitrega, 1910. 409 pp.

Janicki, Stanislaw, editor, *Stosunki rolnicze Krolestwa Kongresowego.* Warszawa: Ministerstwo Rolnictwa i Dobr Koronnych, 1918. 641 pp.

Janik, Michal, *Dzieje Polakow na Syberji.* Krakow: Krakowska Spolka Wydawnicza, 1928. 472 pp.

Kempner, Stanislaw Aleksander, *Rozwoj gospodarczy Polski, od rozbiorow do niepodleglosci.* Warszawa: Instytut wydawniczy "Biblioteka polska," 1924. 345 pp.

_____, et al., *Dzieje gospodarcze Polski porozbiorowej w zarysie.* 2 vols.; Warszawa: K. Kowalewski, 1920.

Kieniewicz, Stefan, Editor, *Galicja w dobie autonomicznej, 1850-1914, wybor tekstow.* Wroclaw: Zakl. Nar. Im. Ossolinskich, 1952. 397 pp.

_____, *Historia Polski, 1795-1918.* Warszawa: Panstwowe Wydawnictwo Naukowe, 1970. 611 pp.

Klobukowski, Stanislaw, *et al., Pamietnik drugiego zjazdu prawnikow i ekonomistow polskich.* Lwow: Drukarnia ludowa, 1891. 302 pp.

Knoke, Anton, *Ausländische Wanderarbeiter in Deutschland.* Leipzig: Deichert, 1911. 108 pp.

Kohler, Max J., *Immigration and Aliens in the United States.* New York: Bloch Publishing Company, 1936. 352 pp.

Kohn, Hans, *Prophets and Peoples; Studies in Nineteenth Century Nationalism.* New York: The Macmillan Company, 1946.

Kolodziejczyk, Edmund, *Ludnosc polska na gornych Wegrach* [Odbitka z "Swiata slowianskiego"]. Krakow: G. Gebethner i Sp., 1910. 34 pp.

Komornicki, Stefan, *Polska na zachodzie w swietle cyfr i zdarzen, czesc I: Zabory i kolonizacya niemiecka na ziemiach polskich, z szczegolnem uwzglednieniem W. ks. poznanskiego do r. 1848* [Odbitka z Ekonomisty polskiego]. Lwow: Ksiegarnia polska, 1894. 351 pp.

Koppelmann, Heinrich L., *Nation, Sprache und Nationalismus.* Leiden: A. W. Sijthoff, 1956. 233 pp.

Koskowski, Boleslaw, *Wychodztwo zarobkowe wloscian w Krolestwie polskiem* [Odbitka z Gazety polskiej]. Warszawa: St. Sadowski, 1901. 62 pp.

Koszutski, Stanislaw, *Rozwoj ekonomiczny Krolestwa Polskiego w ostatniem trzydziestoleciu, 1870-1900 r.* Warszawa: Ksiegarnia Naukowa, 1905. 384 pp.

Kozlowski, Wladyslaw M., *Jak jest za oceanem, urzadzenia panstwowe i zycie spoleczne Stanow Zjednoczonych Ameryki polnocnej* [Ksiazka dla wszystkich, 51]. Warszawa: M. Arct, 1902. 108 pp.

_____, *Z hasel umyslowosci wspolczesnej.* Krakow: G. Gebethner i Sp., 1902. 129 pp.

Kruszka, Waclaw, *Historja Polska w Ameryce.* 6 vols.; Milwaukee: Kuryer Publishing Company, 1905.

_____, *Historya polska w Ameryce; od czasow najdawniejszych az do najnowszych.* Revised edition; Milwaukee: Kuryer Polski, 1937.

Krysiak, F. S., *Hinter den Kulissen des Ostmarken-Vereins. Aus den Geheimakten der preussischen Neben-Regierung für die Polenausrottung.* Posen: [n. n.], 1919. 274 pp.

Krzyzanowski, Adam, *Pauperyzacja Polski wspolczesnej.* Krakow: Krakowska Spolka Wydawnicza, 1926. 153 pp.

Kula, Witold, *Historia gospodarcza Polski, 1864-1918.* Warszawa: Spoldzielnia wydawnicza "Wiedza," 1947. 155 pp.

Kulischer, Eugene M., *Europe on the Move; War and Population Changes, 1917-1947.* New York: Columbia University Press, 1948. 337 pp.

_____, *Jewish Migrations; Past Experiences and Post-War Prospects.* New York: The American Jewish Committee, 1943. 51 pp.

Kuzelewska, Stanislawa von, *Die Landarbeiterverhältnisse im Königreich Polen.* Breslau: Grosser und Comp., 1909. 74 pp.

Laubert, Manfred, *Die preussische Polenpolitik, von 1772-1914*. Krakau: Burgverlag Krakau, 1942. 242 pp.

Lehmann, Max Ludwig, *Preussen und die Katolische Kirche seit 1640*. 9 vols.; Leipzig: S. Hirzel, 1878.

Lewy, Marceli, *Wzajemny stosunek przemyslu Krolestwa Polskiego i Cesarstwa Rosyjskiego przed wojna wszechswiatowa*. Warszawa: F. Hoesick, 1921. 142 pp.

Librowicz, Zygmunt, *Polacy w Syberii*. Krakow: G. Gebethner i Sp., 1884. 373 pp.

Limanowski, Boleslaw, *Szermierze wolnosci*. Krakow: Gebethner i Sp., 1911.

Ludkiewicz, Zdzislaw, *Kwestya rolna w Galicyi*. Lwow: Gubrynowicz i Sp.; Krakow: W. L. Anczyc i Sp., 1910. 276 pp.

——, *Zagadnienia programu agrarnego a emigracja*. Warszawa: Sklad Glowny, Dom ksiazki polskiej, 1929. 95 pp.

Lutoslawski, Jan, *Rolnictwo polskie przed wojna a dzisiaj; szkic okolicznosciowy na podstawie rocznikow "Gazety Rolniczej," 1910-1920*. Warszawa: Ksiegarnia rolnicza, 1921. 75 pp.

Luxemburg, Rosa, *Die industrielle Entwicklung Polens*. Leipzig: Duncker und Humblot, 1898. 95 pp.

Maksimov, Sergiei Vasilevich, *Sibir i Katorga*. 3 vols.; St. Petersburg: A. Transhel, 1871.

Marchlewski, Julian B., *Stosunki spoleczno-ekonomiczne pod panowaniem pruskiem*. Warszawa: T. Paprocki i Sp., 1903. 381 pp.

Martins, Alfredo Romaria, *Historia do Parana*. Second edition; Sao Paulo: Rumo Limitada, 1939.

Maryanski, Modest, *O emigracyi a w szczegolnosci o emigracyi polskiej do Stanow Zjednoczonych Polnocnej Ameryki i o koniecznej potrzebie jej zorganizowania*. Chicago: J. Smolski, 1893. 108 pp.

Milewski, Jozef, *W sprawie utrzymaniu ziemi w naszym reku* [Odbitka z Ziemianina]. Poznan: N. Kamienski i Sp., 1884. 73 pp.

Molicki, Antoni, *Odpowiedz panu St. Szczepanowskiemu na jego Nedza Galicyi*. Krakow: W. L. Anczyc i Sp., 1890. 67 pp.

Myslinski, Jerzy, *Studia nad polska prasa spoleczno-polityczna w zachodniej Galicji, 1905-1914*. Warszawa: Panstwowe Wydawnictwo Naukowe, 1970. 491 pp.

Mytkowicz, Andrzej X., *Powstanie i rozwoj emigracji sezonowej*. Krakow: Instytutu Ekonomicznego N. K. N., 1917. 167 pp.

Nagiel, Henryk, *Dziennikarstwo Polskie w Ameryce*. Chicago: Polish Publishing Company in America, 1894.

Niemyska, Marja, *Wychodzcy po powrocie do kraju; remigranci w wojewodztwie Bialystockiem*. Warszawa: Instytut Gospodarstwa Spolecznego, 1936. 135 pp.

Okolowicz, Jozef, *Wychodztwo i osadnictwo polskie przed wojna swiatowa*. Warszawa: Gebethner i Wolff, 1920. 412 pp.

Oleskow, Jozef, *Rolnictwo za oceanem a przesiedlna emigracya*. Zolkiew: Drukarnia Ojcow Bazylianow, 1896. 48 pp.

Olszyk, Edmund G., *The Polish Press in America*. Milwaukee: Marquette University Press, 1940.

Osada, Stanislaw, *Historya Zwiazku Narodowego Polskiego i rozwoj ruchu narodowego polskiego w Ameryce Polnocnej.* Chicago: Zwiazek Narodowy Polski, 1905. 744 pp.

_____, *Jak sie ksztaltowala polska dusza wychodztwa w Ameryce.* Pittsburgh: "Sokol Polski," 1930. 271 pp.

_____, *Prasa i Publicystyka Polska w Ameryce.* Pittsburgh: The Pittsburger Press, 1930, 96 pp.

_____, *Sokolstwo Polskie; jego dzieje, ideologia i poslannictwo.* Pittsburgh: "Sokol Polski," 1929, 70 pp.

Pankiewicz, Michal, *W sprawie wychodztwa do Sao Paulo.* Warszawa: Polskie Tow. Emigracyjne, 1926. 102 pp.

Papieski, Leon, *Emigracya i kolonizacya oraz zadanie polskiej polityki emigracyjnej.* Warszawa: Tow. Szkoly Nauk Politycznych, W. Rybicki i Sp., 1918. 76 pp.

Park, Robert Ezra, *The Immigrant Press and Its Control.* New York and London: Harper and Brothers, 1922.

Penzler, Johannes, *Fürst Bismarck nach seiner Entlassung. Leben und Politik des Fürsten seit seinem Scheiden aus dem Amte auf Grund aller authentischen Kundgebungen.* 7 vols.; Leipzig: W. Fiedler, 1897–1898.

Pertz, Georg Heinrich and Hans Delbruck, *Das Leben des Feldmarschalls Grafen Neithardt von Gneisenau.* Berlin: G. Stilke, 1880.

Pigon, Stanislaw, editor, *Wybor pisarzy ludowych.* 2 vols.; Wroclaw: Ossolinski Foundation, 1947–1948.

Piltz, Erasmus, *et al., Poland.* London: Herbert Jenkins, Ltd., 1918. 416 pp.

Poniatowski, Jozef, *Przeludnienie wsi i rolnictwa.* Warszawa: Tow. oswiaty rolniczej, 1936. 253 pp.

Poplawski, Jan L., *Galicya w liczbach.* Lwow: Maniszewski i Kedzierski, 1903, 15 pp.

Poschinger, Heinrich von, *Preussens auswärtige Politik, 1850 bis 1858.* 3 vols.; Berlin: E. S. Mittler und Sohn, 1902.

Posner, Stanislaw, *Drogi samopomocy spolecznej.* Plock: Echa Plockie i Lomzynskie, 1903, 361 pp.

_____, *Nad otchlania, w sprawie handlu zywem towarem, czesc I* [Ruch etyczny, III]. Warszawa: Ksieg. Naukowa, 1903, 95 pp.

Pyzik, Estanislao, *Los polacos en la Republica Argentina, 1812–1900.* Buenos Aires: [n. n.] 1944, 334 pp.

Rasinski, Faustyn, *Prace statystyczne, IV. Polska etnograficzna. Czesc I. Stan posiadania.* Warszawa: Gebethner i Wolff, 1915. 126 pp.

Rogmann, Heinz, *Die Bevölkerungsentwicklung im preussischen Osten in den letzten hundert Jahren.* Berlin: Volk und Reich Verlag, 1937. 269 pp.

Rolfe, E. Lloyd, *The State of Parana, Brazil.* Curityba: [n. n.] c. 1920. 60 pp.

Romer, Eugenjusz, *Ilu nas jest?* Krakow: G. Gebethner, 1917. 32 pp.

_____, *Polacy na kresach pomorskich i pojeziernych.* Lwow: Polskie Spolki Oszczednosci, 1919. 162 pp.

_____, *et al., Geograficzno-statystyczny atlas.* Warszawa, Krakow: Gebethner i Wolff, 1916.

Roslaniec, Stanislaw, *Samorzutne scalenie gruntow.* Warszawa: Ministerstwo Reform Rolnych, 1928, 145 pp.

Rothfels, Hans, *Bismarck und der Osten; eine Studie zum Problem des deutschen Nationalstaats.* Leipzig: J. C. Hinrichs, 1934. 104 pp.

_____, *Ostraum, Preussentum und Reichsgedanke; historische Abhandlungen.* Leipzig: J. C. Hinrichs, 1935. 256 pp.

Roucek, Joseph Slabey, *American Lithuanians.* New York: Lithuanian Alliance of America, 1940. 38 pp.

Rozwadowski, Jan, *Parcelacya wielkiej wlasnosci w swietle postepowania pruskich instytucyj posredniczacych.* Lwow: H. Altenberg, 1903. 406 pp.

_____, *Emigracja polska we Francji. Europejski ruch wychodzczy.* La Madelaine-les-Lille: Wydawnictwo P. U. R. we Francji, 1927. 304 pp.

Rutkowski, Jan, *Historia Gospodarcza Polski; Tom II, Czasy porozbiorowe.* Poznan: Ksiegarnia Akademicka, 1950. 452 pp.

Saryusz-Zaleski, Wojciech, *Dzieje przemyslu w B. Galicji 1804-1929.* Krakow: S. A. L. Zieleniewski i Fitzner-Gamper, 1930. 338 pp.

Schiper, Ignacy, *et al., Zydzi w Polsce odrodzonej.* 2 vols.; Warszawa: "Zydzi w Polsce odrodzonej," 1932-1933.

Schlegelberger, Franz, *Das Landarbeiterrecht; Darstellung des privaten und öffentlichen Rechts der Landarbeiter in Preussen.* Berlin: C. Heymann, 1907. 240 pp.

Schmidt, Stefan, *Die Wanderarbeiter in der Landwirtschaft der Provinz Sachsen und ihre Beschäftigung im Jahre 1910.* Berlin: Verlagsbuchhandlung Paul Parey, 1911. 334 pp.

Schroft, Richard, *Die österreichische-ungarische überseeische Kulturarbeit und Auswanderung. Ein patriotisches Mahnwort.* Wien: Konegen, 1894. 56 pp.

Sharp, Samuel L., *Poland: White Eagle on a Red Field.* Cambridge: Harvard University Press, 1953. 338 pp.

Siemiradzki, Jozef, *Polacy za morzem.* Lwow: Gubrynowicz i Schmidt, 1900. 29 pp.

Sienkiewicz, Henry, *Her Tragic Fate* [Za Chlebem]. New York, Chicago and London: T. Tennyson Neely, 1899. 216 pp.

Skowron, Wladyslaw, *Kryzys i skutki emigracji sezonowej.* Warszawa: "Droga," 1932. 32 pp.

Smolka, Stanislaw, *Polityka Lubeckiego przed powstaniem listopadowem.* 2 vols.; Krakow: Akademia Umiejetnosci, 1907.

Spazier, Ryszard, *Historja powstania narodu polskiego w r. 1830 i 1831.* 3 vols.; Krakow: Nakl. Autora, 1933.

Srbik, Franz von, *Die Auswanderungsgesetzgebung.* 2 vols.; Wien: K. K. Hof- und Staatsdruckerei, 1911.

Srodkowo-europejski zwiazek gospodarczy a Polska. Studya ekonomiczne. Krakow: Centralne Biuro Wydawnictw N. K. N., 1916. 215 pp.

Strasburger, Edward, *Stan rolnictwa polskiego w dobie powojennej, a program ekonomiczny Lubeckiego.* Warszawa: Gebethner i Wolff, 1915. 48 pp.

Strzelec, Karol W., *The Burning Bush; Trial and Hope of the Polish People.* Chicago: Church Publishing House, 191-. 36 pp.

Supinski, Jozef, *Szkola polska gospodarstwa spolecznego.* 5 vols.; Warszawa: Gebethner i Wolff, 1883.

Swiatlomir [Stefan Zaleski], *Ciemnota Galicyi w swietle cyfr i faktow, 1772-1902: Czarna ksiega szkolnictwa galicyjskiego.* Lwow: Polskie Towarzystwo Nakladowe, 1904. 212 pp.

Szawleski, Mieczyslaw, *Kwestja emigracji w Polsce.* Warszawa: Polskie Towarzystwo Emigracyjne, 1927. 208 pp.

_____, *Wychodztwo Polskie w Stanach Zjednoczonych Ameryki.* Lwow: 1924.

Szczepanowski, Stanislaw, *Nedza Galicyi w cyfrach i program energicznego rozwoju gospodarstwa krajowego.* Lwow: Piller i Sp., 1888. 218 pp.

Szweykowski, Zygmunt, *Dramat Dygasinskiego.* Warszawa: Gebethner i Wolff, 1938. 95 pp.

Taft, Donald R., *Human Migration; a Study of International Movements.* New York: The Ronald Press Company, 1936. 590 pp.

Targosz, Stanislaw, *Polonia katolicka w Stanach Zjednoczonych w przekroju.* Detroit: Drukarnia Kooperatywna Barc Brothers, 1943. 99 pp.

Tartakower, Ariah, *In Search of Home and Freedom.* London: Lincolns-Prager Ltd., 1950. 96 pp.

Tenenbaum, Joseph, *In Search of a Lost People; the Old and the New Poland.* New York: Beechhurst Press, 1948. 312 pp.

Thomas, William I. and Floryan Znaniecki, *The Polish Peasant in Europe and America.* 5 vols.; Chicago: University of Chicago Press, 1918-1920.

Thugutt, Stanislaw, *Polska i Polacy. Ilosc i rozsiedlenie ludnosci polskiej.* Warszawa: Towarzystwo krajoznawcze, 1915. 30 pp.

Tims, Richard Wonser, *Germanizing Prussian Poland; the H-K-T Society and the Struggle for the Eastern Marches in the German Empire, 1894-1919.* New York: Columbia University Press, 1941.

Treitschke, Heinrich von, *Politics.* Translated by Blanche Dugdale and Forben de Bille. 2 vols.; New York: The Macmillan Company, 1916.

Villard, Oswald G., *Some Newspapers and Newspapermen.* New York: A. A. Knopf, 1923. 345 pp.

Wachtel, Karol, *Z. P. R. K. Dzieje Zjednoczenia Polskiego Rzymsko-katolickiego w Ameryce.* Chicago: L. J. Winiecki, 1913. 575 pp.

Wachtl, Charles Henry, *Polonja w Ameryce; dzieje i dorobek.* Philadelphia: Naklad autora, 1944.

Wajda, Kazimierz, *Migracje Ludnosci Wiejskiej Pomerza Wschodniego w latach 1850-1914.* Wroclaw: Zaklad Narodowy im. Ossolinskich, 1969. 210 pp.

Wakar, Wlodzimierz, *Ludnosc polska, ilosc i rozpostrzenienie.* Warszawa: M. Arct, 1915. 31 pp. and maps.

Wallace, Lillian Parker, *The Papacy and European Diplomacy, 1869-1878.* Chapel Hill: University of North Carolina Press, 1948. 349 pp.

Warchalowski, Kazimierz, *Do Parany.* Warszawa: [n. n.] 1903.

Wasilewski, Leon, *Nationalities in Pomerania.* Torun and London: Baltic Institute and J. S. Bergson, 1934. 54 pp.

Wasiutynski, Bohdan, *Ludnosc zydowska w Krolestwie Polskiem* [Odbitka z Ekonomisty]. Warszawa: E. Wende i Sp., 1911. 99 pp.

Wereszycki, Henryk, *Historia polityczna Polski w dobie popowstaniowej 1864-1918.* Warszawa: "Wiedza," 1948. 374 pp.

Willcox, Walter F., editor, *International Migration.* 2 vols.; New York: National Bureau of Economic Research, Inc., 1929-1931.

Wlodek, Jozef, *Argentyna i Emigracja.* Warszawa: M. Arct, 1923. 513 pp.

Wlodek, Ludwik, *Kolonie polskie w Paranie.* Krakow: G. Gebethner i Sp., 1909. 28 pp.

_____, *Polacy w Paranie.* Warszawa: Wyd. imienia Staszyca, c. 1910. 47 pp.

_____, *Polskie kolonie rolnicze w Paranie.* Warszawa: druk. "Zorza," 1910. 116 pp.

Wloszczewski, Stefan, *L'établissement des Polonais en France.* Paris: Librairie Picart, 1936. 296 pp.

Woycicki, Aleksander, *Dzieje robotnikow przemyslowych w Polsce.* Warszawa: F. Hoesick, 1929. 273 pp.

Wytanowicz, Eliasz, *et al., Studja z historyi spolecznej i gospospodarczej poswiecone Franciszkowi Bujakowi.* Lwow: Drukarnia naukowa, 1931. 314 pp.

Young, Charles Hurlbert, *The Ukrainian Canadians; A Study in Assimilation.* Toronto: T. Nelson and Sons, Ltd., 1931. 314 pp.

Zalecki, Gustaw L., *Studja kolonjalne.* 2 vols.; Warszawa: Biblioteka Polska, 1925–1928.

Zaleski, Witold, *Statystyka porownawcza Krolestwa Polskiego. Ludnosc i stosunki ekonomiczne.* Warszawa: Gebethner i Wolff, 1876. 354 pp.

Zdzitowiecki, Jan, *Xiaze-minister Franciszek Xawery Drucki-Lubecki, 1778–1846.*'Warszawa: S. Arct, 1948. 646 pp.

Zimmermann, Kazimierz, *Frederyk Wielki i jego kolonizacja rolna na ziemiach polskich.* Poznan: Ksiegarnia Sw. Wojciecha, 1915.

Zoltowski, John, editor, *Polish Encyclopaedia.* 3 vols.; Fribourg and Geneva: Committee for the Polish Encyclopaedic Publications, 1922, 1925, 1926.

B. Periodical Articles

_____, "Polacy na tulaczce. Robotnicy polscy w Szwajcaryi," *Straz polska* (Krakow), R. IV, nr. 33, styczen 1911.

_____, "Listy z Brazylii," *Kurjer Warszawski,* nr. 3, 3 styczen 1890, str. 3.

_____, "Znowu wychodztwo do Syberii," *Przeglad Emigracyjny* (Lwow), R. III, nr. 12, 15 czerwca 1894, str. 111–112.

_____, "W sprawie opieki nad Polakami w Brazylii," *Przeglad Emigracyjny* (Lwow), R. III, nr. 18, 1 wrzesnia 1894, str. 174–175.

_____, "Polska kolonizacya nad Oceanem Spokojnem," *Przeglad Emigracyjny* (Lwow), R. III, nr. 19, 1 pazdziernik 1894, str. 180–181.

_____, "Sprawa emigracyjno-kolonizacyjna w sejmie galicyjskiem," *Przeglad Wszechpolski* (Lwow), R. I, nr. 4, 15 luty 1895, str. 56–57.

_____, "Akcya kraju w sprawie emigracyjno-kolonizacyjnej," *Przeglad Wszechpolski* (Lwow), R. I, nr. 7, 1 kwiecien 1895, str. 100.

_____, "Ruch emigracyjny," *Przeglad Wszechpolski* (Lwow), R. V, nr. 4, kwiecien 1899, str. 193–204.

_____, "Komisya emigracyjna w Warszawie," *Polski Przeglad Emigracyjny* (Lwow), R. I, nr. 1, pazdziernik 1907, str. 5–9.

_____, "Przeglad prasy," *Polski Przeglad Emigracyjny* (Lwow), R. I, nr. 1, 10 pazdz. 1907, str. 14.

_____, "Towarzystwo 'Parana'," *Polski Przeglad Emigracyjny* (Lwow), R. I, nr. 1, pazdziernik 1907, str. 9–11.

_____, "Rozmaitosc," *Polski Przeglad Emigracyjny* (Krakow), R. IV, nr. 2, styczen 1910, str. 10.

_____, "Od redakcyi," *Polski Przeglad Emigracyjny* (Krakow), R. VI, nr. 2, 30 styczen 1910, str. 13, 15–16.

_____, "Rozmaitosci," *Polski Przeglad Emigracyjny* (Krakow), R. VI, styczen 1912, str. 23–24; marzec-kwiecien 1912, str. 124ff.

———, "Rozmaitosci," *Polski Przeglad Emigracyjny* (Krakow), R. VI, luty 1912, str. 75–76.

———, "P.T.E., Walne zwyczajne zgromadzenie czlonkow," *Polski Przeglad Emigracyjny* (Krakow), R. VI, nr. 3–4, marzec–kwiecien 1912, str. 77 ff., str. 80 ff., and str. 166 ff.

———, "Mowa posla hr. Baworowskiego," *Polski Przeglad Emigracyjny* (Krakow), R. VI, maj–czerwiec 1912, str. 189.

———, "Mowa posla hr. Lasockiego," *Polski Przeglad Emigracyjny* (Krakow), R. VI, maj–czerwiec 1912, str. 191–193, 195 ff.

———, "Organizacya opieki nad emigrantami zydowskiemi," *Polski Przeglad Emigracyjny* (Krakow), R. VI, maj–czerwiec 1912, str. 234–239.

———, "Ksiadz Anusz," *Polski Przeglad Emigracyjny* (Krakow), R. VI, maj–czerwiec 1912, str. 249–251.

———, "Listy z Brazylii," *Polski Przeglad Emigracyjny* (Krakow), R. VI, maj–czerwiec 1912, str. 252.

———, "Projekt Rosyjskiej ustawy emigracyjnej," *Polski Przeglad Emigracyjny* (Krakow), R. VI, nr. 7, lipiec 1912, str. 257–263.

———, "O tem, jak mozna dawanie 'Napiwkow' na wsi zastapic lub uzupelniac szerzeniem oswiaty," *Polski Przeglad Emigracyjny* (Krakow), R. VI, lipiec 1912, str. 296–298.

———, "Kronika," *Wychodzca Polski* (Warszawa), zesz. 3, grudzien 1911, str. 22–23.

———, "Emigracya polska," *Krytyka* (Krakow), R. I, zesz. I, kwiecien 1899, str. 102–105.

———, "Szkola nauk spoleczno-politycznych w Krakowie," *Krytyka* (Krakow), Rok XIII, Tom XXIX, 1911, str. 333–335.

———, "Szkola nauk spoleczno-politycznych w Krakowie," *Krytyka* (Krakow), Rok XIV, Tom XXXV, 1912, str. 147–149.

———, "V Zjazd Prawnikow i Ekonomistow we Lwowie. Sekcja ekonomiczna. [Stenograficzne Sprawozdanie]," *Ekonomista* (Warszawa, 1913), Rok XIII, Tom I, str. 109–153.

———, IV Zjazd Prawnikow i Ekonomistow Polskich, "Obrady Sekcji ekonomicznej, I Parcelacja, II Emigracya," *Czasopismo Prawnicze i Ekonomiczne* (Krakow, 1907), Rocznik VIII, str. 96–209, 216–221.

———, "Polska polityka w zaborze pruskim; jaka jest i jaka byc powinna," *Przedswit* (Geneva), R. VII, nr. 22, 23, 24, 31 grudnia 1888, str. 1–4.

———, "Emigracya robotnicza," *Przedswit* (London) Serja II, Tom I, nr. 11, 12 wrzesnia 1891, str. 2–3.

———, "Kilka slow o emigracyi polskiej," *Przedswit* (London), Ser. II, nr. 10, pazdziernik 1894, str. 20–22.

———, "Z Poznania; Jeszcze o wydaleniach," *Przeglad Powszechny* (Krakow), listopad 1885, Tom VIII, nr. 23, str. 304–309.

———, "List z Antwerpji, o polskich wychodzcach do Brazylii," *Przeglad Powszechny* (Krakow) kwiecien–czerwiec 1891, Tom XXX, nr. 88, str. 158–160.

———, "W Brazylii. Notatki z podrozy, przez Ks. Zygmunta Chelmickiego." *Przeglad Powszechny* (Krakow) maj 1892, Tom XXXIV, nr. 101, str. 265–267.

288   EMIGRATION IN POLISH THOUGHT

_____, "Dyskusya w kwestyi bojkotu," *Przeglad Powszechny* (Krakow), listopad 1908, Tom C, nr. 299, str. *9-*24.

_____, "Goraczka emigracyjna," *Przeglad tygodniowy* (Warszawa), R. XXV, nr. 44, 20 pazdz. (1 listopad) 1890, str. 517-518.

_____, "Brak rak do pracy," *Przeglad tygodniowy* (Warszawa), R. XXIX, nr. 42, 8 (20) pazdz. 1894, str. 449-450.

Wladyslaw Abraham, "Pierwszy zjazd prawnikow i ekonomistow polskich," *Przeglad Polski* (Krakow), R. XXII, Tom 86, pazdz.-grudzien 1887, str. 151-169.

Jozef Adamczewski, "Walka ekonomiczno-polityczna o ziemie w Ksiestwie Poznanskiem," *Ekonomista* (Warszawa, 1908), Rok VIII, Tom I, str. 313-355; Rok VIII, Tom II, str. 77-103.

Mieczyslaw Ajzen, "Polityka gospodarcza Lubeckiego," *Rozprawy Historyczne*, t. X, zesz. 2 (1931). Warszawa: Tow. Naukowe Warszawskie.

Nicolas Andrusiak, "The Ukrainian Movement in Galicia," *The Slavonic and East European Review*, Vol. XIV, No. 40 (July, 1935).

B., "Polacy w Brazylii. Przez Antoniego Hempla," *Przeglad Powszechny* (Krakow) marzec 1894, Tom XLI, nr. 123, str. 437-439.

Ks. Jan Badeni, "Ruch ludowy w Galicyi," *Przeglad Powszechny* (Krakow) styczen 1895, R. XII, Tom XLV, nr. 133, str. 1-36.

Oswald Balzer, "Drugi zjazd prawnikow i ekonomistow polskich," *Przeglad sadowy i administracyjny* (Lwow), Rok XIV, zesz. X, pazdziernik 1889, str. 721-728.

Roger Battaglia, "Zarys systemu nowoczesnego prawa emigracyjnego," *Przeglad sadowy i administracyjny* (Lwow), Rok XXII, 1897, str. 353-375, 438-458, 525-548, 593-614.

Franciszek Bayer, "Sprawozdanie delegata Warszawskiego Towarzystwa Opieki nad Wychodzcami, Franciszka Bayera, z podrozy informacyjnej po Podlasiu," *Polski Przeglad Emigracyjny* (Krakow), R. V, nr. 17, 1911.

T. Belina, "Na widnokregach," *Glos* (Warszawa), nr. 4, R. XVI, 13 (26) stycznia 1901, str. 52.

Dr. Artur Benis, "Emigracja," [IV Zjazd Prawnikow i Ekonomistow Polskich], *Czasopismo Prawnicze i Ekonomiczne* (Krakow, 1906), Tom VII, 57 stron.

H. Biegeleisen, "Szkoly ludowe w Galicyi," *Biblioteka Warszawska*, t. 178 (1886), 177-187. Warszawa: Gebethner i Wolff.

Dr. A. Bielicki, "Kwestya Rolna w Galicyi. Zdzislaw Ludkiewicz," *Przeglad Powszechny* (Krakow), lipiec-wrzesien 1913, Tom CXIX, str. 110-113.

Richard Blanke, "Bismarck and the Prussian Polish Policies of 1886," *The Journal of Modern History* (Chicago) Vol. 45, No. 2, June 1973, 211-239.

Jan Bloch, "Ziemia i jej obdluzenie w Krolestwie Polskiem," *Biblioteka Warszawska*, t. 202, 203, 204 (1891), 219-270, 549-587. Warszawa: Gebethner i Wolff.

Ks. A. Boc., "Emigracya polska na zachodniem pomorzu," *Przeglad Powszechny* (Krakow), marzec 1900, Tom LXV, nr. 195, str. 495-502.

Richard Bockh, "Die Verscheibung der Sprach-verhaltnisse in Posen und Westpreussen," *Preussische Jahrbücher*, LXXVII (1894), 424-436.

Benedykt Bornstein, "Analiza krytyczna danych statystycznych, dotyczacych ruchu naturalnego ludnosci b. Krolestwa Polskiego," *Przyczynki do statys-*

tyki bylego Krolestwa Polskiego, III (1920). Warszawa: Glowny Urzad Statystyczny.

Aleksander Borowinski, "Sprawozdanie . . . ," *Wychodzca Polski* (czerwiec, 1912). Warszawa: Tow. Opieki nad Wychodzcami.

Eugenjusz Boss, "Sprawa robotnicza w Krolestwie Polskiem w okresie Paszkiewiczowskim, 1831–1855," *Rozprawy Historyczne,* t. X, zesz. I, (1931). Warszawa: Tow. Naukowe Warszawskie.

Feliks Brodowski, "Rosyjski Bank Wloscianski, zasady i metody jego dzialania," *Sprawa Rolna,* zesz. 5–7 (grudzien 1920), 27–59. Warszawa.

Tadeusz Brzeski, "Parcelacya wlasnosci tabularnej w Galicyi," *Wiadomosci statystyczne o stosunkach krajowych,* Tom. XXIII, zesz. II (1911). Lwow: Krajowe biuro statystyczne.

Roman Buczynski, "Nasza wlasnosc ziemska; zarys statystyki rolniczej naszego kraju i ziemianstwa," *Biblioteka Warszawska,* t. 167 (1882), 329–352; t. 168 (1882), 49–64, 255–310, 354–393. Warszawa: Gebethner i Wolff.

Waclaw Budzynowski, "Chlopska posiadlosc w Galicyi," *Krytyka* (Krakow), Rok III, Tom I, 1901, str. 351–359.

Franciszek Bujak, "Maszkienice, wies powiatu brzeskiego; Rozwoj od r. 1900 do 1911," *Rozprawy Akademii Umiejetnosci,* Wyd. Hist.-Filoz., t. LVIII (1914), 1–164. Krakow: Akademia Umiejetnosci.

_____, "Maszkienice, wies powiatu brzeskiego; Stosunki gospodarcze i spoleczne," *Rozprawy Akademii Umiejetnosci,* Wyd. Hist.-Filoz., t. XXXI (1902), 76–182. Krakow: Akademia Umiejetnosci.

Jozef Buzek, "Das Auswanderungsproblem und die Regelung des Auswanderungswesens in Oesterreich," *Zeitschrift für Volkswirtschaft, Socialpolitik und Verwaltung,* X. Band, V. Heft (1901). Wien.

_____, "Rozsiedlenie ludnosci Galicyi wedlug wyznania i jezyka," *Wiadomosci statystyczne o stosunkach krajowych,* t. XXI, zesz. II (1909). Lwow: Krajowe biuro statystyczne.

_____, "Wlasnosc tabularna w Galicyi wedlug stanu z koncem r. 1902," *Wiadomosci statystyczne o stosunkach krajowych,* t. XX, zesz. III (1902). Lwow: Krajowe biuro statystyczne.

Jan Bystron, "Szlaki migracyjne na ziemiach polskich," *Przeglad Socjologiczny,* t. IV, zesz. 3–4 (1936), 110–129. Poznan: Polskie Towarzystwo Socjologiczne.

Leopold Caro, "Das Problem der Auswanderungsfrage," *Volkswirtschaftliche Wochenschrift,* Nos. 1215, 1217, 1218 (1907). Wien.

_____, "Lichwa wiejska i kredyt wloscianski w Galicyi," *Biblioteka Warszawska,* t. 223 (1896), 475–489. Warszawa: Gebethner i Wolff.

_____, "Wychodztwo Polskie," *Ekonomista* (Warszawa, 1907), Rok VII, Tom II, str. 1–14.

_____, "Nasi robotnicy sezonowi," *Przeglad Powszechny* (Krakow), luty 1908, Tom XCVII, nr. 290, str. 181–198.

_____, "Nasi wychodzcy zamorscy," *Przeglad Powszechny* (Krakow), sierpien 1908, Tom IC, nr. 296, str. 149–165; wrzesien 1908, Tom IC, nr. 297, str. 352–372.

_____, "Kwestja obecnego u nas bojkotu," *Przeglad Powszechny* (Krakow) listopad 1908, Tom C, nr. 299, str. *1–*8.

_____, "Miedzynarodowy problem emigracyi," *Przeglad Powszechny* (Krakow) czerwiec 1909, rok XXVI, zesz. 6, str. 321–335.

_____, "Sprawa naszych wychodzcow i robotnikow sezonowych na konfe-rencyi Budapesztenskiej," *Przeglad Powszechny* (Krakow), pazdziernik-grudzien 1910, Tom CVIII, str. 325-347.

_____, "Katolicy niemieccy w Dreznie w sprawie naszych robotnikow," *Przeg-lad Powszechny* (Krakow), pazdz.-grudzien 1911, Tom CXII, str. *7-*26.

_____, "Wspolna akcja w sprawie wychodztwa [referat wygloszony na zjezdzie jubileuszowym Piotra Skargi w Krakowie]," *Przeglad Powszechny* (Kra-kow) listopad 1912, Tom CXVI, nr. 347, str. 140-157.

_____, "Obrona narodowej pracy," *Przeglad Powszechny* (Krakow), marzec 1913, rok XXX, zesz. 3, str. 337-352.

_____, "Unsere Auswanderer in Brasilien," *Oesterreichische Rundschau,* (1 Feb. 1908). Wien.

_____, "Unsere überseeischen Auswanderer und die Enquete vom Jahre 1905," *Zeitschrift für Volkswirtschaft, Socialpolitik und Verwaltung,* (No-vember 1907). Berlin.

S. Chochlinski, "Wychodztwo polskie w Niemczech," *Przeglad Wszechpolski* (Lwow), R. VII, nr. 12, grudzien 1901, str. 739-741.

Chorazy, "Sprawy biezace," *Niwa* (Warszawa, 1885), Rok XIV, Tom XXVIII, zesz. 258, str. 463-467, 527-533, 608-609.

_____, "Interpelacya Polska w parlamencie niemieckim," *Niwa* (Warszawa, 1885), Rok XIV, Tom XXVIII, zesz. 264, str. 923-934.

_____, "Sprawy biezace," *Niwa* (Warszawa, 1886), Rok XV, Tom XXIX, zesz. 275, str. 812-817; Rok XV, Tom XXX, zesz. 278, str. 143-148; zesz. 282, str. 467-471; Rok XVI (1887), Tom XXXI, zesz. 289, str. 66-71; zesz. 292, str. 315-319; zesz. 300, str. 941-947.

Wlodzimierz Czerkawski, "Wysokosc ludnosci miejskiej w Austryi," *Czaso-pismo prawnicze i ekonomiczne* (Krakow, 1901), Rocznik II, zesz. 3-4, str. 391-429.

D., "Drugi zjazd prawnikow i ekonomistow polskich we Lwowie," *Przewod-nik naukowy i literacki* (Lwow, 1889), Rocznik XVII, str. 940-959.

I. D. [Ignacy Daszynski], "Bankructwo demokracyi galicyjskiej," *Przedswit* (London), Ser. III, nr. 1-3, marzec 1895, str. 3-6; nr. 4, kwiecien 1895, str. 1-4; nr. 5, maj 1895, str. 2-5.

John Dewey, "Autocracy under Cover," *The New Republic,* Vol. XVI, No. 199 (August 24, 1918), 103-106.

Roman Dmowski [Skrzycki], "Z Parany," *Przeglad Wszechpolski* (Lwow), R. VI, nr. 2, luty 1900, str. 109-121; R. VI, nr. 3, marzec 1900, str. 172-182; R. VI, nr. 6, czerwiec 1900, str. 359-375.

_____, "Praca polska w Paranie," *Przeglad Wszechpolski* (Krakow), R. IX, 1903, str. 586-599.

A. Donimirski, "Parcelacya," *Biblioteka Warszawska,* t. 220 (1895), str. 305-320. Warszawa: Gebethner i Wolff.

_____, "Parcelacya w Poznanskiem," *Biblioteka Warszawska,* t. 209 (1893), str. 161-173. Warszawa: Gebethner i Wolff.

Emil H. Dunikowski, "O Polskich Koloniach w P. A.," *Przeglad Emigracyjny* (Lwow), R. II, nr. 18, 1893.

_____, "O szkolnictwie w Stanach Zjednoczonych," *Muzeum* (kwiecien 1893), str. 271-283. Lwow: Seyfarth i Czajkowski.

_____, "Z podrozy do Ameryki," *Kosmos,* zesz. I-III (1892), str. 1-57; zesz. IV-V (1892), str. 142-217; zesz. VI (1892), str. 264-298; zesz. VII-VIII

(1892), str. 307–373; zesz. IX–X (1892), str. 420–442; zesz. XI–XII (1892), str. 534–560. Lwow: I zwiazkowa drukarnia.

Wojciech Dzieduszycki, "Sprawy krajowe," *Przeglad Polski* (Krakow), R. XXXVII, Tom 147, 1903, str. 324–339.

Frederyk Engels, "Kwestya wloscianska," *Przedswit* (London) ser. III, nr. 12, grudzien 1894, str. 1–7.

Karl Englisch, "Die Methoden der statistischen Erfassung der Auswanderung," *Statistische Monatsschrift* (Määrzheft 1908). Wien: K. K. statistische Zentralkommission.

———, "Die oesterreichische Auswanderungsenquete," *Arbeitsnachweis* (Mai 1912). Wien.

———, "Die oesterreichische Auswanderungsstatistik," *Statistische Monatsschrift* (Feb.–März. 1913). Wien: K. K. statistische Zentralkommission.

———, "Zu unserer Auswanderungsfrage," *Statistische Monatsschrift* (Feb.–Marz. 1911). Wien: K. K. statistische Zentralkommission.

Wilhelm Feldman, "Proletaryzacya Galicyi," *Krytyka* (Krakow), Rok I, zesz. I, kwiecien 1899, str. 76–85, 129–141.

———, "Ruch Chrzescijansko-spoleczny w Galicyi," *Krytyka* (Krakow), Rok IX, Tom I, 1907, str. 62–69, 230–239.

(f.), [Wilhelm Feldman], "Unarodowienie ziemi jedynem wyjsciem z nedzy galicyjskiej," *Krytyka* (Krakow), Rok XVI, Tom XLII, 15 kwietnia 1914, str. 65–73.

F. Fendi, "Z ekonomiki, IX," *Biblioteka Warszawska,* t. 177 [181] (1886), 84–108. Warszawa: Gebethner i Wolff.

Jozef Frejlich, "Polskie wychodztwo zorobkowe w obwodzie przemyslowem westfalsko-nadrenskim," *Czasopismo Prawnicze i Ekonomiczne,* (Krakow, 1911) Rocznik XII, str. 31–86.

G. Miecz., "Zagadnienia emigracji Zydowskiej z Polski," *Kwartalnik Naukowego Instytutu Emigracyjnego,* Vol. I–II, R. IV (1929), 320–326. Warszawa.

Zygmunt Gargas, "Sprawy krajowe. W sprawie ruchu pienieznego miedzy Ameryka a Galicya," *Przeglad Polski* (Krakow), R. XLI, Tom 162, 1906, str. 518–534.

———, "Kronika literacka," *Przeglad Polski* (Krakow), R. XLIII, Tom 171, 1909, str. 549–552.

———, "R. Dmowski, Wychodztwo i osadnictwo," *Przeglad sadowy i administracyjny* (Lwow), Rok XXIX, 1904, str. 472–476.

———, "Publiczne posrednictwo pracy w Galicyi," *Ekonomista* (Warszawa, 1910), Rok X, Tom IV, str. 45–88; Rok XI, Tom I (1911), str. 56–126.

———, "Reforma konsularna," *Przeglad sadowy i administracyjny* (Lwow), Rok XXXVII, zesz. 12 (grudzien 1912), str. 1133–1151; Rok XXXVIII, zesz. 1 (styczen 1913), str. 55–74; Rok XXXVIII, zesz. 2 (luty 1913), str. 146–155; Rok XXXVIII, zesz. 3 (marzec 1913), str. 181–203.

Kazimierz Gluchowski, "Polacy w Brazylji," *Kwartalnik Instytutu Naukowego do badan emigracji i kolonizacji,* r. II, nr. 2 (kwiecien–czerwiec 1927), 106–137. Warszawa: Polskie Towarzystwo Emigracyjne.

Zofia (Daszynska) Golinska, "Badania nad wsia polska," *Krytyka* (Krakow), rocznik V., zesz. 10, pazdziernik 1903.

———, "Kapitalizm bierny i czynny," *Krytyka* (Krakow), rocznik V, zesz. 2, luty 1903.

292   EMIGRATION IN POLISH THOUGHT

Dr. Z. Daszynska-Golinska, "Z kwestyi rolney," [a review of L. Krzywicki's book of that title], *Krytyka* (Krakow), 1904, rocznik VI, Tom I, str. 433–438.

———, "Utopia najblizszej przyszlosci," *Krytyka* (Krakow), rocznik IX, zesz. I, styczen 1907, 14–22 and rocznik IX, zesz. II, luty 1907, 137–145.

———, "Wlasnosc rolna w Galicyi," *Ateneum* (Warszawa), lipiec 1899, str. 72–108; sierpien 1899, str. 315–339.

———, "Wlasnosc rolna w krajach Austryi," *Ekonomista* (Warszawa, 1904), Rok IV, Tom I, zesz. 1.

Zofia Daszynska-Golinska, "Demografia jako nauka," *Ekonomista* (Warszawa, 1911), Rok XI, Tom III, str. 1–22.

———, "Z demografii wspolczesnej," *Ateneum* (Warszawa), kwiecien 1894, str. 103–116.

Z. D. [Daszynska-Golinska], "Ze statystyki rolniczej," *Ateneum* (Warszawa), sierpien 1892.

Michal Goralski, "Sprawa emigracji i imigracji," *Mysl socjalistyczna* (Krakow), R. I, nr. 4–5, sierpien–wrzesien 1907, str. 154–161.

Ignacy Grabowski, "Bogactwo narodowe," *Slowo Polskie* (14 luty 1907).

Stanislaw Grabski, "Sprawy krajowe. W kwestyi parcelacyi," *Przeglad Polski* (Krakow), R. XXXIX, Tom 154, 1904, str. 99–129.

Tadeusz Franciszek Grodynski, "Ustawodawstwo emigracyjne na tle porownawczem ze szczegolnem uwzglednieniu projektu ustawy austriackiej z r. 1904," *Czasopismo Prawnicze i Ekonomiczne,* (Krakow, 1911), Rocznik XII, str. 87–146.

Wladyslaw Gumplowicz, "Socjalism a kwestja Polska," *Krytyka* (Krakow) R. VIII, zesz. 10, pazdziernik 1906.

———, "Kwestya agrarna," *Przedswit* (London), Ser. III, nr. 6, czerwiec 1899, str. 3–6.

———, "Nasze zadania na wsi," *Przedswit* (London), nr. 1, R. XXV, styczen 1905, str. 16–27; nr. 2, R. XXV, luty 1905, str. 80–86.

William W. Hagen, "National Solidarity and Organic Work in Prussian Poland, 1815–1914," *The Journal of Modern History* (Chicago) Vol. 44, No. 1, March 1972, 38–64.

Korneli Heck, editor, "Editorial," *Przewodnik Bibliograficzny* (pazdziernik 1902), 144–145. Krakow: Gebethner i Sp.

Jan Hupka, "Sprawy krajowe. Wlosci rentowe a parcelacya," *Przeglad Polski* (Krakow), R. XXXVIII, Tom 149, 1903, str. 351–371.

Roman Jablonowski, "Wiejska ludnosc bezrolna," *Roczniki socjologii wsi,* t. III (1938). Warszawa: Instytut Socjologii Wsi.

Michal Janik, "Ludnosc polska w Stanach Zjednoczonych Ameryki polnocnej," *Lud,* Tom XI, zesz. III (1905). Lwow: Towarzystwo ludoznawcze.

Teodor Jeske-Choinski, "Listy z Warszawy," *Przeglad Powszechny* (Krakow), listopad 1908, Tom C, nr. 209, str. 280–284.

Roman Jordan, "Widoki dla wychodzcow w Argentynie," *Polski Przeglad Emigracyjny* (Krakow), R. VI, styczen 1912, str. 4–13; luty 1912, str. 49–62; marzec–kwiecien 1912, str. 92–110.

Junius, "Wspolczesni politycy polacy. Roman Dmowski," *Krytyka* (Krakow), Rok XIV, Tom XXXV, 1912, str. 135–138.

K., "Nowy exodus," *Ateneum* (Warszawa, 1891), Tom LXI, str. 1–7.

Kazimierz W. Kamieniecki, "Szkolnictwo ludowe w Galicyi. Wobec analfabetyzmu," *Czasopismo prawnicze i ekonomiczne* (Krakow, 1905), rocznik VI, zesz. 4.

David Kandel, "Zydzi w Krolestwie Polskiem po 1831 r.," *Biblioteka Warszawska,* t. 279 (1910). Warszawa: Gebethner i Wolff.

Jordan Kanski, "Robotnicy rolni w Krolestwie Polskiem," *Biblioteka Warszawska,* t. 261 (1906). Warszawa: Gebethner i Wolff.

Wladimir W. Kaplun-Kogan, "Die Jüdische Sprache- und Kulturgemeinschaft in Polen," *Zeitschrift für Demographie und Statistik der Juden* (July, August, September, 1915). Berlin: Halensee.

Kazimierz Kasperski, "Wychodztwo polskie i jego przyczyny," *Ekonomista polski,* nr. 39 (1900). Lwow: Drukarnia ludowa.

Stanislaw Kasznica and Marcin Nadobnik, "Najwazniejsze wyniki spisu ludnosci i spisu zwierzat domowych wedlug stanu z dnia 31 grudnia 1910," *Wiadomosci statystyczne o stosunkach krajowych,* t. XXIV, zesz. 1 (1912). Lwow: Wyd. Krajowe biuro statystyczne.

A. Kaupas, "Lithuanians in America," *Charities,* Vol. 13, No. 10 (December 3, 1904), 231–235. New York.

Jozef Kazmierczak, "Wychodztwo do Niemiec," *Praca* (1912). Krakow.

M. Lusnia [Kazimierz Kelles-Krauz], "O naszej taktyce na wsi," *Przedswit* (London), Ser. III, nr. 10, pazdziernik 1899, str. 3–8.

_____, "Nasza praca na wsi; rewizja programu agrarnego?" *Przedswit* (London), nr. 9, R. XXIV, wrzesien 1904, str. 357–370; nr. 10–11, R. XXIV, pazdz.–grudzien 1904, str. 413–421.

Marjan Kiniorski, "Wieksza i mniejsza wlasnosc ziemska," *Ekonomista,* R. III, zesz. I (1903). Warszawa: Gazeta handlowa.

Jozef Kleczynski, "Ceny ziemi wloscianskiej w Galicyi," *Niwa* (Warszawa), R. VIII, 15 kwiecien 1879, str. 553–563.

_____, "Stosunki ekonomiczne w Galicyi," *Wiadomosci statystyczne o stosunkach krajowych,* R. VII (1881). Lwow: Wyd. Krajowe biuro statystyczne.

_____, "Stan ekonomiczny Galicyi," *Przeglad Polski* (Krakow), R. XXII, Tom 88, kw.–czerwiec 1888, str. 209–240.

_____, *et al.,* "Odezwy w sprawie emigracyi polskiej," *Przeglad Polski* (Krakow), R. XXIV, Tom 95, 1890, str. 218–224.

_____, "Z powodu procesu Wadowickiego," *Przeglad Polski* (Krakow), R. XXIV, Tom 96, 1890, str. 375–391.

_____, "Trzeci zjazd prawnikow i ekonomistow polskich," *Przeglad Polski* (Krakow), R. XXVIII, Tom 110, 1893, str. 396–411.

Aleksander Klobukowski, "Wlasnosc ziemska w Krolestwie Polskiem," *Biblioteka Warszawska,* t. 249 (1903), str. 503–531. Warszawa: Gebethner i Wolff.

Stanislaw Klobukowski, "Roczna emigracja polska," *Ekonomista Polski* (Lwow, 1890), Tom I, str. 104–112, 210–243.

_____, "Wedrowka ludu polskiego do Niemiec," *Ekonomista Polski* (Lwow, 1890), Tom IV, str. 57–82.

_____, "Wedrowka ludu Polskiego w glab Niemiec," *Ateneum* (Warszawa, 1890), Tom LX, str. 138–147.

_____, "Roczna emigracja Polska i srodki przeciw niej zaradcze," *Ateneum* (Warszawa, 1889), Tom LVI, str. 283–305, 475–495.

_____, "Wycieczka do Parany," *Przewodnik naukowy i literacki* (Lwow, 1908), Rocznik XXXVI, str. 22–40, 131–153, 237–260, 367–384, 444–455, 535–548,

624–640, 732–740, 828–844, 925–938, 1032–1056, 1158–1187.
Stefan Knauff, "Stefan Zeromski a sprawa emigracyjna," *Kwartalnik Nauko-wego Instytutu Emigracyjnego,* R. III, t. II–III (kwiecien–wrzesien 1928), 424–435. Warszawa.
Dr. Alfred Kohl, "Prady i mysli w naszym kraju w kwestji Zydowskiej," *Ateneum Polskie* (Lwow), pazdziernik 1908, Tom IV, nr. 1, str. 76–83.
Feliks Koneczny, "Konserwatysm chlopski," *Biblioteka Warszawska,* t. 251 (1903). Warszawa: Gebethner i Wolff.
Kor., "Na widnokregach," *Glos* (Warszawa), nr. 17, R. XVII, 13 (26) kwiecien 1902, str. 271; nr. 21, 11 (24) maja 1902, str. 335–336; nr. 29, 6 (19) lipca, 1902, str. 463–464.
Wladyslaw M. Kozlowski, "Stronnictwa polityczne w Stanach Zjednoczo-nych," *Ateneum* (maj 1897), 222–254; (czerwiec 1897), 470–495. Warszawa: J. Cotta.
_____, "Z Ameryki: Biblioteki i czytelnie w Stanach Zjednoczonych," *Biblioteka Warszawska,* t. 228 (1897), str. 141–151.
Adam Krasinski, "Kronika miesieczna," *Biblioteka Warszawska,* t. 247 (1902); t. 249 (1903); t. 264 (1906); t. 266 (1907); t. 268 (1907); t. 269 (1908); t. 270 (1908). Warszawa: Gebethner i Wolff.
_____, "Ludwik Gorski," *Biblioteka Warszawska,* t. 248 (1902), 209–233. Warszawa: Gebethner i Wolff.
Dr. K. Krotoski, "Emigracya polska do Francyi w najswiezszej dobie," *Przeglad Powszechny* (Krakow), kwiecien–czerwiec 1911, Tom CX, str. 26–45, 231–247.
S. Krzeczkowski, "Wychodztwo wloscian z Krolestwa na zarobki," *Biblioteka Warszawska,* t. 243 (1901), str. 47–58. Warszawa: Gebethner i Wolff.
Ludwik Krzywicki, "Kontrola a sprawa emigracyi," *Gazeta Polska,* (Warszawa), nr. 88, 1892.
_____, "Obiezysasi," *Gazeta Polska* (Warszawa), nr. 220, 1892.
_____, "Obiezysastwo," *Gazeta Polska* (Warszawa), nr. 3, 1892; nr. 41, 1899.
_____, "Prawa przeciw wychodztwu," *Gazeta Polska* (Warszawa), nr. 270, 1892.
_____, "Proby powstrzymania emigracyi," *Gazeta Polska* (Warszawa), nr. 87, 1892.
_____, "Wedrowka ludow," *Gazeta Polska* (Warszawa), nr. 86, 1892; nr. 158, 1894.
_____, "Wyludnienie wsi," *Gazeta Polska* (Warszawa), nr. 13, 1895.
_____, "Polacy w zachodnich dzielnicach panstwa pruskiego," *Gazeta Polska* (Warszawa), nr. 135, 1899.
_____, "Wychodztwo za zarobkami," *Glos* (Warszawa), nr. 14, 1887.
[K. R. Zywicki], "Nasi wychodzcy," *Ateneum* (Warszawa, 1901), Tom CI, str. 433–442.
Adam Krzyzanowski, "Osadnictwo polskie," *Przeglad Powszechny* (Krakow), pazdziernik 1900, Tom LXVIII, nr. 202, str. 143–144.
_____, "Jozef Buzek. Das Auswanderungsproblem . . . ," *Przeglad Polski* (Krakow), R. XXXVI, Tom 144, 1902, str. 150–155.
J. Krzyzowski, "Biura posrednictwa pracy i obrony prawnej dla 'obiezysa-sow'," *Glos* (Warszawa), nr. 10, R. XVI, 24 lutego (9 marca), 1901, str. 135.
Tadeusz Kudelka, "Obiezysasi," *Przeglad Powszechny* (Krakow) luty 1900, Tom LXV, nr. 194, str. 208–229.

———, "Wychodztwo i osadnictwo, R. Dmowski," *Przeglad Powszechny,* (Krakow), czerwiec 1900, Tom LXVI, nr. 198, str. 442-445.

R. Kudrzanski, "W kwestyi emigracyjnej," *Przeglad Emigracyjny* (Lwow), R. III, nr. 17, 1 wrzesnia 1894, str. 165-167.

L. Kulczycki, "Emigracja i mniejszosci narodowe," *Kwartalnik Naukowego Instytutu Emigracyjnego,* Vol. III (1927), 17-21. Warszawa.

Eugene M. Kulischer, "Population Changes behind the Iron Curtain," *Annals of the American Academy of Political and Social Science,* Vol. 271 (September, 1950), 100-111.

Kazimierz W. Kumaniecki, "Z naszych spraw spolecznych: Oswiata i emigracya w naszym kraju," *Przeglad Powszechny* (Krakow), pazdziernik 1906, Tom XCI, str. 144-159.

———, "Studya z zakresu statystyki wedrowek," *Czasopismo Prawnicze i Ekonomiczne* (Krakow, 1909), R. X, zesz. 1-3, str. 97-145.

Anastazy Kwiryn, "Stopa procentowa," *Ateneum* (Warszawa, 1877), Tom IV, str. 531-553.

H. Land [Helena Landau], "Ostatni spis ludnosci w Galicyi," *Krytyka* (Krakow), Rok XIV, Tom XXXIII, 1912, str. 139-143.

Dr. Helena Landau, "Parcelacya ziemi w Galicyi," *Krytyka* (Krakow), Rok XIV, Tom XXXIII, 1912, str. 195-199.

———, "Kurya wiekszej wlasnosci," *Krytyka* (Krakow), Rok XIV, Tom XXXV, 1912, str.' 118-123.

———, "Z zagadnien emigracyjnych," *Krytyka* (Krakow), Rok XVI, Tom XLI, luty 1914, str. 164-168.

Ks. Wl. Ledochowski, "Zdjecia cenzur z Ks. Stojalowskiego," *Przeglad Powszechny* (Krakow) pazdziernik 1897, Tom LVI, nr. 166, str. 145-146.

Jacob Lestschinsky, "National Groups in Polish Emigration," *Jewish Social Studies,* Vol. V, No. 2 (April, 1943), 99-113. New York: American Jewish Publications Society.

Zenon Lewandowski, "Wychodztwo polskie i stan Parana w Brazylii," *Roczniki,* Tom XXIX (1902). Poznan: Dziennik poznanski.

Witold Lewicki, "Parcelacya w Galicyi jako objaw spoleczny," *Ekonomista Polski* (Lwow, 1890), Tom I, str. 112-121, 244-261.

Richard H. Lord, "Bismarck and Russia in 1863," *The American Historical Review,* Vol. XXIX, No. 1 (October, 1923), 24-48.

Bronislaw Lozinski, "Agenor hr. Goluchowski w pierwszym okresie rzadow swoich," *Biblioteka Warszawska,* t. 239 (1900), 89-92. Warszawa: Gebethner i Wolff.

B. Lut., "Kronika miesieczna," *Ateneum* (Warszawa, 1892) Tom LXVII, str. 179-183.

Marek Lza, "Zydzi polsko-rosyjscy w Londynie," *Przeglad Powszechny* (Krakow) listopad 1894, Tom XLIV, nr. 131, str. 201-221.

M., "Emigracya naszych wloscian," *Przeglad Powszechny* (Krakow), wrzesien 1885, Tom VII, nr. 21, str. 343-363; pazdziernik 1885, Tom VIII, nr. 22, str. 42-59.

———, "Polacy na obczyznie," *Przeglad Powszechny* (Krakow), sierpien 1899, Tom LXIII, nr. 188, str. 316-324.

F. M., "Ziemia i jej obdluzenie w Krolestwie Polskiem, przez Jana Blocha," *Przeglad Polski* (Krakow), R. XXVII, Tom 108, 1893, str. 144-150.

J.K.M., "Zabor pruski wobec ustawy ekspropryacyjnej," *Krytyka* (Krakow), Rok X, Tom 1 (1908), str. 55–65.

Janusz Machnicki, "Piaty Zjazd Polskich Prawnikow i Ekonomistow," *Ekonomista* (Warszawa, 1912), Rok XII, Tom IV, str. 97–106.

Juliusz Makarewicz, "Walka z spekulacja parcelacyjna," *Przeglad Powszechny* (Krakow), wrzesien 1904, Tom LXXXIII, nr. 249, str. 321–333.

Henryk Maruszczak, "Zmiany w zaludnieniu wojewodstwa Lubelskiego w latach 1822–1946," *Annales Universitatis Mariae Curie-Sklodowska,* Sectio B, Vol. 4 (1949), 61–111. Lublin.

Edward Maurizio, "Przeobrazenie wsi galicyjskiej," *Krytyka* (Krakow), Rok XIV, Tom XXXIII, 1912, str. 227–232.

Antoni Mazanowski, "'Chlopi' Reymonta," *Przeglad Powszechny* (Krakow), lipiec-wrzesien 1909, Tom CIII, str. 317–333.

A. Medeksza, "Wychodztwo i posrednictwo," *Glos* (Warszawa), nr. 15, R. XVI, 31 marca (13 kwietnia) 1901, str. 213.

Barbara Michalowska, "Sprawy ziemstwa i wsi w ekonomiczno-spolecznym programie 'Tygodnika Ilustrowanego,' 1870–1880," *Przeglad Nauk Historycznych i Spolecznych,* t. IV (1954), 198–235. Lodz.

Jozef Milewski, "Kwestya robotnikow rolnych," *Przeglad polski* (marzec 1906). Krakow: Czas.

———, "O kwestyi socyalnej, mowa na wiecu lwowskim," *Przeglad powszechny* (sierpien 1896), str. 244–260. Krakow: Wl. L. Anczyc i Sp.

———, "Ze stosunkow poznanskich," *Niwa* (Warszawa, 1886), Rok XV, Tom XXIX, zesz. 273, str. 601–624.

———, "Pierwszy zjazd prawnikow i ekonomistow polskich w Krakowie," *Biblioteka Warszawska,* t. 188 (1887), 116–126. Warszawa: Gebethner i Wolff.

———, "Sprawy krajowe. Biura postednictwa pracy," *Przeglad Polski* (Krakow), R. XXXVII, Tom 147, 1903, str. 1–24.

———, "Sprawy krajowe. Ustawa parcelacyjna," *Przeglad Polski* (Krakow), R. XXXVI, Tom 151, 1904, str. 544–561.

———, "Sprawy krajowe. Kwestya robotnikow rolnych," *Przeglad Polski* (Krakow), R. XL, Tom 159, 1906, str. 521–544.

Z. Milkowski, "Spolczesne wychodztwo polskie w oswietleniu przydatnosci politycznej," *Przeglad Wszechpolski* (Lwow), R. VI, nr. 2, luty 1900, str. 77–85.

Jozef Modlinski, "Kolonizacya polska w Ameryce Polnocnej," *Wychodzca Polski* (Warszawa), zesz. 3, grudzien 1911, str. 5–6.

F. Morawski, "Przesiedlenie ludnosci z Galicyi zachodniej do wschodniej," *Wiadomosci statystyczne o stosunkach krajowych,* XI. Lwow: Wyd. Krajowe biuro statystyczne.

Ks. Maryan Morawski, "List pasterski biskupow galicyjskich i pisma Ks. Stojalowskiego," *Przeglad Powszechny* (Krakow) maj 1895, Tom XLVI, nr. 137, str. 314–320.

N., "Lichwa, jej przyczyny i skutki," *Przedswit* (London) Ser. III, nr. 9, wrzesien 1896, str. 2–6.

———, "W Brazylii. Notatki z podrozy przez Ks. Zygmunta Chelmickiego," *Przeglad Polski* (Krakow), R. XXVI, Tom 104, 1892, str. 696–699.

D. N., "Syonizm-awangarda pangermanizmu," *Niwa Polska* (Warszawa), 31 sierpnia (13 wrzesnia), 1902, Rok XXX, nr. 37, str. 578–579.

Marcin Nadobnik, "Ludnosc w Galicyi w r. 1910," *Ekonomista,* R. XII, zesz. I (1912). Warszawa: Gazeta handlowa.

———, "Podatki bezposrednie w Galicyi przypisane na rok 1910," *Wiadomosci statystyczne o stosunkach krajowych,* t. XXIII, zesz. III. Lwow: Wyd. Krajowe biuro statystyczne.

Zygmunt Nawratil, "Slowo o robotnikach rolniczych," *Przeglad sadowy i administracyjny* (Lwow), Rok IX, 1884, str. 65–67, 75–77.

J. Nieborski, "Kilka uwag w sprawie kolonizacyi polskiej," *Przeglad Wszechpolski* (Lwow), R. V, nr. 10, pazdz. 1899, str. 588–598.

Wladyslaw Ochenkowski, "O wlosciach rentowych wraz z wewnetrzna kolonizacja," *Przeglad Polski* (Krakow), R. XXXII, Tom 126, 1897, str. 109–118.

Jozef Okolowicz, "Od redakcyi," *Polski Przeglad Emigracyjny* (Lwow), R. I, nr. 1, 10 pazdz. 1907, str. 1–2.

———, "W sprawie noweli emigracyjnej," *Polski Przeglad Emigracyjny* (Krakow), R. VI, luty 1912, str. 33–36.

———, "Prasa Hakatystyczna a P.T.E.," *Polski Przeglad Emigracyjny* (Krakow), R. VI, luty 1912, str. 72–74.

———, "Zmniejszenie emigracyi polskiej do Niemiec i dzialalnosc Polskiego Towarzystwa Emigracyjnego," *Bojkot,* R. II, nr. 8 (sierpien 1912).

Stanislaw Oksza, "Znaczenie polityczne wychodztwa," *Przeglad Wszechpolski* (Lwow), R. I, nr. 9, 1 maja 1895, str. 129–130.

Op., K., "Emigracya polskich robotnikow rolnych w Szwajcaryi," *Przedswit* (London), R. XXX, nr. 1–2, styczen–luty 1911.

St. Os . . . arz., "Z calego kraju," *Przedswit* (London), R. XXX, nr. 4, 1911, str. 180–189.

Zbigniew Pazdro, "Sprawy krajowe. Trzy lata dzialalnosci publicznych biur posrednictwa pracy w Galicyi," *Przeglad Polski* (Krakow), R. XLIII, Tom 169, 1908, str. 502–526.

J. E. Ks. Biskup Pelczar, *et al.,* "Dyskusya nad referatem dra. Caro," *Przeglad Powszechny* (Krakow) listopad 1912, Tom CXVI, nr. 347, str. 158–164.

Zenon Pietkiewicz, "Ruch przesiedlenczy w Rosyi w zwiazku z przemyslem rolnem," *Ekonomista Polski* (Lwow, 1890), Tom III, str. 229–243.

Tadeusz Pilat, "Przeglad pracy Szczepanowskiego," *Biblioteka Warszawska,* t. 190 (maj 1888). Warszawa: Gebethner i Wolff.

———, "Wlasnosc tabularna w Galicyi," *Wiadomosci statystyczne o stosunkach krajowych,* t. XII (1889). Lwow: Wyd. Krajowe biuro statystyczne.

———, "Wybory do sejmu krajowego w r. 1883," *Wiadomosci statystyczne o stosunkach krajowych,* t. VIII, zesz. III (1884), 112–113, 133–136. Lwow: Wyd. Krajowe biuro statystyczne.

B. P-in., "Asymilacya narodowa a socyalizm," *Przedswit* (Krakow), nr. 7, Rok XXXI, styczen–czerwiec 1912, str. 64–74.

J. K. Plebanski, "Kronika miesieczna," *Biblioteka Warszawska,* t. 184 (1886); t. 187 (1887). Warszawa: Gebethner i Wolff.

St. Poraj, "O ruch ludowy w Krolestwie," *Krytyka* (Krakow), Rok XIV, Tom XXXIII, 1912, str. 265–273.

Dr. Bronislaw Potocki, "Kwestya ruska w Galicyi i projekt jej zalatwienia," *Krytyka* (Krakow), Rok X, Tom I, 1908, str. 129–139.

Poznanczyk, "Stosunki ekonomiczne w Poznanskiem," *Biblioteka Warszawska,* t. 241 (1901), str. 433–444. Warszawa: Gebethner i Wolff.

F. R., "Galicyjski apostol Zydow [Ignacy Daszynski]," *Niwa Polska* (Warszawa), 23 listopada (6 grudnia), 1902, Rok XXX, nr. 49, str. 770-771.

Michal Radziwill, "Kronika miesieczna," *Biblioteka Warszawska*, t. 223 (1896); t. 233 (1899); t. 241 (1901). Warszawa: Gebethner i Wolff.

Kazimierz Rakowski, "Poglad na ekonomiczne i spoleczne stosunki w Ksiestwie Poznanskiem," *Przeglad Polski* (Krakow), R. XXXV, Tom 137, 1900, str. 15-49.

_____, "Gospodarcze niedobory naszego kraju," *Biblioteka Warszawska*, t. 263 (1906), 125-164. Warszawa: Gebethner i Wolff.

_____, "Wychodztwo polskie w Niemczech," *Biblioteka Warszawska*, t. 248 (1902), 66-92 and 438-457. Warszawa: Gebethner i Wolff.

_____, "Wychodzcy Polscy w Niemczech" [IV Zjazd Prawnikow i Ekonomistow Polskich], *Czasopismo Prawnicze i Ekonomiczne* (Krakow, 1906), Tom VII, 20 stron.

Albert von Randow, "Die Landesverweisung aus Preussen und die Erhaltung des Deutschtums an der Ostgrenze," *Schmollers Jahrbuch für Gesetzgebung, Verwaltung und Volkswirtschaft im Deutschen Reiche*, X (1886). Berlin: Duncker und Humblot.

C. Reklewski, "O znaczeniu postanowionych reform agrarnych w Cesarstwie rosyjskiem i Krolestwie polskiem, II., Bank wloscianski," *Biblioteka Warszawska*, t. 187 (1888), 209-228. Warszawa: Gebethner i Wolff.

Al. Rembowski, "F. Bujaka 'Rozwoj wsi zachodnio-galicyjskiej'," *Biblioteka Warszawska*, t. 259 (1905), 182.

Jan Rozwadowski, "Znaczenie parcelacyi wiekszej wlasnosci dla Galicyi," *Przeglad sadowy i administracyjny* (Lwow), Rok XXVI, 1901, str. 511-529.

_____, "Znaczenie parcelacyi wiekszej wlasnosci," *Ekonomista* (Warszawa, 1901), Rok I, Tom I, str. 283-304.

Rt., "Adolf Dygasinski. Listy z Brazylii," *Przeglad Polski* (Krakow), R. XXV, Tom 100, 1891, str. 591-592.

Jan Rutkowski, "Licytacye sadowe posiadlosci wloscianskich i malomiejskich, zarzadzone w latach 1910-1912 z uwzglednieniem lat dawniejszych," *Wiadomosci statystyczne o stosunkach krajowych*, t. XXV, zesz. 1 (1914). Lwow: Wyd. Krajowe biuro statystyczne.

C. Rydlewski, "Walka ekonomiczna zywiolu polskiego pod rzadem pruskim," *Ekonomista* (Warszawa, 1904), Rok IV, Tom I, str. 3-8, 238-250.

Martin Schrag, "The Swiss-Volhynian Mennonite Background," *Mennonite Life*, Vol. IX, no. 4 (October, 1954), 156-161. North Newton, Kansas: Bethel College.

Jozef Siemiradzki, "La nouvelle Pologne, état de Parana-Brésil," *Universite nouvelle institut geographique de Bruxelles*, publication no. 1 (1899). Bruxelles: Impr. veuve Ferd. Larcier.

_____, "List z Ameryki," *Przewodnik naukowy i literacki* (styczen 1892), str. 65-83; (luty 1892), str. 174-183; (marzec 1892), str. 268-278; (kwiecien 1892), str. 362-371; (maj 1892), str. 468-475; (lipiec 1892), str. 646-659; (sierpien 1892), str. 738-746; (wrzesien 1892), str. 817-822; (pazdziernik 1892), str. 942-956; (listopad 1892), str. 1033-1042; (grudzien 1892), str. 1188-1202. Lwow: Wl. Lozinski.

_____, "Obrazki z Nowej Polski, I. W puszczy," *Przeglad powszechny* (kwiecien 1899), str. 38-61. Krakow: Wl. L. Anczyc i Sp.

_____, "Pod obcem niebem, szkice i obrazki," *Biblioteka nowa universalna*, rocznik XVIII, ser. 2 (styczen 1904), str. 1-32. Krakow: Spolka wydawnicza polska.

_____, "Stosunki osadnicze w Brazylii," *Biblioteka Warszawska,* t. 205 (1892), str. 104-126. Warszawa: Gebethner i Wolff.

_____, "W sprawie emigracyi wloscianskiej w Brazylii," *Biblioteka Warszawska,* t. 236 (1900), 127-154. Warszawa: Gebethner i Wolff.

_____, "Wychodztwo Polskie w Brazylii," *Przeglad Powszechny* (Krakow) kwiecien 1897, R. XIV, Tom LIV, nr. 160, str. 360-369.

_____, "Polacy w Paranie," *Przeglad Powszechny* (Krakow) sierpien 1897, Tom LV, nr. 164, str. 193-218.

Waclaw Sieroszewski, "Polacy w Rosji," *Biuletyn Polskiego Towarzystwa Emigracyjnego,* nr. 5 (maj 1910); nr. 7 (lipiec 1910); nr. 11 (listopad 1911); nr. 12 (grudzien 1911). Krakow: Polskie Towarzystwo Emigracyjne.

Simonenko, "Nombre et mouvement de la population des dix gouvernements du Royaume de Pologne pour les 27 années de 1867 à 1894," *Trudy Warszawskiego Komitetu Statystycznego,* t. XIII (1895/1896), 144-163. Warszawa: W. K. S., typografia i litografia warszawska.

Tadeusz Smarzewski, "Wiedza prawno-ekonomiczna na zjezdzie naukowym," *Biblioteka Warszawska,* t. 212 (1893), 319-333. Warszawa: Gebethner i Wolff.

Socius, "Straszak Ukrainski," *Krytyka* (Krakow), Rok XV, Tom XXXVII, 1913, str. 19-24.

Socyjalista, "Z galicyi," *Przedswit* (London), Serja II, Tom I, nr. 14, 3 pazdziernika 1891, str. 1-2.

K. Splawski, "Emigracya naszego ludu do Ameryki polnocnej i o wystepku z #45 ustawy wojskowej z r. 1889," *Przeglad sadowy i administracyjny* (Lwow) Rok XVI, grudzien 1891, str. 562-567.

Stanislaw Starzynski, "Pierwszy zjazd prawnikow i ekonomistow polskich w Krakowie," *Przewodnik naukowy i literacki* (Lwow, 1887), Rok XV, str. 953-959.

Wladyslaw Studnicki, "Emigracya," *Krytyka* (Krakow), Rok XIII, Tom XXIX, 1911, str. 70-80.

_____, "Problemat agrarny," *Biblioteka Warszawska,* t. 264 (1906), 1-27. Warszawa: Gebethner i Wolff.

_____, "Swiatlomira 'Ciemnota Galicyi'," *Biblioteka Warszawska,* t. 255 (1904), 179-186. Warszawa: Gebethner i Wolff.

Adolf Suligowski, "Pierwszy zjazd prawnikow i ekonomistow Polskich," *Ateneum* (Warszawa, 1887), Tom XLVIII, str. 298-312.

_____, "Drugi zjazd prawnikow i ekonomistow Polskich i jego znaczenie," *Ateneum* (Warszawa, 1889), Tom LVI, str. 344-355, 496-525.

Zosa Szajkowski, "How the Mass Emigration to America Began," *Jewish Social Studies,* Vol. IV, no. 4 (October, 1942), 291-310. New York: American Jewish Publications Society.

_____, "The Attitude of American Jews to East European Jewish Immigration, 1881-1893," *Publications American Jewish Historical Society,* Vol. 40, no. 3 (1951), 221-280.

Wojciech Szukiewicz, "Sprawa wychodztwa," *Biblioteka Warszawska,* t. 278 (1910), 97-130. Warszawa: Gebethner i Wolff.

_____, "Wychodztwo na Syberje," *Biuletyn Polskiego Towarzystwa Emigracyjnego* (1910). Krakow: Polskie Towarzystwo Emigracyjne.

_____, "Z zagadnien emigracyjnych," *Ekonomista* (Warszawa, 1910), Rok X, Tom II, str. 78–103.

Stefan Szulc, "Wartosc materialow statystycznych dotyczacych stanu ludnosci b. Krolestwa Polskiego," *Przyczynki do statystyki bylego Krolestwa Polskiego,* Vol. I (1920). Warszawa: Glowny Urzad Statystyczny.

Dr. A. Tomaszewski, "Ksiazka o emigracyi [Leopold Caro]," *Przeglad Powszechny* (Krakow), lipiec–wrzesien 1911, Tom CXI, str. 43–57, 229–245.

U., "Kronika galicyjska," *Biblioteka Warszawska,* t. 208 (1892); t. 209 (1893); t. 211 (1893); t. 218 (1895); t. 219 (1895); t. 221 (1896); t. 231 (1898). Warszawa: Gebethner i Wolff.

Wiktor Ungar, "Dwa glosy w sprawie emigracyjno–kolonialnej," *Przeglad Emigracyjny* (Lwow), R. III, nr. 15, 1 sierpnia 1894, str. 141–150.

W., "Emigracya do kopaln westfalskich," *Glos* (Warszawa), nr. 4, R. XVI, 13 (26) stycznia 1901, str. 49–50.

_____, "Hakatyzm i solidarnosc polsko-pruska," *Glos* (Warszawa), nr. 7, R. XVI, 3 (16) lutego 1901, str. 89–90.

_____, "Wychodztwo wiejski," *Glos* (Warszawa), nr. 12, R. XVI, 10(23)marca 1901, str. 165–166.

P. W., "Zydzi w Stanach Zjednoczonych," *Niwa Polska* (Warszawa), 6 (19) lipca 1902, Rok XXX, nr. 29, str. 454–455.

Jozef Warchalowski, "Nowa kolonizacya Brazylii," *Polski Przeglad Emigracyjny* (Lwow), R. I, nr. 1, 10 pazdz. 1907, str. 2–3.

Kazimierz Warchalowski, "Wychodztwo do Brazylii," *Ateneum* (kwiecien 1891), 27–45. Warszawa: J. Cotta.

_____, "Z historyi ostatniego bezrobocia," *Ateneum* (styczen 1893). Warszawa: J. Cotta.

A. Warski, "Z nedzy galicyjskiej," *Glos* (Warszawa), nr. 26, R. XVI, 16 (29) czerwca 1901, str. 389–390.

A. W. [Warski], "Tryumfy hakatyzmu i szlachty polskiej," *Glos* (Warszawa), nr. 38, R. XVII, 7 (20) wrzesnia 1902, str. 580–581.

Leon Wasilewski, "Zapomniani," *Krytyka* (Krakow), R. XIII, lipiec–sierpien 1911.

_____, "Ze stosunkow polsko-ruskich w Galicyi wschodniej, II," *Biblioteka Warszawska,* t. 283 (1911), 455–464. Warszawa: Gebethner i Wolff.

Bohdan Wasiutynski, "Ruch Wychodzczy z Krolestwa Polskiego," [IV Zjazd Prawnikow i Ekonomistow Polskich], *Czasopismo Prawnicze i Ekonomiczne,* (Krakow, 1906), Tom VII, 37 stron.

J. Wasowicz, "O Polskiej wyspie etnograficznej kolo Zytomierza," *Polski Przeglad Kartograficzny,* Tom II, nr. 15–16 (grudzien 1926), 186–191.

_____, "Z geografji osiedli wiejskich na Wolyniu," *Czasopismo Geograficzne,* Tom XII, zesz. 3–4 (1934), 284–293.

Alfred Weglinski, "Rok na wsi: kwiecien," *Glos* (Warszawa), R. XVI, nr. 18, 21 kwiecien (4 maja) 1901, str. 265–266.

Ignacy Weinfeld, "Ludnosc miejska Galicyi i jej sklad wyznaniowy, 1881–1910," *Wiadomosci statystyczne o stosunkach krajowych,* t. XXIV, zesz. II (1912). Lwow: Wyd. Krajowe biuro statystyczne.

J. Weyssenhoff, "Kronika miesieczna," *Biblioteka Warszawska,* t. 201 (1891); t. 202 (1891); t. 203 (1891); t. 206 (1892); t. 207 (1892); t. 208 (1892); t. 213 (1894). Warszawa: Gebethner i Wolff.

Ks. Wiktor Wiecki, "'Charitas' o emigracyi polskiej," *Przeglad Powszechny* (Krakow), sierpien 1900, Tom LXVII, nr. 200, str. 299-301.

Henryk Wielowieyski, "Emigracya ludu i program ochronny," *Przeglad Powszechny* (Krakow), styczen–marzec 1913, Tom CXVII, str. 175-188.

——, "Kolonizacja wewnetrzna i metody jej przeprowadzenia," *Przeglad Powszechny* (Krakow), marzec 1914, Tom CXXI, nr. 363, str. 305-315.

H. Wiercienski, "Proletaryat wiejski i zapowiedziane pozyczki dla wloscian," *Ateneum* (Warszawa, 1886), Tom XLIV, str. 193-200.

Wladyslaw Wislocki, editor, "Editorials," *Przewodnik Bibliograficzny,* V (1882), 71; VI (1883), 76; IX (1886), 34; (czerwiec 1890), 115; (listopad 1895), 206-207; (grudzien 1895), 231-232. Krakow: Gebethner i Sp.

Zd. Wl., "Wychodztwo do Rosyi," *Przeglad Wszechpolski* (Lwow), R. I, nr. 20, 1 listopad 1895, str. 309-311.

T. W-o., "Kwestya zydowska jako zagadnienie narodowe," *Przedswit* (London), nr. 5-6, Rok XXIV, maj–czerwiec 1904, str. 222-229.

Adam Woroniecki, "Polscy obiezysasi w Szwajcaryi," *Ruch chrzescijansko-spoleczny,* Rok IV (pazdziernik 1905). Poznan: Sw. Wojciecha.

Antoni Zabko-Potopowicz, "Wies polska w swietle polskich prac naukowych i publicystycznych z okresu po uwlaszczeniu wloscian," *Roczniki socjologii wsi,* t. II (1937), 67-151. Warszawa: Instytut Socjologii Wsi.

Witold Zalecki, "P. Szczepanowskiego 'Nedza Galicyi'," *Niwa* (1 maj 1888), 209-240. Warszawa: Drukarnia Wieku.

L. Zaleski, "Objasnienie w sprawie emigracyjnej," *Przeglad tygodniowy* (Warszawa), R. XXV, nr. 47, 10 (22) wrzesnia 1890, str. 558-559.

Maurycy Zamoyski, "Kronika miesieczna," *Biblioteka Warszawska,* t. 278 (1910); t. 281 (1911); t. 287 (1912); t. 293 (1914). Warszawa: Gebethner i Wolff.

Wladyslaw Zawadzki, "Kronika Lwowska," *Biblioteka Warszawska,* t. 152 (1878). Warszawa: Gebethner i Wolff.

R. Zm., "Wyznanie wlasnej bezsilnosci," *Niwa Polska* (Warszawa), 7 (20) grudnia 1902, Rok XXX, nr. 51, str. 801-802.

Florian Znaniecki, "Wychodztwo i polozenie ludnosci wiejskiej, zarobkujacej w Krolestwie Polskiem," *Wychodzca Polski* (Warszawa), zesz. 3, grudzien 1911, str. 9-16.

C. Autobiographies, Journals, Diaries, Memoirs and Correspondence

Ballhausen, Robert Lucius von, *Bismarck, Erinnerungen des Staatsministers Freiherrn Lucius von Ballhausen.* Stuttgart und Berlin: Cotta, 1920. 589 pp.

Chelmicki, Ks. Zygmunt, *O Paranie.* Warszawa: [n. n.] 1895.

——, *W Brazylii, notatki z podrozy.* 2 vols.; Warszawa: Wl. L. Anczyc i Sp., 1892.

Daszynski, Ignacy, *Pamietniki.* 2 vols. Krakow: Z. R. S. S. "Proletariat," 1925/26. 266; 346 pp.

Dunikowski, Emil Habdank, *Od Atlantyku poza gory Skaliste, szkice przyrodnicze z dwukrotnej podrozy do Ameryki polnocnej.* Lwow: Seyfarth i Czajkowski, 1893. 354 pp.

302   EMIGRATION IN POLISH THOUGHT

_____, *Wsrod Polonii Amerykanskiej.* Lwow: P. Starzyk, 1893. 171 pp.

Dygasinski, Adolf, *Listy z Brazylii specyalnego delegata Kuryera Warszaw-skiego.* Warszawa: S. Lewental, 1891. 201 pp.

_____, "Na zlamanie karku," *Pisma Wybrane,* Tom V. Warszawa: Ksiazka i Wiedza, 1950. 260 pp.

Dzieduszycki, Wojciech, *Listy ze wsi,* serja I [Odbitka z Gazety narodowej]. Lwow: Gubrynowicz i Schmidt, 1889. 440 pp.

Gerlach, Leopold von, *Denkwürdigkeiten aus dem Leben Leopold von Gerlach.* 2 vols.; Berlin: W. Hertz, 1891–1892.

Hempel, Antoni, *Polacy w Brazylii, przez ... czlonka wyprawy naukowej dra. Siemiradzkiego do Brazylii i Argentyny.* Lwow: Gubrynowicz i Schmidt, 1893. 178 pp.

Hohenlohe-Schillingsfürst, Prince Chlodwig, *Memoirs of Prince Chlodwig of Hohenlohe-Schillingsfürst.* 2 vols.; New York: The Macmillan Company, 1906.

Instytut Gospodarstwa Spolecznego, *Pamietniki Chlopow,* No. 1–51. War-szawa: Drukarnia Gospodarcza, 1935.

_____, *Pamietniki emigrantow. Ameryka poludniowa,* No. 1–27. Warszawa: Instytut Gospodarstwa Spolecznego, 1939. 488 pp.

_____, *Pamietniki emigrantow. Francja,* No. 1–37. Warszawa: Instytut Gospo-darstwa Spolecznego, 1939. 702 pp.

Jordan, Roman, *Argentyna jako teren dla polskiego wychodztwa. Sprawo-zdanie z podrozy informacyjnej.* Krakow: Polskie Towarzystwo Emi-gracyjne, 1912. 44 pp.

Klobukowski, Stanislaw, *Wspomnienia z podrozy do Brazylii, Argentynie, Paragwaja, Patagonia i Ziemi Ognistej.* Lwow: Gazeta handlowo-geo-graficzna, 1898. 192 pp.

_____, *Wycieczka do Parany.* Lwow: Gubrynowicz i Syn. 1909. 213 pp.

Kropotkin, Petr Aleksievich, *Memoirs of a Revolutionist.* Boston and New York: Houghton Mifflin Company, 1899. 502 pp.

Lansdell, Henry, *Through Siberia.* 2 vols.; London: S. Low, Marston, Searle and Rivington, 1882.

Milkowski, Zygmunt [T. T. Jez], *Opowiadanie z wendrowki po koloniach polskich w Ameryce Polnocnej.* Paris: Goniec Polski, 1901. 266 pp.

Pankiewicz, Michal, *Z Parany i o Paranie.* Warszawa: Gebethner i Wolff; Krakow: G. Gebethner i Sp., 1916. 79 pp.

Polskie Towarzystwo Emigracyjne. *Czwarty rok dzialalnosci Polskiego To-warzystwa Emigracyjnego w Krakowie, 1912.* Krakow: Polskie towarzystwo emigracyjne, 1913. 89 pp.

Popiel, Pawel, *Pamietniki.* 2 vols.; Krakow: Krakowska Spolka Wydawnicza, 1927.

Siemiradzki, Jozef, *Szlakiem wychodzcow. Wspomnienia podrozy do Bra-zylii* [Biblioteka dziel wyborowych, nr. 133 and 134]. Warszawa: A. T. Jezierski, 1900. 160 pp.

_____, *Za morze, szkice z wycieczki do Brazylii.* Lwow: Jakubowski i Zaduro-wicz, 1894. 100 pp.

_____, *Z Warszawy do rownika, wspomnienia z podrozy po Ameryce poludniowej, odbytej w latach 1882/83 ....* Warszawa: Ignacy Zawiszewski, 1885. 226 pp.

Waldersee, Alfred Grafen von, *Denkwürdigkeiten des General-Feldmar-*

schalls Alfred Grafen von Waldersee. 3 vols.; Stuttgart und Berlin: Deutsche Verlags-Anstalt, 1923-1925.

Whyte, William Athenry, *A Land Journal from Asia to Europe.* London: S. Low, Son, and Marston, 1871. 336 pp.

D. Government Publications, Parliamentary Deliberations, and Statistical Compilations

Austria. K. K. Handelsministerium. *Protokoll der im K. K. Handelsministerium durchgeführten Vernehmung von Auskunftpersonen über die Auswanderung aus Oesterreich.* Wien: K. K. Hof- und Staatsdruckerei, 1912.

Austria. Statistische Centralkommission. *Oesterreichische Statistik.* Wien: K. K. Hof- und Staatsdruckerei, 1884, V. Band, 3. Heft; 1913, N. F., 8. Band, 1. Heft; 1914, XCII. Band, 1. Heft.

Austria. Statistische Zentralkommission. *Oesterreichisches statistisches Handbuch.* Nebst einem Anhange für die gemeinsamen Angelegenheiten der osterr.-ungar. Monarchie. 1-32, 1882-1913. Wien: Holder, 1883-1915.

Austria. Statistische Zentralkommission. *Statistische Monatsschrift.* Wien: K. K. statistische Zentralkommission, Jhg. I, 1875- N. F., Jhg. XVIII, 1913.

Austria. Statistische Zentralkommission. *Statistische Übersichten über die Bevölkerung und den Viehstand von Oesterreich nach der Zahlung vom 31. Oct. 1857.* Wien: Holder, 1859.

Austria. Statistische Zentralkommission. *Statistisches Jahrbuch der oesterreichischen Monarchie fur das Jahr 1863, . . . 1864, . . . 1865, . . . 1866, . . . 1867, . . . 1868, . . . 1869, . . . 1870, . . . 1871.* Wien: Holder, 1864-1873.

Austria. Statistische Zentralkommission. *Tafeln zur Statistik der oesterreichischen Monarchie.* Wien: K. K. Hof- und Staatsdruckerei, 1861-1871.

Austria. Statistische Zentralkommission. *Übersichtstafeln zur Statistik der oesterreichischen Monarchie für die Jahre 1861 und 1862.* Wien: K. K. Hof- und Staatsdruckerei, 1863.

Galicia. Krajowe Biuro Statystyczne. *Wiadomosci statystyczne o stosunkach krajowych.* Lwow: I zwiazkowa drukarnia, R. I, 1876- R. XXV, 1914.

Galicia. Sejm. *Alegata do sprawozdan stenograficznych sejmu krajowego . . . .* Lwow: I zwiazkowa drukarnia, 1873-1914.

Galicia. Sejm. *Stenograficzne Sprawozdania sejmu krajowego Krolestwa Galicyi i Lodomeryi z Wielkiem Ksiestwem Krakowskiem . . . .* Lwow: I zwiazkowa drukarnia, 1869-1914.

Germany. Reichstag. *Stenographische Berichte über die Verhandlungen des Reichstages.* Berlin: W. Moeser Hofdruckerei, 1886-.

Germany. Statistische Landesamt. *Statistik des deutschen Reiches.* Berlin: Puttkammer und Mühlbrecht, Band XIV, 1876- Band CCXL, 1915.

Germany. Statistische Landesamt. *Vierteljahrshefte zur Statistik des deutschen Reichs.* Berlin: Puttkammer und Muhlbrecht, Jahrgang 1897, II Heft; 15. Jahrgang, 1906, IV. Heft; 20 Jahrgang, 1911, IV. Heft.

Poland. Glowny Urzad Statystyczny. *Rocznik statystyki Rzeczpospolitej Polskiej, 1926-1927.* Warszawa: Glowny Urzad Statystyczny, 1927. 320 pp.

Prussia. *Gesetz-Sammlung für die königlich preussischen Staaten, 1806 bis*

1886. Berlin: Carl Heymanns Verlag, 1887.

Prussia. *Gesetz-Sammlung für die königlichen preussischen Staaten, 1898.* Berlin: Gesetzsammlungsamt, 1899.

Prussia. *Gesetz-Sammlung für die königlichen preussischen Staaten, 1902.* Berlin: Gesetzsammlungsamt, 1903.

Prussia. *Gesetz-Sammlung für die königlichen preussischen Staaten, 1904.* Berlin: Gesetzsammlungsamt, 1905.

Prussia. Herrenhaus. *Stenographische Berichte über die Verhandlungen des Herrenhaus, Landtag.* Berlin: W. Moeser Hofdruckerei, 1883–.

Prussia. Königlichen statistischen Bureau. *Preussische Statistik.* Berlin: Königlichen statistischen Bureau, Band XVII, 1870– Band XLVIII, 1879.

Prussia. Königlichen statistischen Landesamt. *Zeitschrift des königlich preussischen statistischen Landesamts.* Berlin: Koeniglichen statistischen Landesamts, Jhg. IX, 1869; Jhg. XLVII, 1907.

Prussia. Landtag. *Stenographische Berichte über die Verhandlungen des Haus der Abgeordneten, Landtag.* Berlin: W. Moeser Hofdruckerei, 1883–.

Prussia. *Preussische Gesetzsammlung, 1908.* Berlin: Gesetzsammlungsamt, 1909.

Prussia. *Übersicht über die Geschäftstätigkeit des preussischen Hauses der Abgeordneten in der III. Session der 17. Legislaturperiode vom 12/XI/1890 bis zum 20/VI/1891.* Berlin: H. Moeser Hofdruckerei, 1891.

Prussia. *Verhandlungen des königlichen Landes- Ökonomie-Kollegiums.* Berlin: Unger, 1913.

United States. Bureau of the Mint. *The Monetary Systems of the Principal Countries of the World, 1913.* Washington, D.C.: Government Printing Office, 1913. 85 pp.

Warszawa. Warszawski Komitet Statystyczny. *Trudy Warszawskiego Komitetu Statystycznego.* Warszawa: W. K. S., typografia i litografia warszawska, t. XIII–XXXIX, 1895/1896–1910.

E. Pamphlets, Brochures and Emigration Handbooks

Dunikowski, Emil H., *Program wycieczki polskich turystow pod przewodnictwem ... do Chicago i w glab Ameryki.* Lwow: K. Tuszynski i Sp., 1893. 15 pp.

Ferreira Correia, Manoel F. and Serro Azul, *Opis stanu Parana w Brazylii wraz z informacyami dla wychodzcow* [dla wystawy kolumbijskiej w Chicago z polecenia Rzadu paranskiego]. Lwow: Polskie Tow. Handlowo-Geograficzne, 1896. 80 pp.

Kolonizacya polska zamorska, kilka slow o potrzebie organizacyi wychodztwa i skupienia polskiej ludnosci wychodzczej w brazylijskiem stanie Parana, Nowa Polska, wraz z mapa sytuacyjna kolonij rolniczych w poludniowych brazylijskich stanach, rzecz wydana staraniem Towarzystwa kolonizacyjno-handlowego we Lwowie. Lwow: Gazety handlowo geograficznej, Gubrynowicz i Schmidt, 1899. 41 pp.

Odezwa w sprawie wychodztwa polskiego do Danii. Poznan: Ksiegarnia Sw. Wojciecha, 1913. 16 pp.

Polish Emigration Land Company in Virginia. *By-Laws, Charter, Prospectus and "Odezwa."* Washington, D.C.: P. L. Schriftgiesser, 1870.

Appendix A
Prussian Poland

REGIERUNGSBEZIRK DANZIG

Year	Total Population as per Censuses[1]	Total Births[2]	Total Deaths[3]	Natural Increase	Actual Increase	Immigration or Emigration (-)
1816	237,980					
1817		12,724	6,819	5,905		
1818		13,007	7,059	5,948		
1819	265,582	13,250	8,388	4,862		
1817 to 1819		38,981	22,266	16,715	27,602	10,887
1820		13,895	7,779	6,116		
1821		14,774	8,094	6,680		
1822	294,803	14,473	8,766	5,707		

1820 to 1822	43,142	24,639	18,503		29,221	10,718
1823	14,312	7,682	6,630			
1824	14,381	8,107	6,274			
1825	15,052	8,564	6,488	317,066		
1823 to 1825	43,745	24,353	19,392		22,263	2,871
1826	15,158	8,843	6,315			
1827	12,652	10,165	2,487			
1828	13,594	11,068	2,526	329,938		
1826 to 1828	41,404	30,076	11,328		12,872	1,544

307

REGIERUNGSBEZIRK DANZIG

Year	Total Population as per Censuses	Total Births	Total Deaths	Natural Increase	Actual Increase	Immigration or Emigration (-)
1829		12,670	13,235	-565		
1830		12,123	13,308	-1,185		
1831	326,549	13,021	18,376	-5,355		
1829 to 1831		37,814	44,919	-7,105	-3,389	3,716
1832		12,236	12,500	-264		
1833		13,655	11,258	2,397		
1834	332,667	14,755	11,128	3,627		

Year						
1832 to 1834		40,646	34,886	5,760	6,118	358
1835		13,444	10,306	3,138		
1836		14,154	8,989	5,165		
1837	349,218	14,908	11,538	3,370		
1835 to 1837		42,506	30,833	11,673	16,551	4,878
1838		13,953	10,000	3,953		
1839		14,413	12,935	1,478		
1840	366,685	15,648	12,268	3,380		
1838 to 1840		44,014	35,203	8,811	17,467	8,656

309

REGIERUNGSBEZIRK DANZIG

Year	Total Population as per Censuses	Total Births	Total Deaths	Natural Increase	Actual Increase	Immigration or Emigration (-)
1841		15,437	11,117	4,320		
1842		16,311	10,308	6,003		
1843	387,306	16,770	11,198	5,572		
1841 to 1843		48,518	32,623	15,895	20,621	4,726
1844		16,960	10,016	6,944		
1845		17,346	11,886	5,460		
1846	405,805	17,262	15,175	2,087		

1844 to 1846	51,568	37,077	14,491	18,499	4,008
1847	16,055	12,777	3,278		
1848	15,552	17,565	-2,013		
1849	19,858	16,687	3,171		
	404,667				
1847 to 1849	51,465	47,029	4,436	-1,138	-5,574
1850	18,786	11,524	7,262		
1851	19,365	11,700	7,665		
1852	19,835	21,916	-2,081		
	423,928				
1850 to 1852	57,986	45,140	12,846	19,261	6,415

REGIERUNGSBEZIRK DANZIG

Year	Total Population as per Censuses	Total Births	Total Deaths	Natural Increase	Actual Increase	Immigration or Emigration (-)
1853		18,820	16,402	2,418		
1854		18,718	14,416	4,302		
1855	435,896	18,804	19,766	-962		
1853 to 1855		56,342	50,584	5,758	11,968	6,210
1856		17,562	14,420	3,152		
1857		19,498	16,270	3,228		
1858	453,626	20,813	15,161	5,652		

1856 to 1858	57,883	45,851	12,032	17,730	5,698	
1859	21,175	14,937	6,238			
1860	21,538	14,202	7,336			
1861	20,416	14,514	5,902			475,570
1859 to 1861	63,129	43,653	19,476	21,944	2,468	
1862	20,832	15,788	5,044			
1863	22,455	16,637	5,818			
1864	23,946	13,153	10,793			502,820
1862 to 1864	67,233	45,578	21,655	27,250	5,595	

313

REGIERUNGSBEZIRK DANZIG

Year	Total Population as per Censuses	Total Births	Total Deaths	Natural Increase	Actual Increase	Immigration or Emigration (-)
1865		23,177	17,650	5,527		
1866		23,180	19,213	3,967		
1867	515,222	22,568	16,195	6,373		
1865 to 1867		68,925	53,058	15,867	12,402	-3,465
12/1/1871	525,012[4]					
12/1/1867 to 12/1/1871		86,468[4]	66,294[4]	20,174[4]	9,790[4]	-10,384[4]
12/1/1875	542,316[5]					

Period					
12/1/1871 to 12/1/1875	95,749[5]		65,236[5]	30,513[5]	17,304[5]	-13,209[5]
12/1/1875 to 12/1/1880	125,300[6]	569,181[6]	85,634[6]	39,666[6]	26,865[6]	-12,801[6]
12/1/1880 to 12/1/1885	122,898[7]	578,770[7]	83,213[7]	39,685[7]	9,934[7]	-29,751[7]

REGIERUNGSBEZIRK DANZIG

Year	Total Population as per Censuses	Total Births	Total Deaths	Natural Increase	Actual Increase	Immigration or Emigration (-)
12/1/1890	589,176[8]					
12/1/1885 to 12/1/1890		126,048[8]	82,313[8]	43,735[8]	10,406[8]	-33,329[8]
12/2/1895	618,090[9]					
12/1/1890 to 12/2/1895		126,798[9]	78,801[9]	47,997[9]	28,914[9]	-19,083[9]
12/1/1900	665,992[10]					

12/2/1895 to 12/1/1900	137,093[10]	83,099[10]	53,994[10]	47,902[10]	-6,092[10]
12/1/1900 to 12/1/1905	709,312[11]				
12/1/1900 to 12/1/1905	143,283[11]	84,234[11]	59,049[11]	43,320[11]	-15,729[11]
12/1/1905 to 12/1/1910	742,619[12]				
12/1/1905 to 12/1/1910	141,290[12]	78,388[12]	62,902[12]	33,307[12]	-29,595[12]

317

REGIERUNGSBEZIRK OPPELN

Year	Total Population as per Censuses[1]	Total Births[2]	Total Deaths[3]	Natural Increase	Actual Increase	Immigration or Emigration (-)
1816	524,784					
1817		29,783	21,739	8,044		
1818		31,304	22,144	9,160		
1819	561,173	33,747	20,098	13,649		
1817 to 1819		94,834	63,981	30,853	36,389	5,536
1820		32,403	18,176	14,227		
1821		33,979	17,841	16,138		
1822	617,379	33,095	21,210	11,885		

Year						
1820 to 1822	99,477	57,227	42,250		56,206	13,956
1823	33,057	25,516	7,541			
1824	35,066	21,557	13,509			
1825	36,395	21,786	14,609	656,539		
1823 to 1825	104,518	68,859	35,659		39,160	3,501
1826	37,142	23,676	13,466			
1827	35,528	25,932	9,596			
1828	35,590	26,753	8,837	694,251		
1826 to 1828	108,260	76,361	31,899		37,712	5,813

319

REGIERUNGSBEZIRK OPPELN

Year	Total Population as per Censuses	Total Births	Total Deaths	Natural Increase	Actual Increase	Immigration or Emigration (-)
1829		35,309	26,873	8,436		
1830		36,265	24,945	11,320		
1831	730,044	34,096	27,351	6,745		
1829 to 1831		105,670	79,169	26,501	35,793	9,292
1832		34,374	28,341	6,033		
1833		38,195	30,560	7,635		
1834	757,986	38,152	29,927	8,225		

Year						
1832 to 1834	110,721		88,828	21,893	27,942	6,049
1835	35,153		27,550	7,602		
1836	36,461		28,508	7,953		
1837	39,247	807,393	29,207	10,040		
1835 to 1837	110,861		85,365	25,595	49,407	23,812
1838	38,140		27,187	10,953		
1839	40,626		31,310	9,316		
1840	41,198	906,010	26,780	14,418		
1838 to 1840	119,964		85,277	34,687	98,617	63,930

REGIERUNGSBEZIRK OPPELN

Year	Total Population as per Censuses	Total Births	Total Deaths	Natural Increase	Actual Increase	Immigration or Emigration (-)
1841		40,778	24,470	16,308		
1842		44,542	29,235	15,307		
1843	939,624	40,776	33,425	7,351		
1841 to 1843		126,096	87,130	38,966	33,614	-5,352
1844		43,845	27,981	15,864		
1845		44,194	30,074	14,120		
1846	987,318	42,871	30,321	12,550		

1844 to 1846		130,910	88,376	42,534	47,694	5,160
1847		38,567	44,526	-5,959		
1848		31,531	50,751	-19,220		
1849	965,912	48,379	33,819	14,560		
1847 to 1849		118,477	129,096	-10,619	-21,406	-10,787
1850		44,691	27,911	16,780		
1851		46,842	29,946	16,896		
1852	1,005,609	45,920	38,343	7,577		
1850 to 1852		137,453	96,200	41,253	39,697	-1,556

323

REGIERUNGSBEZIRK OPPELN

Year	Total Population as per Censuses	Total Births	Total Deaths	Natural Increase	Actual Increase	Immigration or Emigration (-)
1853		46,017	35,160	10,857		
1854		42,939	38,104	4,835		
1855	1,014,383	40,149	41,952	-1,803		
1853 to 1855		129,105	115,216	13,889	8,774	-5,115
1856		40,564	36,909	3,655		
1857		52,204	30,504	21,700		
1858	1,077,663	53,545	34,004	19,541		

Year						
1856 to 1858		146,313	101,417	44,896	63,280	18,384
1859		54,489	32,462	22,027		
1860		52,856	29,007	23,849		
1861	1,137,844	49,182	34,478	14,704		
1859 to 1861		156,527	95,947	60,580	60,181	-399
1862		51,777	29,900	21,877		
1863		55,891	36,328	19,563		
1864	1,192,384	55,443	36,700	18,743		
1862 to 1864		163,111	102,928	60,183	54,540	-5,643

325

REGIERUNGSBEZIRK OPPELN

Year	Total Population as per Censuses	Total Births	Total Deaths	Natural Increase	Actual Increase	Immigration or Emigration (-)
1865		56,480	35,672	20,808		
1866		56,917	40,866	16,051		
1867	1,237,969	55,106	39,983	15,123		
1865 to 1867		168,503	116,521	51,982	45,585	-6,397
12/1/1871	1,309,563[4]					
12/1/1867 to 12/1/1871		229,029[4]	145,652[4]	83,377[4]	68,243[4]	-15,134[4]

Date						
12/1/1875	1,376,362[5]					
12/1/1871 to 12/1/1875		247,167[5]	166,070[5]	81,097[5]	66,799[5]	-14,298[5]
12/1/1880	1,441,296[6]					
12/1/1875 to 12/1/1880		306,895[6]	201,834[6]	105,061[6]	64,934[6]	-40,127[6]
12/1/1885	1,497,595[7]					
12/1/1880 to 12/1/1885		313,342[7]	222,699[7]	90,643[7]	56,299[7]	-34,344[7]

327

REGIERUNGSBEZIRK OPPELN

Year	Total Population as per Censuses	Total Births	Total Deaths	Natural Increase	Actual Increase	Immigration or Emigration (-)
12/1/1890	1,577,731[8]					
12/1/1885 to 12/1/1890		343,178[8]	216,468[8]	126,710[8]	80,136[8]	-46,574[8]
12/2/1895	1,710,181[9]					
12/1/1890 to 12/2/1895		381,682[9]	230,305[9]	151,377[9]	132,450[9]	-18,927[9]

Period						
12/1/1900	1,868,146[10]					
12/2/1895 to 12/1/1900		415,433[10]	231,278[10]	184,155[10]	157,965[10]	-26,190[10]
12/1/1900 to 12/1/1905	2,035,601[11]	432,445[11]	240,838[11]	191,607[11]	167,455[11]	-24,152[11]
12/1/1905 to 12/1/1910	2,207,981[12]	439,635[12]	236,235[12]	203,400[12]	172,330[12]	-31,070[12]

REGIERUNGSBEZIRK POSEN

Year	Total Population as per Censuses[1]	Total Births[2]	Total Deaths[3]	Natural Increase	Actual Increase	Immigration or Emigration (-)
1816	575,341					
1817		29,775	18,565	11,210		
1818		30,238	17,884	12,354		
1819	604,612	30,759	16,705	14,054		
1817 to 1819		90,772	53,154	37,618	29,271	-8,347
1820		29,404	14,538	14,866		
1821		31,164	15,805	15,359		
1822	655,434	31,581	19,604	11,977		

1820 to 1822		92,149	49,947	42,202	50,822	8,620
1823		28,753	18,054	10,699		
1824		29,918	18,807	11,111		
1825	712,786	31,216	18,858	12,358		
1823 to 1825		89,887	55,719	34,168	57,352	23,184
1826		30,820	21,421	9,399		
1827		26,878	28,951	-2,073		
1828	730,862	25,150	31,801	-6,651		
1826 to 1828		82,848	82,173	675	18,076	17,401

REGIERUNGSBEZIRK POSEN

Year	Total Population as per Censuses	Total Births	Total Deaths	Natural Increase	Actual Increase	Immigration or Emigration (-)
1829		27,884	26,200	1,684		
1830		27,988	25,775	2,213		
1831	730,047	25,161	32,668	-7,507		
1829 to 1831		81,033	84,643	-3,610	-815	2,795
1832		25,296	28,657	-3,361		
1833		32,263	24,824	7,439		
1834	758,284	32,106	23,497	8,609		

1832 to 1834		89,665	76,978	12,687	28,237	15,550
1835		29,954	20,930	9,024		
1836		31,221	20,313	10,908		
1837	788,578	32,864	24,720	8,144		
1835 to 1837		94,039	65,963	28,076	30,294	2,218
1838		33,611	20,265	13,346		
1839		35,088	25,480	9,608		
1840	824,875	36,167	24,727	11,440		
1838 to 1840		104,866	70,472	34,394	36,297	1,903

333

REGIERUNGSBEZIRK POSEN

Year	Total Population as per Censuses	Total Births	Total Deaths	Natural Increase	Actual Increase	Immigration or Emigration (-)
1841		36,758	23,452	13,306		
1842		38,833	25,509	13,324		
1843	857,230	36,553	28,971	7,582		
1841 to 1843		112,144	77,932	34,212	32,355	-1,857
1844		39,644	24,826	14,818		
1845		42,417	24,266	18,151		
1846	900,430	40,447	26,824	13,623		

334

1844 to 1846		122,508	75,916	46,592	43,200	-3,392
1847		34,889	29,809	5,080		
1848		33,772	38,267	-4,495		
1849	897,339	42,024	36,466	5,558		
1847 to 1849		110,685	104,542	6,143	-3,091	-9,234
1850		41,412	28,618	12,794		
1851		39,290	27,309	11,981		
1852	906,743	40,018	52,290	-12,272		
1850 to 1852		120,720	108,217	12,503	9,404	-3,099

335

REGIERUNGSBEZIRK POSEN

Year	Total Population as per Censuses	Total Births	Total Deaths	Natural Increase	Actual Increase	Immigration or Emigration (-)
1853		38,421	32,665	5,756		
1854		38,410	33,252	5,158		
1855	909,551	33,342	37,889	-4,547		
1853 to 1855		110,173	103,806	6,367	2,808	-3,559
1856		31,677	35,985	-4,308		
1857		39,445	33,170	6,275		
1858	918,222	42,256	32,385	9,871		

1856 to 1858		113,378	101,540	11,838	8,671	-3,167
1859		41,358	25,964	15,394		
1860		39,146	23,012	16,134		
1861	963,441	39,019	27,057	11,962		
1859 to 1861		119,523	76,033	43,490	45,219	1,729
1862		41,318	26,994	14,324		
1863		42,950	29,051	13,899		
1864	978,268	44,023	27,556	16,467		
1862 to 1864		128,291	83,601	44,690	14,827	-29,863

337

REGIERUNGSBEZIRK POSEN

Year	Total Population as per Censuses	Total Births	Total Deaths	Natural Increase	Actual Increase	Immigration or Emigration (-)
1865		43,921	28,893	15,028		
1866		43,934	43,507	427		
1867	986,443	43,906	29,495	14,411		
1865 to 1867		131,761	101,895	29,866	8,175	-21,691
12/1/1871	1,017,194[4]					
12/1/1867 to 12/1/1871		177,681[4]	118,111[4]	59,570[4]	30,751[4]	-28,819[4]

Date						
12/1/1875	1,033,747[5]					
12/1/1871 to 12/1/1875		191,343[5]	127,695[5]	63,648[5]	16,553[5]	-47,095[5]
12/1/1880	1,095,873[6]					
12/1/1875 to 12/1/1880		242,308[6]	149,622[6]	92,686[6]	62,126[6]	-30,560[6]
12/1/1885	1,106,959[7]					
12/1/1880 to 12/1/1885		233,265[7]	154,352[7]	78,913[7]	11,086[7]	-67,827[7]

REGIERUNGSBEZIRK POSEN

Year	Total Population as per Censuses	Total Births	Total Deaths	Natural Increase	Actual Increase	Immigration or Emigration (-)
12/1/1890	1,126,591[8]					
12/1/1885 to 12/1/1890		240,902[8]	143,426[8]	97,476[8]	19,632[8]	-77,844[8]
12/2/1895	1,173,211[9]					
12/1/1890 to 12/2/1895		241,441[9]	136,047[9]	105,394[9]	46,620[9]	-58,774[9]
12/1/1900	1,198,252[10]					

12/2/1895 to 12/1/1900		252,817[10]	134,947[10]	117,870[10]	25,041[10]	-92,829[10]
12/1/1900 to 12/1/1905	1,262,672[11]	255,733[11]	135,381[11]	120,352[11]	64,420[11]	-55,932[11]
12/1/1905 to 12/1/1910	1,335,884[12]	252,935[12]	127,472[12]	125,463[12]	73,212[12]	-52,251[12]

341

REGIERUNGSBEZIRK BROMBERG

Year	Total Population as per Censuses[1]	Total Births[2]	Total Deaths[3]	Natural Increase	Actual Increase	Immigration or Emigration (-)
1816	244,835					
1817		14,802	8,323	6,479		
1818		16,162	8,374	7,788		
1819	279,360	15,879	7,863	8,016		
1817 to 1819		46,843	24,560	22,283	34,525	12,242
1820		15,845	7,694	8,151		
1821		16,836	8,238	5,598		
1822	303,372	16,470	10,492	5,978		

1820 to 1822		49,151	26,424	22,727	24,012	1,285
1823		15,587	8,612	6,975		
1824		16,490	9,162	7,328		
1825	327,144	16,821	10,793	6,028		
1823 to 1825		48,898	28,567	20,331	23,772	3,441
1826		17,055	12,336	4,719		
1827		14,026	14,864	-838		
1828	333,644	14,393	13,208	1,185		
1826 to 1828		45,474	40,408	5,066	6,500	1,434

343

REGIERUNGSBEZIRK BROMBERG

Year	Total Population as per Censuses	Total Births	Total Deaths	Natural Increase	Actual Increase	Immigration or Emigration (-)
1829		14,682	13,336	1,346		
1830		14,148	13,563	585		
1831	326,231	13,584	23,433	-9,849		
1829 to 1831		42,414	50,332	-7,918	-7,413	505
1832		12,524	15,436	-2,912		
1833		16,174	13,462	2,712		
1834	362,384	16,386	12,991	3,395		

1832 to 1834	45,084	41,889	3,195		36,153	32,958
1835	15,435	10,221	5,214			
1836	16,575	10,091	6,484			
1837	16,739	12,336	4,403	381,128		
1835 to 1837	48,749	32,648	16,101		18,744	2,643
1838	17,611	9,693	7,918			
1839	17,949	13,130	4,819			
1840	18,875	12,107	6,768	408,975		
1838 to 1840	54,435	34,930	19,505		27,847	8,342

345

REGIERUNGSBEZIRK BROMBERG

Year	Total Population as per Censuses	Total Births	Total Deaths	Natural Increase	Actual Increase	Immigration or Emigration (-)
1841		19,473	13,015	6,458		
1842		20,629	13,293	7,336		
1843	432,957	20,772	14,354	6,418		
1841 to 1843		60,874	40,662	20,212	23,982	3,770
1844		21,072	12,876	8,196		
1845		22,963	12,870	10,093		
1846	463,969	21,846	14,273	7,573		

1844 to 1846		65,881	40,019	25,862	31,012	5,150
1847		18,494	16,842	1,652		
1848		18,357	24,663	-6,306		
1849	454,675	22,759	25,058	-2,299		
1847 to 1849		59,610	66,563	-6,953	-9,294	-2,341
1850		23,278	14,894	8,384		
1851		22,375	14,173	8,202		
1852	475,002	23,571	21,083	2,488		
1850 to 1852		69,224	50,150	19,074	20,327	1,253

348

REGIERUNGSBEZIRK BROMBERG

Year	Total Population as per Censuses	Total Births	Total Deaths	Natural Increase	Actual Increase	Immigration or Emigration (-)
1853		22,113	16,852	5,261		
1854		21,585	15,164	6,421		
1855	483,085	21,783	22,101	-318		
1853 to 1855		65,481	54,117	11,364	8,083	-3,281
1856		20,810	15,908	4,902		
1857		22,941	17,222	5,719		
1858	498,933	23,333	16,808	6,525		

Year						
1856 to 1858		67,084	49,938	17,146	15,848	-1,298
1859		24,059	17,237	6,822		
1860		24,070	14,847	9,223		
1861	522,109	23,918	14,908	9,010		
1859 to 1861		72,047	46,992	25,055	23,176	-1,879
1862		23,743	16,457	7,286		
1863		26,221	16,387	9,834		
1864	545,461	25,897	16,391	9,506		
1862 to 1864		75,861	49,235	26,626	23,352	-3,274

349

REGIERUNGSBEZIRK BROMBERG

Year	Total Population as per Censuses	Total Births	Total Deaths	Natural Increase	Actual Increase	Immigration or Emigration (-)
1865		26,685	18,282	8,403		
1866		26,061	27,203	-1,142		
1867	550,895	25,120	17,632	7,488		
1865 to 1867		77,866	63,117	14,749	5,434	-9,315
12/1/1871	566,649[4]					
12/1/1867 to 12/1/1871		101,435[4]	67,101[4]	34,334[4]	15,754[4]	-18,580[4]

12/1/1875	572,337[5]				
12/1/1871 to 12/1/1875	108,236[5]	76,814[5]	31,422[5]	5,688[5]	-25,734[5]
12/1/1880	607,524[6]				
12/1/1875 to 12/1/1880	142,714[6]	87,535[6]	55,179[6]	35,187[6]	-19,992[6]
12/1/1885	608,659[7]				
12/1/1880 to 12/1/1885	136,969[7]	90,052[7]	46,917[7]	1,135[7]	-45,782[7]

REGIERUNGSBEZIRK BROMBERG

Year	Total Population as per Censuses	Total Births	Total Deaths	Natural Increase	Actual Increase	Immigration or Emigration (-)
12/1/1890	625,051[8]					
12/1/1885 to 12/1/1890		142,734[8]	84,915[8]	57,819[8]	16,392[8]	-41,427[8]
12/2/1895	655,447[9]					
12/1/1890 to 12/2/1895		141,708[9]	79,861[9]	61,847[9]	30,396[9]	-31,451[9]
12/1/1900	689,023[10]					

Period						
12/2/1895 to 12/1/1900	152,808[10]		84,137[10]	68,671[10]	33,601[10]	-35,070[10]
12/1/1900 to 12/1/1905		723,965[11]				
	153,553[11]		82,044[11]	71,509[11]	34,950[11]	-36,559[11]
12/1/1905 to 12/1/1910		763,947[12]				
	151,272[12]		75,860[12]	75,412[12]	39,982[12]	-35,430[12]

353

REGIERUNGSBEZIRK MARIENWERDER

Year	Total Population as per Censuses[1]	Total Births[2]	Total Deaths[3]	Natural Increase	Actual Increase	Immigration or Emigration (-)
1816	333,101					
1817		19,835	11,340	8,495		
1818		20,454	11,350	9,104		
1819	367,495	21,069	11,678	9,391		
1817 to 1819		61,358	34,368	26,990	34,394	7,404
1820		20,935	10,501	10,434		
1821		22,259	12,086	10,173		
1822	403,300	22,585	12,949	9,636		

1820 to 1822	65,779	35,536	30,243	35,805	5,562
1823	21,799	11,413	10,386		
1824	22,131	13,187	8,944		
1825	23,509	12,723	10,786	434,310	
1823 to 1825	67,439	37,323	30,116	31,010	894
1826	23,248	14,233	9,015		
1827	19,613	16,229	3,384		
1828	20,720	17,087	3,633	462,269	
1826 to 1828	63,581	47,549	16,032	27,959	11,927

355

REGIERUNGSBEZIRK MARIENWERDER

Year	Total Population as per Censuses	Total Births	Total Deaths	Natural Increase	Actual Increase	Immigration or Emigration (-)
1829		20,264	21,903	-1,639		
1830		19,045	19,981	-936		
1831	455,807	20,141	30,186	-10,045		
1829 to 1831		59,450	72,070	-12,620	-6,462	6,158
1832		19,059	20,142	-1,083		
1833		22,549	18,918	3,631		
1834	471,488	23,132	16,802	6,330		

Year						
1832 to 1834		64,740	55,862	8,878	15,681	6,803
1835		21,421	14,027	7,394		
1836		22,068	13,507	8,561		
1837	499,001	23,394	17,162	6,232		
1835 to 1837		66,883	44,696	22,187	27,513	5,326
1838		22,333	15,275	7,058		
1839		23,786	19,281	4,505		
1840	549,697	25,472	17,578	7,894		
1838 to 1840		71,591	52,134	19,457	50,696	31,239

357

REGIERUNGSBEZIRK MARIENWERDER

Year	Total Population as per Censuses	Total Births	Total Deaths	Natural Increase	Actual Increase	Immigration or Emigration (-)
1841		25,267	16,922	8,345		
1842		27,314	17,815	9,499		
1843	577,575	27,910	18,316	9,594		
1841 to 1843		80,491	53,053	27,438	27,878	440
1844		28,492	17,385	11,107		
1845		29,500	19,033	10,467		
1846	613,300	29,066	19,907	9,159		

Year						
1844 to 1846	87,058	56,325	30,733		35,725	4,992
1847	26,308	21,077	5,231			
1848	25,170	27,679	-2,509			
1849	31,914	25,046	6,868	621,046		
1847 to 1849	83,392	73,802	9,590		7,746	-1,844
1850	31,579	20,101	11,478			
1851	31,095	20,942	10,153			
1852	32,619	30,621	1,998	649,548		
1850 to 1852	95,293	71,664	23,629		28,502	4,873

359

REGIERUNGSBEZIRK MARIENWERDER

Year	Total Population as per Censuses	Total Births	Total Deaths	Natural Increase	Actual Increase	Immigration or Emigration (-)
1853		30,362	25,424	4,938		
1854		28,945	21,981	6,964		
1855	658,436	29,703	27,981	1,722		
1853 to 1855		89,010	75,386	13,624	8,888	-4,736
1856		28,281	21,473	6,808		
1857		31,740	23,994	7,746		
1858	682,032	32,518	24,289	8,229		

1856 to 1858	92,539	69,756	22,783		23,596	813
1859	33,370	22,135	11,235			
1860	32,736	21,245	11,491			
1861	32,829	20,868	11,961	712,831		
1859 to 1861	98,935	64,248	34,687		30,799	-3,888
1862	33,149	22,892	10,257			
1863	36,143	23,446	12,697			
1864	37,194	20,774	16,420	750,298		
1862 to 1864	106,486	67,112	39,374		37,467	-1,907

REGIERUNGSBEZIRK MARIENWERDER

Year	Total Population as per Censuses	Total Births	Total Deaths	Natural Increase	Actual Increase	Immigration or Emigration (-)
1865		36,811	24,072	12,739		
1866		35,784	30,804	4,980		
1867	767,620	35,146	23,761	11,385		
1865 to 1867		107,741	78,637	29,104	17,322	-11,782
12/1/1871	789,599[4]					
12/1/1867 to 12/1/1871		138,931[4]	96,356[4]	42,575[4]	21,979[4]	-20,596[4]

12/1/1875	800,434[5]				
12/1/1871 to 12/1/1875		150,027[5]	101,568[5]	48,459[5]	10,835[5]	-37,624[5]
12/1/1880	836,717[6]				
12/1/1875 to 12/1/1880		194,666[6]	125,145[6]	69,521[6]	35,976[6]	-33,545[6]
12/1/1885	829,459[7]				
12/1/1880 to 12/1/1885		189,540[7]	127,776[7]	61,764[7]	-7,603[7]	-69,367[7]

REGIERUNGSBEZIRK MARIENWERDER

Year	Total Population as per Censuses	Total Births	Total Deaths	Natural Increase	Actual Increase	Immigration or Emigration (-)
12/1/1890	844,505[8]					
12/1/1885 to 12/1/1890		193,620[8]	113,453[8]	80,167[8]	15,046[8]	-65,121[8]
12/2/1895	876,270[9]					
12/1/1890 to 12/2/1895		189,773[9]	109,488[9]	80,285[9]	31,765[9]	-48,520[9]

12/1/1900	897,666[10]					
12/2/1895 to 12/1/1900		195,118[10]	109,860[10]	85,258[10]	21,371[10]	-63,887[10]
12/1/1905	932,434[11]					
12/1/1900 to 12/1/1905		192,830[11]	106,494[11]	86,336[11]	34,760[11]	-51,576[11]
12/1/1910	960,855[12]					
12/1/1905 to 12/1/1910		185,704[12]	97,653[12]	88,051[12]	28,293[12]	-59,758[12]

NOTES

1. Total population, from census of 1816 to 1867, in *Preussische Statistik* (Berlin: 1879), Band XLVIII A, Anlagen, Tab. VI, 8–9.

2. Total births, from 1817 through 1867, in *Ibid.,* Tab. VIII, 11–12.

3. Total deaths, from 1817 through 1867, in *Ibid.,* Tab. XXII, 34–35.

4. *Vierteljahrshefte zur Statistik des deutschen Reiches, 1875,* in *Statistik des deutschen Reiches* (Berlin: 1876), Band XIV, Heft III, P. VI, 154. Population of 1,241,320 within new territorial boundaries of Oppeln District as of December 1, 1867 used in computations of excess of emigration in December 1, 1867/December 1, 1871 period.

5. *Monatshefte zur Statistik des deutschen Reiches fur das Jahr 1877,* Juli-Dez. Heft, in *Statistik des deutschen Reiches* (Berlin: 1877), Band XXV, 44–45.

6. *Statistik des deutschen Reiches* (Berlin: 1883), Band LVIII, 1, 16–17. Population of Marienwerder District in December 1, 1875, within boundaries existing in December 1, 1880, established at 800,741.

7. *Statistik des deutschen Reiches* (Berlin: 1888), N.F., Band 32, 1, 18–19. Population of Danzig District in December 1, 1880, within territorial boundaries during census of December 1, 1885, established at 568,836; that of Marienwerder, by same process, established at 837,062.

8. *Statistik des deutschen Reiches* (Berlin: 1894), N.F., Band 68, 18–19.

9. *Vierteljahrshefte zur Statistik des deutschen Reiches* (Berlin: 1897), Jahrgang 1897, II Heft, 166–167.

10. *Statistik des deutschen Reiches* (Berlin: 1903), N.F., Band 150, 2–3. Population of Marienwerder in December 2, 1895, within territorial boundaries extant in December 1, 1900, established at 876,295; that of Bromberg in December 2, 1895, by same process, established at 655,422.

11. *Vierteljahrshefte zur Statistik des deutschen Reiches* (Berlin: 1906), 15. Jahrgang, 1906, IV. Heft, 298–299. Population of Marienwerder in December 1, 1900, within boundaries extant in December 1, 1905, established at 897,674; that of Bromberg in December 1, 1900, by same process, established at 689,015.

12. *Ibid.* (Berlin: 1911), 20. Jahrgang, 1911, IV. Heft, 150–151. Population of Marienwerder in December 1, 1905, within boundaries extant in December 1, 1910, established at 932,562; that of Oppeln District in December 1, 1905, by same process, established at 2,035,651.

The above figures do not always correspond to those of Heinz Rogmann in his *Die Bevölkerungsentwicklung in preussischen Osten* (Berlin: 1937), 232–233. Though the different final totals between Rogmann's and the above are not sufficient to change the pattern of the general trend toward development of emigration, as indicated by that author, it is felt that they nevertheless should be explained. Thus, Rogmann's figure of -3,279 for the 1862/1864 period in Reg. Bromberg appears to be a typographical error. The excess of emigration figures for Regs. Posen and Oppeln in the 1865/1867 period are more difficult to explain. In the case of the former, he reaches his total emigration figure of -23,257 by accepting Boeckh's data for total deaths at 27,929 in 1867 *(Zeitschrift des königlich preussischen statistischen Bureaus* (Berlin: 1869) 9. Jahrgang, 1869, 215), as against those in *Preussische Statistik* (Berlin: 1879), Band XLVIII A, Anlagen, Tab. XXII, 35. Since Boeckh's figure for total deaths does not correspond with the figure given in both *Preussische Statistik* (Berlin: 1879), Band XLVIII A, Anlagen, Tab. XXII, 35 as well as in *Preussische Statistik* (Berlin: 1870), Band XVII, 284, and since the latter two publications both agree on 29,495 as total deaths in Reg. Posen in 1867, this latter figure was accepted in the computation of excess of emigration for that period (1865/1867).

The difference in the above table for excess of emigration from Oppeln District in 1865/1867 stems from Rogmann's acceptance of the above cited Boeckh's census figure for 1867 of 1,241,320 as against 1,237,969 given in *Preussische Statistik* (Berlin: 1879), Band XLVIII A, Anlagen, Tab. VI, p. 9. This error is a result of acceptance of population census for that year in newly established territorial boundaries and not the more accurate one of total population in 1867 within boundaries of 1864 census. (Sometime in the latter part of the 1865/1867 period, an area totalling 3,351 population in 1867 was detached from Liegnitz District and added to Oppeln District.) Hence, Rogmann's (and Boeckh's) error leads him to compute total emigration from Oppeln District in 1865/1867 period as -3,046 and not -6,397 as in the above table.

Rogmann's error in total emigration from Marienwerder District in the 1865/1867 period is the result of his acceptance of Boeckh's erroneous summation of total deaths for the 1865/1867 period (*Zeitschrift des königlich preussischen statistischen Bureaus* (Berlin: 1869), 9. Jahrgang, 1869, 214–215), which leads to his (Rogmann's) erroneous conclusion of an excess of emigration of -16,781 rather than -11,782 during that period.

POPULATION BORN IN THE EASTERN MARCHES LIVING IN STADTKREIS BERLIN, BRANDENBURG, WESTPHALIA AND RHINELAND

PLACE OF BIRTH

PLACE OF RESIDENCE	YEAR	East Prussia	West Prussia	Posen	Silesia
Stadtkreis Berlin	1871	32,095	(1)	29,217	64,946
	1880	30,991	31,628	47,967	85,044
	1890	71,342	57,882	76,876	123,514
	1900	91,898	72,612	95,366	137,961
	1907	98,205	80,359	103,793	142,215
Brandenburg	1871	12,491	(1)	21,617	43,666
	1880	12,011	11,574	32,005	54,014
	1890	34,122	26,611	55,181	78,329
	1900	60,334	48,997	85,484	115,815
	1907	83,411	76,298	119,037	155,135

Westphalia				
1871	1,630	(1)	1,007	4,499
1880	6,271	5,405	4,225	10,205
1890	36,624	14,569	13,875	21,599
1900	102,244	33,832	57,347	43,086
1907	114,871	43,551	83,873	50,710
Rhineland				
1871	3,699	(1)	1,535	6,561
1880	10,251	4,450	3,244	10,268
1890	28,551	9,717	7,562	16,460
1900	64,489	22,248	28,269	29,505
1907	73,428	35,736	46,915	42,931

1. Included in East Prussia.

Sources: *Zeitschrift des königlichen preussische statistischen Landesamts* (Berlin: 1907), XLVII, 38–39 and *Statistik des deutschen Reiches* (Berlin: 1910), Bd. 210, 1, Abt. IX, Teil I, 68ff. For more detailed compilation on all the provinces of the German Reich see Heinz Rogmann, *Die Bevölkerungsentwicklung im preussischen Osten* (Berlin: 1937), tab. 27, 244–247.

369

Appendix B
Russian Poland

RUSSIAN POLAND

Year	Total Population on Jan. 1 [13]	Births	Deaths	Natural Increase	Actual Increase	Immigration or Emigration (–)
1868	5,705,607[1]	243,782[1]	158,690[1]	85,092[1]		
1869	5,800,438	247,402	161,509	85,893	94,831	8,938
1870	5,903,391	272,965	166,427	106,538	102,953	–3,585
1871	6,087,866	266,629	151,481	115,148	184,475	69,327
1867 to 1870		786,996	479,417	307,579	382,259	74,680
1872	6,193,712	258,929	186,865	72,064	105,846	33,782
1873	6,337,316	273,074	239,573	33,501	143,604	110,103
1874	6,398,731	277,369	185,222	92,147	61,415	–30,732
1875	6,515,153	268,264	168,879	99,385	116,422	17,037
1876	6,639,846	273,620	159,954	113,666	124,693	11,027
1877	6,771,574	268,554	165,738	102,816	131,728	28,912
1878	6,860,127	266,495	184,715	81,780	88,553	6,773

Year						
1879	6,977,897	283,253	181,622	101,631	117,770	16,139
1880	7,104,864	279,255	185,278	93,977	126,967	32,990
1881	7,232,292	276,548	194,342	82,206	127,428	45,222
1871 to 1880		2,725,361	1,852,188	873,173	1,144,426	271,253
1882	7,328,731	290,287	206,062	84,225	96,439	12,214
1883	7,422,325	290,769	185,709	105,060	93,594	-11,466
1884	7,545,142	292,307	183,916	108,391	122,817	14,426
1885	7,687,893	307,298	205,306	101,992	142,751	40,759
1886	7,851,700	314,242	194,773	119,469	163,807	44,338
1887	7,990,752	325,562	199,514	126,048	139,052	13,004
1888	8,166,708	334,587	204,031	130,556	175,956	45,400
1889	8,124,878	352,405	220,721	131,684	-41,830	-173,514
1890	8,256,562	349,807	217,509	132,298	131,684	-614
1891	8,440,698	357,961	207,775	150,186	184,136	33,950
1881 to 1890		3,215,225	2,025,316	1,189,909	1,208,406	18,497

RUSSIAN POLAND

Year	Total Population on Jan. 1 [13]	Births	Deaths	Natural Increase	Actual Increase	Immigration or Emigration (-)
1892	8,624,834	349,382[2]	246,099[2]	103,283[2]		
1893	8,808,969	375,660	233,358	142,302		
1894		396,652	247,523	149,129		
1895		406,697	229,554	177,143		
1896		403,091	224,453	178,638		
1897		403,563	228,189	175,374		
1898		407,170	235,102	172,068		
1899		418,605	246,001	172,604		
1900		431,031	241,684	189,347		
1901		431,005	250,227	180,778		
1902		447,117	246,509	200,608		

Year						
1903		436,714	252,371	184,343		
1904		436,510	264,205	172,305		
1905	11,312,275	422,023	261,055	160,968		
1891 to 1904		5,765,220	3,406,330	2,358,890	2,871,577	512,687
1906	11,370,444	430,938	248,275	182,663	58,169	-124,494
1907	11,505,112	435,820	244,170	191,650	134,668	-56,982
1908	11,687,853	438,248	245,421	192,827	182,741	-10,086
1909	11,935,318	452,081	253,693	198,388	247,465	49,077
1910	12,204,446	443,118	246,445	196,673	269,128	72,455
1911	12,463,830	439,040	244,734	194,306	259,384	65,078
1912	12,782,347	442,008	236,242	205,766	318,517	112,751
1905 to 1911		3,081,253	1,718,980	1,362,273	1,470,072	107,799

NOTES

1. Simonenko, "Nombre et mouvement de la population des dix gouverne-ments du Royaume de Pologne pour les 27 années de 1867 à 1894," *Trudy Warszawskiego Komitetu Statystycznego* (Warszawa: 1895/1896), t. XIII, 144–163. The annual population schedules, without the data on births and deaths, are also available for the 1868–1890 period in Wladyslaw Grabski, *Rocznik Statystyczny Krolestwa Polskiego, Rok 1914* (Warszawa: 1915), 15, and correspond with the above in all cases except for the year 1889. Grabski's figure of 8,124,868, checked against the data available for the ten districts and the city of Warsaw, in Simonenko, *loc. cit.,* appears to be a typographical error. Jozef Buzek, apparently using the same annual population schedules for the periods 1871–1880 and 1881–1890 arrived at the same actual increases as those above. There are, however, differences between the births, deaths, natural increases and, therefore, immigration totals for the two periods in question (2,715,440 births, 1,809,330 deaths, 906,110 natural increase and 238,316 immigration for 1871–1880; 3,133,810 births, 2,011,880 deaths, 1,121,930 natural increase and 86,476 immigration for 1881–1890). Since the author did not include either the annual figures from which the natural increases had been computed or cite their source, it is impossible to explain this considerable disparity. See his, *Poglad na wzrost ludnosci ziem polskich w wieku 19-tym* (Krakow: 1915), 11, 26. The remaining population schedules, from 1892 until 1913 are from: Stefan Szulc, "Wartosc materialow statystycz-nych dotyczacych stanu ludnosci b. Krolestwa Polskiego," *Przyczynki do statystyki bylego Krolestwa Polskiego* (Warszawa: 1920), Vol. I, table XIV, 212.

2. Benedykt Bornstein, "Analiza krytyczna danych statystycznych, do-tyczacych ruchu naturalnego ludnosci b. Krolestwa Polskiego," *Przyczynki do statystyki bylego Krolestwa Polskiego* (Warszawa: 1920), Vol. III, 25.

Because of the questionable credibility of the statistical data on the natural movements of population in Russian Poland in the years preceding the first World War, the above figures are advanced with considerable reservations and only because they are the only ones to be had for that period. All are based on civil registers maintained by local civil officials who were required by law to make periodic reports to the next higher administrative authorities until they ultimately reached the provincial level. The data received at the provincial level were summarized and forwarded to St. Petersburg by the provincial governors as annexes to their annual reports to the Emperor. *(Obzor . . . gubernii za . . . god. Prilozenije k wsiepoddanjejszemu otczotu.)* These statis-tics, begun in 1867 in Russian Poland, were regarded as "classified" informa-tion by the authorities until 1896 when they were published by the Warsaw Statistical Committee in its publication *Prace Warszawskiego Komitetu Statystycznego (Trudy Warszawskago Statisticzeskago Komiteta)*, T. XIII.

Other sources of statistical information on the natural movements of population during varying parts of this period are the *Annual Reports*... of the Central Statistical Committee in Petersburg, the *Reports on the State of the Public Health (Sprawozdania o stanie zdrowotnosci publicznej)* published by the Public Health Inspector in St. Petersburg and finally, the *Prace*... *(Trudy)* of the Warsaw Statistical Committee (established in 1889).

The *Reports*... of the Public Health Inspectorate are quite obviously based on the *Reviews*... *(Przeglady*..., *Obzory*...*)* submitted by the provincial governors. What makes them less creditable than the *Reviews*... on which they are based is the considerable evidence that frequently they included data for former years in their latter listings. At other times they were extremely careless in their calculations of data drawn from the *Reviews*. ...

The *Annual Reports*... of the Central Statistical Committee issued several publications prior to 1897 and up to 1904 published annually data based on tax schedules, police information and some local registers — all of questionable value. Other information was drawn from the *Reviews*... *(Obzory*...*)* of the provincial governors. Up to approximately 1890 the local civil registers, on which the *Obzory*... were based, were concerned only with the "legal" population of the local administrative units. Therefore, people born elsewhere but residing in that community were not included while those born in that community but long since removed elsewhere in Russian Poland — or even abroad — were most frequently included in the registers. As a result of this practice, communities which had some immigration were very likely to have listed population in their registers that was much smaller than the actual, resident population. The contrary was the case in communities with an excess of emigration. There the emigrants, long since departed — and possibly deceased — were still carried on the civil registers of their native communities.

After approximately 1890 there was a greater effort, at the instigation of the Warsaw Statistical Committee, to revise local registers to include legal population present, legal population absent and resident population born elsewhere. Unfortunately, shortly thereafter several provinces ceased their statistical operations and thereby destroyed the continuity of the data on natural movements of the population for the whole of Russian Poland. The Warsaw Statistical Committee partially filled the lacuna caused by cessation of certain provincial statistical reports. It collected and published population data for 1890, 1893 and from 1905 annually until 1913. These last, though still imperfect, are much more creditable than all previous information. Based as they were on the local civil registers — as were the *Obzory*... — they also inherited many of the latter's shortcomings, but by diligent effort they frequently were able to correct some of the more flagrant errors forwarded by keepers of local civil registers. Nevertheless, critical researchers in this area of study conclude that by 1913, because of the crescive growth of error — especially by including on the registers legal population no longer living in a given community — the total population of Russian Poland, as compiled from the civil registers, was approximately a million in excess of the actual population living in that area at that time. This probably explains the apparent paradox of Russian Poland, on the basis of the statistical data available, appearing to be an area of immigration while the large volume of emigration to the westward, apparent to contemporary observers, indicating it to be an area of emigration. Competent statisticians have remained divided upon interpretation of the available statistical data insofar as they pertain to emigration or immigration. Thus, Grabski maintained that Russian Poland, in contradistinction to the other sectors of prewar Poland, was an area wherein the actual increase of population exceeded the natural increase (with the exception of the years 1888–1889 and 1904–1905) and hence was predominantly a country of immigration. Szulc, however, argued that since at least 1893 Russian Poland was an area in which emigration predominated. The one based his stand on the evidence of questionable statistical data, the other made his case partly by establishing the questionable credibility of the statistics and partly on the basis of "the fact [of emigration] well known to all." Neither proved his case conclusively largely because of the unavailability of incontrovertible data and the inability to correct available statistics. Grabski, by the uncritical acceptance of data of questionable validity, appears to have over-simplified his case for Russian Poland as a country of immigration. Szulc, on his part, seems to have refused even to consider the total effect of the large volume of immigration into Russian Poland, especially from adjacent Russian territories — a volume of sufficient size to counterbalance the volume of emigration from the Kingdom. Szulc, *op. cit., passim* and Grabski, *op. cit., passim.* See also, Edward Grabowski, *Wplyw wedrowek na skupienie sie ludnosci w Krolestwie Kongresowem, 1816–1913* [Praca referowana na posiedzeniu Wydz. hist.-filoz. Akademii Umiejetnosci w Krakowie, 22/XI/ 1915] (Warszawa: 1916), 102, representing the immigration thesis and Stefan L. Zaleski, "General Demography of Poland," *Polish Encyclopaedia* (Geneva: 1925), Vol. II, No. 2, fn. 1, 151, representing the emigration thesis. For a more detailed critical analysis of the statistical data on the natural movements of population in the Kingdom, see Bornstein, *op. cit.*

Appendix C
Austrian Poland

AUSTRIAN POLAND

Year	Civil Population as per Censuses	Births	Deaths	Natural Increase	Actual Increase	Immigration or Emigration (-)
Oct. 31, 1857	4,597,470[1]	18,565[2]	22,824[2]	-4,259		
1858		217,502[3]	141,657[3]	75,845		
1859		228,018[3]	152,236[3]	75,782		
1860		222,511[4]	148,962[4]	73,549		
1861		208,390[4]	161,998[4]	46,392		
1862		222,972[5]	166,165[5]	56,807		
1863		240,755[6]	175,305[6]	65,450		
1864		255,871[7]	158,365[7]	97,506		
1865		211,860[8]	176,913[8]	44,947		
1866		216,554[9]	218,446[9]	-1,892		
1867		228,700[10]	166,707[10]	61,993		
1868		229,170[11]	164,954[11]	64,216		
Dec. 31, 1869	5,418,016[12]	254,055[12]	174,792[12]	79,263		

Oct. 31, 1857 to Dec. 31, 1869		2,764,923	2,029,324	735,599	820,546	84,947
1870	5,491,675	252,800[13]	178,962[13]	73,838		
1871	5,546,330	242,726[14]	187,891[15]	54,835[16]		
1872	5,576,786	242,386	211,750	30,636		
1873	5,512,613	245,027	309,019	-63,992		
1874	5,552,204	247,391	207,619	39,772		
1875	5,615,146	260,593	197,469	63,124		
1876	5,679,331	256,748	192,380	64,368		
1877	5,743,861	256,938	192,226	64,712		
1878	5,807,844	259,146	194,980	64,166		
1879	5,881,277	271,632	198,016	73,616		
Dec. 31, 1880	5,926,172[17]	251,305	206,227	45,078		
Dec. 31, 1869 to Dec. 31, 1880		2,786,692	2,276,539	510,153	508,156	-1,997

AUSTRIAN POLAND

Year	Civil Population as per Censuses	Births	Deaths	Natural Increase	Actual Increase	Immigration or Emigration (-)
1881	5,964,689	256,370	209,651	46,719		
1882	6,017,892	278,415	217,011	61,404		
1883	6,071,385	269,004	207,309	61,695		
1884	6,136,739	269,988	196,432	73,556		
1885	6,179,596	261,030	210,000	51,030		
1886	6,245,564	273,976	199,720	74,256		
1887	6,314,678	286,699	209,384	77,315		
1888	6,391,738	287,991	202,738	85,253		
1889	6,484,471	293,072	192,096	100,976		
Dec. 31, 1890	6,554,415[18]	286,618	208,492	78,126		

Dec. 31, 1880 to Dec. 31, 1890		2,763,163	2,052,833	710,330	628,243	-82,087
1891	6,616,815	303,519	208,942	94,577		
1892	6,651,187	276,133	209,604	66,529		
1893	6,731,045	307,384	195,407	111,977		
1894	6,772,180	289,672	216,461	73,211		
1895	6,884,539	310,792	219,397	91,395		
1896	6,964,562	314,763	202,751	112,012		
1897	7,047,275	312,703	198,337	114,366		
1898	7,116,113	297,478	196,733	100,745		
1899	7,207,610	324,125	200,759	123,366		
Dec. 31, 1900	7,245,074[19]	324,168	201,520	122,648		
Dec. 31, 1890 to Dec. 31, 1900		3,060,737	2,049,911	1,010,826	690,659	-320,167

AUSTRIAN POLAND

Year	Civil Population as per Censuses	Births	Deaths	Natural Increase	Actual Increase	Immigration or Emigration (-)
1901	7,401,332	322,340	187,354	134,986		
1902	7,469,006	327,199	210,272	116,927		
1903	7,537,840	315,469	197,719	117,750		
1904	7,610,122	323,027	202,164	120,863		
1905	7,660,219	312,129	213,783	98,346		
1906	7,740,964	329,133	200,470	128,663		
1907	7,818,169	321,412	196,617	124,795		
1908	7,896,764	317,399	191,539	125,860		
1909	7,962,701	317,319	204,441	112,878		
Dec. 31, 1910	7,962,426[20]	310,553	193,342	117,211		
Dec. 31, 1900 to Dec. 31, 1910		3,195,980	1,997,701	1,198,279	717,352	-480,927
1911	8,019,180[20]	309,193[20]	197,897[20]	111,296[20]		-54,542[20]
1912	8,097,534[21]	316,859[21]	184,366[21]	132,493[21]		-54,139[21]
1913	8,148,570[22]	295,170[23]	190,393[24]	104,777[22]		-53,741[22]

NOTES

1. The total civil population present *(der ganzen anwesenden Bevölkerung)* in October 31, 1857. This includes resident foreigners and excludes military personnel. *Statistische Übersichten über die Bevölkerung und den Viehstand von Oesterreich nach der Zahlung vom 31 Oct. 1857* (Wien: 1859), 5.

2. Live births and deaths for November and December, 1857. *Tafeln zur Statistik der oesterreichischen Monarchie* (Wien: 1861), N.F., III. Band, 84, 97.

3. *Ibid.* (Wien: 1862), N.F., V. Band, 1. Heft, 55.

4. *Uebersichtstafeln zur Statistik der oesterreichischen Monarchie für die Jahre 1861 und 1862* (Wien: 1863), 8, 23, 34, 49.

5. *Statistisches Jahrbuch der oesterreichischen Monarchie für das Jahr 1863* (Wien: 1864), 18, 33.

6. *Ibid.,* 1864 (Wien: 1865), 18, 33.

7. *Ibid.,* 1865 (Wien: 1867), 18, 33.

8. *Ibid.,* 1866 (Wien: 1868), 18, 33.

9. *Ibid.,* 1867 (Wien: 1869), 20, 35.

10. *Ibid.,* 1868 (Wien: 1870), 20, 35.

11. *Ibid.,* 1869 (Wien: 1871), 24, 39.

12. *Ibid.,* 1870 (Wien: 1872), 15, 26, 43.

13. *Ibid.,* 1871 (Wien: 1873), 24, 41, 43.

14. Live births per annum from 1871 through 1910 in *Oesterreichische Statistik* (Wien: 1913), N.F., 8. Band, 1. Heft, 15*.

15. Deaths per annum from 1871 through 1910 in *Ibid.,* 17*.

16. Natural increases, per annum, from 1871 through 1910 in *Ibid.,* 20*.

17. *Ibid.,* 112–113.

18. *Ibid.*

19. *Oesterreichisches statistisches Handbuch* (Wien: 1903), 21.

20. *Oesterreichische Statistik* (Wien: 1913), N.F., 8. Band, 1. Heft, 33*. The figures for excess of emigration in 1911, 1912 and 1913 are estimates arrived at by means of coefficient of emigration established on the basis of data for the previous decade. Thus, the coefficient of emigration for Galicia is established by the formula

$$W = \sqrt[10]{\frac{B_{10} - (L - G)}{B_{00}}},$$

in which W is the coefficient of emigration, B_{00} the civilian population in the 1900 census, B_{10} the civil population in the 1910 census, L the total live births

during the decade and G the total deaths during the decade. For further details
see *Oesterreichische Statistik* (Wien: 1913), N.F., 8. Band, 1. Heft, 30*-31*
and *Ibid.* (Wien: 1914), XCII. Band, 1. Heft, XXXII-XXXIII.

21. *Ibid.,* N.F., 8. Band, 3. Heft, 42*.
22. *Ibid.,* N.F., 14. Band, 1. Heft, 16*
23. *Ibid.,* 32*, 274.
24. *Ibid.,* 53*, 274.

A number of writers had occupied themselves with the subject of population
movements and emigration from Galicia in the several decades preceding the
outbreak of the first World War. Of these, a number compiled tables of
immigration or emigration based on the differences between natural and
actual increases between census years. The more scholarly availed themselves
of whatever primary statistical data was accessible to them. Others contented
themselves with acceptance of findings of the former. Unfortunately, a certain
amount of error found its way into the computations of the more reliable
authorities which was perpetuated by those who accepted them uncritically.
The following is an attempt to appraise critically the various statistical
conclusions reached by these researchers.

Perhaps the most diligent and widely accepted authority in this area of
research was Jozef Buzek. His *Poglad na wzrost ludnosci ziem polskich w
wieku 19-tym* (Krakow: 1915), has been frequently regarded as the most
comprehensive work on population movements in the three sectors of pre-
World War I Poland. The frequency with which it is cited by other writers
touching on the subject of population growths and movements is testimony of
the recognition accorded to his authority in that province of research.

The differences between the above table and the several compiled by Buzek
largely devolve upon the census figures accepted in computation of actual
population increases in inter-census periods. If the total population at each
census is accepted, the differences at times are considerable. This writer has
preferred to base his computations exclusively and, of course, consistently on
schedules of civil population. This was done both for purposes of convenience
(the 1857 census does not enumerate the military personnel present in Galicia
at that time nor do the available data on the annual natural increases include
military personnel) and because it was felt that periodic shifts in military
personnel stationed in Galicia during the period under consideration do not
validly fall into the purview of a study of population movements and,
especially, immigration or emigration.

Buzek considered the problem from both points of view. In his *Poglad na
wzrost . . . ,* 16, he based his computations on censuses of total population (that
is, including military personnel in Galicia) and reached the totals: -61,421 for
the 1881/1890 period; -302,826 for the 1891/1900 period, and -488,543 for the
1901/1910 period. However, on this basis, the total emigration for the
1891/1900 period should have been 302,703. In two earlier essays, however, he
based his calculations on actual increases of civil population as has been done
in the above table. One, entitled, "Das Auswanderungsproblem und die
Regelung des Auswanderungswesens in Oesterreich," in the *Zeitschrift für
Volkswirtschaft, Socialpolitik und Verwaltung* (Wien: 1901), X. Band, V.
Heft, 444, his final figures are: 67,415 in the 1857/1869 period; -1,997 in the
1870/1880 period; -81,997 in the 1881/1890 period, and -340,833 in the

1891/1900 period. His figure for the 1857/1869 period does not correspond with those in the above table, because it is based on percentages of immigration and emigration calculated on the basis of total population. (See: *Oesterreichische Statistik* (Wien: 1884), V. Band, 3. Heft, IV–V.) His final figures for 1881/1890 and 1891/1900 likewise differ from the above table, the one slightly, the other more significantly. Since Buzek did not give the sources of his statistics or the calculations by which he reached the figures for emigration totals, it is impossible to explain the differences. In another entitled, "Rozdiedlenie ludnosci Galicyi wedlug wyznania i jezyka," in *Wiadomosci Statystyczne o stosunkach krajowych* (Lwow: 1909), t. XXI, zesz. II, 200, fn. 1, Buzek again included data on excess of immigration or emigration which are somewhat at variance with both his conclusions in his essay in *Zeitschrift* . . . and in the above table. This time his calculations for the 1869/1880 period are -1,897 as against those in his essay in *Zeitschrift* . . . of 1,997 which corresponded with conclusions in the above table. The error appears to be the result of his acceptance of 2,786,592 instead of 2,786,692 as total live births for that period, which caused an error in his calculations of natural increase and ultimately in the amount of emigration. (See *Supra,* fn. 13 and 14.) The difference between Buzek's figure of -320,290 for the 1891/1900 period and the one in the table above resulted from his acceptance of 3,060,860 rather than 3,060,737 as the figure for total live births during that decade.

The tables of total immigration and emigration compiled by Stefan L. Zaleski in his, "General Demography of Poland," *Polish Encyclopedia* (Geneva: 1921), Vol. II, No. 2, 144, are identical reproductions of those of Buzek in his *Poglad na wzrost* . . . , 16 and subject therefore to the same criticism. Brzeski's calculations in his, "Parcelacya wlasnosci tabularnej w Galicyi," in *Wiadomosci Statystyczne* . . . (Lwow: 1911), t. XXIII, zesz. II, 12, also on the basis of total rather than civil populations during respective censuses, are correct for the 1869/1880 and 1891/1900 periods, but his emigration total of -67,460 for the 1881/1890 period does not correspond with either the corrected (that is, on the basis of civil population) or uncorrected (that is, on the basis of total population) totals. Since he gave no indication of how he arrived at his final figure for that decade, it is difficult to trace the exact origin of his data. It appears to be, however, based directly on computations of Edward Czynski and T. Tillinger whose statistics not only for natural increase during the 1881/1890 period are erroneous (710,240 as against 710,330 in the above table), but whose figure of 642,780 for actual increase during that decade was simply an error in arithmetic (6,607,816 minus 5,958,907 equals 648,909). See their, *Etnograficzno-statystyczny zarys liczebnosci i rozsiedlenia ludnosci polskiej,* Wyd. II (Warszawa: 1909), Tab. XVI, 37.

Ignacy Weinfeld in his, "Ludnosc miejska Galicyi i jej sklad wyznaniowy, 1881-1910," in *Wiadomosci Statystyczne* . . . (Lwow: 1912), t. XXIV, zesz. II, p. 5, 10, Tab. VII, has two emigration totals for the 1901/1910 period (based on total, that is, uncorrected, population)differing with each other in the same essay. In one place he listed totals of natural increase as 1,198,270 and actual increase as 709,736, which would have given him a total emigration of -488,534. Had he used the more precise figure of 1,198,279 for natural increase, he would have arrived at the exact total of -488,543 emigrants calculated on that basis (that is, total population). In another part of the essay, however, he reached the conclusion that total emigration during that decade reached 488,416. This figure does not correspond with either corrected or uncorrected totals of emigration for that decade and, inasmuch as the author did not indicate how or where he got that figure, it is impossible to trace the disparity.

Stanislaw Kasznica and Marcin Nadobnik in their, "Najwazniejsze wyniki spisu ludnosci i spisu zwierzat domowych wedlug stanu z dnia 31 grudnia 1910," *Wiadomosci Statystyczne* . . . (Lwow: 1912), t. XXIV, zesz. 1, pp. XVIII–XIX, based their calculations for the 1901/1910 period on both tentative totals of natural increase (1,191,282 — tentative; 1,198,279 — final) as well as on an erroneous total of actual increase during that decade (713,448 as against the corrected actual increase of 717,352 in the case of civil population or 709,736 if based on total populations). By this means they arrive at a total emigration of 477,384 which corresponds neither to the corrected nor uncorrected totals of emigration for that decade. This error was repeated by Nadobnik in his essay entitled, "Ludnosc w Galicyi w r. 1910," in *Ekonomista* (Warszawa: 1912), R. XII, zesz. I, and accepted as accurate by Adam Zakrzewski in his, "Emigracya Polska" in Stanislaw A. Kempner (ed.), *Dzieje gospodarcze Polski porozbiorowej w zarysie* (Warszawa: 1920), Vol. II, 55–56. The latter, in his emigration table covering the decades 1881/1890, 1891/1900, 1901/1910, accepted the uncorrected conclusions of Buzek, *Poglad na wzrost* . . . , 16, for the first and second decade respectively and the erroneous one of Kasznica and Nadobnik, *loc. cit.*, for the third decade. H. Land [Helena Landau] in her essay, "Ostatni spis ludnosci w Galicyi," in *Krytyka* (Krakow: marzec 1912), R. XIV, 140, is guilty of the identical misjudgment on all three counts also. Mieczyslaw Szawleski, in his *Kwestja emigracji w Polsce* (Warszawa: 1927), 51, accepted uncritically the conclusions reached by Czynski and Tillinger, *loc. cit.*, for the decades 1881/1890 and 1891/1900, and the more erroneous conclusion of Weinfeld, *loc. cit.*, in the case of the decade 1901/1910. Leopold Caro and Karol Englisch, in their *Emigracya i polityka emigracyjna* (Poznan: 1914), 21, like Szawleski, *loc. cit.*, accepted the findings of Czynski and Tillinger, *loc. cit.*, for the 1881/1890, 1891/1900 periods and those of Weinfeld, *loc. cit.*, for 1901/1910.

The above writers were concerned specifically with the subject of population movements. Others just treated it in passing in broader more comprehensive studies. Franciszek Bujak's comprehensive study of Galicia, a milestone in the regional history of nineteenth century Poland, gave round figures for total emigration from Galicia during the 1881/1890 and 1891/1900 periods. See his, *Galicya* (Lwow: 1908/1910), Vol. I, 55. His figures appear to be approximations of those of Czynski and Tillinger, *loc. cit.*, and therefore subject to the criticism of their calculations. Stanislaw A. Kempner, likewise a scholar on a broader scale, estimated that there was a total emigration of 480,000 in the 1901/1910 decade and about 856,000 in the two decade period of 1891/1910. By his reckoning there should have been a total of 376,000 excess of emigrants in the 1891/1900 decade, a figure which does not correspond with either the uncorrected or corrected emigration totals for that decade. See his, *Rozwoj gospodarczy Polski, od rozbiorow do niepodleglosci* (Warszawa: 1924), 178.

Jan Rutkowski, in his multi-volume economic history of pre-war Poland, likewise ventured round figures of average annual total emigration from

Galicia, during the last three decades. See his, *Historia gospodarcza Polski; Tom II, Czasy porozbiorowe* (Poznan: 1950), 233. As approximations of total emigration from Galicia during these decades they may be accepted as fairly creditable. Since, however, he regarded them as average annual total emigration from Galicia to the United States, and since there is no existing statistical basis on which such estimates could be based, his figures must be regarded as arbitrary.

INDEX

A